THE
SERPENT
HANDLERS

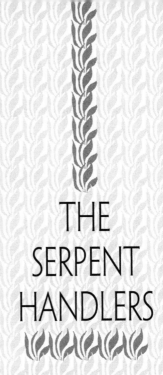

THE
SERPENT
HANDLERS

*Three Families
and Their Faith*

FRED BROWN
AND
JEANNE McDONALD

John F. Blair, Publisher
Winston-Salem, North Carolina

The paper in this book meets the
guidelines for permanence and
durability of the Committee on
Production Guidelines for
Book Longevity of the
Council on Library Resources.

Library of Congress Cataloging-in-Publication Data

Brown, Fred W., 1941–
    The serpent handlers : three families and their faith / Fred Brown
and Jeanne Mcdonald.
        p.   cm.
    Includes index.
    ISBN 0-89587-191-2 (alk. paper)
    1. Snake cults (Holiness churches) 2. Appalachian Region, South-
ern—Religious life and customs. 3. Brown family. 4. Coots family. 5.
Elkins family.   I. McDonald, Jeanne, 1935–   II. Title.

BX7990.H6 B76 2000
289.9—dc21
[B]
00-020601

Cover photograph by Verlin Short
Design by Debra Long Hampton

This book is dedicated to our children,
who have vastly enriched our lives—

Amanda, Cameron, Kathleen,
Melissa, Shannon, and Sumner—
and to our
beloved granddaughter, Sydney.

CONTENTS

The Brown Family

The Coots Family

The Elkins Family

FOREWORD

Nowhere is the diversity of American life better expressed than in the variety of religions that thrive in a land that has, historically, nurtured religious freedom. Thus, it is ironic that what is likely America's most unique sect, the serpent-handling religion, is so poorly understood and its followers so often maligned.

Since its inception at the beginning of the twentieth century, serpent handling has had many a day in court. Several states have passed laws against handling serpents in religious services; and in the case of Punkin Brown, the court has established a precedent in ordering the Brown family not to take its children to churches where serpents are handled. Despite this obvious obstruction of religious freedom, there is no public outcry or concern for the constitutional rights of these believers. How is it that a Bible-based religion has come to suffer so much opposition in a country where religious liberty is cherished?

Serpent handlers are integrally related to three great strands of American Protestantism: Holiness, Fundamentalism, and Pentecostalism, although they generally identify themselves as Holiness. Within the American religious experience, Holiness is often associated with the doctrines of Wesley and the early Methodists. Today, of course, the Methodists are a large, long-accepted, and hardly controversial denomination. The serpent handlers, on the other hand, are small, fiercely independent groups scattered primarily throughout Appalachia, although such churches are to be found in many other states as well. Despite the controversy surrounding their religion, serpent handlers interpret the Holiness faith as a way of life in which one is committed to being obedient to God in all things. This commitment explains their modest dress, the length of their hair (short for men, no beards or mustaches; uncut for women), and their dedication to living by the Word and refusing to accept many aspects of modern culture and "worldly ways."

Fundamentalism, a modern religious movement within American Protestantism, emerged in the second decade of this century to defend the Bible as God's word, not simply as another text to be interpreted by modern critical scholarship. While many eschew the label, the term rightly applies to those who wholly and unconditionally accept the Bible—more precisely, the King James Bible—as the Word of God. While serpent handlers do not identify themselves as Fundamentalists, they do insist on structuring their lives as mandated in the Scriptures.

Every weekend throughout Appalachia, preachers and elders arrive at serpent-handling churches with a Bible in one hand and a serpent box in the other. The serpent boxes are set near the front of the church, almost as a preview of what is to come later in the service. Often, the preacher begins by stating what all believers know: "There is death in that box."

But handling dangerous reptiles is the Word. Pentecostals know it, too. Pentecostalism is the link that serpent handlers have with mainstream American Protestantism. The great modern Pentecostal denominations, such as the Church of God, trace their origins to the day of Pentecost, when the Holy Spirit possessed the apostles. Historians place the emergence of modern Pentecostalism in the early part of this century, when believers sought to experience their faith in intense emotional terms. In fact, they were not simply content to affirm a series of beliefs; rather, they literally wished to possess the Holy Ghost. As believers pursued Biblical justification for a wide range of emotional experiences, they focused on verses across Scripture from Acts to Mark.

Speaking in tongues, a gift that remains central to many Pentecostal denominations today, is accepted as evidence of receiving the Holy Ghost. Serpent handlers obey this Sign as well, but they also refuse to exclude the Sign that tells them to pick up serpents, as it is so clearly mandated in Mark 16: "They shall take up serpents."

Their connection to Holiness, Fundamentalism, and Pentecostalism might explain some aspects of the serpent handlers' behavior to those unfamiliar with the faith—the "sinner people," as believers call them. Especially in their obedience to the Word, believers reveal their Holiness roots, and in this sense, serpent handling is no different from any other Holiness practice. Pentecostalism reminds us that to be filled with the Holy Ghost, we must be receptive to God's Word. And to be obedient to God's Word is "joy unspeakable." There is passion in life, there is fire in the blood, and only God will determine the moment of death, whether by serpent or by other means.

But it is not death that is of concern to serpent handlers; it is eternal life. In this respect, serpent handling has firm ties to movements within Protestantism. Therefore, its followers should have a legitimate voice within the Christian tradition. But the serpent-handling churches are often portrayed by the popular media in distorted terms. Newspapers typically report on the deaths or bites of handlers but seldom on the actual practice of the faith, simply because death under unusual circumstances sells more copies than the straightforward explanation of religious beliefs. In popular fiction, serpent-handling believers are described as uneducated people mired in poverty and provincialism. Mainstream religious leaders tend to dismiss such churches as cults and sensationalist splinter groups.

It is no wonder, then, that serpent handlers generally shun publicity. Seldom are they given a real voice. Others usually speak *for* them, interpreting their behavior to reflect preconceived story lines. Rarely can they recognize themselves in what has been televised or written about them. That is why this book is so significant. Fred Brown, a newspaper reporter who has earned the handlers' respect from years of unbiased reporting, and his wife, Jeanne McDonald, a novelist, have combined their talents in a remarkable way. Within a framework that provides a background on the serpent handlers' lives, they have allowed the handlers to tell their own stories, in their own words, with their own voices, and without editorial comment. All those included have been allowed to read the finished text of their taped interviews before publication, in order to eliminate misconceptions and philosophical errors. Thus, they are assured, as is the reader, that it is their own true stories that are being told in this book.

These stories present the handlers as real human beings with real dreams, real problems, and immovable faith. It is highly unlikely that the reader will come away believing that he or she should pick up serpents. But that is not important. What *is* important is that this faith be understood and respected. A powerful faith is revealed by these interviews; a spiritual engagement is illuminated. These are touching stories of extreme passion and uncompromising commitment, stories of people willing to risk their lives to follow what they believe to be God's mandate.

Dr. Ralph W. Hood, Jr.
Professor of Psychology
University of Tennessee, Chattanooga

Ralph Hood is a past president of the Division of Psychology of Religion of the American Psychological Association and is the recipient of the association's William James Award for research in the psychology of religion. He has published over 150 articles and five books on the psychology of religion. He has served as the editor of The International Journal for the Psychology of Religion and The Journal for the Scientific Study of Religion.

PREFACE

It was fall, and a cold breeze was blowing down from the great mountain behind the Carson Springs Church of Jesus Christ. The spring-fed creek in front of the church had risen almost to the point of overflowing the wooden footbridge leading from the road to the church. The trees were exploding in a brilliant show of color. It was a peaceful and idyllic setting, but I was apprehensive. I was there that night because Charles Prince had called the newspaper I work for and asked if anyone wanted to cover a serpent-handling service. I had jumped at the chance. Growing up in Cedartown, Georgia, I had heard about snake handling all my life, but I'd never had an opportunity to attend a service.

The year was 1984, and Charles Prince was just beginning his triumphant return to the Signs Following religion. He had grown up listening to the sound of his father's voice as Ulysses Prince preached the Word wherever and whenever he found a crowd that would listen. Kitchens, street corners, tents, pulpits—it didn't matter, as long as there was a chance he could turn one single soul to God. Charles and his brothers and sisters were accustomed to being uprooted and dragged from one town to the next. They were also accustomed to going to sleep to the sound of rattlers buzzing beneath their beds, where their father stored his snake boxes to get the children familiar with the serpents.

When he was older, Charles Prince strayed from the holy life for a few years. He opened a bait shop in Canton, North Carolina, and married a fourteen-year-old girl. But in 1984, the year of my initiation, he had a resurgence of faith. He sold his bait shop, gave his second wife half of the fifty thousand dollars from the sale, and gave away the other twenty-five thousand. He then returned to the church with a passion so intense that he usually followed all the Signs at every service. That meant picking up serpents, drinking poison, laying on hands, handling fire, speaking in tongues, and sometimes casting out devils.

On that particular night at the Carson Springs church, Prince brought with him a large, contentious Eastern diamondback rattlesnake. It was more than six feet long and weighed nearly a hundred pounds. Its flat, triangular head was bigger than a grown man's fist. It was a mean snake, that was clear. Charles, sounding pleased, said, "It comes out of the box biting at the wind." To hoist the deadly rattler into the air, he had to lean at an angle in order to keep the snake from dragging on the floor. Not satisfied with a merely victorious handling of the Eastern diamondback, he draped the huge snake around his neck and hopped on one foot across the church floor, holding up the first finger of his right hand. Then he reached into a snake box and took out a canebrake rattler. Prince danced and swung the canebrake through the air like a skip rope.

He not only handled snakes at that service. He also drank a jar filled with strychnine, handled fire, and laid his hands on some of the ailing members in the congregation.

I was impressed enough to want to find out what made people like Charles Prince put their lives on the line for God two or three times a week. It was the beginning of my fifteen-year odyssey to get to the heart of the serpent-handling religion. I followed Charles Prince for a year or so, intrigued by his ability to withstand bites, to survive lethal gulps of strychnine, and to hold a burning jar of kerosene beneath his chin until his lips turned sooty black. I asked him if the strychnine was potent enough to kill. "I don't want it if it isn't," he said. I once had a small dose of it tested by a toxicologist, who pronounced it decidedly potent enough to kill. Charles once told me that the strychnine in the jar was lethal if the undiluted crystals floating in it gave it a smoky appearance. "It's still got the feathers in it," he said.

I came to know Charles Prince well. I watched him perform the unexplainable. I saw him walk barefooted up the length of a canebrake rattler, hold a deadly scorpion in the palm of his hand, lift a rattler to his head and wear it like a coiled cap. He helped me gain access to many churches throughout eastern Tennessee.

I was on the way to discovering the depth of the religion across the Southeast when, in 1985, Charles was bitten in the Apostolic Church of God near Greeneville, Tennessee. His trademark was to grab armfuls of serpents and hold them in a kind of embrace close to his chest. On the fatal night near Greeneville, Charles had his usual armload of deadly serpents, but this time, several bit him on the shoulders and hands. Undaunted, he grabbed his Mason jar of strychnine from the pulpit and slugged it down. "It's the feathers of strychnine!" he shouted. After the first swallow, he shouted, "He's a good God. He don't put out the flames. He just takes away the pain."

Two days later, Charles Prince died. His pain was excruciating, but he refused to be taken to a hospital. At the end, blood spouted from his pores as the venom destroyed nerves, bone, and tissue. A coroner said later that it was as if a bomb had detonated inside his body.

Since then, I have come to know many more serpent handlers, but only John Wayne "Punkin" Brown, Jr., has come close to the charisma and religious intensity possessed by Charles Prince. Punkin, too, died following the Signs. The most likely candidate to step into Punkin's shoes is Jamie Coots of Middlesboro, Kentucky. Like Punkin, Jamie is a devoted father, husband, and son. He is young. He owns his home. He makes a living driving a rock truck. He loves his life and his family. But because he loves God above all, he, like Punkin Brown and Charles Prince, puts his life on the line by picking up serpents in church.

Outsiders call serpent handlers exhibitionists, showmen, cultists, and charlatans. They claim that serpent handlers milk their snakes of venom, defang them, or feed them just before handling so that they will not strike. None of this is true. What can be greater proof of the serious intentions of these believers than death itself?

Although many serpent handlers are uneducated, they are neither ignorant nor crazy. They handle snakes not to test their faith but to confirm God's Word as set forth in Mark 16. Their speech, which might sound ignorant to the uninformed ear, is the result of a long cultural heritage. It includes a dose of the Scots-Irish dialect of their ancestors, a smattering of Biblical terms, and a generous helping of colorful idioms handed down through generations. Their grammatical constructions, syntactic patterns, and idiosyncrasies of language also stem from the geographic isolation of the mountains in which they live. This isolation has tended to preserve and concentrate all these linguistic features into a rhythmic, lilting expression unique unto itself.

After years of hearing my stories about the Signs Followers, my wife, Jeanne, also a writer, suggested that we do a book together in which serpent handlers could tell their stories in their own words, without editorial comment. She was especially interested in the involvement of women in the church. She wanted to learn how, as wives and mothers, they were able to demonstrate a faith as bold and enduring as the men's.

During the interviews we conducted over the next year, and on the occasions when we joined the serpent handlers in their services, in their homes, at their dinners on the grounds, at their homecomings, at their revivals—and yes, unfortunately, at their funerals—we have come to know them in a very personal way. They opened up their hearts to us without compensation or reward. They talked candidly about their successes and failures, their victories and their heartbreaks, sparing no details. All they asked is that we tell the truth as they have told it. Our contact with them has given us an inestimable respect for the sacrifices of their faith.

In the following pages, we tell the stories of three serpent-handling families. After introducing the person who is the subject of each chapter, we present a memoir related by the believer himself or herself. Their accounts are printed here as closely as possible to the way they gave them to us, in their particular idioms and with the honesty and fervor that characterize this unique group. The profiles of Punkin and Melinda Brown differ from the others in form because the two are no longer here to speak for themselves. We relied on taped personal interviews with Punkin and on family accounts of the couple's faith and their often unsettled relationship. And as long as the unresolved custody of their children remains an issue in the courts, their names will stay in the public forum.

The serpent handlers practice their religion daily in thought, word, and deed. When they fail, they suffer, pray, and try harder the next day. Their religion demands a price too high for most of us to pay. Imagine having enough faith to pick up a deadly reptile to confirm God's Word, knowing that a bite could be crippling or even fatal.

What about the miracles? How can they be explained? We have seen people hold flame in their hands and dance on fire without being burned. We have witnessed believers drinking strychnine with no ill effects and handling poisonous snakes without being bitten. Other miracles are related in this book—healings, casting out devils, baptism by an unseen spirit. Even these stories seem plausible because we believe in the veracity of the people who witnessed such events firsthand.

In Galatians, Paul wrote, "The fruit of the Spirit is love, joy, peace longsuffering, gentleness, goodness, faith." All these words define the character of the serpent handlers, who deserve respect for their bravery in following their heartfelt convictions.

Fred Brown
Knoxville, Tennessee
October 1999

And the Lord God said unto the Serpent, Because thou hast done this, thou art cursed above all cattle, and above every beast of the field; upon thy belly shalt thou go, and dust shalt thou eat all the days of thy life.

Genesis 3:14

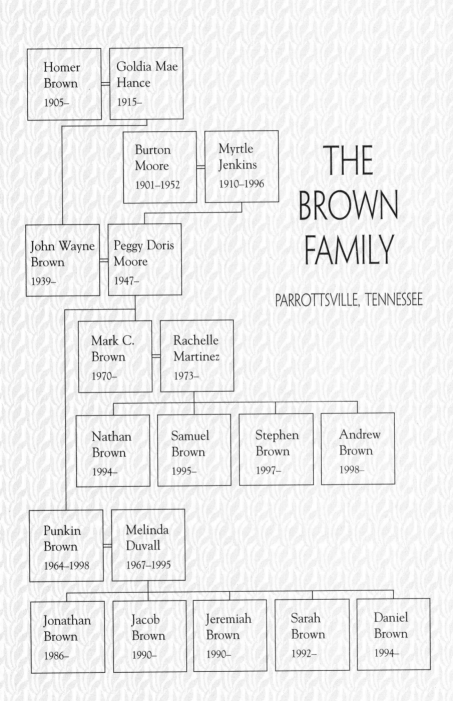

THE
BROWN
FAMILY

PARROTTSVILLE, TENNESSEE

Homer Brown 1905–
Goldia Mae Hance 1915–

Burton Moore 1901–1952
Myrtle Jenkins 1910–1996

John Wayne Brown 1939–
Peggy Doris Moore 1947–

Mark C. Brown 1970–
Rachelle Martinez 1973–

Nathan Brown 1994–
Samuel Brown 1995–
Stephen Brown 1997–
Andrew Brown 1998–

Punkin Brown 1964–1998
Melinda Duvall 1967–1995

Jonathan Brown 1986–
Jacob Brown 1990–
Jeremiah Brown 1990–
Sarah Brown 1992–
Daniel Brown 1994–

COCKE COUNTY,
TENNESSEE

It was the beauty of the lush hills and valleys and the abundant water resources that gave Cocke County its economic boost. Just as the French Broad made Newport a vital river port in the 1700s, the rivers have made tourism a profitable business in more recent years.

ON THE OUTSKIRTS OF NEWPORT, TENNESSEE, an immense roadside billboard reads, "That 'Love thy neighbor' thing . . . I meant that. *God*."

The sign represents radical change in an area that once had the reputation of being the meanest place in Tennessee. Cocke County, which straddles Interstate 40 between Knoxville, Tennessee, and Asheville, North Carolina, has frequently been the scene of drunken brawls, drug trafficking, murders, cockfighting, beatings, and grudges settled by gunfights. Its wild history of lawlessness was inherited from the region's days as a rough frontier town, when Cherokee Indians rode the rolling hills and William Cocke, a companion of Daniel Boone, crossed the Allegheny Mountains into Kentucky and Tennessee.

Though Cocke County has yet to completely overcome its reputation, it is not without its positive history. It is the birthplace of both Metropolitan Opera star Grace Moore, who was born in Slabtown, now known as Nough, near Del Rio, and Kiffin Yates Rockwell, the first American aviator to shoot down an enemy plane in World War I. And just outside Del Rio is Christy Mission, where a North Carolina girl named Catherine Marshall came to teach mountain children a hundred years ago. Her story, *Christy*, was turned into a novel, a Broadway musical, and a television series.

Things have begun to turn around for Cocke County in the last two decades. Circuit-court judge Kenneth Porter, a lifelong resident, said in 1990, "There are signs that Cocke County is living down its reputation. We went the past two, three years without a homicide. Most of the old saloons we had in Newport have been closed."

And as saloons closed, churches opened, some in town and some in outlying areas like Parrottsville, where serpent-handling preacher John Brown and his family live. In this little community located along Highway 321 between Newport and Greeneville, the 250 residents live mostly by farming beef cattle, tobacco, and grain. John Brown has held a multitude of jobs during his sixty years—farmworker, landscaper, gravedigger, salesman—but he is presently a carpenter.

If progress has not moved as quickly in Cocke County as in other Tennessee counties since the early 1800s, that is due in part to the fact that more than a hundred thousand acres of its land lie in Cherokee National Forest and the Great Smoky Mountains National Park, making the entire south end of the county rural mountain land that is off the tax rolls. This rurality brings both isolation and insulation for many of the people who live in the area. Small Fundamentalist churches spring up as social and religious havens, giving their members a sense of comfort and community and bringing together cluster groups of people who don't fit into the larger outside world.

In Newport, the county seat and the area's largest town, churches are interspersed among other old buildings along the main street in the downtown area and out past the city limits—Liberty Temple, Full Gospel, Gethsemane Free Will Baptist. In the old business district, carpet and furniture stores are sandwiched among crumbling bars and lounges, abandoned buildings with brick fronts and gracefully arched windows, and an occasional Holiness church. There is an atmosphere of decay along these streets. One store still has Christmas decorations in the window in June; the windows are grimy; the buildings are generally neglected. Newer and brighter shopping malls on the outskirts of the city have lured customers away from downtown businesses and introduced a vast new world of modern consumer products.

At one time, Newport was a big canning center; Stokely Van Camp employed hundreds of local residents. Another once-thriving business, furniture making, still provides a living for many citizens. In the 1990 census, the numbers showed that the main occupations were sales work, clerical work, service work, precision work, line production, and repair work. Topping the list were machine operators, assemblers, and inspectors. Jobs in farming, forestry, and fishing—previously a much greater source of employment in the area—had dwindled to 389.

Cocke County was created in 1797 when a triangular piece of Jefferson County was chopped off and named after the distinguished general William Cocke, who helped settle the territory. It is bounded by the counties of Hamblen and Greene to the north and by Jefferson and Sevier to the west and southwest. The base of the triangle rests on the edge of the Great Smoky Mountains National Park. Two rivers—the French Broad and the Pigeon—flow through the area, and the Nolichucky River creates the northern boundary. After eighty-two years of toxic dumping by the Champion Paper Company upstream in Canton, North Carolina, bitter litigation and negotiation have recently led to a cleanup that is still in progress.

Following World War I, the county earned a reputation as the nation's moonshine capital. And in the late 1980s, it became notorious as a champion grower of marijuana. The town's relative isolation has left little room for anything except logging and apple growing in earlier days and factory work—at Quaker Oats, Stokely Van Camp, and various furniture factories—today.

The population of Cocke County is an amalgam of Dutch, Irish, French, German, African, and Scottish immigrants. To their land, the people gave names like Dutch Bottom, Irish Cut, Pig Trot, Bat Harbor, Sunset Gap, Frog Pond, and Purty Holler Gap. Insulated on small farms, isolated by both poverty and geography, they turned to family, neighbors, and God for sustenance. The church, especially, gave them the opportunity to come together, to sing and enjoy fellowship, and to forget, for the duration of the service, their daily hardscrabble lives. "We didn't know there was a depression here in the country," says Lucy Black Ownby, who grew up in and eventually inherited her grandfather's house beside Caney Creek in Cosby. "We lived like there was a depression all the time. It was just all hard, but we got by. We grew what we ate and ate what we grew. We never did go hungry or naked. I never had to eat cornbread for breakfast. You got to know, though, that there wasn't nothing else around here. You either farmed or you made moonshine to feed your family. Some women made it, too."

It was the beauty of the lush hills and valleys and the abundant water re-sources that gave Cocke County its economic boost. Just as the French Broad made Newport a vital river port in the 1700s, the rivers have made tourism a profitable business in more recent years. Outdoor recreation and resorts are the big draws; hiking, camping, kayaking, and whitewater rafting attract nature lov-ers from all over the country.

Once you cross the Pigeon River on the way out of town, you begin to notice well-kept old Victorian houses with wraparound porches and beautifully manicured lawns. Real estate is cheap in this land-rich county. The average cost of a two-bath, two-bedroom house is seventy-five thousand dollars.

Farther out, where the country is more mountainous, house trailers cling to the steep, rocky hills. Along the roads are more churches—Free Will Baptist, Victory Baptist, Community Chapel Worship Center, Assembly of God, all set against a breathtaking backdrop of emerald-colored mountains and gleaming riv-ers. Farmhouses anchored on acres and acres of land dot the rocky landscape. Some modest houses beside the road boast healthy vegetable and flower gar-dens, while others grow a rusty crop of abandoned automobiles and broken and discarded appliances. On the left is a brand-new barn, on the right a dilapidated structure where cows wander in and out between sagging boards. An ancient Ford truck, rust-eaten except for a trace of green paint, and an old, bowlegged wringer washer on the makeshift porch of a trailer are evidence of the area's tenacious connection to the past. Satellite dishes in hillside yards show the resi-dents a more prosperous outside world than they previously could have imag-ined. In the case of the serpent handlers who live in this area, it is a world they shun.

Isolation has also led to high levels of unemployment and illiteracy. Today, Cocke County's population of just over thirty-one thousand is heavily weighted toward the thirty- to thirty-four-year-old age group, which may indicate an opti-mistic trend for the area. The average income in 1994 was $14,139. The unem-ployment rate in 1995 stood at just over 11 percent. Many Cocke Countians are retired or disabled. Payments for retirement and disability insurance, unem-ployment, income maintenance, and veterans came to $122,356,000 in 1995. That figure included $17,267,000 for unemployment insurance benefits.

Illiteracy is a decisive factor in the socioeconomic problems of Cocke County. A third of the residents have less than a ninth-grade education; only half of those who remained in school longer have earned high-school diplomas; and six of every hundred have a bachelor's degree. These numbers help explain the endurance of remnants of the original Scots-Irish dialect, the preservation of inherited colloquialisms and grammatical forms, and a stubborn adherence to old customs and beliefs.

For the serpent-handling believers especially, there is resistance to being out in the world. Members seldom travel far beyond their own community of fellowship except to attend revivals in neighboring states among their inner circle of churches. To the Signs Followers, the outside world is negligible; the real reward lies in what God offers above and beyond this present life. For them, Cocke County is only a rest stop on the long, hard highway to eternity.

Punkin Brown in Kingston, Georgia, with Carl Porter in the background
Photo by Ralph Hood

MANNER OF DEATH: ACCIDENT

JOHN WAYNE "PUNKIN" BROWN
1964—1998

*For misery does not come from the earth,
nor does trouble sprout from the ground;
but human beings are born to trouble just
as sparks fly upwards.*

Job 5: 6–7

THE DEATH

NOBODY KNOWS IT YET, but the video camera set up in the back of the Rock House Holiness Church of God is recording the last two hours of John Wayne "Punkin" Brown's life. Punkin, from Newport, Tennessee, is thirty-four years old. He's one of the favorite evangelists on the serpent-handling circuit, a dedicated young man with an outgoing personality and an energetic style of preaching. Charismatic—that's what they call him. In the seventeen years he has been in the Signs Following religion, Punkin has never refused a call to preach, to save, to heal, or to rededicate a single soul. He's known for his unique style of bouncing across the front of churches and skipping up and down the aisles. When the spirit of God covers Punkin Brown, you know it. You hear it, you see it, you feel it. It's so palpable you can almost taste it.

It is October 3, 1998, a warm autumn evening in Macedonia, Alabama. Punkin is one of the featured evangelists who will be preaching at the evening program, but he has still not arrived at the church when the service begins.

Later, when he pulls into the parking lot, he will tell a friend that he stopped alongside the road to clean out his snake boxes.

The crowd that has gathered is small—mostly women and children. A few men sit on the stage and on the benches against the side wall. Three snake boxes are pushed against the pulpit. Occasionally, one of microphones on the stage picks up the dry, deadly sound of a rattle.

The Signs Followers adhere to what they believe is a mandate in Mark 16: 17–18, which reads, "And these signs shall follow them that believe; In my name shall they cast out devils; they shall speak with new tongues; They shall take up serpents; and if they drink any deadly thing, it shall not hurt them; they shall lay hands on the sick, and they shall recover."

The service is slow to start. People wander around the church, a small one-room building with a dozen or so pews. A guitar tunes up; a baby cries. Several people join in a hymn—"I'm on My Way to Heaven." On the stage, a man in a white shirt and cream-colored pants does a few halfhearted dance steps, but nobody seems enthusiastic. The spirit is lacking. God hasn't moved, not yet. There is more music, more singing; a few women begin to clap. Some push their hands out into the air or raise their arms over their heads. "He'll be there to help you if you call upon His name," proclaims the next hymn. Children, rest-less and expectant, wander among the pews. A woman stands and rocks back and forth with her child on her shoulder.

Billy Summerford, the minister, is preaching about the spirit of God. "I've seen it float into a church like a big blue cloud," he says.

But not tonight. Something's different tonight. There's a pall hanging over the Rock House Holiness Church of God, as if all the energy has been sucked from the building by some unseen force. The congregation is waiting for Punkin— Punkin and Jamie Coots, a serpent-handling preacher from Middlesboro, Ken-tucky. When the two men come into the church a half-hour later, things pick up a little, but something still doesn't feel right. Jamie Coots greets the men on the stage, gives the holy kiss to a couple of them. Punkin sits behind the pulpit, his head framed by the small window behind him. A woman sings "I'm Going Home to Be with Jesus," and the young mother with the child rocks a little harder, gaining momentum. A few other women come forward now, barefooted, prepared for the rocking-step dance they perform in front of the altar. One seems to swoon. Her knees fold; she sways, then rights herself. In a minute, she twirls in a circle with arms extended. God has arrived.

The woman with the baby brings the child forward, and a healing circle forms around her. Those in the circle raise their hands, touch the child, and offer prayers. One is ululating, singing out a high-pitched, incomprehensible lament, but no one pays much attention. A young woman with long, dark hair walks to the pulpit and sings "He Didn't Have to Do It, But He Did."

The snake boxes are pushed back toward the prayer bench. Again, a microphone picks up the sound of a rattle, but so far, none of the boxes has been opened. No one has been anointed or been covered up by the spirit. Punkin sits on a bench behind the altar tuning his guitar and occasionally whispering to his friend Jamie Coots. Finally, he steps forward and begins to play his guitar. He sings "I'm Gonna Let It Shine." Still, everything appears to be happening in slow motion. The minister invites Jamie Coots to preach—a respectful convention in the serpent-handling churches—but Jamie shakes his head no.

"We're letting Satan control the service tonight," proclaims the minister. "We need to get up and start performing for the Lord."

Punkin, too, seems dispirited, tired. "We need to get stirred up," he tells the people. He asks someone to read from Romans, the New Testament book that is a message from the apostle Paul to the Christians of Rome. Punkin asks for chapter 13. As the reader shouts out the lines, Punkin repeats them, stalking back and forth behind the pulpit.

"Let every soul be subject unto the higher powers. For there is no power but of God," says the reader.

"No higher power," Punkin echoes. Head down, concentrating, he seems to pick up a little energy.

"Whosoever therefore resisteth the power, resisteth the ordinance of God: and they that resist shall receive to themselves damnation."

"Whosoever resisteth the power of God," Punkin repeats. He circles restlessly.

There are calls from the men on the stage, a Greek chorus. "Come on, come on. Tell it."

"Those who resisteth receive damnation," says Punkin.

"Amen. Come on."

The reader continues. "For rulers are not a terror to good works, but to the evil. Wilt thou then not be afraid of the power? do that which is good, and thou shalt have praise of the same."

"We're fixing to find out what the power was," Punkin avows.

Excitement rises.

The reader continues. "But if thou do that which is evil, be afraid; for he beareth not the sword in vain: for he is the minister of God, a revenger to execute wrath upon him that doeth evil."

Punkin looks back at the reader. "A what?"

"A revenger."

"A revenger," Punkin repeats. He perks up, performs a simple hop-skip dance step, paces some more. Behind him, a guitar riff ripples and drifts off into silence. A cymbal crashes, then echoes into stillness. Punkin's voice gains depth, rhythm. His words, singsong now, are interspersed with a sound—*heh*—that is half bark and half cough. It is his particular way of emphasizing his message. "You hear me good—*heh*. We better be scared of the terror."

"Bring it on!" someone calls. "Yeah. Come on."

Punkin hops on both feet. He holds his hand to his mouth and coughs. "Thank you, Jesus."

"Come on. You got that right. Think about it," cries the chorus.

Punkin wipes his face with a white handkerchief and executes another dance step. "I'm ready to go," he says. "I ain't afraid to die. *Heh*. Come on down." He walks up and down the steps that lead from the floor of the church to the stage.

Punkin handling snakes at a revival. His father, John, stands behind him.
Photo by Ralph Hood

He's still talking about the higher power. "You gonna be judged for the deed that you've done," he warns. "Heh. We need to be ready to go." Suddenly, with a burst of enthusiasm, he runs off the stage, down the aisle, and back again, then sinks down on the steps as if he is short of breath. But his litany continues. "Bless Your holy name, Jesus. Satan's shedding big ole tears." He gets up and begins to pace again. The fire has not yet fully caught in the congregation.

One woman claps a few times, waves her arms. The chorus continues, supporting Punkin's message. "Bless you. Come on. Praise the Lord," the people cry.

"He said ask—heh—and you shall receive," says Punkin. "He said seek and ye shall find." He hops on two feet. His shirt is soaked with sweat. His face gleams. "You people know I'm going to a better place." A rattle sounds as if to emphasize his words. "If the Lord didn't visit you, you wouldn't be here."

"Amen," says the chorus. "Think about it."

"You can't have Jesus—heh—and hold on to the world." Punkin points to the snake boxes. "When they go in this box and get bit, they got a good excuse. No matter how much they ridiculed the apostles—heh—they kept right on preaching."

Now, the people are beginning to feel the spirit. Some yell. Some stand and wave their arms, then sit down again. Punkin sinks again on the bench in front of the pulpit, as if his legs will no longer support him. Again, he swipes the handkerchief across his forehead. But just when he seems to be losing momentum, he rushes to the snake box and pulls out a thick, yellow timber rattler three or four feet long. The snake arches and coils in his hand, and the congregation comes to attention. Mothers call their children from the front rows and send them to the back of the church. A few women rush outside with their babies.

"If they don't bite," says Punkin, "ain't no need to be scared." Holding the snake aloft, he circles behind the pulpit, hurries down the stairs on the left, crosses in front of the pulpit, rushes up the stairs on the right, then skips behind the pulpit again. The microphone is in his right hand, the rattler in the left. On the return circuit, he swings the serpent high in the air, and the snake swiftly coils back toward the hand that holds it. This seems to be the moment of the strike. Punkin barely flinches. Few notice that he has been bitten. Punkin looks at his hand briefly and continues to preach. "God don't ever change," he says. "It's gonna be all right."

But something has changed in Punkin. Suddenly, he seems stunned, though he continues to proclaim: "No matter what comes, God's still God." He quickly hands the snake off to Gene Sherbert, a handler from Georgia, who stuffs it back into its box. Punkin walks behind the pulpit, circles back to the steps, and again glances at his right hand. He staggers, turns pale, then raises his arms. A man on the stage rushes toward Punkin, begins to rub his neck and back, and spouts a wild litany of indecipherable wails. Punkin stumbles down the steps and collapses. The men gathered at the altar support him for a moment, then clear a space on the floor to lay him down. They fall to their knees and crowd around him, praying, shaking, and speaking in tongues.

"Jesus, have your way!" someone shouts.

"Right now, God! Right now, Jesus!" a man cries. "Help my brother right now. I'll glorify You. I'll praise You for it."

Children are crying, women screaming. Now, there is total chaos in the church. Women run back and forth from the bathroom, bringing wet paper towels, an electric fan. Some stand over Punkin waving makeshift paper fans, moaning, and praying. People bend forward to lay hands on him. "Jesus, Jesus, have your way," somebody calls. One woman claps her hands as if to get someone's attention—maybe Punkin's, maybe to help keep him conscious. When asked if he wants medical help, Punkin manages to point toward the ceiling, meaning that he will depend on the Lord to save him.

"Praise His name," cries Billy Summerford, a voice of authority in the confusion. "Everybody keep your mind on the Lord."

The young woman who earlier sang at the pulpit wanders up and down the aisle in shock, wringing her hands and crying, "Jeeee-sus. Jeeee-sus. Jeeee-sus."

Children are weeping inconsolably now. Some are removed from the church by their mothers. A few people hurry out in distress. Near Punkin's outstretched body, a woman swoons. Others rush to hold her up. One man gets down on his knees, stretches out his arms, and puts his face to the floor in a supplicating position. A woman speaks in tongues. Jamie Coots makes an effort to lift Punkin, then gives up and lays him down again.

Now, the woman walking the aisle picks up her child and continues her lament as he sleeps against her shoulder, unaware of the confusion around him. "Jesus. Jesus. Jesus."

All is bedlam, despair. Above the din, there is a long, drawn-out cry, a wail that floats above the room like a dirge. Then, over the noise, a loud entreaty: "Praise His name."

The group around Punkin grows quiet. They hold hands and sway together. Then Billy Summerford steps onto the stage and picks up his snake boxes. Gene Sherbert takes his box out, too, as if to say that it is all over. A small girl walks toward the back of the church crying and wiping her eyes on the long collar of her white sailor dress.

And then, suddenly, the video camera goes blank.

Punkin Brown has gone to meet his maker.

THE AFTERMATH

In his official statement to Scottsboro district attorney Charlie Rhodes, Jim Grigg, coroner in the Jackson County, Alabama, Department of Forensic Sciences, reports that John Wayne "Punkin" Brown, Jr., was transported on October 3, 1998, from the Rock House Holiness Church of God to Jackson County Hospital in Scottsboro, where he was pronounced dead at 11:12 P.M. Central Standard Time.

Five minutes. That's how long it took Punkin Brown to die. It was his twenty-third snakebite, a bite much less serious than others he had suffered in his seventeen-year serpent-handling career.

The Brown family is reluctant to agree that the bite was what killed their beloved child and brother, even though Punkin had often said he would be happy to die with a snake in his hand. No other family member was in attendance at the Rock House Holiness Church of God that night, but Punkin's father, John, and his brother, Mark, have studied the video taken by the camera set up in the church. Mark comments that in the video, you can see Punkin holding the microphone in one hand and the snake in the other. "It [the rattler] is sticking out. You just see Punkin [jerk his hand]. Then he comes back around in front of the pulpit again, and when he comes back, Gene gets [the snake] from him and puts it up. I don't think it got a good bite on him."

Carl Porter, the Georgia evangelist who eulogized Punkin's wife, Melinda, when she died three years earlier, says that in all his years of handling snakes in church services, he has never seen anyone die so quickly from a bite. "No one has ever known anything like this. It was just unusual."

Punkin's mother, Peggy Brown, agrees, although she has not been able to gather the strength to look at the video. But when she saw her son's body, she, too, was not convinced that the bite was what killed him. "It was like it scratched him. It wasn't bad. His right arm was swelled so he couldn't hardly meet the buttons in his cuff. The left one [the side that was bitten] was fine."

Mark adds another strange piece of evidence. "The right side of his face was hard, and the left side was soft. The last thing he said was, 'No matter what happens, God is still God.' He walked behind the pulpit and never said no more after that."

"That's why we can't believe," Peggy explains. "I wouldn't even say [it was] a bite, 'cause [the snake] didn't bite. It *hit* him. That's why we just cannot believe that's what did it. It was too fast. I've seen ones that they have had to *pull* off."

Punkin's father joins in. "I had one to bite me [on the finger] with one fang. [For] about fourteen hours, my arm was [swollen] up like this."

"John was black from his neck all over," adds Peggy.

"I was swelled all the way down in here," affirms John, rubbing his hand from chest to groin. He was sick for nine days.

The Browns believe a heart attack killed their son. The family and close friends had often seen him clutch his chest in pain or swell up with fluid, but no one could convince him to seek medical help.

Yet there is evidence that the rattler sank its fangs into Punkin's left middle finger. The Alabama state medical examiner's conclusion that snakebite was the cause of death comes as a disappointment to the family members, who want Punkin to have enjoyed victory over the serpent. Still, they all agree that when it is your time to go, God takes you home, no matter the form in which death arrives.

"The preliminary report turned out inconclusive," says coroner Grigg after Dr. Stephen Pustilnik's autopsy on Punkin the Monday following his death.

Pustilnik's findings indicate that Punkin suffered from arterial sclerosis and an enlarged heart, possibly caused by hypertension, but that neither would have caused death. "Brown did not die of a heart attack," Pustilnik emphasizes.

Jim Grigg expresses a commonly held conception about snakebites. "If you have been bitten twenty-two times by venomous snakes, you should be fairly immune," says Grigg. "I have been a coroner for sixteen years, and this is the first death [of its kind] I've seen since I became coroner."

However, Pustilnik disagrees with Grigg's theory about venom immunity. He says that instead of setting up an immunity to the venom, Punkin probably had a *sensitivity* to it, and that it would likely have taken *less* venom to kill him than it would a person who had not previously suffered a bite.

During his seventeen-year career in the serpent-handling church, Punkin Brown handled more snakes than most people care to think about, including puff adders, Southern copperheads, Western diamondbacks, Eastern diamondbacks, timber rattlers, canebrake rattlers, cottonmouth moccasins, pygmy rattlers, tiger rattlers, rock rattlers, Great Basin rattlers, Mojave rattlers, sidewinders, and assorted cobras. And with twenty-two previous bites recorded, perhaps Punkin's system was indeed sensitive to venom.

Stephen Pustilnik feels that even though Punkin had an enlarged heart, the snakebite was certainly the catalyst that triggered his collapse and therefore must be considered the official cause of death. Although he did not test for snake venom in the autopsy, he says that the video of the bite proves that it was the cause.

There were, he claims, many factors that contributed to the death. "It was the combination of his active mode when he was preaching. His heart rate was up, and the heart was enlarged—and it takes years for the heart to get enlarged. He probably had hypertension, which is the most common cause of heart enlargement. At that point, he was undoubtedly pumping the dose of venom around in his body. He was preaching, and the [excitement] allowed the toxin to reach his heart very quickly. He was definitely bitten by the snake. His finger was hemorrhagic. There looked to be puncture wounds. It was probably a combination of the two [the enlarged heart and the bite]. If the venom was not a lethal dose, it probably started an aberrant electrical activity of the heart. If it *was* a lethal dose, then that is what did it. The snakebite is what decided his final demise. The fingers have marvelous veins and arteries on either side—digital arteries and digital nerves. If the fang gets into one of those nice vessels, [the venom] has a free highway into the circulatory system. The fingers are very vascular. The enzymes in the venom help destroy the flexor tendon or extender tendons.

"It's just a combination of stuff. The snake was especially agitated. If it squirted [released its venom], he got a larger dose. It could have hit one of the vessels in the finger and [been given] free access to the heart. Maybe his heart got to be larger over the years, and that combination—with the jumping around and with the snakebite—might have caused an increased cardiac demand and required increased blood flow to his heart and body and [sent] the heart rate up."

The official amended autopsy report signed by Pustilnik on October 5, 1998, reads as follows: "Decedent John Wayne Brown, age 34, race W, sex M, length 69 in., weight 223 lbs. *Autopsy Findings*: I. Puncture wounds on left third finger with soft tissue hematoma of the left third finger. II. Visceral congestion. III. Cardiomegaly (500 grams). IV. Bilateral pulmonary consolidation. V. Cerebral edema, mild (1450 grams). *Cause of Death*: Snake bite to hand. *Contributory Cause*: Hypertensive cardiovascular disease. *Manner of Death*: Accident."

The report concludes, "The postmortem examination demonstrated apparent puncture wounds on the left third finger associated with soft tissue hematoma of the left third finger. An abrasion on the dorsum of the left hand was suspicious for a bite mark without evidence of puncture wounds in that area. Also identified was cardiomegaly with mild atherosclerosis. Also identified was bilateral pulmonary consolidation and mild cerebral edema. Visceral congestion was also seen. Toxicology demonstrates no arsenic, strychnine, lead or mercury."

Punkin Brown's family wants to know why a test for venom in his system was not administered, but Dr. Pustilnik and the district attorney are satisfied with the official findings. "An enlarged heart is an unstable heart," says Pustilnik, "and [Punkin's] was a significantly enlarged heart. Not just a little bit large, a *lot*. Oh yeah, on the way to serious trouble."

Punkin's earthly troubles ended that night on Sand Mountain, but Peggy and John Brown's continue. The day before Punkin's funeral, his children are removed from their paternal grandparents' home by a Cocke County juvenile-court judge and given into the temporary custody of Melinda Brown's mother, Frances Goswick of Plainville, Georgia. Within a few brief days, the Browns thus lose both their son and the five grandchildren who have lived with them most of the time since the death of their mother three years earlier. At first, funeral arrangements keep them occupied, but the judge's decision represents another enormous loss to a family that has suffered more than its fair share of grief.

Punkin's parents choose to bury their son at Carson Springs, the site of the church to which Peggy and John first took their seven-year-old boy. Peggy recalls that by the time Punkin was twelve, he would curl his hands in excitement when he watched members handle serpents.

It is the site of the church of famous serpent-handling preacher Charles Prince, though it came to be known by a different name after Prince's death. The church building is no longer there, having been destroyed by fire years back, but the spot is a peaceful, quiet place. Punkin Brown will be buried there in the Holiness Church of God in Jesus' Name Cemetery beside his wife, Melinda, on a high ridge that looks down into a quiet valley. After three years of turmoil during which he lost his wife, struggled with severe financial problems when he was denied disability payments for his work-related back injury, and was the victim of vicious gossip in the serpent-handling community, Punkin Brown will finally be at rest.

THE FUNERAL

On a cold October morning in 1998, John and Peggy Brown prepare to bury their firstborn son. Rain sweeps in early, a cold, windy onslaught that hints at the approach of winter. The skies seem to be weeping for Punkin Brown, a man who lived by the faith and died by the faith. The mourners include friends and members of churches in Tennessee, Kentucky, North Carolina, Georgia, Alabama, Virginia, and West Virginia.

Punkin's five children—Jonathan, age twelve; twins Jacob and Jeremiah, seven; Sarah, five; and Daniel, four—attend the funeral-home service in Newport, Tennessee, and are then taken back to Parrottsville by their grandmother Peggy Brown. Before they leave, John Brown takes their hands and leads them to Punkin's silver casket, where he lifts them up so that they can kiss or caress their father. Then, after patting his son's arm, John Brown looks down at Punkin for the last time, turns slowly, and walks to his wife's side.

Peggy Brown spends a few final minutes alone with Punkin, leaning over the casket, sobbing. Tenderly, she cups his face in her hands and kisses his forehead. He is her baby, her first child, born when she was only sixteen years old.

The mourners who have filled the chapel to overflowing touch Punkin's body and weep as they file past the satin-lined casket. Propped on either side of Punkin's head are two black-and-white photographs of him handling serpents.

The chapel service is simple, consisting of only two songs and a brief eulogy listing the family's names. No serpents are handled at the funeral home.

The cemetery is located on a steep hill between the prongs of a V-shaped road. There is only one road leading into the hollow below the ridge, and on the day of the funeral, it is mired in mud. The hearse carrying Punkin's body slips and swerves as it makes its way cautiously up the grade to the burial site.

Once the mourners have gathered, several pull rattlesnakes from boxes placed on the vault and begin to sing and pray. Some hold them close to their faces, as if searching for an answer to the tragedy in the serpents' slitted eyes. Some rub the serpents' heads with open palms as rain slashes down.

Lydia Elkins Hollins, from the well-known church in Jolo, West Virginia, cradles a large black timber rattler in her arms as if she is rocking a baby. Covered with the spirit, she begins to dance in the rain and to speak in tongues.

Mark Brown picks up a rattler as the hundred or more people begin to sing "Lord, Have Your Way."

Then John Brown raises his arms toward the emptying heavens and walks toward the snake boxes. He hoists a large rattler up to eye level, then raises it above his head. As he returns to the protection of the green tent covering the grave, he stares out across the closed casket. What he sees there, only he knows, but his face is etched in anguish.

Jamie Coots, minister of the church in Middlesboro, Kentucky, where Punkin's wife was bitten in 1995, shouts into the wind, "He's not laying there. He has done gone on to meet God, and you need to rejoice. Brother Punkin was a hard man who didn't compromise. He was going Saturday night, whether he was right or whether he was wrong."

Many of the ministers gathered at the grave echo the church's belief that Punkin died that Saturday night in Alabama because it was his appointed time to go. "I believe we were predestined before the foundation of this world," proclaims Carl Porter. "I believe God knew us before this world was ever born. It was Punkin's time to go. He was really looking forward to [this] day."

"This wasn't a *test* of faith," adds Jimmy Morrow, minister of a serpent-handling church in Del Rio, Tennessee. "This *is* our faith."

The Reverend Billy Summerford, minister of the church where Punkin was fatally bitten, assures those gathered that Punkin has crossed over: "He is walking on streets of gold. Punkin Brown and I walked a lot of miles together. We got a lot of other preachers here today, but we are going to miss him, because he was always there for us."

At the end of the burial service, John Brown asks the gathering to pray for

Punkin Brown, about four years old
Family photo

Punkin with daughter Sarah and son Daniel, 1995
Family photo

John and Peggy Brown with Punkin's children in 1999 in their back yard
Left to right: Jonathan, twins Jacob and Jeremiah, Daniel, and Sarah
Photo by Fred Brown

The Brown Family 21

his five grandchildren. "Remember Punkin's children," he says. "Keep fasting and praying. There is nothing too great or too small for God to do."

And then a great chorus of mingled voices rises in the hollow, and Punkin Brown is left to make his way into the next world.

A TONGUES-TALKING, SERPENT-HANDLING HOLINESS WOMAN

MELINDA DUVALL BROWN
1967–1995

"I have never danced like that before."

SHE WAS HANDLING SNAKES when he met her, and she was handling snakes when he lost her. And then he lost his five children in a custody battle that pitted his esoteric religion against society's broader and more conventional yardstick.

From the beginning of their tumultuous thirteen-year marriage, Punkin Brown and Melinda Duvall were destined to be star-crossed lovers. And just when they seemed to be getting it right, both met up with deadly timber rattlers—one black, one yellow—and the lives of the remaining Brown family members were forever changed.

When he was seventeen, Punkin met Melinda Duvall at a Kingston, Georgia, serpent-handling homecoming service. Gene Sherbert was the pastor of the church at the time. Melinda, a pretty, brown-eyed, brown-haired fourteen-year-old, was a girl after Punkin's own heart. She was an active member of a Signs Following church and was already handling serpents. "Punkin had seen her down there handling big rattlesnakes, speaking in tongues, and shouting," says Mark Brown. "He seen all that and that just hooked [him] right there. He found a woman that liked to do the things that he liked to do."

When Punkin returned to Parrottsville after the revival, he told his brother,

"I've met me a tongues-talking, serpent-handling Holiness woman, and I'm going to marry her."

A year later, four months after Punkin celebrated his eighteenth birthday, the couple did marry. It was 1982. Melinda was fifteen years old. "I tried to talk them out of getting married that young," says Peggy, "but her mama and daddy encouraged it."

"When they first got married, Melinda handled serpents a lot," Mark says. "Just on her own. Punkin said he'd come home from work and she'd be setting on the porch and have a pile of copperheads laying in her lap. That was down there at her mom and dad's house. When she got older, she quit handling them as much. I think she got around the women up here and sort of backed off. [At first,] she kind of felt like she'd just handle them the way she wanted to handle 'em. The Lord didn't have to move or anything. If she wanted to handle them, she'd handle them. She'd go to the boxes herself and get 'em. But it got to where it started worrying Punkin a lot. I guess he may have talked to her and told her she needed to pray and slow down a little or something. I don't know. But it got to where she didn't handle them like that anymore."

Punkin and Melinda lived in Georgia for about three years. "They moved back and forth a couple of times," Mark recalls. "They'd live there for a while and then come back, and then they went back down there and got in that motel."

"There was times in their marriage when they lived in Georgia that Punkin would call us and they would have no money, no food," says Peggy.

Shell, Mark's wife, nods. "She told us she lived on potatoes and soup beans and biscuits and cornbread."

"One week, they'd eat it [fixed] one way," adds Mark, "and then next week, they'd alternate and eat it another way."

"Every two weeks, we'd take them something to eat," says John. "And then they come back and got that trailer. That's when Punkin worked in the mill. He worked in the yarn department. He was laying up yarn, taking material to the machine, and taking it off the machine. After it was produced, he would take it back."

"That's one thing they thought might of could happened to his back," Peggy adds. "Pull around on that, it weakened his back."

"After he worked in the cotton mill, we built him this house down here, just right below us," says John. "He moved back here, and he was working over

Four generations:
Peggy Brown (holding
Sarah), Myrtle Moore
(Peggy's mother),
Melinda Brown, and
Rachelle Brown
Family photo taken in 1992

in Morristown then, and going to church. Melinda started working, too. They had some problems, Melinda and Punkin did." Punkin came home from the late shift one night and found Melinda and Jonathan gone. Jonathan was thirteen months old. "Punkin was working in a furniture factory then. It was six months before we got to see Jonathan. The law wouldn't do nothing about that."

At the beginning of the marriage, Punkin worked for Melinda's father. The two men soon had a disagreement about tithing. "They found out when we got married that they weren't going to tell me what to do," said Punkin in an interview shortly before he died. "I wasn't going to live by their rules. And everything changed. I went to work for her daddy, and he told me on payday when we come in, he said, 'You got to give me your 10 percent out of your check every week, your tithes.' I said, 'I don't pay my tithes to no man. If I pay my tithes, I'll pay them to the church.' Well, that was the end of that move. From then on, I wasn't nothing but dirt. Melinda's grandfather cussed me like a sailor, but he never mistreated me. Whatever I wanted, he'd give it to me. He called me, begging me not to handle serpents. Which, that don't bother me none. People don't understand it. That don't bother me."

From then on, the couple struggled over their differences with Melinda's parents and the resulting stress on their own relationship. A separation ensued, then a divorce that caused backsliding not only by Punkin and Melinda but also by John Brown, whose faith was shaken by all the family problems.

"Punkin got a lawyer, and Melinda come down here and got one," Peggy recalls. "They went to court that time. Punkin was wanting custody of Jonathan then, which he didn't get, but he got visiting every two weeks. He'd go pick Jonathan up at the Adairsville exit. They went on like that. Punkin would call Melinda at work." Peggy nods toward the kitchen. "Her phone number is still in there in the phone book."

It was a year before the couple got back together, a dark year filled with tragedy and suffering. "Punkin kind of lost it for a while," Peggy says. "He was out of the church. His life was a big mess."

"He went to work in Asheville, North Carolina, in Burlington Mills," Mark recounts. "And then somehow he quit working up there, and it wasn't long after that that he got down in his back. For seven months, he walked humped over. He was drinking and everything. The pain of [his back] and the pain of not seeing Melinda as often, he just didn't care about nothing, more or less."

"He was going to a doctor in Greeneville [Tennessee]," John adds, "and they kept telling him, 'Well, it is a pinched nerve.' He slept in a chair for one year, right here [in the living room of his parents' home]. He couldn't lay down in the bed. Finally, he got a specialist, and they done surgery, and he got to where he would walk and straighten up."

Peggy Brown wrings her hands. "Yeah, he was drinking [and] into drugs. One time, he had been out running around with some boys about his age. He come in over here, and he kept walking. He'd go through the house, and he'd walk. What he had done, he had drank and mixed it with some pills. So he got scared. And he told me he thought he was going to die. I was going to take him to the emergency room, and he was ready to go. He told me, 'Mama, I don't want to die like this.' Now, I said, 'Punkin, if you don't want to die like this, you better do something about it.' He said, 'I know it, Mama.' I was going to take him [to the hospital], and I said, 'Now, you will have to tell them what you took. 'Cause if they don't know what you took, they'd give you the wrong thing. It could kill you.' He wouldn't tell *me*, but I said, 'You got to tell *them*.' He said, 'Okay, I'll tell the doctors.' So I couldn't tell you right now what he took. Whatever it was, it scared him pretty bad. I respected that he didn't want me to know, and I kindly stayed back. They started an IV for whatever he would have to have. They kept him so long that it scared him pretty bad.

"But he didn't straighten up right away. Melinda was messed up during this time, too. [Her parents] kept Jonathan, but they wouldn't take her in because of what she was doing. She'd gotten down there and gotten into drugs. Punkin told her just to come on home. She didn't at first. [But then] some things happened, and she called him and wanted to come back. She had got down in Chattanooga and got assaulted. Four men. And throwed her out of the car after they did it."

John Brown is shocked by this terrible news. "Well, how come y'all never did tell me about it?"

"We thought you knowed it," says Peggy, abashed.

"Melinda didn't tell too many about it," Mark says to his father. "She told Shell. I didn't know about it until Shell told me."

John is upset. "I thought we didn't have no secrets."

"Now, I didn't know that," Peggy replies.

Shell breaks in. "Melinda sat me down and told me about it."

"I just more or less caught it later," Peggy says to John.

John turns his head and looks off into the distance. "Naw. I wouldn't have wanted to know anyway."

After a brief and uncomfortable silence, Shell continues. "Punkin went after her. He did. Knowing what happened and everything, he still went and got her. He loved her that much."

After Melinda's disastrous experience in Chattanooga, she and Punkin remarried, and the family was complete again. Mark tries to pin down the year. "It was during the summertime. I was in college, so I didn't know a lot of what was going on down here. I stayed in Johnson City [Tennessee]. It was early in 1989."

Shell agrees. "It *was* early 1989, because Melinda's twins were born in October of 1990. They were premature, just seven months when they were born."

"Punkin had started back to church before they got remarried," Mark says.

"Frances [Melinda's mother] had lost a son," Shell says. "And Melinda told me she always felt like her mother tried to replace that son with Jonathan." She stops to think. "That's when I first met [Punkin]. I met him in June—no, May—of 1990."

That summer, in Evarts, Kentucky, Punkin was bitten by a canebrake rattler. Ironically, he wasn't even handling serpents at the time. Another man was trying to put the rattler in its box. Punkin squatted on the floor, and the rattler arched and bit him on the leg. "Melinda was pregnant with the twins. She was with him," Mark remembers. "He looked at her and told her, 'I love you.'"

Shell nods. "He walked over to her and kissed her on the cheek. And he said, 'I love you, Melinda.' That's the first time I ever seen anybody get bit."

"That was dangerous," Mark says. "He wasn't handling. He said the Lord spoke to him and told him he was going to get bit. He said he had made up his mind he wasn't going to handle no more, because he didn't want to get bit. That's the first [time] he had been bit bad, and it affected him bad. He got numb, tingly all over. Slurred when he was talking. They said he got like he was drunk at one point and raised up in the bed and looked in the mirror and said, 'That man is bit.'"

Punkin later told his wife that the first thing that came to his mind was that he might not get to see those babies she was carrying. But he recovered from that bite and later that same year—1990—began his work as an evangelist. He started holding revivals, mostly in Kentucky. "That's when we first started videotaping the services, revivals and such," says Mark.

Once they returned to the church, Punkin and Melinda found a better life. The year after the twins, Jacob and Jeremiah, were born, Sarah came along. Daniel joined the family three years later. Punkin was fast gaining a reputation as one of the most prominent evangelists in the Southeastern serpent-handling churches.

Then came the book *Salvation on Sand Mountain*, by Dennis Covington, who was later criticized as having libeled Punkin Brown's reputation. "Of all the handlers I'd run into," Covington wrote, "Punkin Brown seemed to be the one most mired in the Old Testament, in the enumerated laws and the blood lust of the patriarchs. His sermons [were] preached in guttural monotone while he walked in front of the congregation with a rattlesnake draped over one shoulder. He didn't have much to say about redemption. And he was unpredictable and combative, the handlers' equivalent of a mad monk."

Covington also repeated some unsubstantiated gossip about Punkin in his book that strained Punkin's marriage and blemished his reputation in the serpent-handling churches. "Dennis Covington wrote all this stuff in that book about me [messing around with another woman]," Punkin said. "What it was, it was after Middlesboro [Kentucky] homecoming in 1992. We was handling serpents, we was drinking strychnine—doing, you know, regular meeting." One of the people attending the homecoming was Elvis Presley Saylor. When Covington left the meeting, he picked up Saylor, who was hitchhiking along the highway, and drove him back to Harlan County, Kentucky. On the way there, Saylor told Covington that his wife, influenced by Punkin's preaching against adultery and fornication, wanted a divorce because Saylor had been married before. According to the beliefs of the serpent handlers, his previous marriage made their relationship adulterous. Saylor thought that Punkin wanted his wife for himself, and Covington printed Saylor's speculation without verification and without asking Punkin for his own version of the story. Punkin didn't hear the gossip until nearly a year later, even though it was circulating throughout the serpent-handling community. When he did find out, Melinda laughed at the story because, she joked, Punkin was "hot" now. But Punkin maintained that the rumors definitely damaged his marriage.

"Melinda was a good person, a good mother," says Peggy. "She took care of her kids. She didn't go anywhere she couldn't take the kids. They came first. But if I got sick or something, even her [with] them kids, she'd try to help me. She was just a giving person. She had her own car. She went wherever she wanted to go, 'cause Punkin liked to hunt and stuff. She had her car, [and] she'd go visit or go to town and shop. Whatever she wanted to do, she done as she pleased. And she had her own checking account, she had her own money. She had her own will. If she wanted to go, she went."

And then, in 1995, things began to fall apart again. On August 6, Melinda was bitten by a black timber rattler during services at the Full Gospel Tabernacle in Jesus Name in Middlesboro, Kentucky. She was twenty-eight years old and the mother of five. Before she reached for the serpent, she had begun to speak in tongues, which meant that she was fully anointed. The family grieves that it was her husband, Punkin, who handed her the snake, just as he had handed Melinda dozens of serpents in the past, and just as he himself had received them hundreds of times.

"I didn't really see it bite her, but Mark told me it had bit her," John says. "Bit her in the forearm."

Melinda's nine-year-old son, Jonathan, was in the back of the church and did not see his mother bitten. Melinda was struck in the manner that the serpent handlers call being "dog-bit," which means that the snake sinks its fangs into the flesh and refuses to let go, causing considerable bleeding.

Once the snake was taken back, Melinda continued to dance. John approached her and asked if she wanted to go to the doctor. "She said no," John recalls. "[I] went outside, and I asked her again, 'Do you want to go to the doctor?' 'No,' she said. She looked at me and she said, 'I have never danced like that before.'"

John had no intimations of Melinda's death, but only a few days before the incident occurred, Punkin had suffered a disturbing dream that his friend

Cameron Short, who interprets dreams and visions, warned him contained a symbol of death. Short himself also had a dream indicating trouble for Punkin's family.

When Melinda began to feel ill, she was taken to the nearby home of Jamie Coots and his wife, Linda, who lived in a public-housing apartment in Middlesboro. By that time, Melinda had lost the use of her legs. Linda Coots heard Punkin beg his wife to seek medical help. "I was in there, and he was crying," says Linda. "He said, 'Melinda, we got them kids.' She said, 'Punkin, I trust in the Lord.' "

"Punkin begged her to go to the doctor," John Brown verifies. "He certainly did. [It was rumored] that he didn't, but he cried and begged. He'd tell her to think about the children. She wouldn't [seek medical attention]."

John returned to Tennessee to get Peggy and promptly drove her back to Kentucky. It was Sunday evening, and Peggy had been working all day in the nearby mountain resort of Gatlinburg, cleaning motel rooms. She didn't know about Melinda's misfortune until that evening, when John arrived home to get her.

When Peggy walked into the bedroom where her daughter-in-law lay, watched over by Signs Followers, someone asked Melinda, "Do you know who that is?"

"That's Mama," said Melinda.

Peggy, too, was a witness to Punkin's pleas to Melinda to go to the hospital. "Punkin come in there and got down on the floor beside the bed Sunday night and begged her to go. She wouldn't go."

"She'd holler," says Shell, who also shared the bedside vigil. "She'd holler, 'Punkin, go get yourself something to eat. Go lay down, rest. I'll be all right.' "

Punkin kept trying to convince Melinda to go for treatment. "Think about the kids," he said.

But Melinda asked, "Have you lost your faith?"

Punkin was stymied. "Well, they wouldn't have treated her as long as she *refused* treatment," he later said. "She was twenty-eight years old, buddy. They wouldn't have took her. She never lost her mind, never was out of her head. Yes, sir, I guarantee you she would have refused treatment at the hospital. She done *did* [refuse treatment]. That's why we didn't take her. I got bit [one time], and they called the ambulance to come and get me. I don't know who called them. But they come. I was living in a little ole trailer, and the ambulance driver stuck his head in. He wouldn't even come in the door. That was in Georgia. He said, 'We hear there was a snakebite victim here.' I was laying on the couch. I said, 'Yeah, me.' He said, 'Do you want treatment?' I said, 'No, I don't want no treatment.' I said, 'I got bit in church. That's what I believe in [serpent handling].' He said, 'Well, we had to come and ask you. Do you care to sign this paper releasing us, saying that we come?' I said, 'No, I'll sign your paper, but leave your medicine outside.' So he come in, and I signed his paper, and he set there a minute, and he left. What the EMT in Middlesboro told Jamie Coots was that as long as Melinda was in her right mind and she refused treatment, there wasn't no way they could of took her, no matter what nobody wanted to do. She wouldn't go. The EMT told Jamie, 'You could of put her out and made her went to the hospital. But if she lived, she could of sued you for what you done.' Now, ain't that ridiculous? That's stupid, buddy."

Thinking that Melinda would recover, John returned to Parrottsville that evening. Punkin had already driven back to care for the children. When John got home and took over the child care, Punkin started the hour-and-a-half drive back to Middlesboro.

Peggy remembers how Melinda was sitting up in bed with her arm in a pan of cold water. "Honest, I thought she was going to be all right," says Peggy, her bright eyes darkening with the recollection. "It done something to me when she died. I was right there. I never will forget it. She was telling a friend how to do something with his truck. Yeah, his fan wouldn't go off. When he cut the motor off, the fan was still running. She told him he was going to have to get down there and unhook that wire. Now, if she was delirious, she wouldn't know that."

Punkin was ten minutes too late to see his wife before her head fell back on the pillow. He rushed on to the hospital where she'd been taken, but Melinda was already dead.

Little did anyone know that Melinda Brown's death would set off a blast of public criticism about serpent-handling churches and parental responsibility and lead to a custody hearing in which Punkin would temporarily lose his five children to Melinda's sister, Angela Ashe of Cleveland, Tennessee. Cocke County Juvenile Court judge Phil Owens made his ruling on the argument that the children were being endangered by attending church services where deadly snakes were present.

Punkin Brown was too immersed in his beliefs to make a compromise, even for his beloved children. "I'll teach them what the Bible says," he declared. "I don't care what nobody else says. When they made that [custody] order, there was never a judge to sign that paper. Never. But because I handle serpents and go to church, they took my children away from me. My wife died for what she believed in. *She believed it.* They can say that she didn't believe, they can say that all they want to, but she believed it. *She died, didn't she?* I mean, they can't change that, can they? She was my *wife.* [Her parents] holler what they lost— their daughter. I lost my *wife,* my *companion.* I ain't got her no more. Ain't even got my *kids* no more. They'll have to answer *to the Lord* on it, buddy. They can holler they got that judgment over there in that courthouse. But when [that judge] goes before God, there'll be nobody to plead his case, praise the Lord. Well, it don't make no difference what they do, what they say. Whatever Phil Owens does, he can't change the Bible. You turn to Mark 16, and it still reads, *"They shall take up serpents."* They can't change it. They can change their laws, make the law, but they can't change the Word of God. And they won't change me for what I believe in."

The Browns had to deal with both grief and exhaustion; Peggy and Punkin had sat up for two days and nights while keeping watch and praying over Melinda. Yet the very morning after Melinda's death, Owens removed the five children from their paternal grandparents' care. Peggy Brown says she will never forget that day. "We had set up with Melinda from Sunday to Tuesday. We just catched catnaps. See, the way it happened, we were all exhausted, and then, losing her, we were just all to pieces. *I* was. And right the next morning, here they come to get the children. What can you do? You can't think.

"When [Deputy Steve Johnson] come to Punkin's trailer that morning, [the children] was eating, and there was no reason to come in. He told [the court] the house was clean. I said the twins didn't want to go out. They was crying. They were scared. He come inside the door there. I was standing there, and I said, 'They are not going out there with you unless you tell them you aren't going to take them anywhere.' That's what got him, too. He told them he wasn't taking them anywhere and went to town and had to come back and get 'em."

"The trailer was cleaned up," Punkin remembered. "We didn't know they was coming. It was like that. Melinda cleaned the house before she went to church [the day she was bitten]."

"Melinda always kept her house clean," says Peggy. It is a matter of pride for the entire family.

The enmity that had developed between the two families over the years was never more evident than at Melinda's funeral. The families did their mourning on separate sides of the chapel in the Manes Funeral Home, a low brick building next to the courthouse in Newport. The Reverend Carl Porter of Kingston, Georgia, one of the ministers eulogizing Melinda, portrayed her as a stalwart member of the church. He had been present at the service when the black rattler sank its fangs into her left arm just below the elbow. He noted that when she died, Melinda was following the Signs, as proclaimed in the Bible. "Sister Melinda lost her life because she believed in the Lord," he said. "And anyone who does not know the Word should respect those who do. She put everything on the line. All of it was on the line as her husband tried to get our sister to go to a doctor. She refused, because she said she would trust in the Lord [to heal her]. Sister Melinda is in a better world. She will be missed, but this is a short time here and a long time over there. Some of us go ahead of others, but after a while, we go the same way. I'm not telling you to handle snakes. There is death in it, you make sure. Sister Melinda stood for it."

Bruce Helton, a snake-handling minister from Evarts, Kentucky, and a snake-hunting friend of Punkin's, called Melinda "not only a believer but a doer. She loved Brother Punkin, but she was the Lord's, who holds the key and the breath of life. Sister Melinda got hers over with. I've got a hope that as long as we serve the Lord, there are people who will die for this." He added, "This is sad, people. Today, we got grief, but one thing's for sure, hold on to the Lord, and He will bring us through."

During this part of the service, Punkin stood up and performed a halfhearted version of the unique, energized hop he always executed when he was anointed by God. But his spirit was sapped by grief and exhaustion, and he sat down, limp and overwhelmed.

Since Punkin had not been able to afford insurance on his wife, Helton asked for an offering to help defray the cost of the funeral.

Members of Melinda's family from Plainville, Georgia, and Cleveland, Tennessee, escorted the children. The younger children wept as their grandfather John Brown led them to the open casket to take a final look at their mother.

Cocke County chief deputy Blaine Hartsell and members of the Newport Police Department were present to provide an escort for the funeral services and to prevent hard feelings from arising between the two families. And indeed, tension thickened in the small chapel. Melinda's family objected to the presence of a newspaper reporter friend of the Browns, and the Browns, already grieving over the loss of Melinda and the removal of the children, were appalled when one of Melinda's relatives entered the chapel wearing shorts.

The issue of the children remained to be settled. Under Tennessee law, once the juvenile court intervenes in a case, whoever has the children—parent, relative, or someone outside the family—has only temporary custody. "Once it comes under the purview of the juvenile court, we have jurisdiction of those children until they reach age eighteen," said Phil Owens at the time. "And [the Brown children] are under our jurisdiction now. I want to be open-minded about this. People are free to express their religious beliefs, but I feel we have to waive that [right] when it comes to the welfare of the children."

Punkin said in an exclusive interview that he feared he would lose his children permanently because of his religious beliefs and because his in-laws took a dim view of his faith, even though some members of Melinda's family had formerly handled serpents themselves. He accused the court of putting stumbling blocks in his path in his attempts to regain custody of the children. He maintained that he had complied with all court orders but had never been served with any legal documents showing why his children were removed from his home the day before Melinda's funeral. In fact, he said that he didn't even know where his children were until the funeral, and that he wasn't allowed to see them even on that day. "I wasn't able to hold them until I got visitation rights August 18. That was almost two weeks after Melinda's death."

Punkin admitted that he had kept poisonous snakes in his home in the past. He also confirmed that in 1991, a rattlesnake had escaped from its box in a side room. His oldest son, Jonathan, about seven at the time, jumped over the reptile in the hall to avoid it. After that, Punkin removed the snakes from his trailer.

Owens appointed Vida Bell, a Newport attorney, as guardian ad litem. Ironically, it was her husband, juvenile-court judge John Bell, who later removed the children from the elder Browns' home after Punkin's death. Judge Owens also ordered home studies and psychological examinations for both families and the children. "No doubt, this is one of the toughest cases I have ever had," said Owens.

Punkin won the first round in October 1995, when Owens restored full custody of his children to him. However, Owens ordered that Punkin never again take his children to a church where snakes were present. Nor could Punkin even have the children *outside* the church if, on the inside, believers were handling or transporting snakes. "I enjoin you from having a child around snakes or any other dangerous animal, and that includes church service," said Owens at the conclusion of the six-hour hearing in Cocke County Circuit Court. "I can't tell you how to practice your religion, but I can protect the children, and that is what I'm going to do." Handling snakes in a manner that endangers people is a misdemeanor in Tennessee.

In testimony during the first custody trial, Vanessa Butler, a psychologist from Athens, Tennessee, evaluated the mental health of five-year-old Jacob and three-year-old Sarah. She found that Jacob had significant emotional problems and was "an extremely anxious little boy. He has an extreme preoccupation with the fear of snakes and talked about snakes being hidden in different places in the house." Butler testified that Sarah did not fully understand that her mother was dead and that she would not be returning home.

However, Vida Bell, the children's court-appointed guardian in the first custody hearing, recommended that they be returned to Punkin. She reported that the children seemed happy and wanted to be with their father. Furthermore, she said that she did not believe that Punkin Brown kept poisonous snakes in his home.

Two Department of Human Services social workers said that they did not find a threat to the children's well-being in Punkin's home and that they saw no reason not to return the children to him.

After the trial, Punkin told a newspaper reporter, "I'm just glad to have my children back, and I will do whatever [the court] wants me to do."

John Brown, however, was not so pleased with the outcome, since the children would not be able to go to church if snakes were handled. "I think not to let the children come to our churches is a violation of our religious rights," he said.

But Melinda's father, Lewis Duvall, once a serpent handler himself, said after the trial that he feared for his grandchildren's safety. "They will die from snakebite before they are twelve years old," he said.

According to published accounts, Melinda Brown was the fourteenth snake handler to die in Tennessee, and hers was the seventy-sixth church-related snakebite death officially recorded since the turn of the century.

And then, in October 1998, Punkin Brown also became a statistic—victim number seventy-seven.

Seventeen-year-old Peggy Brown holding one-year-old Punkin in 1965.
Family photo

TO SPEAK
IN TONGUES

PEGGY MOORE BROWN
B. 1947

"You feel so clean after the spirit leaves you. You feel so clean."

WHEN YOU ASK PEGGY BROWN what it's like to handle serpents, she points to her youngest grandson, Andrew, who sleeps soundly in his carryall across the room. "See that baby over there?" she says. "You can't hardly keep from picking him up, can you? Well, that's the way it is with serpents when God moves on you. You can't keep from picking them up."

That feeling—anointment—is a general emotional and physical sensation that leaves you unable to resist, she says. The serpent handlers call it "the word of knowledge," God's permission to let you handle snakes.

To look at her, you'd never guess that serpent handling is part of Peggy Brown's personal religious creed. She's a dark-eyed, big-boned woman with the compassionate expression of one who has experienced her own troubles and is thus sympathetic to those of others. She has been there. She understands. From the moment you walk into her house, she makes you feel welcome. She sometimes takes in virtual strangers who profess an interest in her church or need a place to sleep before the long ride home.

Peggy's dark, graying hair, now well below her waist, has been cut only once in the thirty years since she joined the church. At home, she winds it into a thick, neat bun at the back of her head, but for services, she combs it out and lets it flow down her back. When she goes to church, she dresses in the same simple way she does at home—blue denim jumpers or flowered dresses, no makeup, no jewelry except for her wedding ring. She offers herself up to God just as she is—no frills, no strings.

When Peggy laughs, she covers her mouth and lowers her eyes, giving an impression of shyness, but when she goes to the rostrum to sing during services, the volume and depth of her voice are surprising. It is in church that her inner strength is most evident. She sings with a rich, throaty gusto, standing with her back to the congregation or in profile, gazing up at the ceiling. At those times, people who know her suspect that she is singing to her firstborn son, Punkin. Tears roll down her cheeks. Sometimes, she is crying inconsolably by the time the hymn ends. The wound of losing her child is still fresh in her heart, and now her pain is compounded by the ugly custody suit that has snatched away the grandchildren, who call Peggy "Mama." For Daniel, the youngest, who was still a baby when his mother died, Peggy is the only maternal figure he can remember.

Punkin's death and the removal of his children from Peggy's care have been like a nightmare she is unable to wake from. "I try to live a good life," she says, "but I'm afraid I sometimes feel bad toward Frances [Mary Frances Goswick of Plainville, Georgia, the maternal grandmother, who was awarded half-time custody of the children], and I worry that God might not forgive me for that."

The custody suit filed by Mrs. Goswick compounded the inestimable grief the Browns felt after that terrible night when their son died on Sand Mountain. Chuck Phillips of the Jackson County Sheriff's Department, the chief investigator of Punkin's death, said that no charges would be filed. "The only thing we did was write this up as a matter of record. It is not against the law in Alabama to handle snakes in church."

But that wasn't the end of it, not for Peggy and John Brown. Almost immediately, juvenile court judge John Bell placed the children in the temporary custody of Melinda's mother, who claimed that the children were endangered by attending serpent-handling services. In particular, the judge was concerned that the children had accompanied the Browns to services where snakes were handled even after the court had ordered Punkin to keep them away following the death of his wife.

Peggy Brown was torn between loyalty to her son's wishes and adherence to the court's order. She told the judge that since Punkin had been determined to give his children the kind of religious education he believed in, she had to comply with his wishes. "My son wanted them to be in church," she said. "And that was one night a week. My son was thirty-four years old. He had the say-so. The children were with me in the back of the church. Children are not allowed in the front [where the snake boxes are kept]."

Fletcher Ervin, court-appointed guardian for the children, then told Judge Bell that in his interviews with the children, they had told him they wanted to return to the Browns. "I think this opinion has to be given some weight by the court," he said. "These are beautiful children, and they have to be kept together. I think it would be criminal to break them up."

But Bell was adamant. "The choice is not for the children to make," he declared. "It is for the court to decide what is in the best interest of the children."

Peggy Brown was devastated when the judge, in a decision reminiscent of the Biblical Solomon, ruled that custody be shared between both sets of grandparents. It was especially painful for Peggy because she knew that Frances Goswick had herself attended a serpent-handling church in Georgia with her former husband, Lewis Duvall, for several years, and that Melinda had handled serpents in church as early as age fourteen, when Punkin first met her.

The Browns were convinced that the court's decision was influenced by the fact that they are serpent-handling believers. In a rare show of anger, John Brown stood up and shouted after the ruling. "My son gave his life for what he believed!" he exclaimed. "Is this the freedom that we are guaranteed by the Constitution?"

But the judge replied that, because of the trauma from the deaths of both their parents, continuity in the children's lives was more important than the Browns' feelings. "I expect strict compliance with the court order," the judge said. "Like it or not."

When the judge struck his gavel, Frances Goswick whisked the children away before Peggy Brown had a chance to say good-bye to them. Grief-stricken, the Browns drove home alone. They were left waiting for the children's visits on the first and third weekends of the month. Since then, Peggy has spent all of her free time consulting lawyers and social workers in an attempt to bring the children home. She fired her first lawyer and hired another. She also assumed much of the record gathering and legwork herself, in an effort to save legal fees. And she prayed. Most of all, she prayed.

Then, in August 1999, her first reward came when, at the end of summer vacation, which the children spent with Peggy and John, Jonathan, then fourteen, adamantly refused to return to the home of Frances Goswick. Consequently, Judge Bell ruled that Jonathan could remain permanently in the custody of the Browns. It was a step that renewed Peggy's energy and gave her the first real hope that the family might one day be together again.

From the time she was a child, all Peggy Brown ever wanted was to marry and have children. Early on, she planned a career in nursing, but in the tenth grade, she dropped out to care for her ailing mother, even though she had eight brothers and sisters to help out. For Peggy, the youngest girl, it was a burden of love, and she was her mother's favorite.

Peggy Doris Moore, daughter of Burton and Myrtle Moore of Cocke County, was only fifteen the first time she set eyes on John Brown, but it was love at first sight. The courtship was barely three months long. Both she and John were living in Parrottsville when they met. "I knew his uncle," says Peggy. "I knew a lot of John's relatives. We lived up the road from his family. [One day,] I ran out of cigarettes, [and] my mother never did drive. She said, 'Go down there and ask one of Mr. Brown's boys if they are going to the store.' So I went down there and asked them. [John] was working on a car out there. His big blue eyes is what I saw. He was all greasy when he looked up at me, and that was all I saw, was those big blue eyes. That was that. He was twenty-three when we got married. We got married the twenty-third day of May, and John turned twenty-four the twenty-fifth day. I wanted to wait till his birthday, but he didn't."

The following year, Peggy gave birth to a boy she named John Wayne Brown, Jr. The couple called the baby "Punkin," a nickname that stuck with their son until the day he died.

This weekend, with Punkin's five children visiting for Easter and three other guests in her little hillside house in Parrottsville, Peggy has cooked a pot roast, mashed potatoes, green beans, and cornbread. For dessert, there is chocolate cake, one of her grandchildren's favorites. While she dishes out food and cuts up meat for the children as they dress for church, she spontaneously grabs up one child and kisses him, admonishes another for getting shoe polish on the rug, and then in the next breath tells him she loves him.

There will be no serpents in John Brown's church service tonight, not with the children there. Although they hope that their grandchildren might someday decide to become members of their church, the Browns are adhering strictly to the Cocke County Juvenile Court order against taking the children to services where snakes are present. John Brown believes this ruling is an infringement of his religious freedom, but he says he will do nothing to risk losing visitation rights.

Waiting to leave for services, freshly bathed and in clean clothes, the four youngest children sit on the front porch and play with Yoda, the new bulldog puppy John has bought for them. Jonathan has gone to visit his uncle and aunt, Mark and Shell Brown, who live ten minutes away. Jeremiah, Jacob, Sarah, and Daniel chatter about their grandmother's pet parakeet, which recently flew outside and was lost, and the two new birds Peggy has bought to replace it. Below the porch of the modest, gray one-story house with cream-colored shutters, the children's toys and bicycles are scattered among the flower beds, where spring roses and purple and yellow irises are blooming.

Peggy loves flowers, especially roses. Her curtains and slipcovers are printed with roses, and a vase of artificial roses sits on a table in her immaculately clean living room, where dozens of family photos hang on the walls—Punkin, Mark, Shell, the grandchildren, nephews, nieces, and other relatives. Peggy earns extra money by cleaning houses. And when she's not contacting people who might help in the custody suit, she quilts and sews, keeping her hands busy.

From the very beginning, the Browns have "fleeced the Lord" to advise them about what is best for the children. This means asking God to send them a sign. Peggy's son Mark explains what she means: "That's like when they took the kids. My dad put a fleece before the Lord [to ask] if the Lord wanted them to fight for 'em, [and to] let them have the money [to hire a lawyer] on a certain day [if He did]. Not by *their* money, but by *His* means. Come that certain day, they had the money they needed."

When Peggy and John talk about that experience, tears glitter in their eyes. "We asked the lawyer what the fee was," says John. "He told us. We said, 'Well, we'll put it like this. In three days, if we've got the money—not our own money—but if we've got the money on that day, then we will fight it.' On that day, we had it."

"People just give it to us," says Peggy.

"We didn't ask. We didn't *tell* nobody," John says, smiling. "We didn't put out the word. We didn't *ask* nobody. There was envelopes that come in here with twelve hundred dollars, one hundred dollars. One time, two thousand dollars. Sure did. That's why we went ahead with it. We weren't going to fight at all. We were just going to set up visiting rights, 'cause these children been through enough. God is God. There is none like Him, unto Him, and never will be. They might can take the children away from the home, but they won't take the home away from the children. That's the way of the spirit of God. They might take them away from the religion, but they'll not take the religion out of the children."

Peggy nods. "Those children weren't brainwashed or anything. When our own boys was old enough, if they would say, 'Mama, we don't want to go [to church],' they didn't go. We went by ourselves. That is what John was trying to get across to them. They had their own choice. Because if we had *made* them go to church, that wouldn't have put the Lord in their life. They had to *choose* the Lord. When you repent, you choose your life, you see. So that is what we give [our children]. They had to do it on their own. We couldn't make them. What [Melinda's family] is trying to say is that we *made* them be in our faith—to take up serpents—which we didn't."

Mark joins in. "I was never *taught* serpent handling. But I went to serpent-handling churches. . . . That is as far as it went. I didn't know anything about it until I got in it and started finding out for myself. Reading on it, studying it out."

How many of the Browns' nine grandchildren will follow in the serpent-handling tradition, no one knows, but on the night of Mark's ordination as a minister in the Marshall, North Carolina, church, John stood at the altar and looked down at the congregation. "These children setting here tonight are the future of the church," he said. But he also urged patience and caution, telling those who would handle serpents in the future to make sure they are anointed. John and Peggy Brown do not want to lose another loved one to a serpent's bite.

IN HER OWN WORDS
PEGGY BROWN

Punkin was five years old when we got in the church. Liston Pack [former minister of a church in Carson Springs] started coming by to talk. He and John went way back, to their mean days when they were young boys. So Liston invited us to church at Carson Springs. Then finally we did [go], and we repented . . . and started going to church there. That was September of '69.

The first time that anybody picked up a serpent at Carson Springs was when Jimmy Williams was the pastor there. They preached it—Mark 16—but that was the first time [serpent handling] was done in the church. They had been praying that if [that was what God wanted them to do, He should] send them a sign, if that's what [the verse] meant. We went to church on Saturday night, and Brother Jimmy Ray Williams—the one that died with strychnine—his daughter got up to go to the bathroom, which was outside, and there was a copperhead crawling in the door. And it had oil around it. They had been asking God for signs, *and there it was laying there in the doorway.*

That right there is why we have been so strong in believing the Scriptures. That's why our faith started to grow. After that, if we did anything, we prayed about it before we did it and asked God to show us. We put a fleece out. That was to show us that God was in that. That was the sign. It is an affirmation, so that we would know that it was God's will for us to do whatever we are asking Him. See, when you start praying to God to do something like that, what else can you do but believe it? Who else can do it except God, who you're asking? And I've never doubted it. The oil may have represented that [the snake] was sacred. It was God-sent. Jimmy Ray Williams handled the serpent that night.

The first time I handled, I could not tell you. You know, I can't remember exactly when. It was a rattlesnake, the first snake that I picked up. It was after my children were born. I was probably standing there singing or something. The feeling is like you really start feeling the spirit of the Lord. It is a good feeling. It is a peaceful feeling. You are rejoicing, and you love everybody. There is just no worry there. You feel protected.

I haven't been bitten, [but] I haven't taken up the serpent many times. Maybe a dozen times in twenty-nine years. I won't handle until I feel anointed. It's like, in my mind, I want to, but I won't do it. But every time I have done it, before I would go get [the snake], there was no fear, and I just had to get it. You want to hold it. I'm trying to think of words to describe it. It's in my legs; I can't stand still; I'm gone. It's an assured fact that it is okay, I'll put it that way. You just love everything. You love everybody. You don't see everything. It's not real. Like if there was somebody there that you knew didn't like you, you love them to death. You're not flesh anymore. You're not thinking *flesh* anymore. You see, it's spiritual. It's not fleshly, it's spiritual.

[Outside of being anointed,] I'm bad scared of snakes. And especially since John was bit and Punkin was bit. I have taken care of a lot of people that have been bit, but I've never been bitten. I'm just scared. I have to know that it is a sure fact that it is okay before I'll go.

Somebody asked me do I worry about my kids. I say, "Well, it worries me a lot." This was our greatest fear with Punkin. But we believe the Bible, and if you deny any part of the Bible, you'd be lost. We believe *every single word*, and if I tell [my children], "You're not supposed to do that," they're going to look at me and say, "Mama, the Bible says . . ." I would be denying the Bible.

[When John handles,] I do worry. When he got bit—he has been bit three times—I knew that he wasn't going to go to the doctor. I knew that. What else I knew was that I was going to depend on other people to pray. I begged the Lord, but as far as get down and pray, I didn't, 'cause I took care of John, plus my kids were small, too. And I knew that if God didn't heal him, there was a chance he would die. I mean, you know that. But it would be like John wanted it. He wouldn't go to the doctor. I even got accused by his family that I wanted him to die because I wouldn't take him to the doctor. But they know better than that now. He told them, "I won't go." They expect that now. This was cousins and that. But they found out better, and they don't say anything now, because they know how we believe.

[As a child,] Punkin would sit in the front of the church, right where he could see. Every time they'd ask if anyone wanted prayer, he was in the prayer line. From the time he was six up until the time he was maybe eleven or twelve, I never stopped him. He would just always go. He was always wanting in the prayer line. I believe [that] in his heart, he wanted to work for the Lord. That's what I always thought, right from the beginning. Now, he learned to play the guitar by watching them chord it. That's how much attention he paid. He just took everything in.

[When Punkin started handling serpents, I was] scared to death. It never goes away. Except that I have been in services when he took serpents up, but the fear would leave me. I knew it was all right. I felt safe for him. Well, he drank strychnine one night, and it hurt him. I never got scared. I was fine. It was buckling his legs, and he went outside, and I was walking behind him praying. I wasn't scared. We got home, *he* was fine. I got home, *I* went all to pieces. Because what it was, the spirit of the Lord was gone, the peace in me was gone, and I was the mother again.

There have been services we've been in before where there was a haze in the room when the serpents was into it—not necessarily if I [handled that night], or even when the spirit was moving. There been people in that church that got healed, and when that happened, it was like there was a haze. Now, Liston Pack's wife had a blood disease. They wasn't sure if it was leukemia or not, but she was going to the doctor getting tests done. She got healed [in church]. And this one time, Eunice Ball, Alfred Ball's wife, she hadn't eat. I can't remember how many days she'd went without eating. Her throat got bad, and they prayed over her, and she instantly got up and wanted to eat. Her throat was healed. Of course, people had got bit after that, [and] they got healed. People had come from out of state. There was one woman came in a wheelchair, and she got up and walked out. See, a lot of these things have happened.

I've always believed in the Lord, I *always* have. And even when I was small, I would try to figure out why there was God and why there was Jesus. They would teach you about God, and then they would say, "Praise Jesus." I wanted to know, "Why did you do that?" I was wondering in my youngun's mind, "Why did you do that?" As we got older and we got in our faith, we learned that Jesus Christ *is* God. So that wasn't hard to understand.

I was born in Bridgeton, New Jersey, third of July 1947. There were nine of us. I lived in New Jersey till I was five and my daddy passed away. I was the youngest girl. Mama and Daddy was from down here. How we got to New Jersey was, my oldest brother had gone up there to work—that's how it got started—and [he] had got Daddy a job in the apple and peach orchards, taking care of the trees. My brother was in the Korean War. The orchards furnished you a house to live in—like farming is here. We lived in a shack on the orchard. And when Daddy passed away, Mama had four kids left at home. Daddy had cancer and what the old people called dropsy, and now they call it congestive heart failure, you know, where your feet would swell. The rest [of the children] were married when Daddy died. Mama moved back down here [to Tennessee] 'cause it was cheaper living here.

One of my sisters passed away after her son was born. [The son,] Chris Austin, [is] the manager of a funeral home [now]. When he was six weeks old, my sister hemorrhaged. That was when they had to send after the plasma in North Carolina, and it didn't get back in time. I was three—two or three—at the time.

When we moved back down here, Mommy worked and drawed Social Security on us. She worked cleaning the WLIK radio station to make ends meet. We moved to different places to get a better house. I grew up in and around Newport. I had more or less a happy childhood. We didn't have anything. We didn't have any money. Mama got a check once a month—that's when you got groceries. Then she run a bill at the store. Where we lived, we lived in Edwine most of the time. This man owned a store up there, and he'd let us [run up a bill]. She wouldn't get anything except flour and milk—things you had to have. And then she'd pay for it when she got the check.

The [New Jersey] house was in the orchards, so all you had to do if you wanted fruit was go outside and get it. I was little then, and before [Daddy] passed away, we had moved to a township, Shiloh, and Daddy would go back and forth to work. Mommy worked in the field cutting asparagus for a canning company, McCormick.

Like I said, when we come down here [to Tennessee], it was cheaper living, and she didn't have to work as hard. And we got pretty decent housing then. It was just like fifteen, twenty dollars a month rent. The most we paid for one was thirty a month. It wasn't anything fancy, but it had enough room. Plus, it was warm.

Mama was married to Daddy twenty-six years. Daddy was mean. Daddy beat her, but I don't remember that. The other kids have told me that. He wasn't a drinker, but he was mean. About all I remember about my daddy was him picking me up and carrying me. And he petted me. I was the baby girl. That's what I remember, and that's really all I care to remember. Daddy was real jealous of Mama, and [that's why] he used to beat her. [After he died, it was] good and bad. Mama had a boyfriend. And this man, he drank. He wasn't abusive. He didn't hit her or anything, but he drank. I just didn't like drinking.

Mama always taught us about the Lord. She didn't go to church that much, but I did. I always went to Bible school. Every time they had vacation Bible school, I was ready. And I went to Sunday school, but even when I was growing up, I didn't like Sunday school. I would go to hear the preaching, but I didn't like Sunday school, and as I got older, I thought how odd that was, because usually a kid won't sit and listen to preaching. I loved to hear the preacher. Mama never kept us from going, and once in a while, she might go, but she wasn't one to go all the time. But she did believe in the Lord, and she taught us. You was not allowed to use cuss words, not around my mother. None of her kids were allowed to say any cuss words when they were home. [Long after] my sister was married and had four kids, she came out with a big [cuss word], and I saw Mama smack her mouth. But she was in Mama's house, and Mama said, "You do that in your home, but you don't do it here."

She taught us about the Bible, but [she] didn't read it to us. But I did. I read the Bible when I got old enough to pick it up. Mama's relatives were Pentecostal Holiness, her sister and them. And Mama never did say that much, but I heard that's what she was, growing up. That's how she talked. And somewhere, I was taught—I guess it was [by] my mother—that [people are] married one time, and no matter what, we stay married one time. No divorce. Now, I never did believe in divorce either, even growing up. Which, my brothers and sisters, they *have* divorced. Well, they always told me, my older sisters and brothers, "You're so down-to-earth, you're so down-to-earth." I always took everything serious. That's how I was. To have fun, I had a playhouse built on the creek bed, and I played with dolls till I was twelve. I always loved dolls.

When I quit school, I was in the tenth grade. Now, I was a straight-A student, never failed a year from kindergarten on. Well, my mother had a stroke when I was in the tenth grade. She had two. She hemorrhaged twice through her nose from blood pressure. I talked her into letting me quit school and stay home and take care of her. It scared me because she lived by herself. Now, I loved my mother, was close to my mother. She was arguing with me about it. She wanted me to go on, because my brother was going to take me to go to nursing school. I loved to care for kids, I loved to care for people, so I talked her into letting me quit. I said, "All I want to do is get married and have kids." I done had my mind made up, and that's what I wanted. So she said okay, and I quit in the tenth grade. We had moved back to New Jersey, but we didn't stay long, and after she hemorrhaged, she thought maybe [living there] was what had brought it on, and she wasn't satisfied there. My [oldest] brother more or less talked her into trying it for a while, because the majority of my relatives lived up there, so she tried it for a while, and we moved back. [Then] she had a real bad stroke, and she called and asked me if I would come and take care of her. John and I lived in Michigan then. Now, mind you, I had sisters here, but I was always the one that took everything serious. And that's what she depended on. I took care of a lot of her bills.

After we got married, John and I went to New Jersey. He went up there [first] and got a job. He had friends up there, and he had lived up there before. I'd been married one month when I got pregnant, and my mother wouldn't let

me go. Now, I'm married, but she wouldn't let me go on the bus by myself. She rode all the way up there on the bus with me, spent the night, and rode all the way back, just to make sure I got there. That's how she was.

We moved up there when I was about four months pregnant—I was showing a little bit—and we lived up there until Punkin was six weeks old, and we moved back here [to Tennessee]. And then [when Punkin] was a little over a year old, we moved back to Michigan. John was landscaping. He worked for a fellow at this great big cemetery, and they did the landscaping, fixed the graves real pretty. The man that run it was a friend of his daddy's. He worked there for years and then worked at another landscaping job after that.

We lost a baby up there—five months old. They called it crib death. His name was Greg. I had him to the doctor that day. I slept with him all night because he was sick. They gave him a shot, said he had a cold. Up there, they had an osteopath. That's who I took him to. And they sent him home, and that night, I was up with him almost all night. And I put him to bed and laid down for a while. And I got up to see about him, and he was dead. I blamed myself for a long time, but they had to do an autopsy. The coroner come to the house, and he took the medicine [the doctor had prescribed for the baby], and he asked me had the doctor give him a shot, and he took [the doctor's] name and all that, and the coroner told me it was the doctor's fault. The baby had pneumonia, and his lungs filled up when I laid him down, which I didn't know. The coroner said that when I took him to the doctor that day, he should have been put in oxygen. They took [the doctor's] license, but I didn't find this out for a long time. [Greg] was five months old the day we buried him. He was born in July, and that was in December.

I lost another one after him. I've had five. Five births. I had two were still-born. The doctor told me that the last one [after Mark] was a girl. I remember it like it was yesterday. I was twenty-six years old, and I begged him to tie my tubes. And he said no. He was a Seventh-Day Adventist. I liked him real well. And he said, "No, you found out you can have a girl. You don't want to do that [have your tubes tied] after all these boys." But I started hemorrhaging, all night long. And John said, "No more." But the doctor told me that if I wanted to have another baby, he couldn't find nothing wrong other than when the baby would start gaining weight, I would give way, and then the labor started, depending on the weight of the baby. Then he said I would have to stay in bed. And John was scared. He said, "No. No more." He said, "We have Mark and Punkin, and we need you." Like I said, the doctor was Seventh-Day Adventist, and they don't believe in blood transfusions, but if you need one, they do it. But he knew that we were really religious about that, too, so John's brother had the same type blood that I had, and [the doctor] told John, "If it comes down to it, that she has to have [a transfusion], tell [your brother] that he has to stay here." He was going to take it right from him and put it in me. Now, they don't do that now, but then they did. So John's brother stayed with me all night. And finally, [the doctor] told John, "She's really weak." But he had a nurse, and she sat by my bed all night. All night long. And [then the doctor] said, "If I see that she's going to have to have [a transfusion], then we'll do it, but if we can get past it, we won't." And I got past it. I was weaker than all get-out, but I got by it.

Jacob, the third one, weighed three pounds, ten ounces, and I held him.

They let me hold him. I couldn't go to the funeral, but John showed me everything, what he picked out [for the baby to wear].

After I lost Greg, I put everything on Punkin. I mean, he was my son, my love. He was all I had.

I tried to get pregnant after I lost Jacob, 'cause Punkin was five, and I wanted another baby, and there was nothing to keep me from it. I was healthy. But after we were in church a month, I got pregnant. *One month*. See, God wouldn't let me have one till we straightened up. Before I joined the church, something was missing.

I don't like to talk about John when I tell it as he told it, but John was an alcoholic. See, I knew that when I married him, but I mean, I *loved* him. But he did change. And I wasn't no angel or anything. But of course, I was a kid. When I left home, I was fifteen. I'd never had a chance to be in no bars. But my mother, in her own right, she was strict. The only places I went was [to] spend weekends with my sister.

But mostly [the thing missing in our lives] was that John was an alcoholic, and he would leave and stay gone, two or three days at a time. Now, he always worked good. He was a good provider. But sure as the weekend come, he'd leave. See, I didn't drive a car till Mark was two years old. I never drove. So where I was [when John went off], that's where I stayed, unless I could get somebody to come and take me home. So when I got my own home, I stayed home, me and Punkin. I had my baby, I was fine, and I loved John. He did that right on up to when Punkin was a baby. But like I said, he always worked hard. He never drank on the job. He got his check and took me to the grocery store. We always had groceries. He'd give me the money. He kept what he wanted, and he was gone. That's the way it was.

But John changed, and I got pregnant. And honest, this is the truth. When I'd start feeling the Lord, Mark would do didos [somersaults] like he was feeling it, buddy. He would flip. When I'd start feeling the Lord, he would feel it, too. If you'd had music with it, it wouldn't have been no better. And that's the truth. And when I told him that later, he would just grin. Because they loved the Lord, both my kids did. And that story thrilled him, because he felt the Lord. See, I almost lost him. I got scared. I was begging the Lord. Another thing. When Mark was born, he weighed four pounds. His lungs collapsed, and we had to take him to the University of Tennessee Hospital and put him in intensive care. The nurses brought him to let me hold him, 'cause they didn't think he

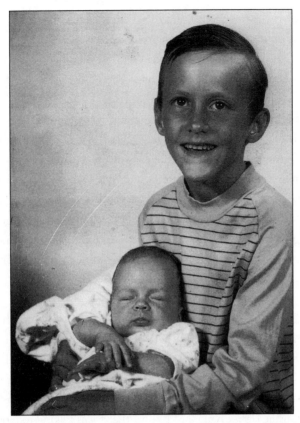

Six-year-old Punkin holding his newborn brother, Mark in 1970
Family photo

was going to live. His lungs weren't developed.

But God showed me my baby was going to be all right. I had a dream before I had him. I had a dream that I was in this room, and there were babies in caskets, but they wasn't dead. And then when he was born, they took him to the university hospital. They was supposed to keep him until he weighed five pounds. Everybody went to pray for him—Jimmy Williams, Joe Williams. When I went to get him, he was in those incubators. Those babies were sitting all around [in bassinets], but they wasn't dead. You see, that was the dream. The doctor looked at me, and he said, "There is nothing wrong with this baby." He smiled. "You can take him home." There was another doctor there who didn't agree with that. [But the first] doctor said, "She'll take better care of him than we will." I brought him home. He weighed three pounds, ten ounces. His head was [tiny]. You couldn't hold him. I had to hold him on a pillow to burp him.

And then when I went down there to get him, I knew my baby was all right. God has blessed me with him for twenty-nine years.

To me, that's miracles. When you got God in your life, you see the miracles. They's people who prayed so hard for him. There's been a lot of things happen like that down through the years.

Speaking in tongues, I guess you could say, is my Sign. See, in the Bible, it says "the gift of diverse kinds of tongues." What it was, when I went out there [to Carson Springs] and heard them other women speak, I wanted to do that. I went out there for a long time before I did it, but I kept praying [that] the Lord would let me do it. It's beautiful. So one night there at the church, God moved on me, and it was like I was carried away, boy. I started speaking in tongues at the first of the service and was still speaking in tongues at the end of the service, and that's like talking from seven-thirty to nine or ten o'clock. And then it clicked off. It was like a dream. I mean, I was there, but I *wasn't* there. And I'm telling you, I *loved* it.

You feel so clean after the spirit leaves you. You feel *so clean*. That's the best way to put it. I was so tired, and the pastor of the church come over, and he said, "Did you pray for the gift of diverse kinds of tongues?" I said, "No, I just wanted to speak in tongues." He said, "You must have spoke in four or five." And they still say that God give me the gift of different kinds of tongues. I didn't know what I was saying, but I know that I was talking to God.

In the Scripture, there's an unknown tongue which you're speaking directly to God, and then there's a tongue that you interpret. And see, I prophesy and interpret. There was something happened in church one day, and I had heard gossip, but I didn't know nothing about it, 'cause we wasn't going there, we was going to the Marshall church, and [this brother they were talking about] had a church in another town. And some of the brothers was praying about something. They'd been told this gossip but didn't know if it was true or not, and they asked the Lord to tell them. *Through me.* Because I didn't know all this. And one night, John said, "Let's go to this other church." We still didn't know anything about this gossip. And God spoke through me to this brother and told him to leave us, gave him Scriptures and everything. See, when God uses me to do it, I can't remember everything I said. It's like I'm standing here, and it's coming out of my mouth. I couldn't tell you everything I said. Bits and pieces, but not what I'm saying in a row. God told me Scriptures. God told [the brother] to depart from that building and not to come back. And after church, [the other brothers] told me what it was. Because it scared me, saying things about this man I didn't even know, so God sent us there for that purpose that night.

Now, this has not just come since I got in this faith. This is my belief ever since I've been big enough to realize that God existed: That everybody is put here for a purpose. And for me, my purpose has always been to have children and take care of my children. That's always been my purpose.

Back when we first started in the church, there was people that I got really upset with because they wouldn't take their kids to a doctor. I got all tore up because they wouldn't take them. I don't believe that way. A child is innocent. Adults are old enough to make a decision. That is up to you, but I don't believe you should do a child that way. Which I didn't mine, but I saw people when we first started out, like I said, their kids' eyes would be glassy [with fever]. I didn't like that business. I never could do that, because I couldn't stand to see my kids suffer like that. I took mine to the doctor.

We take care of our children. We love our younguns and our grandchildren just as much as anybody else loves their children, now.

Mark and John Brown at Mark's ordination in 1999
Photo by Fred Brown

AVOIDING THE LAKE OF FIRE

JOHN BROWN
B. 1939

"God spoke to Brother Pack and said, 'There will be a sign, and around where the sign's at, there will be oil.' About a week or two after that, . . . [a member] was going out the church door, and there was a copperhead crawling in the door . . . [and] there was oil all the way around it. . ."

THIS WAS IN BAXTER, KENTUCKY, sometime in the 1980s. It was a hot summer night, and there were very few open spaces on the old-fashioned oak pews. John Brown was behind the pulpit, preaching in his personal fashion—soft, reassuring, persuasive. He is a slender, wiry man with thinning hair and the leathery skin of someone who has worked outdoors most of his life. Outside the church, he looks like a grandfatherly type, but when he stands behind the pulpit and speaks, it is with an authority that is delivered so earnestly that it seems impossible to deny. When John Brown talks about God, he makes the news seem fresh, as if he has just spoken to his Lord and is relating that heavenly message to the congregation as it has come to him. He has been reading and studying the Bible for so long that he can quote any chapter and verse. The words weave themselves into his everyday conversation so smoothly and thoroughly that almost everything he says has a spiritual tone.

Brown has not always followed the religious precepts he preaches today, but the message means more to the congregation coming from someone who was once a sinner and has now turned the sharp, hard corner to righteousness.

As John Brown preached that night, darkness rose around the tiny church. The service had begun in daylight, but now it was growing late. The building pulsated with singing and shouting. The rattle of a tambourine mingled with the rattles of serpents coiled and waiting in boxes near the altar. The first was a joyful, man-made noise, the other a dangerous warning. Suddenly, as if propelled, John Brown scurried to the front of the pulpit, where a row of long, dark boxes was lined up. Some ornate, some carved with *Mark 16* on their lids, the boxes were filled with an assortment of deadly reptiles—copperheads, yellow rattlers, timber rattlers. The copperheads were thin and long and the rattlesnakes thick and sinewy, marked with black and brown diamonds. Their triangular heads swayed from side to side as their tongues flicked out and up, testing the air or, as the late serpent handler Charles Prince used to say, "biting at the wind."

On that night, John Brown opened not one but two boxes and pulled out two enormous rattlers, one in each hand. He held them close to his chest, and as he watched them, his expression began to change. His mouth clenched, his forehead tightened, and his complexion turned a deep red. Not once did he take his eyes off the snakes. And then, in one lightning-quick motion, he gave both rattlers an abrupt and vehement shake. As if charged with an electric jolt, the snakes shot upright into the air above Brown like pieces of twisted iron. Then, just as abruptly, he shook them once more, and the reptiles fell limp in his hands, hanging to the floor like lifeless ropes. A third shake sent them straight up again, stiff and startled. A final shake, and the snakes dropped to Brown's side like cut vines. Finally, calmly, he put the snakes back into their boxes and continued his sermon.

Afterward, he explained his facility with the serpents. "It is the power of God," he said. "God did that."

You have to accept some of the unbelievable things that take place in serpent-handling services because you have seen them with your own eyes. And when such an account comes from John Brown, you believe him, for he is a man of God who knows the long, hard road he has climbed and the even longer path he must take to salvation. Like Job, he has experienced heartache and turmoil for following the mandates of his religion. And like Job, he has wondered and sometimes wandered. But John Brown has never completely put aside his beliefs. He has lost several friends and two beloved family members to the snake-handling religion, from either snakebite or strychnine. His most heart-wrenching loss came with the death of his older son, Punkin.

Now, on another summer night, at his own church in Marshall, North Carolina, Brown is participating in an ordination service for his son Mark and a favorite nephew, Steve Frazier. You can't help seeing a tinge of worry in John's faded blue eyes. He is proud but somehow wary as he urges the two young men to "wait on the Lord to move" before picking up serpents. "With the Lord, everything is possible," John Brown says. "Without Him, danger lurks. With God, there is power and glory."

He compares life without God to what Job called "the land of gloom and chaos, where light is like darkness." Brown has witnessed both the glory of God and the gloom of chaos. He has watched churches come and go and seen faithful members slide back into the world. He himself once turned from the church to walk in the gloom, only to return to the religion that nurtures him. John Brown, like John the Baptist, has walked in the wilderness, has been baptized in the name of Jesus Christ, and has urged repentance. He believes firmly in the tenets of the snake-handling churches, that Mark 16 is the true Word. To believe otherwise, he says, is to deny God's proclamations. In this quest for obedience to the Word in Mark 16, Brown has been bitten three times. He once hovered between life and death for nine days, swollen from navel to neck. Although he believed then that he was about to meet his maker, he knows now that God had other plans for him. Those plans include not only Peggy, his wife of thirty-six years, and his son Mark and daughter-in-law Rachelle, but also his nine grandchildren.

John Brown was born in Cocke County, which still has a reputation for spawning tough, independent, and sometimes lawless people who are wary of the outside world. Most of the residents are of Scots-Irish descent, and like their ancestors, they are used to hard times. John and Peggy have had to work hard all their lives to support their family and their church.

John was brought into the serpent-handling religion by Liston Pack, one of the county's reformed tough guys. Pack founded the Carson Springs Church in Jesus Name after a life of rugged individualism and innumerable clashes with law enforcement. One day, while the two men were traveling in South Carolina, Liston convinced John to be baptized. It was a turning point in John's tumultuous life, the first step away from his old ways to where he is today. His past was not much different from that of hundreds of other Cocke County boys brought up on sharecropper farms with little hope and even fewer dreams. He just found something better to look forward to.

IN HIS OWN WORDS
JOHN BROWN

I was somewhere around thirteen or fourteen years old when my grandfather died. Oh, Lord, I was close to him. His name was Jake Hance. He meant a lot to me. He'd take me to church with him anytime I wanted to go. That was often. About every week. If Pa went, I went. He lived with Dad and Mom, and when he'd go to church, I would go. When he died, I missed him a lot. But I'd try to remember what he taught me and everything. I'd always think, "Well, if I do right, and if I live right, then I'll be with him again someday." But [it] didn't happen until later on that I changed my ways.

Pa always went to different denominations. He'd go to Church of God, he'd go to Baptist, the Holiness—just wherever he could get a service that day, that's where he'd go. I never did hear him say anything harsh or anything about a minister or anything like that. I'd ask him sometime, I'd say, "Pa, what do you think about this preacher?" He'd say, "Son, he's a good 'un." And that is the only thing I ever heard him say.

He would stand and testify, and I remember the words that he would say. He'd testify about what a glorious time he was going to have when he reached heaven. There he'd be with his heavenly father forevermore. And there would be times I'd ask him, I'd say, "Pa, if you are sick, aren't you going to the doctor?" He'd say, "Yeah, I'm going to *my* doctor." And I'd see him slip off. He had a place in the woods. We lived down in the lower part of Cocke County in Rankin on a farm down there. I followed him one time [and] hid behind a tree. He was out there praying. He was seeking the Lord to heal him. Out in the woods, on his knees praying. And, Lord, it wouldn't be long until he'd be better. I guess that is where I get a lot of my faith from. Sometimes, I don't think I have much of that. But anyway, that is where I get a lot of that from, because of the things that he did and the things that he taught me to believe in—that God was able to do all things, just not *some* things, but *all* things.

But Pa would not go to a doctor. When he died, he was working. He had a stroke. His children took him to the doctor then. That's the only time I can ever remember him going to a doctor. He lived about ten days after the stroke. But he never regained consciousness. He was sixty-five years old when he died.

He wasn't an old man. He was retired, but he was a sharecropper, and he still done a little farming and stuff like that.

I was born in Cocke County. I have two sisters and four brothers, and I am the third child. My parents, Homer and Goldia Mae, were sharecroppers in Cocke County. Both of them were born in Cocke County. Dad and Mom went up north in the early 1960s. Dad went to work on a farm. I continued going to church until I was maybe about seventeen years old, [and then] I got out. I joined the service. That was 1956. I went in the army [for four years], and then I went into the navy for four years. I was on the USS *Alfred A. Cunningham*, destroyer. We were out of the West Coast. I did think about making a career out of the military. You know how a young man is. He thinks twenty years is a lifetime, which is not even a drop in the bucket, so I changed my mind and got out and went into carpentry.

After my grandfather died, I had some wild years. *Really* wild. I was *wild*, I'd just soon tell you. I was overseas a lot, had my good times. I enjoyed what I was doing, enjoyed my time in the service. When I got out, I went to work here in Tennessee.

Peggy and I lived near each other in Parrottsville. She was really pretty. We was married in 1963, May 23. I was twenty-three years old at the time. I just known I needed me a wife, and that was it. I was working on the farm at the time. I worked for the Stokely Brothers. I transplanted just about everything— cabbage, tomatoes, corn, all that. And then for a while, I did remodeling. I sold insulated windows, replacement windows while I was working at Stokely. Then we left and went to Michigan. I came back here off and on from Michigan for about twelve years. There was no work around here. We moved to Michigan, and I landscaped, done construction, worked in the cemetery. That's what I did when we first went up there. We dug graves and kept maintenance on the cemetery, things like that. I done repair work. They'd hold the services there, and we'd put the people away, you know. Dug the graves. And then I went into landscaping. Worked that a few years, and then I went into injection molding, plastics. I worked there until I come back to Tennessee permanent. That was in 1973. I never did work in the car industry. I made parts for them, but I didn't work in it. We molded parts for the car. That was the injection plastics. We took contracts through them.

I got into snake handling around 1968 or 1969. I was dating a girl around 1961 or 1962, [and] her family went to the serpent-handling church, and her dad had gotten bitten and died. I went to church with them and got acquainted with this serpent handling, but you know, I didn't pay much attention to it then, because I wasn't interested. But later on, I got to reading the Word of God and studying, even before I become a Christian. I understood about the Godhead and about serpent handling, and then later on, Liston Pack—he was the main inspiration in my life, I guess—[brought] me into it.

At that time, about 1967, I was an alcoholic. Liston got interested and [prayed] for me. He'd come to my house, and he'd stay hours at a time. He even lost his job over it, talking to us about the Scriptures and about the Bible and about the love of Jesus. Then me and him went on a trip to South Carolina, and we stopped on Sunday morning down there at a little church. It was the Assembly of God or Pentecostal Holiness, something like that. That is where I repented at. This was in Greenville. Liston was going visiting people, and I was just going with him. It was not a Signs Following church. It was a Pentecostal church. It was before Liston had a church here in Newport. Then, gradually, I got to going out there [to Carson Springs] and got into serpent handling. Since then, I've been in it.

[The way it got started,] Brother Pack was up here on the mountain praying. We had been praying about the Lord letting us take up serpents. There might have been one or two who had taken them up, but there had never been any in [that] church. God spoke to Brother Pack and said, "There will be a sign, and around where the sign's at, there will be oil." About a week or two after that, we went to church on Saturday night, and Brother Jimmy Ray Williams— the one that [later] died with strychnine—his daughter was going out the church door, and there was a copperhead crawling in the door. That snake just came in by itself. It happened like God said it was to beforehand, and it come to pass. It crawled back out into the yard, and where the serpent was at, there was oil all the way around it. This was not car oil. It was just oil. I don't know how it got there. It was fresh oil. Sure was. Brother Jimmy took and put [the snake] in a paper bag, took it in the church, and handled it.

What we did, we put what we call a fleece out. Let me give you an example. In the days of Gideon, the angel of the Lord come unto Gideon and said that God had chose him to deliver Israel out of the hands of the Midianites, their enemies. So Gideon fleeced the Lord. He put a piece of wool out on the ground and said, "Now, Lord, if this is You, let all the ground around this wool be wet, but let the fleece of wool be dry." So next morning, he got up. The ground was wet, and the wool was dry. So he prayed again and said, "Lord, don't be angry at me," but he put it out there again and said, "Now, let the *wool* be wet, and let the *ground* be dry." So the next morning, the wool was wet, and the ground was dry. So that is why we say a *fleece*. We put it before the Lord, and if that comes to pass, we go ahead and mind the Lord. So that copperhead was a fleece.

Brother Jimmy Williams, he was the one who took it up that night. That was the first time I had ever saw serpents taken up. He come in, and he opened the bag, and he reached his hand down in the bag and took the serpent himself. Oh, Lord, I wasn't afraid. I never felt the power of God so strong in my life. The Lord had me *covered* up that night. Lord. There was nothing going to happen to me. Jimmy was the only one who handled it that night, though.

It was a year after that [when] Brother Buford Pack—he's the [other] one who died with the strychnine—he was coming to my house. He wasn't a Christian then, but he'd keep me up all night long talking about the Word of God. I was working every day. This is *night after night*. Finally, I got down and prayed and said, "Lord, if you are going to save him, *save* him." Buford said, "I understand the Godhead now, but I'm not sure about these snakes. I'm going to go catch one and see if they'll handle them."

They was having a revival starting on Saturday night in Carson Springs Holiness Church of God. Me and Buford went to the mountains. We hunted all day, and late in the evening, we found one. Little ole black rattler. They brought it out there, and Brother Mark Doyle Morrisy from Middlesboro, Kentucky, and Brother Tommy Coots, they were the ones holding the revival. We had [the snake] in a paper bag. We didn't know no better then. We'd just throw them in a paper bag or anything. We took it out there, and Brother Jimmy, he just took that bag, shook it out, and took that rattler up. It was just as calm as it could be. Well, it was about an hour before church service started, and Brother Buford, he said he had to run to North Carolina and get his family. He said he'd be back. By the time church service started—it might have been started five minutes— Buford and his family come through the door, and Buford went straight to the altar and prayed [repented his sins] that night. That serpent was taken up, but I still didn't handle serpents that night.

It was about a month or so later the Lord let me take them up. I believed it ever since. Mostly, I handle them when I am anointed. Well, it moves on people in different ways. Sometimes, I've handled them just through the word of knowledge, that God will speak to your mind and you just take them up. But now, there is an anointing of God that can move in your life, and you just *know* it. You can't keep your hands off of [serpents then].

The first time I got bit, Mark was about a month old. I was the first one of them that got bit out there in Carson Springs. By a rattler. I was in bed one morning about four. The Lord woke me up and spoke. He said, "There is a sign on the mountain." So I called another brother, and I said, "I want you to go on the mountain with me. The Lord spoke to me and told me there is a sign there." So I drove up on the mountain. We had a place there where we parked when we'd look for serpents. I looked. We walked around there for maybe three or four hours and got down and prayed, and I said, "Lord, I know you spoke to me. You told me there was a sign here." He spoke again and said, "A little higher on the mountain." So I got in my car and started up the mountain and went around a curve, and there it laid, just stretched out in the road. It was the prettiest little light rattler you ever saw—a timber rattler. I had a paper bag. I went back, and the brother said, "We better get us a stick or something." I said, "No, the Lord give this 'un to me. It'll be all right." I walked back, reached down, picked it up, put it in the bag, and went on top of the mountain, and the Lord give me victory over that.

We come back off and took it down to Brother Jimmy's, and he handled it. He said, "That one will bite somebody." I said, "Lord, brother, don't tell me that." He said, "Yeah, that one will bite somebody."

So I got ready and went on to church and had it in a box. When I went to church, I just set it up on the car hood, and they was a Baptist sister there that night. She walked by it and said, "If that one bites somebody, the undertaker will take him out of here." It was a pretty good-sized rattler. When she said that, I just went out. I mean, there was the greatest feeling come over me that I'd ever had. And the Lord began to speak to my mind [to] tell me what to do.

The service was going good and the Lord said, "Take it out [of the box]," and said, "When you take it out, it is going to bite you, and it is going to swell you from one joint to the other." Church was full. I reached my hand down there and took it out. It bit me right there. And for a long time, nobody known I's bit. It didn't even swell. It didn't do anything. Finally, Don Pack told Brother Jimmy, said, "Brother Brown's bit." It wasn't bothering me until I looked back at Punkin setting there. Punkin was about five or six years old. He was setting about middleways in the church. Fear come upon me, because I had been told that it would take about forty-five minutes or an hour for a serpent bite to kill you. I said, "Lord, is this my time?" and he said, "Not yet, my son."

Brother Jimmy Williams began to preach. The spirit of the Lord was just carrying me across that floor and back. [The bite] swelled from here to here. But not much—'bout like a wasp sting. I let them know that I had been bitten. Naturally, I'm going to fear. It is just a natural man's fear. But then the spirit of the Lord moved on me, and it'd carry me across the floor and back. I felt real good, and the only thing that I felt out of that [bite] was a little numbness across the top of my lip. My arm didn't hurt. Didn't get sick. Nothing. It didn't hurt me, so I went on to bed and went to sleep. The next morning, I went to North Carolina. I preached up there on the mountain the next day. That made my faith stronger. But I been bit twice since then. I got hurt real bad one time. Through it all, I've had my trials and my tribulations. And I'm still holding on.

It's not hard to keep the faith if you really trust in the Lord, and I trust in the Lord. All things, I trust in the Lord. I did get out of the church one time. This was about 1985. Not for long, though. When you aren't going to church, then you are backslid. That's the way I feel about it. If you are not going forward, then you are backing up. I got out then because that was when Punkin's mother-in-law come and took Jonathan away, see. We had quite a few problems. I'm not proud of that. Not at all. But anyway, it wasn't for long, and I got back in the Lord, and I've been there ever since. I was out for about a year or so. I didn't do anything wrong—you know, bad wrong—but still yet, if you are not in the church, you are not doing the things you ought to do. That's the way I look at it.

Before that, we had built a church in Marshall, North Carolina, in 1974. I had been a minister since 1970, and I was minister in Marshall in 1974. But there was a time when I closed the church down for a few years because there was a lot of envy and strife and jealousy going on. So I shut her down. That was probably in 1983. I opened it back up about 1986. Lester Ball took it over. After he left, I didn't feel led to go back at that time, because there was so much confusion and stuff going on. But later on, I did, and we've been there ever since. I didn't take it back over until somewhere around '86 or '87. What was going on most of all, it was jealousy between the people. And God don't work at all in that. Because you got to take up serpents, and working the Signs of the Gospel, or to win anybody unto the Lord, you've got to have perfect love. You've got to have that in your heart.

We lost a few members, and I have lost members since Punkin's death in October [1998]. Probably because of fear. I don't know whether it is something to do with the law, but there has been one or two call me and told me that they probably wouldn't be back. They didn't give that reason [fear of the law], but you could read between the lines. But that goes on. I mean, it is understandable. The ones that left the church, they didn't have any children. So I think it is just being involved maybe with the law that they were afraid of. At one time, back before Lester took over, I probably had forty members. It is down to probably fifteen now. When Punkin and Melinda got serpent-bit and died, that caused a lot of fear among the people. That is normal. If you had children going to church like that, and if the law began to come in and say, "Well, this is it, we are going to take your children because of what you believe," you know you are going to have fear.

The fifteen members who come there now are solid. They have been with me for a long time. We are trying to build the church back up right now. We have some come and go, you know. You might go one night and have five or six, and the next night, you might have thirty or forty. We have Baptist people come and visit. There is one Baptist minister who comes there, and he ministers sometimes. He's more of a hard-shell Baptist. He's not a serpent handler, but he's coming along. He's getting more involved, you know.

Both Punkin and Mark came up in the church. But now, they also went to the church of their choice. I never did encourage them. When they come to be fourteen or fifteen years old, they were out with ball games, and they went where most of the other children went. I never made them go to church.

Punkin, I believe, was seventeen when he got in the church. And the first time he was bit, it was by a copperhead. [Punkin was away from home at the time.] Before that, that week, I dreamed that Punkin got bit but wasn't handling a serpent. He'd just got through preaching, and he went over to help—this was in the dream. Somebody had had the serpents out, and they was trying to get them back into the box, and he went over to help to get them back, and one jumped out on the floor and hit him on the leg. But I saw in the dream that no harm come to him, so I known it would be all right.

And when he called and told me he was going to die, that was exactly how it had happened. I got tickled and laughed. I known he was just scared, you see. He said, "Daddy, you better get up here in a hurry. If you want to see me again, you better get up here in a hurry." But the Lord had already showed me that

Punkin was going to be all right. I got tickled. Me and him both were laughing. We couldn't help it, you know. It tickled me real good. I had already saw that he was all right. I laughed and said, "Well, we are on our way." I said, "Raise your hand and praise the Lord, and thank the Lord for that bite." By the time we got up there, he was all right. We come home the next night. He was doing all right. It swelled up in [his chest]. He had never been bitten by a rattler before. This was in 1990, and Melinda was pregnant with the twins.

This is also when he began holding revivals. Now, he would hold revivals for two, three weeks at a time. No telling how many souls were saved in those revivals, [how many] people healed. He'd tell about people being healed, and people being saved, and people coming back to the Lord that had fallen away, you know. And really, that was his desire. He would hear maybe somebody in the church was having trouble, and then you'd find Punkin there. He would be trying to get it straightened out. He'd pray. He'd go to Georgia, Tennessee, North Carolina. That's where his ministry was, mostly. He was the evangelist of our little church. He would go. If somebody asked him, he would be there. He was not only an evangelist, but he was an apostle of the church. The apostles' job was to establish the church and to work Signs and miracles and wonders. Whatever was wrong in the church, then they would try their best to get that out, so that the spirit of the Lord could move freely. More or less, Punkin did that job. [When] he would hear about two brothers having trouble or something, he was there.

In the last three or four years, Punkin probably only preached one or two times at our church. He was more outgoing than we were. Yeah, he was a member of our church, but he was gone most of the time. Mark is there about every service. Now, Mark was around nineteen, maybe, when he come into the church. But there was never any pressure on my children to go to my church. It was by their own choice they're in it. That's just like by my own choice that I'm into it. It was of their choice. I never did push them.

It was like when Melinda got bit. Handling was her choice. She was twenty-eight years old, and she had been handling serpents since she was fourteen years old. She was handling when she was bit in Middlesboro. She come up speaking in tongues [and] took the serpent. I didn't really see it bite her, but Mark told me it had bit her. I didn't feel no fear at all. I had no fear on me whatsoever. I asked her, I said, "Do you want to go to the doctor?" She said no. [I] went outside, and I asked her again, "Do you want to go to the doctor?" No, she said.

[Then] she looked at me, and she said, "I have never danced like that before."

The serpent bit her in the forearm. Now, that was a big serpent. It never even acted like it was going to bite. Punkin was singing. I didn't handle that serpent, but I had handled serpents that day. A lot of us had—Bruce [Helton], Punkin, Allen [Williams], Brother [Carl] Porter. Oh, there were a bunch of them. I don't understand it to this day. She had never been bitten before. They took her to over at Brother Jamie's [Jamie Coots, the minister of the church]. And Punkin begged her to go to the doctor. He certainly did. [Some people] told that he didn't, but he tried and begged. He'd tell her to think about the children. She wouldn't do it.

I had to come home. I brought Punkin over to get the children. He went back, but I didn't go back because I thought she was going to be all right. She wasn't delirious. I felt like that she was going to be all right, and I was going to go to work next day. I said [to Melinda] before I left, I said, "You know who I am, don't you?" She looked at me and grinned and said, "Yeah, I know who you are."

Now, they got me over here in court because of this right here, Mark 16: "They shall take up serpents." But yet they preach from the same Bible, deliver the same Bible. They preach the same Word of God, but when they come down to the Signs of the Gospel, they'll leave this out, say it's not right. Now, if I believed that, if I believe the Signs of the Gospel was not right, then what about John 3:16, where it says, "[For] God so loved the world that he gave his only begotten son that whosoever believeth in him should not perish, but have everlasting life"? Now, would that give me room to doubt that also? You see? How come that if they got a right to preach this other, how come I've not got a right to preach the Signs and practice them? They practice Matthew 28:19, where it says, "Go ye therefore and teach all nations, baptizing them in the name of the Father, and of the Son, and of the Holy Ghost: Teaching them to observe all things whatsoever I have commanded you; and, lo, I am with you alway even unto the end of the world." Now, they preach that, and they practice that. Why am I not allowed to practice Saint Mark 16 and 18, "They shall take up serpents," or laying hands on the sick, and them being healed? Why should there be controversy there anywhere? The same God said it all. And if there's something in here that's written that He didn't say, then we need to hunt us another one. Is that the truth?

I've not only got my life in this world in this [belief], but I got life everlasting. That's my hope. I'm not worried about *this* life. It is only temporal. *This* life, the Bible says, is a vapor that is here for a little while and then vanishes. And that's a proven fact. It's proven every day that we are not here eternally. But now, I've got the promise of eternal life for ever and ever, that I'll never have to die. I also believe that our eternal life will be just like it is here. We just won't have these mortal bodies. We'll have a body likened unto Him, which the Bible says we will. We will have a body like unto the Lord, a spiritual body, when we are changed from mortal to immortal. What we are is spirits. We are spirits, just clothed with a body of clay. If you will take notice, when a man dies, he's planted into the earth. If you go back and dig him up a year later, he's decayed, isn't he? [He] went back to the dust of the earth. But the spirit lives. The soul of a man lives.

What the law can do, the courts of this land, they can put a judgment on you for so long, but one day after a while, you are going to leave that judgment one way or the other. You will either die or they'll either drop it. The only reason they didn't try Punkin [was that] they could not try a man from the grave. They could not put judgment on *him*, so they took the closest thing to him—me and Peggy. And that's why they tried us.

Stop and think. The children were not taken [by the court] until he died. Think about that. Why weren't they taken before? Why wasn't all this brought up before? He didn't die in a state where there is a law against [serpent handling]. So he wasn't breaking no law. *He was not breaking no law.* Neither have I. The only thing that I can think of, I broke *their* law, what they *say* is the law, when I took up serpents. That's the only one, because I try my best to abide by the laws of the land, which God tells me. God says to submit yourself unto every ordinance of man which is pleasing to God. Where that crosses His law, then we ought to obey God rather than man.

Our name wasn't in the court order. *Punkin's* was. He was not supposed to take the children to church if [the members] was handling serpents. Well, the way it read, our names weren't in it. But it says, whoever takes them. Whoever takes them breaks the court order. But we can go back now. There is a privacy act pertaining to the parents and their children that [says] we cannot tell *our* children how to raise *their* children, see. We did not have custody of the children. *Punkin* had custody of them. He had full custody, and we could not say whether they went to church or whether they didn't go to church. That was up to Punkin. I told them I didn't agree with Punkin about taking them to church.

If it had been me, what I would have done, I would have took it back to court. I would have tried to get that overturned. I talked to some that says it *can* be overturned.

Punkin took them to Middlesboro and Morristown. He took them to the church where he wanted to take them. And we *did* take them to church. After he had broke the court order, *we* took them to church. But it was on his say-so, not on ours. Not before. See, children have rights, too.

Now, the judge said in his ruling [that] their grandfather—me—says that it is all right for them, [that] they are old enough to make their choices at thirteen or fourteen years of age whether they want to handle serpents or not. *I did not say that.* This is what I said: I said they's some children at the age of even younger than this, at twelve or thirteen or fourteen, they come to the knowledge of good and evil. But anyone knows that a child, until they are eighteen, they are under the jurisdiction of the parents. I believe that they's some that's even forty and fifty years old that's not come to the age of accountability. I know when Mark was seven years old, I had an electric heater here, and it was cold, and I was heating with a stack heater, and it burned out. I'm a licensed electrician, and I couldn't fix it. I told Peggy, "Let's run to town and get one." Mark said, "I'm going to stay here." He is seven years old. When we come back, he had the heater fixed and running. He had tore it down and put it back together and plugged it up, and it was running. So how can we say [what the age of accountability is]? In the Word of God, we find in Jeremiah that God told Jeremiah, he said, "I knew you from your mother's womb."

So the age of accountability is knowing good and evil. That's what that is. I don't think they should be able to make a choice of whether they are going to take up serpents or whether to drive a car or not. I could put that in there, but it wouldn't have done no good. Even if they know between good and evil at an early age, I would not allow children to take up serpents. I would not allow it in my church. I think it should be eighteen years of age, despite the fact whether they understand good and evil.

We are not trying to prove our faith when we take up serpents. It is *not* for a blessing. It is *not* to prove your faith, but it is to *confirm* the Word of God. I can take you today and find a snake show where somebody that don't even go to church is taking up serpents. You ever been to one of those roundups down in Georgia? You see how they take 'em up. That don't prove nothing to me. But when that spirit moves in my life—the anointing of God, Christ in you, the hope of glory, unspeakable and full of joy—[when that] moves in your life, you know it is all right then. That is a sign unto the unbeliever that the Word of God is right. It is for the believers to take them up, but it is [also] a sign to them that don't believe.

Not everyone in my church takes up serpents, even. Peggy has handled serpents, but Lord, it's been years since she handled them. I've got brothers that goes up there. It's been a long time since they took up serpents. Anyway, it will work. God will work in the midst. I believe it is a gift. I believe in the gift of the spirit, that there is a gift of healing, there's gift of tongues, there's gift of knowledge, there's gift of wisdom, different things. I could go down here and handle serpents on the streets until I turn blue, but if God wasn't in it, I wouldn't accomplish a thing. People would probably pay to come to see it. That's right. But this is freely give, you see. But when that right thing moves in your life, it'll let the other people know. That's where the Bible says, "Let the need be preached in the anointing, and the demonstration of the spirit, and it will not become void unto you."

That's what Punkin was doing. He was taking it out to the people. He took it. And he stood upon it. Yes, he did. He died believing. If you noticed in the videotape, after he was serpent-bit, he said everything was all right. I don't believe the serpent bite hurt him, don't believe it hurt him one bit. I been with him too many times when it hurt him. But there was something else that took place. Five minutes. They said [he died in] eight minutes, but I got it confirmed that it was five minutes. Snakebite won't kill you in that length.

Like I said, the judge didn't understand what I was talking about, [that] we are free mortal agents. God gave you a mind, that you can choose which way you want to go. That's up to you. I can preach to you and preach to you, but you'd have to make that choice. I can tell you what the Bible says, and I can preach to you what the Bible says, but to make you do it? No way. It's got to be your choice. I believe there's people gets down and starts praying, and when the spirit begins to move, tongues may come upon them, and they are speaking directly to God. They don't know what they are telling God, but the spirit knows it. That's what Paul teaches. He says for us to pray in the spirit, because the spirit knows our needs, wherein we might be asking for new homes, new cars, and all of that stuff. That's this wantonness of the flesh, you see. But the spirit knows our needs, and that's where it's at.

I don't believe it's meant for everybody to preach. I don't believe everybody is an apostle, and I don't believe everybody is a prophet or a teacher or an evangelist. But I believe God's got some that'll lead the way.

The only way I can find to enter the kingdom of heaven is by God's plan, not by man's plan. And if you don't enter the kingdom of heaven, you are going to hell. That lake of fire is where you are going if you aren't right with the Lord. The lake of fire is forever and ever. The Bible says, "Where the worm dies not, and the fire is not quenched." It is forever and ever. Just as sure as there is a heaven, there is a lake of fire. They teach now that there are degrees, according to how much sin. It is not like that. The Bible said no sin shall enter there. He said *none*. No sin.

I was praying about why Punkin died, what caused his death. I dreamed that I was talking to Punkin, and he had a sand rattler—they call it a rattler serpent, but it don't have no rattles. I asked him, "Is that a bad serpent?" And he said, "No, this seems to be all right, Daddy." In the dream, he took and put it to his ear three times. And then the third time, they was a little serpent crawled out of his ear. I believe that the Lord was showing me that it wasn't the one that he had on the *outside*, it was something on the *inside* [some internal problem] that caused his death.

Punkin was always a daddy's boy. Mark, I always said, was a mama's boy. Punkin went everywhere I went. If the wheels rolled, Punkin went. Mark'd stay home. I've started places with Mark, he'd cry. He'd want to go back to his mama. But Mark is smart. He's intelligent as all can be. More of a serious type, I guess. He had two years at East Tennessee State. I think he lacked one semester [of] finishing. I don't know today why he quit. I never did question him about it. I figured he was old enough to make his own decision, and he was. He was over eighteen. So all at once, he dropped out. He was going to Kentucky to church quite often, and that is where he met Rachelle, at Shields, Kentucky, at Bruce Helton's church. They ended up getting married, and now they got four kids. Mark is the manager of produce over at Wal-Mart. So he's not done too bad. But he got interested in the church somewhere around the age of twenty. He never took up serpents for a while. But I guess he's been more active in it here lately, since Punkin's died. Probably more active in it than he was before. Mark has only been bitten one time. But it didn't hurt him. It was probably two, three years ago. I believe it was in Morristown. I wasn't with him. They told me weeks later. Punkin told his mama. It was just a bite that didn't hurt him. It was a copperhead.

It does worry me that he is the last of my children. I worry about him. That's just nature. That is the flesh part. I don't worry more about Mark than I did Punkin. I've always feared for both of them, that the day would come—a car wreck or whatever. You know. But I was hoping they would be burying *me*, rather than me burying *them*. That's what I always hoped for. Death doesn't have no age limit on it. They's nowhere that I can read that it has an age limit on it. This is what Jesus said. He said, "My time has not yet come, but your time is anytime." So we don't have the promise. I hope Mark lives to be of old age, but I don't know that. I hope that he's able to put me away, instead of me having to put him away. But who knows?

Rachelle Brown at a revival in Kingston, Georgia—
Jamie Coots is in the background on the left.
Photos by Fred Brown

THE LORD JUST
SHOUTED ME

RACHELLE "SHELL" MARTINEZ BROWN
B. 1973

*"I'd see serpent handling, and . . . I
thought, 'Oh, Lord, I'd like to feel that.
I'd like to feel what they're feeling'."*

WHEN SHELL BROWN SITS AT THE PIANO BENCH in the
House of Prayer in the Name of Jesus Christ, she seems to take on a new persona. Music spills from her fingertips; hymns explode from her lips. Her body sways as she leans across the piano and pounds out songs for Jesus. "Without the Lord, I couldn't do nothing," she says. "He gave it all to me."

In the little white church perched high on a remote mountainside in Marshall, North Carolina, Shell seems to settle into her natural element, as if she was born to serve God through her music. Her dark hair and eyes are a striking contrast to her pale skin. Her demeanor is open and friendly. When she smiles, two long dimples appear in her cheeks. The devoted mother of four energetic boys and the obedient wife of a young preacher, she loses her shyness in church and gives herself completely over to the spirit.

As the service begins, expectation lights a fire in her dark eyes. She dips her head, shifts a little on the piano bench, straightens her print cotton dress, and lifts her long, brown hair off her neck. She glances at her husband, Mark, who stands nearby on the church stage tuning his amplified rhythm guitar. They whisper a few words, nodding at each other and at the other two men who will also be playing guitar for the service.

Then the music begins. Two microphones are positioned strategically on the stage, and when the guitarists burst into the opening bar of the hymn, the sound is magnified to a deafening volume, bouncing against the walls and windows of the church, making a joyful noise unto the Lord, as the Psalms command.

Shell doesn't use sheet music; she plays by ear, and she seems to have an instinctive feel for the key of the hymn. Her small hands fly across the keyboard, the fingers bent the way piano teachers always tell students to hold them. Chords seem to be presented to her out of the blue. As she belts out the song, she shakes her head, raises a hand in the air occasionally to praise God, and stops to wipe away a tear. Her energy and enthusiasm at the keyboard combine to make a riveting performance, but Shell Brown is not playing for an audience. She's playing for the Lord.

For the most part, the music is an amalgam of old camp-meeting songs, revival songs, rock-'n'-roll, rhythm-and-blues, and gospel. Everybody on stage and most of the congregation put their hearts and souls into the hymns, leaning into the rhythm, swaying, clapping, dancing, hopping, banging cymbals and tambourines. As they sing, some of the worshipers weep, their faces contorted with emotion. Others squeeze their eyes shut in concentration and tap their feet in time with the music. A few look toward the ceiling, as if they can see something or somebody there above them—Jesus, or maybe a loved one who has passed over. Whatever they see or feel, their energy illustrates the words of Preacher John Brown, Shell's father-in-law. "I'm not asking anybody to understand," he says, "as long as God understands."

They sing, "Jesus is a-coming back,/That's one thing I know./I wanna put on a long white robe,/A robe as white as snow./I don't wanna miss heaven,/No, no, no, no, no./I don't want to miss heaven and its beauty there./I got a mansion in that city/So bright and fair./I want to put on a long white robe/That is white as snow./I don't want to miss heaven,/No, no, no, no, no."

The next hymn is the one that makes Shell cry. Everybody seems to be thinking about Punkin. Everybody's wiping away tears as they sing, "Some call it heaven/But I call it home./Some call it dreaming/So let me dream on./Some call it paradise/Somewhere beyond the skies./Some call it heaven/But I call it home."

A woman hands Shell a tissue from the box that always sits on the pulpit. She wipes her eyes and manages to smile as her son Steven toddles up to the front of the church, climbs the first step to the stage, then jumps down again, grinning as if he has achieved a giant victory. Shell's mother-in-law, Peggy Brown, holds baby Andrew. Other women in the congregation are keeping their eyes on the two oldest boys.

Church services are one of the few times Shell is free of a child tugging at her skirt or her hand. During the week, she has hardly a minute to herself. Andrew, ten months, is the baby; Steven is almost two; Samuel is four; and Nathan is five. Nathan and Andrew have the dark eyes and dark hair of their mother, whose father was Mexican, while the other boys favor their light-haired father.

Shell, born in Scottsburg, Indiana, in 1973, has been a Signs Follower since high school. God has been a constant force in her life—in the way she talks, the way she behaves, and the way she brings up her children. "Before I had kids, I really did have a close relationship with God," she says. "I mean, that's all I had. All the time. I loved being with the Lord. But now, I can't give God as much time as I want to because I have four kids. That's kind of hard. My husband says, 'You're doing God's work because He gives you these blessings, and you're taking care of them, and God understands that.' And I believe that, because the Lord blesses me greatly. He's really good to me." Still, she seems wistful, thinking of how this important aspect of her life has changed. She stands in her immaculate kitchen, preparing supper for guests and family before it is time to leave for Saturday-night services at the family church in Marshall, almost an hour away over mountainous roads. She slices off a piece of the potato she is peeling and hands it to Steven, who can't wait for supper. He munches on the raw, white chunk and toddles away, looking for excitement with his older brothers, who are playing with wooden guns and toy cars in the living room.

Shell handles the children with grace and patience. She is soft-spoken and matter-of-fact. The bluish gray, white-shuttered ranch house where she, Mark, and their boys live has five rooms and two baths and sits on a quiet road in Parrottsville, just outside Newport. Toys litter the porch and yard, announcing that children live here. A broad lawn stretches behind and in front of the house, but the family complains of the odor from the nearby chicken farm. The children would rather play inside than out.

The neighbors know that the Browns handle serpents in church, but for the most part, they respect their right to worship as they please. When Melinda, their sister-in-law, died of snakebite, the family was criticized but never ostracized. Formerly, when Mark kept snakes in boxes in the basement, a woman down the road refused to let her children play at the Browns' house. The snakes have now been removed to a cousin's home, and the friendship has resumed.

Two hours before the church service, Shell stands barefooted in the kitchen. She has several pots and pans cooking on the stove at once—fried potatoes, fried fish, beans—and cornbread baking in the oven. While she cooks, she puts away groceries she has just bought at the market. Andrew crawls into the kitchen, crying, and Shell settles him in his high chair, gives him juice in a bottle and a jar of peas and carrots, and goes back to the stove. Placated, Andrew dips his fingers into the jar. Shell starts filling plates for the older boys. She'll also serve her three guests and her husband when he comes home from work, but she has too much to do to eat supper herself. She'll wait until after the church service, which could be as late as midnight. One of the guests, an old family friend, is Cameron Short from Evarts, Kentucky. He was a close friend of Punkin's and now spends a lot of time with Mark. Cameron says he'll wait for supper, too. He might drive home after church instead of spending the night. Earlier, when he came into the house, he took off his shoes. "It's a sign of respect, in a way," Shell explains. "So you don't track in dirt from the outside. And it's just more comfortable."

Shell sends the older boys into the bathroom to clean up for church. They emerge damp and shiny, carrying their shoes, struggling into clean clothes. The service is scheduled to begin at seven o'clock, though Shell says that nobody ever gets there until seven-thirty. Samuel, the four-year-old, needs help. He has dressed himself but put his shoes on the wrong feet.

The boys are excited when, a little after five-thirty, Mark comes in from his job at the local Wal-Mart, where he is manager of the produce department. He swoops Steven up in his arms, rubs the heads of the two oldest boys, and coos to the baby. Then he goes into the kitchen to see what Shell is cooking.

Once he has changed his clothes, he sits to wait for his supper. On the wall of the comfortable living room are trophies from Punkin's hunting trips—the heads of six- and eight-point bucks and several hooves that serve as gun racks and hatracks. "Mark loves to hunt, too," says Shell. "But the way he works, it is hard. He does have a deer in the freezer that he has killed, but he hasn't had a chance to mount it yet."

Mark and his cousin Steve Frazier are to be ordained as ministers in the church tonight. If Mark is nervous, he doesn't show it. He sinks into an easy chair in the living room and pushes a button on the remote control for the television set. He and his parents have dozens of videos of family events and church services, especially ones in which Punkin participated. This particular evening, Mark seems to find comfort in a video of Punkin playing his guitar while Punkin's daughter, Sarah, the next-to-youngest of his five children and a toddler when the film was made, lays her head on his shoulder. Sarah is the only girl among the nine grandchildren in the Brown family, and the camera lingers on her lovingly. Now eight years old, Sarah always prefaces her stories about her father with the phrase, "When my daddy was alive . . ."

The next sequence shows Sarah's first birthday party. The camera swings back and forth between Sarah and uncles, aunts, cousins, and grandparents. There's a closeup of Melinda, Punkin's wife.

In the video, Shell is newly pregnant with her first child, Nathan. "Melinda and I were best friends," says Shell. "More like sisters. She was always there for me. All the years that I knowed her, we had only one argument, and it didn't last long. She was also a good wife. She always stood by Punkin in whatever he wanted to do. Melinda would always take Punkin's side in everything—she loved him that much. And as for a mother, she was excellent. [The children] came first in everything.

"I never did work after I got married," says Shell. "Mark didn't want me to." The church says that the husband is the head of the household, period, amen. Shell has no problem with that mandate. Her mother and stepfather, Sharon and Otis Napier, are also Holiness, so the same sort of hierarchy existed at home when she was growing up. "It was easy for me because that's the way we always lived," she says.

Shell brings Mark a plate. He eats supper in his easy chair while he watches a tape of Punkin catching snakes to be used in services. The clock is ticking, and everyone is getting anxious to leave for church. Finally, Shell emerges in a green plaid dress, her hair freshly combed. She wears no makeup or jewelry. She put those frivolities behind her when she made her decision to join the church. Her long, curly hair is brushed out. She has not cut it since pledging her life to Jesus in 1990.

Miraculously, by six-thirty, the kitchen is clean, the dishes washed, the counters wiped. While Cameron Short and Mark leave for services in Cameron's truck, Shell fastens her four children into car seats in the family van. The family also makes this long, winding trip on Sunday and often at other times during the week, but it's one that Shell always looks forward to. It's a long journey, but one that, each and every time, puts her closer to Jesus.

IN HER OWN WORDS
RACHELLE BROWN

I'd seen serpent handling, and it was just like a fascination at first. I thought, "Oh, Lord, I'd like to feel that. I'd like to feel what they're feeling." I play the piano, so I was playing, and God moved on me to walk around the pulpit, and I was wanting to handle then. I'd been praying anyway. Me being young in the Lord, I didn't know if it was okay or not. I felt the Lord great, but I didn't know for sure. But when the Lord moved on me to do it, an elderly sister in the church brought the serpent to me, and she prophesied to me and laid it in my hand. The Lord just shouted me. I felt the Lord real strong. I felt like I was out of this world. The serpent, when I first got it, it felt scaly, but I didn't pay no attention to that. When the Lord moves on you real strong like that, you forget. I can't remember. You just know it's there, and that's all you know. I remember it was a rattler. They said I held it for a while, but I can't remember, the Lord was on me so strong. The Lord covered me up, and I shouted, and then I just [blacked out] like that, and I laid down on the floor, and [the snake] laid down in my lap, and I had it in my hand. Have you ever heard about "going out in the Lord"? It was something like that. I didn't know nothing, and a brother came and got [the snake] from me. I was weak as water, and they said they thought [the snake] was dead 'cause it was like a shoestring. So when they come to get it, it raised its head up. They said, "Oh, she killed my snake [when] the Lord moved on her," but when they got it, they knew it was alive, and they put it back in the box.

The first time the Lord ever moved on me to go to the box, we was at Bruce Helton's church house, and I was scared. God wanted me to go into the box and prophesy for a witness, and I was so scared. The Lord moved on me so strong, and [still] I didn't do it. And after church, the women told me, "You're supposed to do that [when God commands you to]," but I didn't, and I [got] a whupping for a week over it, laid up on the couch for a week. That's when I fell off the tractor. It rolled over my foot. I didn't get hurt; I just couldn't walk. I was chastised [by God]. I knowed it was coming. The reason why I didn't [handle the serpent] that time was I was afraid, because I had never really seen a woman go in the box except for Sister Bobbie and Sister Gracie. So I asked the Lord to give me one more chance. After I got better, I went to church the next week. I think it was on a Wednesday. We'd had a real good meeting, and God spoke to me again, and I went and got [the serpent]. And it's just like before—it went like a dishrag. The Lord moved so good, and His voice was so strong. He just shouted me. I just put [the snake] back in the box and went on. They's no difference, really, in taking it out of the box and putting it back in. It's just taking that first step. You never know what's gonna happen.

After [I handled the first time], I did it every once in a while when the Lord would speak to me. I've only went in the box to get 'em one time myself. I always receive 'em from [other] people. Around through here, yeah, you can't really find a woman that'll go into the box. They just won't do it. Now, they do at Jolo. But around here, [the women] wait on another preacher or somebody to get one out before doing it theirself. And there's so much fear now in the churches [because of recent bites]. That's why women's afraid. It scared me at first, and I prayed, and God helped me to overcome that fear. It's human nature. You know, of course. You think about it. And a lot of women, they hesitate. But the men tends to move faster when the Lord speaks.

If you wait on the Lord and wait until He speaks to you, that would be okay, but if you don't wait on God, if you [handle serpents] when you *want* to, that's when the fear comes in. When you feel it strong inside, when you feel like you're about to burst, when your heart starts pounding so hard, that's when you know it's okay. It's going to be all right. As for me, my arms get numb and tingly when God moves on me. My hands get numb—like ice. It don't happen to me all the time, but most of the time, that's how I feel. And that's when it's time to go pick up a serpent.

I'm Mexican. My [biological] father's name was Senon Martinez. I have no idea [what part of Mexico he was from] because my mother met him in Indiana. My real father did not go to church, but my mother was Holiness. My stepdad worked in the coal mines until he got disabled. He got black lung and ruptured a disk in his back and couldn't work no more. Mom didn't start working outside the home till I got married. Then she worked in a sewing factory for three years. My stepdad didn't go to church in the beginning. He really didn't know much about God, [but] Mom went to church about all her life, so she would teach him about it, and he'd take her to church, [and] he would sit out in the car. And one night, the Lord moved on him to pray, and he went to the altar, and he began to learn then. And he's been living right pretty much ever since, and he preaches now. My mom is from Austin, Indiana. [She's] a serpent handler now. When I first prayed [repented, joined the church, and got baptized], she hadn't got into it. We went to a few churches where they had serpent handling, but she never really got into it until I prayed. I guess I was sixteen, maybe seventeen. We knowed about [serpent handling], but she was always afraid. I have two sisters. My sister [Angie], she was in the church, but now she's backslid. And Janice, yeah, she's in the church, she's living right. She goes to a serpent-handling church, too. My stepfather is an evangelist. He moves around to different churches and holds tent revivals, and he's a serpent handler now, too. He started about [1990].

I met Mark at Bruce Helton's church [in Evarts, Kentucky]. Bruce and Brother Punkin were holding a revival. And I repented. And it weren't like they said it was. [John Brown likes to tease Shell by saying that Punkin announced in church that Mark needed a wife, and that Rachelle declared herself a candidate.] First time I met him, I wasn't living right. I'd seen him once or twice. We just said hi, and that was it. So when I prayed, I had a little criticism in high school, not necessarily over serpent handling. My teacher asked me about it. She was amazed [when I stopped wearing makeup and jewelry and certain clothes], but as far as criticism, they wouldn't ever criticize. It was the way I dressed [that surprised people]. I changed my talking. I didn't act like I used to.

Mark come back again for his brother's revival, and I really got to know him then. We talked and everything, and Punkin kindly encouraged it. He egged it on a little bit. We got together in July of '90, I believe it was, and Punkin got bit, and [his family] come down to see him, and that's how me and Mark got together. He was going to school in Tennessee at the time. It was really odd. Punkin got bit, and it scared him because he wasn't handling the serpent when it hit him. Another brother was trying to put it in the box, and it jumped from the floor where Punkin was crouched down, and it bit him on the leg. So he called his mom and dad and his brother, [and] when they come down, I was sitting up with Punkin, and Mark come in. I fell in love with him that moment when he walked into Bruce Helton's house. Mark had everything that I had prayed and asked the Lord for. I loved the way he loved the Lord and did for the Lord. He made me laugh. I always wanted someone that could make me laugh.

The next day, we prayed and said, "Thank God, Punkin's gonna be all right," and Punkin was laughing and kidding, and he was feeling better, and Punkin started telling Mark things about me and trying to get us together, but at first Mark wouldn't because he had a girlfriend at school. But me and Mark still went out to dinner and stuff. And when he come back later that month, he'd broke up with her, and then we got together in September, so it worked out good. I was a senior in high school. [But] me and Mark broke up in December.

During those months [we were apart], I was confused. I [had been] thinking he was the one, but I guess not. I was very depressed. I had lost a lot of weight. What got us back together was, I had some wisdom teeth pulled and had gotten sick from infection, and they had put me in the hospital. And Brother Cameron [Short] and Mark came to pray for me. After that, we started actually talking again as just friends. After I got out of the hospital, he came down, and we hung out the whole weekend, and then he asked if I would like to come to Tennessee for the week just to get away from things, and I said, "Yeah, sure." So I came down and stayed with Punkin and Melinda, and we just hung out and talked a lot. He took me home that weekend, and before he left, he reached over and kissed me, and that opened a door to conversation for about two or three hours in the car. We talked about taking it slow, but actually it went fast, 'cause a month and a half [later], we was married. We had got back together in April, and then after the Lord gave Mark the okay, we got married in June of '91. We wanted to make sure this was it. We eloped.

Mark had been raised in the church all his life, but he never prayed until a year before I did. I prayed in March of '90, and he prayed in '89. So he prayed a year before I did. Mark was going to East Tennessee State University. He's working for Wal-Mart now. He is a very bold and independent person, a great husband and father. He is wonderful with the kids and does with them every chance he gets. [He has a] great sense of humor. He likes to laugh and have fun when we're together or with friends. He is a good person. We really don't have time to do much as a family, but when we do, he just takes us to wherever he thinks of first. He is very spontaneous. Me, I don't really get to have what you call fun. I'm just happy to get thirty minutes alone by myself. That's fun for me.

[I started prophesying] in March of '92. [When the] woman handed me the snake and brought me prophecy, the Lord spoke to me and told me He had moved on me to do His Signs. He had told me that He loved me, and He was going to use me in His Signs [taking up serpents].

Yeah, oh yeah, I have spoken in tongues. The Lord give me that, too. The only times I remember the meaning of what I said is when God uses me to prophesy. Like if I was speaking in tongues and God uses me to go to somebody, then he'll speak through me to them, and I'll know what the interpretation of the tongues is. But the Lord has not give me the gift of interpretation. Sometimes I don't understand it unless God uses me, but sometimes if somebody's up preaching, God begins to move upon me, and I begin to speak in tongues, and then sometimes the Lord will give me the interpretation of what he's saying, but other than that, I just prophesy.

Sure, I have friends outside the church. We're not as close as the ones in church. Not that many. Like my neighbor Pat. We're real good friends. And another woman up the road. A few friends here and there, and relatives. My neighbor knows we do it [handle serpents], and when this case with Punkin come up, she got fighting mad. She said, "This is what you-all *believe*. You got freedom of religion, and to me, it ain't nothing to nobody and the way they believe." She did, she got upset over it. She said, "For all this time, you-all have took care of the younguns [Punkin and Melinda's children], and they [the court] come out and snatch them out from under you." Now, she did get ill with that. She knows what I believe. But she don't ever fight it. She says she don't understand, but she says, "Now, that's *you*," and she respects that. She does. She can't stand nobody coming against nobody because we don't come against nobody else."

[It doesn't worry me to think about my boys handling serpents when they get old enough] because I look at it differently. When it does happen, it might scare me. It don't worry me for the [men] to *handle*, but [it does worry me] when they go out in the woods and *catch* them. That part worries me. That I kindly dread. When they're doing that, they don't have the Lord on them. But [when they're] in the church service, and God's moving, that does not scare me. Because if they die, it's their time to go. That's how I feel about it. I'd rather [my children handle serpents] than be out in the world doing drugs and stuff they shouldn't be doing.

But [if anything happened to them,] it would still grieve my heart.

MY HEART'S DESIRE

MARK BROWN
B. 1970

"He took this old heart and everything I had done, cast it away, and gave me a new one."

SINCE HIS EVANGELIST BROTHER, PUNKIN, DIED FROM SNAKEBITE in 1998, Mark Brown is the lone surviving child of one of the best-known serpent-handling families in the Southeast. Now Mark is more wary, but not afraid. He is too intent on following the will of the Lord.

Mark Brown is twenty-nine years old and the father of four boys. He is thin as an ice skater's blade, tall, broad-shouldered, and handsome, with wavy brown hair, dark eyes, and a compelling smile. On weekends, he devotes his life to church and family. During the week, he works hard to make a living for his wife and children. He has held his job as manager of the produce section at a Wal-Mart store for four years, and he is good at it, so good that his superiors would like him to move into corporate management. But Mark wants to stay where he is, because this way, he can give more time to the church and his family. He is now an ordained minister in the House of Prayer in the Name of Jesus Christ, and success in the corporate world is far less important than success in his spiritual world. "Oh, yeah," he says. "People at work know about my church, but I've never been openly criticized for it."

To look at Mark Brown, a gentle, reflective, and compassionate young man, you would never guess that on Saturdays and Sundays, he handles deadly snakes in the name of his religion. He doesn't fit the stereotype of the snake handler.

Shell and Mark Brown with their children
Left to right: Nathan, Andrew, Steven, and Samuel
Photo by Creative Touch Studios, Newport, Tennessee

Like his father, John Brown, minister of the family church in Marshall, North Carolina, Mark has a slow, measured approach to everything he does. Since his brother's death, he is more cautious when he handles serpents, but his faith is unaltered. He says he rarely considers whether he might one day follow his brother to the grave while practicing the fundamental tenets of his religion. Nor will he ever shrink from doing what God tells him to do, even if it means picking up the deadliest snake in the world.

Mark Brown was born into the serpent-handling church he attended with his father and mother, the Carson Springs Church in Jesus Name. That church, built by its former minister, Liston Pack, was for years one of the leading refuges for serpent-handling believers. From his earliest years, Mark sat in a pew and watched his father grab up large, deadly rattlesnakes. Unlike his older brother, who was itching to become part of those ceremonies, Mark at one point in his young life ran away from the church and straight into the clutches of drugs and alcohol. But there was always something at the back of his consciousness that kept him from going too far. And when he returned to the church, he was back to stay. Those days when he abandoned his church are not among his proudest, but he does not deny those experiences, either. Mark learned from his wild days, which now seem a life as foreign as a weekend without church.

Because he is the brother of one of the religion's legendary preachers, there are inevitable comparisons, but Mark says he is now his own man with his own style of preaching, his own insights, his own message, and his own dreams for a ministry that will always include the Signs and handling fire. While Punkin's preaching style was old-school, fire-and-brimstone evangelism, Mark's approach is more reserved, though he is still new to the ministry. Where Punkin was outgoing, full of energy and practical jokes, capable of tossing harmless yard snakes on friends while they were in the shower, Mark is serious, studious, cautious. Where preaching came easily and naturally to Punkin, it is sometimes awkward for Mark. And where Punkin was fearless when it came to handling dangerous reptiles in religious services, Mark rarely makes a move unless he is sure that he is fully anointed with God's protective covering.

Because his family has endured Job-like calamity over the past several years, Mark feels a compelling responsibility not only to carry on the family tradition but also to protect his parents, his wife, and his sons from further tribulation. But like his brother, Mark does not ever intend to lay down the Bible or alter the practice of handling snakes in church. He believes that he has a personal mandate from God, told through a prophecy related to him by family friend Cameron Short. "The Lord told me that my hands would do the work of the Signs," he says, his brown eyes glimmering in the soft light of his living room. One of his boys dances through the room, throwing a rubber ball at any target that catches his interest. Mark seems unconcerned about where the ball might land.

Children are adored in this house. Life revolves around them. Every time Mark and Shell go to church, the children go, too. Sometimes, the two oldest boys, Nathan and Samuel, are allowed to sing at the end of the service while their mother plays piano and their father accompanies them on his guitar. Meanwhile, baby Andrew is likely being passed from woman to woman and Steven is toddling back and forth among his grandmother Peggy and various other women sitting with the children rows back from where serpents might be handled. Ironically, snakes are rarely taken from the boxes during services at the Marshall church. Often, an entire service will pass without snakes being handled.

A few weeks before he eloped with Shell in 1991, Mark felt the stirrings of the Lord in his soul. It was at a revival in Evarts, Kentucky. He couldn't go forward, and he couldn't go back. He felt as if he was stalled in a squall in the middle of a storm of Scripture. "I'd be a-praying for people, and I'd just felt like I wanted to holler," he remembers. "Just like a strong praise coming out of my mouth. And then that night, it got to feeling that way, and then it just worked into tongues, and I started speaking in tongues. It was like turning water on and not being able to turn it off. I mean, that is how I felt. It was right at the end of service when we were praying, and it started rolling, and I sat down. They took a few testimonies, and I was setting there, and the spirit just kept rolling in me. I was [still] setting there, and they dismissed service, and they were shaking hands, and Cameron come over to shake my hand. Under my breath, I was speaking in tongues. Cameron looked at me. 'Obey the Lord,' he said.

"When he said that, it just broke free. And I walked over, and I flipped the box, and I pulled out two black rattlers. That's the first time I went to the box, too, [although I had handled before]. I spoke in tongues, and the first time I went to the box—all in the same night—and I pulled out two rattlers. I don't even remember holding them. I just remember going in and getting them, and I remember having them. And people were [leaving] church, so Cameron's prophecy that the Lord would use me to work his Signs [came true], and people would stand in the aisles a-gazing. They were all standing in the aisles of the church where they were dismissing, a-watching. I was the only one handling serpents. I handled them, I don't know, it seemed like five or ten minutes. And I felt like in my heart, [the serpent] was for somebody else if they wanted it. Somebody that hadn't never done it before.

"I told them, 'This is for somebody.' I said, 'If you want this, this is for somebody.' Nobody handled them, and I put them back up, and we was walking out of the church, and it was still rolling on me. As I was walking out the door, I said, 'This is for somebody tonight.' And it just hit me. And I said, '*It still is,*' and I went back up and got them back out again, and everybody come back in again. I sat down over on a bench, and I was just speaking in tongues. I mean, that's just all I *could* do. I was setting there holding [the serpents], just had them in my hands. I was setting there, and it come to me that [the serpent] was for Shell's daddy. If he wanted to handle them that night, he could. He had never done it before. I was young, and I didn't want to offer it to him, because I just felt like I was a young person at church. So in my mind, I said, 'Lord, if it is for him, you let one of the elders offer it to him.' I hadn't no more thought that in my mind than Cameron said, 'Otis, this is for you tonight if you want it.'

"He didn't take it, but later I found out—Shell told me—that he said if *I* would have offered it to him, he would have taken it, because he knew the Lord was moving on me. I mean, that is how the Lord was working it out. But he didn't handle serpents that night. He didn't take them, so I put them back up. We put them back up, and after church, we'd always go down to one of the sister women's house and eat. We were sitting down there, and one of the brothers had his rattlers sitting over there [in a box] in the living room, and we were sitting down there, and everybody was talking, and that spirit was still rolling. I was speaking in tongues, and I almost got [the serpents] out then. I stared at that box for a long time. I wish now that I would have, because it was just the Lord working. It would have been just as wonderful. When the flesh comes in, it holds you back from doing some things. That was a wonderful night there, too."

IN HIS OWN WORDS
MARK BROWN

My earliest memories [of church] were out in the hollow over here in Carson

Springs. Me and another boy, Tracy Click, we'd sit on the front bench. His dad had cymbals, and one of us would play cymbals, and one of us would play tambourines. We swapped the instruments back and forth. He'd play one, and I'd play the other one.

Punkin was there, too. He'd just started playing the guitar. He started trying to learn when he was twelve. Music is important in the church. One part is the praise part. We do it as a praise. But, too, I think it sort of gives the people a chance to just let go. To worship. The music sort of sets an overtone. You could pray out loud but not be heard, because the music is going, and singing. Or you could sing. Music just lets you get into praising the Lord.

I started trying to learn in college. I pecked around on the keyboard some when I was younger, learning chords and stuff. I learned some on the guitar, not a lot. But when I was in college, I took a course where I learned. I knew the basic chords, but it helped me more or less as practice. Then I started playing at Bruce's [Bruce Helton's church in Evarts, Kentucky], when I'd go up there around 1990. Daddy tried to play guitar, but he can't, really. The young members more or less had to learn, and then it just kind of went in that direction. Growing up, I guess the music gave us something to do.

But looking back, watching Daddy in church, I really don't think it affected me, because I don't remember anything really going on in church. I mean, to me it was just normal routine singing, preaching, whatever. As far as serpent handling, I don't really remember any serpent handling until on up when I was around ten. This would be at Marshall.

I was always fascinated with snakes, as far as snakes themselves. Just like a lot of kids are fascinated with bugs, snakes, and stuff like that. My cousin Tommy Moore and I would go out, and if we seen a garter snake, we'd catch it. This was just being a little kid. We was into all that—bugs, birds, snakes, dogs. We hunted rabbits and things like that. It was just me and him being out and being in the wild. We were nature nuts, I guess. So seeing snakes in church was just normal to me. I guess that's about the only word I can think of. *Normal.*

Even seeing my father handling serpents didn't worry me. Not really. I don't remember him handling too many. My memory is after he got bit and suffered for nine days. After that, it took him a long time before he ever really got back into handling them. So it was two or three years before he ever went back into a box and got one. I mean, he'd handle one when someone else got them out, but it was a long time before he ever actually went into a box and got one out.

I guess he was worrying with some fear there, so he didn't handle them a whole lot after that, for me to remember. The most serpent handling I remember was when Brother Charles Prince got into the church and started coming to the church at Marshall. He went to Marshall, Morristown, and Carson Springs. That's probably when I began to see a lot of serpent handling. I was about ten or eleven. It was around about the time that Punkin started handling them, too.

Being Punkin's baby brother wasn't all that bad. Mama says he always picked over me. Like if Mama was going to whup me for something, he'd ask her not to whup me, and he'd pet on me. As we got older, when I was about eight to twelve, we played peewee basketball. He was into basketball, and we played a lot of basketball together. The guys in the neighborhood would get together, and we'd play. I'd go to elementary-school basketball practice with him and shoot ball with them. And he picked on me. That was just his nature. He *liked* picking on people. He picked on me, but nobody else could. They could aggravate me so far, but when they really got to me, he'd take up for me. I remember one time on the school bus, they were picking at me over this little girl on the bus. Three or four of them. He told them to stop, and they wouldn't. He almost fought over me then.

I looked up to Punkin a lot. I watched a lot of things he did, like playing ball and things like that. I didn't play sports much. In elementary school, I played ball, but I broke my leg in the seventh grade in elementary school playing base-ball [and] didn't play any more baseball after that. I played basketball until the last of the eighth grade, and then going into high school, I didn't do anything like that. I didn't consider myself the caliber for moving up into that. In high school, mainly I just focused on studies and making good grades.

I was an A and B student. I graduated fourth in the class. I liked biology, math, and French, mainly because of the teacher. He was a great teacher. And I liked graphics. In the first three years of high school, I didn't really socialize. I'd go to school and come home. What friends I had [were] my cousin or people in church. I had a few friends in school. My senior year, when I was able to drive, I got a job in town. I was getting out more and making more friends. That's when, I guess, I got wild. We drank and run around, mostly just right around town. Cruise and listen to music. I'd say most of the time my senior year, I'd hang out at my best friend's house. I tried pot then, but it didn't have any effect on me. I didn't care much for it. I just tried it 'cause of the mood I was in. I was drinking at the time. So I just thought, well, no big deal. I just never did fool with it [any more]. I was too scared to get into any kind of hard drugs. I think I took some caffeine pills once, and they made me feel like my head was crawling. That scared me. So I didn't care nothing for that neither. We drank and run around, but as far as getting drunk, I guess I only got drunk maybe six or seven times.

This [was during] the time that Punkin and Daddy were out of the church. Melinda and Punkin were separated, and our whole family life was in turmoil anyway. I spent a lot of time away from the house, running around with my friends. I guess I really never did think what Mama or Daddy thought about it. But I always knew that I wanted to go to college. Punkin hadn't gone. Neither had Mom or Dad. It was just something I was going to do. I think I was the only one of the immediate family to ever go to college.

In the fall of 1988, I entered East Tennessee State University in Johnson City. I went through the fall of '90. When I quit, I was majoring in industrial technology. I originally went in under a pre-pharmacy major, but I did that out of setting a goal on something, not something I was really interested in, just something that was a good profession. But I just couldn't take an interest in it. That's probably because of the chemistry and the science. I had to be able to comprehend what I was doing, and I just couldn't do it. I always loved designing and drafting and drawing, so I switched over to [an] industrial technology major. I enjoyed that. I liked it a lot. [I thought] it would lead me into a manufacturing career somehow.

I didn't finish because I just got tired. Lots of things started happening in school. A lot of the guys I hung out with were going in directions that I didn't care to go in. During the year of 1989 was when I prayed, when I dedicated my life back to the Lord. In '89, I started going to church, and by '90, that's all I wanted to do. I just wanted to go to church and travel. Not that I wanted to go on the road and be a minister or anything. My roots were getting more settled into church than running around at school and stuff. My friends weren't doing drugs or anything, nothing like that. They [just] weren't the same way [as] when we first started running around.

Things began to change in the summer of '89. I was a cook in Gatlinburg at Shoney's Restaurant. There was a guy who lived in Punkin's trailer, the trailer Punkin eventually moved into. Him and his wife worked at Shoney's. I had worked at three or four different Shoney's since I was sixteen. And this guy, when I first met him, in '87, I believe, he was doing drugs, his life was in a bad way. He'd moved into that trailer and married this girl that he had met up there.

I was riding to work with him in '89, and they had just given their life to the Lord. He had quit drugs and drinking, and his life was just completely different. And all we talked about was going to church, the Lord, and the Bible, and things like that while we were going to work. Well, all that got to rolling in my mind and in my heart and made me want to start going back to church.

After I got to college, I more or less quit the wild life. The guys I hung out with, they didn't drink. We would just more or less pal around. My roommate was a member of a Christian fellowship group. I got to going with that group with him, and they were just college students who were Christians and didn't party and stuff like that. It was more like a fellowship, and we'd play intramural sports—basketball, football. The next summer, the summer of '89, I got back down here and got to riding with that guy to church, and we talked about the Lord and the Bible, and it just made me long to go to church.

At the time, I was in a relationship with a girl. The relationship we had, I knew I couldn't go to church and maintain that relationship, too. We were doing things that I knew we couldn't do if I was living for the Lord. I had talked to her about the church, told her what type of church I went to, and she didn't like it. I told her my ways would change, the language I used. [I told her] that there was a lot of things I was doing that I wouldn't do if I went back to church. We'd drink every now and then, nothing major. My hair was down past my shoulders, and I told her I would cut my hair. [My] whole way of living would be different. I was going to clean up my life, and she couldn't understand it. She was afraid my personality would change. That scared her. She kind of talked me out of it. She was a Catholic. Our ways were different, as far as religion. She lived in Newport, and we had been going together for about seven months when we broke up.

I was coming back from work one day on the way to her house, traveling down this back road. It was about a lane and a half wide. I come around just a slight curve, and the car did a complete 180 in the middle of the road. There was a bank on one side and about a hundred-foot drop-off on the other side. I wasn't going fast. There was nothing to cause me to do that, and the car just did a complete 180, and when it stopped, I knew in my mind, I said, "Thank you, Lord. I hear you." The Lord was just sending me a message: *Either you are going to have to go one way, or you are going to end up in trouble.* I went on to her house, and that whole night, I just thought about what had happened. I knew I was in a situation where I wanted to go one way, but I felt like I couldn't. So I just left it up to the Lord. I prayed. I prayed twice at the house. But I just couldn't get satisfied. Then I just went back and did whatever it was I was doing [before].

About the first of July, my girlfriend was talking to me about breaking up. I talked her out of it. This was after the car incident. I talked her out of it, and about two weeks later, it just hit me: That's what I needed to do.

We broke up probably about the first part of July, and that was a pretty emotional deal. Then after we broke up, within a week, I went to church. Punkin was back in church. I was riding to church with him, and all the way to church, all I could do was cry. I mean, he was listening to a gospel tape, and I'd just look out the window, and all I was doing was just crying. We got to church, [and] I went up and set behind the pulpit beside Allen [Williams], a friend. Church hadn't started yet, and I looked at Allen, and I said, "Let's start this one out right," and I went to praying. I remember kneeling down at the altar and crying. I didn't really know what to say, and I just asked the Lord to forgive me. And the rest is a blur. I remember getting up and hugging one or two of the guys, and I remember singing with them on a couple of songs in the service, but the rest of it was just a blur. I didn't handle serpents then, though. It was years before I handled serpents.

The Lord had just saved me. He had forgiven me of all my sins, and all that was gone. He made a new man out of me right there. He took this old heart and everything I had done, cast it away, and gave me a new one. After that day, I loved everybody. You are just joyful. It is almost hard to explain. You are joyful. Nothing bothers you. You feel overwhelmed. Later on, when I tried to think back on what all really happened at that service, it kind of amazed me, because I couldn't remember anything. I was so overwhelmed. In a sense, I was transported to another place. I knew what I was doing and everything, but I was so overfilled with joy and the spirit, I guess I didn't notice anything going on around me. There has only been one other time really that I been that way. And that was the one time I handled fire. That was around July 15, 1989. But coming out of that service, I knew my life had changed. I knew that I was going to have to walk by what I'd been taught all my life by my mother and father and the church.

Serpent handling is how we believed and what we practiced, but what I knew I had to walk by was cleaning up my life as far as in this world. Going back to school, I was going back a different person. It kind of scared me at first, because I didn't know what the guys would think of me. I guess the Lord worked that out, because it wasn't even a problem. They were all surprised when I come back. When I left school, my hair was way below my shoulders, and when I came back, it was real short. When they asked me what happened, that gave me a chance to tell them that I had been born again.

That fall and spring semester, it went pretty good. I hung around with the guys, and we played ball a lot, and, too, I started dating a girl that I had met at Shoney's. Her family was in the Church of God. Their ways and everything was pretty close to ours. We only dated for about four months. Then, during the Christmas break from college, I went to one or two revivals with Punkin. That summer, I didn't travel much to revivals. In fact, I worked with Dad for a while, about a month or so. Then I went back to Shoney's for the last part of the summer to work. When I started back to school that fall [1989] after Punkin got bit, that is when I met Shell. That was in Shields, Kentucky.

Punkin was playing matchmaker with us. He was trying to hook us up. I was dating this other girl at the time, so I wouldn't fool with [Shell] much. I would talk to her, but as far as any kind of closeness or dating, we wouldn't do [it] because I was dating this other girl. Come to find out, Shell said that's why she got a lot of respect for me, because she knew I wouldn't cheat on her, because I wouldn't with that other girl.

I started back to school that fall and broke up with that other girl right after I went back to school. Then me and Shell started talking. I don't know, when I went to school that fall, things just seemed different. Everybody just seemed different, the way they were doing things. I didn't feel like I belonged there anymore. I didn't have a desire to be there. I didn't know where I wanted to be. I just felt like I didn't belong *there* anymore. I just prayed about it. It started about the middle of the semester. I just prayed about it, whether I should come back for the spring or not.

One day, I was sitting there, and I was looking in the local paper, and there was a job in there at a engine-works place, where they make cams for racing cars. I told the Lord, I said, "Lord, if it is all right for me to leave school, let me find a job, a pretty good-paying job where I can work and I won't have to come back." That place up there called me for an interview. I left school one day early and came down for the interview. And I told the Lord, "If this is it"—I think I had two weeks left in school—"if this is it, and if it is all right for me to leave school, and this is the job, let [them] wait until I get out of school to hire me." I said, "Let everything work out just where it will all fall right in place." So I went and talked to [the woman doing the hiring], and she looked at my application, and she told me, "I'd like to have you." She said I was basically what they needed. She said, "I'll tell you what, I don't normally do this, because I need somebody now, but if you want the job, I'll wait until you get out of school to start."

So I knew right then. Everything just fell into place. I loaded up, finished out that semester, and told the guys I probably wouldn't be back. That was it. I was dating Shell at the time. We dated that last semester of school, and then we broke up around the first of December. I just had a lot on my mind, I guess. I wondered about school and things with her. I was traveling back and forth. See, during that semester, every weekend, I was going to Kentucky to church at Evarts and Shields. That's how we were seeing each other. But I was going for church. Punkin was preaching there off and on. He'd preach a revival or something. After Shell and I dated for about a month, I told everybody, "Shell's the one." Because what I had in my mind for a wife . . . It's kind of odd, but all the other girls I dated, I knew they weren't the one, because they didn't match up to what I had in my mind. That was somebody that would be a good wife, a mother, cook, clean house, and [liked] to do those things. And someone who played the piano. That was just in my mind, I don't know why. I guess that is what the Lord put in there. All the other girls I'd date, some of them might cook and they'd clean and be good and stuff like that, but they couldn't play the piano. I said I knew they were not the one.

And when I met Shell, I *knew* she was the one. I told *everybody* she was the one. Everybody was telling *her* that. This was '90. God had put it together. But I just had so much going on in my mind, I guess I couldn't handle it all. We broke up. I just had to clear my head. There were just a lot of things going on in my mind that I couldn't understand, and what direction I was going in. So I just needed to step back and take a look at what all was going on.

And then when I got out of school and started working, then in my mind, I guess I had a sense that I would start back just talking with her. I went to church in Kentucky, and when I got up there, I found out that she had started talking to somebody else, so I just withdrew myself. I still went up there to church off and on. She was dating this other fellow. Not really dating, just talking.

That was going into '91 then. Then in April, we talked. She had her wisdom teeth cut out, and they had set up infection and swelled her up real bad. Then Cameron and Punkin went to Georgia for services, and when I took Cameron home, we stopped by over at the hospital to pray for her. And then I took Cameron home and came back, and I called her at the hospital, and we talked. After she got home, we started talking on the phone and stuff, and then things just kind of fell back into place.

I think with her, it was love at first sight. I think [for me], it was just more of a sense that she was the one. I guess I was so involved with doing for the Lord at the time, it just felt right and fell right into place. Some people you just feel comfortable with, and I was that way with her. She is easy to talk to, and she laughs and cuts up and plays. She just all around suited what I needed. I tried to make it a little romantic. I'd go in on Friday evenings. I'd get there for church. We'd hang out Fridays, and then we would usually go around to church people. And then Saturday night, we'd have service. Then Sunday night, we'd have service. Then I'd go back home after church Sunday. So the majority of the time was spent in church or around church people. We didn't spend a whole lot of time alone.

But I knew she'd be a good wife. Her mama would make [the children] get up in the morning, and they'd clean house. So I knew right there, her background on keeping up a house would be good. And she did the majority of the cooking for [her family]. I mean, when we got married, her daddy said he hated to see their cook leave. Their mama could cook, but Shell would do most of the cooking. That let me know that she'd keep home and cook and clean. And then I'd watch her with everybody else's kids. She'd help people in the church with their kids. You could just tell. Her ways and actions with people and how she dealt with and tended to the kids and played with the kids, you could just tell that she'd be good. She has been a good wife. Yeah, it'd be hard for anybody to match up to her. So on June 11, 1991, right after we got back together, it wasn't but two or three months [before] we married.

She was in a serpent-handling church in Shields. She handled before we got married. See, when Punkin got bit, when me and Shell met, that's when she had just started going to church up there. I think she had just been going for like a week or two before then. So it all kind of fell in right there at the same time. When Punkin was bit, we walked in, and I went straight to where Punkin was at. That's where my attention was focused. Then after he got better and everything, he started joking around. He'd say, "You see Rachelle in there? She's pretty, ain't she? You ought to talk to her." I said, "I can't talk to her. I'm dating somebody else." Punkin said, "No, you ought to talk to her." He said, "She'll make a good 'un. I'll tell you, she'll make a good 'un." He was probably one of the biggest influences on knowing what kind of person she was, because Punkin just didn't say that about anybody. You had to really strike him pretty good. He didn't down nobody, don't get me wrong. Finally, I ended up taking her to the store to get some ice [for Punkin], so he'd hush and leave us alone. He was the matchmaker that got us together.

We began going to church at Morristown [Tennessee]. We traveled to Kentucky and went to Morristown. The Marshall church was closed down at the time. I was already handling serpents. Not often. The first time I handled them, I believe, was in '90. I was in school. It might have been the early part of '90. I handled a copperhead over in Morristown. We'd had a pretty good service all night, and they'd preached, and they'd taken prayer requests. And I was setting there, and there was a burden in my heart and in my mind to sing another song. I sat there. You just feel like you got to do it or you are going to bust. That's how you feel. If you don't do it, in here your heart is a-pounding. So I said, "I feel like singing a song." And everybody said, "Well, sing it." I got up and sang a song. I can't really remember what I sung. But I started singing, and everybody started shouting and praising the Lord, and they were handling serpents. One of the brothers had a copperhead. I was over there singing. And he had a copperhead, and he brought it over there and reached it out to me. I took it from him and handled it. I give it back to him, and they handled on. The service just died down, and that was it. And we talked afterward that we just felt like the Lord wanted the service to go a little bit more. That was the first time I handled a copperhead. I mean, the spirit was moving good, but looking back now and comparing it to what I know now, I wasn't really what you'd say anointed that time. I could feel the Lord, but it wasn't like a deep anointing.

Now, before that, about three months before that, we were at the church at Morristown, me and Punkin. I was standing up in front, and the spirit was a-moving pretty good, and I just remember standing there in my mind praising the Lord, and the next thing that I remember was I had a fire bottle, reaching for somebody to light it. Finally, I think somebody gave me a lighter, or they lit it, and the Lord let me handle fire. From the time walking from where I was at, over there to get the fire bottle, I don't remember. I just remember having the fire bottle, and in the meantime, Punkin—I didn't know it—but Punkin was a-shouting around, and he was drinking strychnine. Somebody told me that later. The Lord let me handle that fire. I remember taking the fire bottle and holding it to my hand, and I just let it lick up between my fingers. I rubbed it around my hand. This was the early part of '90. I was wearing a brown sweater that my aunt gave me for Christmas. So it was probably January of '90. See? That was my heart's desire. After I got in church and praying and everything, I'd always had it in my mind and I'd even told the Lord a couple of times I'd like to handle fire before I handle serpents. I don't know why. I was just fascinated with handling fire. And that is the only time I have ever really handled fire like that. I've tried it a couple of times since then, but that is the only time under the anointing of God. I handled fire to where you just hold it there and it didn't do nothing. But I'd prayed and asked the Lord to let me handle fire before I handled serpents.

And also my heart's desire—I'd like to pray for people. The Lord used me a lot to pray for people, more so than handling serpents. He lets me pray for people just for different things. I'd just be in church, and the Lord would move on me to go pray for somebody and not really know why. The Lord used me a lot in that. Somebody might be sick, or just down and weak, or sometimes the Lord would move on me to pray and anoint all the people in the church, and then the church would go for a little while, and everybody would break loose. Everybody would shout and get in real good. The Lord was working through me to anoint the entire church congregation. I mean, it might just be for an obedience, to see if I'd do it, as my part. And then, you know, He could work in the rest. There's times I went to pray for somebody, and the Lord [would] just fall right then, and they'd take off shouting. There's been times [when] people told me later they'd asked the Lord to send me to pray for them for one reason or another. I think the Lord picked me because it was my heart's desire. I wanted to do that.

At the time, after I prayed to God, there was a little bit of controversy in the church and division over serpent handling. Some were saying we was doing it too much and we needed to wait more on the Lord and things like that. So I mean I wanted to do that, but I set my heart's desire on different things. I wanted to do all, but my heart's desire was to pray for people, and I wanted to handle fire before I handled serpents.

Before I ever handled fire or handled serpents, Brother Cameron over in Morristown, he got a yellow rattler one night, and he come and had Punkin pour oil in his hands. The Lord moved on him to come anoint me and tell me some things. Well, he come over and poured the oil on my head, and when he did, I just started squalling. I heard him say, "The Lord spoke, and I heard him say, 'I'll use your hands to work my Signs.'" And then after that, I didn't hear any more. Cameron told me later that the Lord also said he would use me to work his Signs, and that people would stand in the aisles a-gazing. See, I didn't hear that part. I've had many nights like that since then. Yeah, there's been many now. But I have to have an okay from the Lord. I'm not just going to go up to the box and get [a snake] out. Not because I might want to. Well, I won't say that I won't, but I try not to. I feel like you are subject to get hurt that way. You may or you may not. Just depends. See, I like to have an okay from the Lord, either by His spirit or His word working in me to do it, or Him speaking to me and telling me it is okay. I've had Him to do that with me a couple of times. Speak to me. I mean, the spirit will be a-moving good, and the Lord speaks to you and tells you it is okay. I hear words from the Lord. There is a voice. Then there is a feeling, too. Your heart is a-pounding here, and you just can't, like Daddy says, you just can't stay out of it. You got to [pick up serpents] or bust.

Then there is also just standing there. I mean, the spirit will be a-moving good, and you might shout a couple of times or something or other and just have your mind working, and the Lord of Lords will speak to you. It is a voice that you hear. Just a small, still voice. I mean, you just know it. That's what I try to wait on. I mean, like, if I'm cleaning [the snake boxes] or looking at them around the house, or if I'm getting ready to go to church, I might want to see how [the snakes] are acting. I'll get them up on a hook and look at 'em. I might pick them up off the hook just to see how they are acting before I take them to church. But as far as in church, I pretty much try to wait on the Lord.

Sometimes, before church, I want to see if the serpents I have are acting real bad. Like when you get them up on the hook, they might try to turn on you, just constantly turn on you or try to get away from you. If you pick them up off the hook, they might try to squirm out of your hands, or weave a lot, or stuff like that. You just see how they are acting. And if they are acting that way, I won't take them, not unless the Lord tells me it is okay. I just feel like if the Lord wants them to be handled, if you've got several, He might just want certain ones, [or] He might want them all. I just kind of test to see which one He wants me to take. Cameron, he taught me this—he used to lay a box out, and if he had two or three, he'd lay them all out there, and he'd tell the Lord, whichever He wanted him to take, let them crawl in the box. He might have a den box, where you have two or three together. Then you have the boxes you are going to take them in. He'd lay them out in the floor, and he'd say, "Lord, whichever you want me to take, let it crawl in the box." And he'd say the one the

Lord wanted him to take would crawl into the box. It might be two of them, or three of them, or whatever. It is just different ways.

Last Wednesday, I took one to Middlesboro, and they were all in there, and in my mind, I thought, "Well, Lord, the one's not singing [rattling]. That is the one I'll take." They were all singing but one. I got him out, picked him up on the hook and everything. He didn't sing, so I stuck him in the box. The one I wanted to take, that's the first one I got out, and he was singing up a storm. I told the Lord, "Lord, let him stop singing if it is all right to take him," and he never did stop singing, so I put him back in there. We didn't handle serpents that night. It is just sort of being sure what God wants us to do.

I wait on the anointing, because it is dangerous otherwise. Well, you really don't think about it being something dangerous. You just don't want to miss the will of the Lord. If you did, then fear might creep in. So when the Lord is on you real strong, you are more or less at peace with this enemy. I mean, since the Garden of Eden, God put enmity between man and serpent. You are just at complete peace with the serpent. And it is not just the serpent. You are at peace with *everything*. You don't feel no harm. It is just kind of hard to explain. You are just full of joy, and it is a power. It is not like, "Oh, look at this power I've got." But it's a power that is within you that's not of this world that lets you do it. And it is the same thing for praying for somebody that's sick and they get healed. It's a power that comes forth while preaching the Word or testifying. It is a power of the spirit of God that's nothing of this world. It is just completely different. You are not really thinking about what you are doing. You are just happy and joyful because of that spirit that is stirring within you, allowing you to do these things.

And if you are bitten, you know it is okay. I've been bitten only once. I had a copperhead bite me at Morristown, but it didn't do nothing. I was anointed that night. I think that was February or March, around '94. It bit me right there on the right hand on the ring finger. It didn't swell or do nothing. It didn't even hurt. I didn't even feel it. Actually, I was standing over toward the front, and I was praying, and it was one of those feelings where you just feel like you got to go [to the snake box]. If you don't, you are going to bust. I was wrestling around with it for a little bit, and I started feeling it so strong that I just went.

When I went, the Lord overtook me. It wasn't like [an] another-world experience, but it was pretty close. I opened the lid, and there were six or seven copperheads in there, and I reached in to get them out, and somehow I was going to separate them. I went to pull them apart, and they said that's when one bit me. I didn't see it. The pastor and his son seen it. It snapped me on the finger. I ended up with them all in one hand, and I went off a-shouting, and I raised them up [over my head] and was shouting, and I looked and there was blood coming down my finger. I seen that, and I come back in my mind to a certain degree. I looked around, and I said, "Well, I better put these up now." So I stuck them up, and nobody else seen it. I went back over, and I stuck my hand in my pocket to stop the blood. I'd look, and it was bleeding. It was bleeding pretty good. I thought, "Well, if I'm bit, I'll know here in just about a minute."

Bryan Gregs, he was walking around. He's circling around the pulpit, and he walked up, and he prayed for me. And when he prayed for me, I knew I was going to be all right. I mean, me and him both, the Lord just covered us up. I stuck my hand in my pocket. I stood there. I'd look at it, and I'd put it back in my pocket. I [kept thinking], "Well, if I'm bit, I'll know." I figured that it would swell or something. I sat there. They started preaching. It quit bleeding, and I got up, and I looked at it. I got to wondering. I thought, "Well, maybe I scratched it on the screen, or something on the box, or a screw sticking up." I looked at the box, and I thought, "Well, I don't remember it scratching or nothing."

When the preaching got done, or toward the end of the preaching, I went over and sat beside Bryan. I asked him, "Did one of those bite me?" He said, "Yeah, didn't you see it?" I said, "No, I didn't know." He told me what happened. In my mind, I'd been asking the Lord for a good anointing testimony, where you testify and everybody feels it and shouts and stuff. So we are sitting there, and they got done with preaching, and the pastor said, "Well, Mark, I know *you* got a good testimony." Everybody is kind of looking around. I stood up, and I said, "God's power is real. One of those copperheads bit me tonight, and you can look. It didn't do nothing to me." Well, when I said that, everybody took off shouting. All but Shell. She was sitting back there pale as a ghost. It scared her. She didn't know it until then. We all shouted awhile and stuff.

The next day, I went back to work, and there was just like a little scab there. I was working and doing something, and I hit this finger, scratched it on a staple or something. It hurt like the dickens. It come to me, yeah, "Now look at what the Lord done for you, and look what this little staple done to you." That made me appreciate what the Lord had done even more then.

Now, I haven't handled any exotic serpents. No, 'cause we've not had them around in the church much where I've went. Just rattlers and copperheads. Before I got in church up in Evarts, they had the puff adders and the green mambas and cobras. Those guys [the men who owned them] moved somewhere else, and the rest of the church people up there, they didn't have the money or the means to get a-hold of anything like that. I guess that puff adder is about the only thing that we've really had since then. I didn't handle it, *uhhh, uhhh*. No, Punkin was the only one that handled it around here. He never handled it in church, either. It was just one day. He never carried it to church. Oh, it [would have] scared everybody to death if he'd carry that thing in. It could be in the bedroom, and you could hear it go *scruuussssss*. It would go *whoooooooosssssssh*. [One] day Punkin called me. He was all excited—you could just feel the Lord in his voice. He said, "The Lord let me handle that [puff adder]. Strongest I ever felt." He said it didn't even blow or nothing. He was just all excited.

It is something I've thought about, dying by a serpent bite. I don't think it means it is a victory of evil over good. I've heard many church members say that, say they'd like to go by a snakebite. Punkin said he'd rather go that way as any other way, and the only reason we questioned his death is that we just felt from the beginning that wasn't what killed him. With Melinda, it was the snakebite that killed her. With Jim Ray [Williams], when he died, it was just a matter of thirty minutes or so. There wasn't no way around it. Now, Brother Prince, I'm not sure. His [death] was sort of like Melinda's. See, he had drunk strychnine, too. So I'm not real sure which one caused his.

Punkin always said it didn't matter to him if he went by a snakebite or a car wreck. Either one, it was all the same to him. It didn't make no difference. The only reluctance to say that it was the snakebite that got Punkin is because he died too fast for the type of bite he had. It would have been all right if it had been the serpent. That would have been accepted as well as anything else. We'd accepted, right at the shock of it. But then once we seen him [in the video of the service], how and where it bit him, and the type of bite he had, and as fast as he died, then we just said there was no way. If it had bit him and really sunk into his hand or his arm or somewhere fleshy where it could get in and really bite, then we could have understood it. In a place where it didn't really bite him hard—the finger—we just couldn't accept that. And to die in five minutes, there is no way. Out being in the wild—somebody not in church or [who doesn't] even know anything about the Lord or anything and gets bit in a good place—they won't die that fast.

If the serpent bites you and you die, then for us, that is God's will for taking you out. It doesn't matter whether it was a car wreck, snakebite, heart attack, stroke. It was God's will, and you were going that day, that hour, that minute. And Punkin was going that day. There is no question in my mind. No doubt about it. Nope. See, his heart's desire was to go preaching the Word. In the last few years, he said when he died, he wanted to go feeling what he's feeling. He usually said it when he was preaching. He said, "When I die, I want to go feeling the Lord. I want to feel this anointing." He felt like if you *didn't* feel that when you died, it wasn't there to carry you over. So [the anointing] would keep you from feeling any harm. I mean, no matter if you were in a car wreck or somebody shot you full of bullets, if you was feeling the Lord, you wouldn't feel no pain. That's how you get victory over death, is the Lord's anointment covering you when you die. You don't feel no pain, and then you go in to be with Him.

I guess I feel like that was the Lord's way of letting him die, feeling what he was feeling. As far as the serpent bite with him, I just feel like that was for more purposes than him dying. In my mind, I really don't even think him being bit played any part in him dying. I think it'll play out with all this to-do with the kids and stuff. I feel like that's what this is about. I believe it plays a part in all this custody hearing over the kids. And, too, I've thought about it. A month or so after he died, I thought, "Now, if Punkin had been preaching and died, just fell over from a heart attack from preaching, there wouldn't have been no big deal." And there was a lot of people out there that Punkin knew in the press and things like that, that would have never knowed he died unless it happened the way it happened. You know, it became a media deal. In some ways, I feel like that God used it, too, to let a lot more people know about it. There's a purpose in it. We may not never know, but there is purposes that I feel will play out within the next year or so.

Now that Punkin is gone and I'm the last son, I don't think about being the last one left. In my mind, I want to take more caution about what I do and how I do things, so as not to put no more on Mama and Daddy. And more so, like when we are in church, I want to be sure that is what God's wanting me to do, 'cause I know when I go that there'll be a sense of worry there with them.

I'm really waiting on the Lord, not so much for myself, but for them. Mom and Dad both worry. I don't feel so much pressure, just more of a willing desire to take more caution. Shell and I haven't talked about it much, either. We've talked about [the fact] that Mom and Dad will worry more, and we have to watch what we do so they won't worry.

Now that I'm an ordained minister, I just want to do whatever the Lord wants me to do. I like to travel, so I'd like to go visit churches, hold revivals. In my mind, I'd sort of like maybe to hold tent revivals every now and then. I've just never really been in what you say is a tent revival, and I've heard people talk about that. The idea is kind of fascinating to me.

But preaching doesn't come easy for me. So far, it is something I have to work at. Now, some people, it comes easy and natural. Punkin was a natural. But I felt like back around '91, if I'd probably followed the Lord like I should have, it would have come natural to me. There was several times there when the Lord was moving on me to get up and talk about the Scriptures, and I just set still, and I didn't get up. I feel like that He pulled that back from me. For about two or three years there, I was what you would say spiritually struggling, *wanting* to do more but didn't *feel* like I could do more. I'm trying to seek out and work it and get to where God wants me to do what He wants me to do.

There are times now when I miss Punkin. I will be listening to a tape and something will just strike me, and I miss him. We'd get out and be serpent hunting or going to church somewhere, and I miss that. But I can't pattern myself after Punkin. I can't do that. I can follow his teachings and what he preached and what I know is right, but I can't pattern myself after him. That was *his* job. I can't do what he did, unless God gives it to me to do. That's like serpent handling. I feel like God gave that to him to do. He could do it whether he was feeling it or whether he wasn't feeling it. The Lord would allow him to do it. Unless God gives that to me, it is hard for me to do that. But I want to evangelize like Punkin. Yeah, anything to do with preaching and going for the Lord. To me, that's my desire—if it is going from church to church, or evangelizing, or at Marshall, just whatever the Lord wants me to do.

That's my heart's desire.

For there is one God,
and one mediator
between God and men,
the man Christ Jesus;

Cameron Short holding a serpent at Middlesboro in 1999
Photo by Fred Brown

FROM VIOLENCE
TO VICTORY

RICHARD CAMERON SHORT
B. 1955

*"I talked to that old preacher, and he told
me I was chosen of God and if I didn't
give over to God, I would probably suffer
a whole lifetime of misery."*

*Though not a member of the Brown family, Cameron
Short was a close friend of Punkin's and spent a great
deal of time with him during the last years of his life.*

THROUGHOUT HIS YOUNG ADULTHOOD, while he struggled with drugs, alcohol, guns, and violence, Cameron Short had a recurring vision—that of his mother treading barefooted across a six-foot rattlesnake. This was no dream; this was reality. His mother was a serpent handler. He remembered the scene from a church service when he was three years old. "She was holding that thing above her head, and its tail [was] dragging the floor," he recalls. "I had been around [snakes] off and on during my childhood. I knew people never pulled [the snakes'] teeth, and I knew they never took the poison out. And due to the fact that I saw that kind of power that I didn't understand and kept that vision in my mind, it was just enough to keep me from committing suicide." It is ironic that the serpent—the very creature he considers the representation of Satan—has helped give Cameron Short a reason to live, but that's exactly the way it happened.

The first thing you notice about Cameron Short is the serious expression on his face. Since suffering a gunshot wound when he was twenty-one, he has lived in almost constant pain from the bullet he still carries in his back. Add heart disease and spinal problems and you get an idea of the physical disabilities he deals with on a daily basis.

He is a compact man with a round face, a receding hairline and long, graying sideburns. His piercing, dark eyes and his fierce demeanor immediately put strangers on guard, but what initially seems threatening is only a stubborn determination to keep his religion from being exploited. He is wary of strangers in church.

What Cameron Short is really made of comes through when he sings a solo derived from an old Irish hymn he heard years ago. He does not sing this hymn with the usual explosive musical background heard in Holiness churches, but only with the soft and simple accompaniment of his guitar and a genuine sorrow for the man he worships: "Talk about suffering here below,/Can't you hear him, Father?"

Cameron has spent much of his life wrestling the demons that led him away from his religious upbringing. He was born in Norton, Virginia, in 1955. His father, Kenneth Cameron Short, was a disabled veteran who lost his hand in the army in 1941. In 1964, the family moved to Harlan County, Kentucky, because Cameron's mother, Bobbie Jean Posey Short, was from Evarts and didn't care much for Virginia.

Like his father, Cameron entered the military. He came out in 1976. That fall, at the age of twenty-one, he was accidentally shot at a town hangout. It was an incident that precipitated years of medical problems and an anger fueled by drugs and alcohol. "Couple or three of the men at a party got outside having a disagreement, and I stepped out to see if I could calm them down before it got too loud and the police were called," he says. "And just as I stepped out the door, one of them shot at another one and hit me. The bullet nicked my kidney and cut apart my intestines in five places. I'd lost so much blood that the doctor said they were afraid to mess with it anymore, so they left [the bullet] in there and told me I would probably have a lot of problems when I got up in my thirties, and they were very correct.

"After I healed up, I returned to work operating a billiard parlor—a pool room—which I did off and on. During that time span, I got involved in drug trafficking, illegal whiskey, gambling, beer—however I could survive. I was pretty mean. You can go to Harlan County, Kentucky, and you can stop about anyplace up there, and if you say my name, they'll tell you, 'That was one of the meanest men that ever come to Harlan County.' I had a bag of pot in one pocket, a bag of assorted drugs in another, a pistol in each of my back pockets, and a pair of nun-chucks. And I used one or the other of 'em almost every night."

Suicide seemed like the easiest way out of a violent, dead-end life that for a time cost him his daughter, his wife, his entire family. But whenever he tried it, the vision of his mother and the serpent came back to him, and he nurtured the vague hope that there might be something else out there.

Then he met evangelist Punkin Brown.

IN HIS OWN WORDS
CAMERON SHORT

The first time I ever saw Punkin was in church in Morristown, Tennessee. I found out after a while that the life that I was living wasn't nothing but a lie, a nonrealistic lifestyle that wasn't intended for man to live. I done all kinds of street drugs. I'd been on 'em for years except for when I was in the military. I only done cocaine one time, but I had a lot of experience with LSD, THC—hallucinogenic drugs—amphetamines, marijuana, whiskey, beer. I started watching too many people die in that type of lifestyle, people close to me, a couple of my friends, people I cared about committing suicide. And I began feeling that something was out of place, and I started having a whole lot of dreams that were bothering me very bad. I knew that there was something abnormal about [these dreams], and I knew it wasn't drug related. I talked to an old preacher about one of the dreams I'd had, and he had interpreted it. It was a terrible dream. I dreamed of the sky being red with blood and seeing three crucifixes about twenty to forty feet high. The wind was blowing, and there was real loud music coming out of the blood-red sky. I talked to that old preacher, and he told me I was chosen of God and if I didn't give over to God, I would probably suffer a whole lifetime of misery. There are some people that are preordained and chosen to do work for God from the time they are born or from the foundation of this world, and they don't have any choice in the matter. Many are called, but few are chosen, and some people don't have a choice.

[The preacher] told me I was fixing to go through three of the hardest things that I would ever go through in my life. And then I watched those three events unfold. My common-law wife left and took my daughter that I didn't see again for years. A woman I loved died in a bad sort of manner. And I stood and watched my best friend shoot his brains out—from drugs and alcohol and divorce problems and things of that nature. He was a very talented man. He was a good singer, had made a couple of records. He was a good carpenter, electrician. For several days, he had been using a wide measure of drugs, mixing LSD with Valium. I found out later he had been suicidal for a lot of years, and I never knew it. [He and my brother-in-law and I] were out target shooting, and he told us he couldn't hit the small targets. He got the gun, walked out about ten feet, and shot himself in the head.

It just changed something. I saw the waste. I was twenty-five when that happened. And really, that began the turning point. I stopped using drugs then, but I drank more heavily, and it was still a couple or three years before I started going to church. I played music all the time for small, private parties in small bars and what have you, and had a big variety of friends in all walks of life—some rich and some poor—and lived that kind of atmosphere, chasing women and fighting. And all my friends chauffeured me around in new cars and give me money and drugs and all kinds of enticing things that a sinner man would want.

But after that friend of mine killed hisself, because we were kind of mean—although the police didn't suspect us at all, quite the contrary—people started pointing the finger at me and my brother-in-law, and then all these so-called friends that we had disappeared. Everything disappeared, and then after a few months, I found myself sitting on the railroad track with a pistol to my head.

I was about twenty-seven at that time. And then I realized how artificial everything had been up to that point. I realized that man had not been born to suffer and be in the kind of shape that I was in. There was something inside me, way down deep, and several times, I started to commit suicide, but I kept seeing in the back of my mind this image of my mother [with the rattlesnake]. She had been a serpent handler and still is today. She's sixty-eight now. She was in the Church of Jesus Christ with Signs Following in Big Stone Gap, Virginia, but when I was a teenager, I stopped believing in it. I didn't believe it at all. I was two or three years old when I first saw [my parents handling serpents], but the time I remember most of all, I must have been nine or ten years old.

I had a very volatile temper. I got so violent that almost all my family was afraid of me. I'd had to take care of myself for a lot of years, since I'd been fourteen or fifteen. I never gave anybody a hard time, but if I was around a situation where there was somebody trying to do something to me or somebody I liked, usually there would be trouble. So I lived here in Kentucky, and I wandered and played music, and there was no more drug use, but the drinking became more obsessive, and I became a full-blown alcoholic. I was put in the hospital a couple of times, and none of it did any good. I got to running around with another man who's still a sinner man at this time. I was twenty-eight years old, and I went to a Pentecostal church for about six months. At this time, I wasn't married. And I just quit going to church, and I told the Lord that I needed a good wife and I would resume my life with Him. After being in church, the violent man [inside me] was gone, [but] then I started drinking again and got kind of violent again and wound up having some pretty serious problems. I was accused of shooting a man, and it was two years before the grand jury failed to indict me on grounds of no evidence and no eyewitnesses. It gave me two years to think about it, and it got the gun-carrying out of my life. That was ten years ago. [But even] that never got me in church. The thing that got me in church was, I just couldn't get away from God. He started showing me things. He started calling me then. I've not preached at this point, but the Lord has used me in some of the spiritual gifts and almost all the Signs—the Bible Signs.

The first time I saw Punkin was, my mother had talked me into coming to church in Morristown. I was twenty-eight or twenty-nine, and he was still a teenager, I presume, because he was real young. He was kind of hopping around like a jackrabbit, he was feeling so good that night. John Brown, his father, was there. That's the one thing that I can never seem to shake out of my memory, the strange, invisible power that I seen burning in his father's eyes. He was up there in the pulpit handling a three- or four-foot rattlesnake, and he was dancing in the spirit beside Punkin, and there was a luminous, red light coming out of his eyes that you can't see with the natural eye. That pulled my thoughts into it more than ever. I had never handled any serpents, but that night, I felt the anointing to do it, but I didn't do it.

And then a couple of years down the road, when I really got to know [Punkin], he started coming up to the House of Prayer in Jesus Name in Lejunior, Kentucky, about a mile from my home. We became closer than brothers within a month or two's time. The following spring and summer, he found out that I had a pretty wide knowledge of reptiles and catching reptiles—I've done that even when I was a sinner. I done it because I enjoyed it. My sister's husband and

I caught them for seven or eight years. Sometimes we sold 'em, sometimes we gave 'em to preachers, but we really just liked the sport.

Punkin knew a method of hunting in country like this and [in] flat country. And the method of hunting here and up there in the mountains are two different types of hunting. In the flat country like down in southern Alabama and lower, you go out early in the morning, and you flip pieces of tin, and you'll find 'em (underneath) getting out of that hot sun. But up there [in the mountains], you've got to go up high to get rattlesnakes. Copperheads can be found most anywhere, but they're still in the rocks. [Catching them] in the mountains is very dangerous. Sometimes, you have to go out on the edges of cliffs, and you got to hang by tree limbs sometimes and reach down and get your serpents, and then you got to watch another [snake trying to] bite you in the process and [worry about] losing your foothold. There's a whole variety of ways you can get hurt.

Punkin and I did this together up until his death. We [became close] in about 1988 or 1989. When we first met, there was just something about him that was different. A lot of people thought I loved him more than I did the other brothers. I didn't love him more than I did other brothers or sisters in the church, but shortly after I met Punkin, I knew that he wasn't going to last very long, because the Lord's got ways of showing people things, and He can let you know things. When we first met, Punkin talked about the possibility of moving up [to where I lived], and I thought about moving down there, because we had so much in common. He never knew it back in the beginning, but I told my wife that he wouldn't live very long, and at one time, it bothered me so bad [that] I didn't think about *dissolving* our friendship, but I thought about spacing it out and us seeing a little bit [less] of each other, because I knew it was going to hurt so bad when he died. It was just something I knew inside. He just had this look in his eye that he wasn't sent in this world to stay here long. I've seen that look in people's eyes before. I think every man is sent here for one specific purpose or another, and when that purpose is fulfilled, I think he or she dies.

I knew Punkin in a lot of ways better than his own family. He could make you laugh no matter how you felt, and make you mad at the same time. He was good at both of them. But now, I'm not [saying this] to praise Punkin above any other Christian man. He was just a brother that I loved very much and a very close friend. And [there were] many times when I probably would not have been able to hold on without him and for the faith of Jesus Christ. I did backslide several times. Everybody else just wanted to kick me down in the mud, but he would always try to pull everybody back in the boat. The Lord working through him [brought me back several times]. He loved everybody enough so he would have come and helped them whether the Lord moved on him or not. That's the type of fellow he was.

He spent about a month with me every summer. We hunted serpents, and he would come up and hold revivals. He liked to get a lot of serpents because he traveled to a great number of places. He was what the old-timers called a circuit rider, and they thought it was part of their duty that there was an ample supply of serpents for them. I went with him as much as I could, but the last three or four years, I've had a lot of health problems—my spine is crooked and I've got a coronary [problem]—and it got so sometimes I couldn't go with him. But our home was his home.

I worried about him sometimes. Me and him differed a little on the way serpents were handled. I had handled them on faith when I first got started, and there was one time when I picked up one without the Lord moving on me, and it bit me and almost killed me. And after that, I just started waiting on the spirit of God. I've been bitten a few times since then, but I've not been hurt. Punkin believed [in handling] serpents just simply because the Book says to take up serpents, whether anointing was present or whether it wasn't. And that worried me sometimes. That's between him and God, because when a man gives 100 percent of his time to God, he's gonna have a lot more power with God than a man who gives Him 30 or 60 percent. He was the type of man that if he saw somebody with a serpent in their hand and he knew it was going to bite him, he would reach and get it. He would take it and be bit in their place. He took a couple out of my hand when he thought I was in danger. Why, sure, he would die for you if you were a brother or sister in the Lord. That's how much love the man had. It didn't matter if you'd done something to him the day before.

[I've had this ability to interpret dreams] thirteen or fourteen years. I'd had a few as a child, you know, and then after I got saved and got the Holy Ghost, I even knew what the ones had meant when I was a child. And when I first got in church, I was fascinated with the [ability of the pastor to interpret] the dreams that I had. For the first few months of church, I could tell this man the dreams I had, and they would come out just exactly as he had said. And that was beyond my wildest imagination, so I wanted [that gift]. I didn't want it to make money with or anything like that. I wanted it where I could stay out of trouble and [help] other people and keep them out of trouble.

So I started fasting, and I went hungry three days a week for six months. And then the Lord let me understand a lot of dreams [but] not all of them. He tells me things in dreams and puts me in trances and shows and tells me things in visions from time to time. Visions of things about government, the Judgment, things about the church, things about my children, grandchildren, people in general. Yes, I had visions about Punkin. Several times, Punkin came to me with a dream and said, 'What does this mean?' He had a lot of dreams off and on about church-related things. The Lord wanted him not to go to certain places at certain times, or [the dreams showed] when there was trouble coming.

Three years prior to Melinda's death, at Punkin and Melinda's trailer, her mother, Frances [Goswick], had been there, and she knew then that Melinda and Punkin were actively handling serpents, because me and Punkin were out catching them. You know she knew it, and she got up and [later, in the trial for custody of Punkin's children] testified under oath that she didn't know [the snakes] were there, and she did.

The second day I was there, she came to me and said, "Can I talk to you a minute?" and I said yes. She said, "Do you handle serpents, too? Melinda tells me you have an understanding of visions and dreams." And I said, "Yes, ma'am, [but] not always, and it's not because I'm above anybody else, but just because He decided to do it." And she wanted to tell me this out-of-ordinary dream she had had. She told me she dreamed she had looked up in the sky and seen a huge golden head—it looked like the head of a man up there—and she said she saw this woman on the earth, and the woman's head was missing. And [the woman on earth] had three iron rods coming up out of her neck, and she said all of a sudden, this woman lifted up off the face of the earth and went up, and her body connected with that golden head, and then it went on up out of her sight. She asked me what I thought about [the dream], and I really didn't want to answer it. But she said, "Our pastor thinks if the three rods are three years, then the church is going to get raptured out of here in three years. If Christ is the head, then the church is going to get raptured out of here."

I've read my Bible enough to know that the *Rapture* is a man-made word, and it's not going to take place in that form, as a lot of people think it is. I knew that her interpretation was wrong to start with. And I didn't know *who* it was, but I knew what the dream meant. It meant that the three iron rods were three years. I said, "In three years, if my understanding of this is correct, there's a woman in your family who's going to go home to meet God." And she just said, "Well," and shook it off. And three years later—within a two-week span of time [of Frances's dream]—Melinda was snakebit and died. So I perceive that it was God trying to show her what was going to happen to her daughter, and she just disregarded it. She may never even have thought of it again. Maybe it would comfort her some if she knew it.

We're all members of each other's body, in the body of Christ. According to Scripture, one person can be the foot, another person can be an ear, a hand, just the same way with the family unit. You know they all come out of the mother and the father, but they're really all one body.

In the month before Melinda died, Punkin came up twice to try to catch more serpents, and he had another dream, and he thought it was a good dream. He had dreamed of having a white mamba in his hand. And they're deadly—it's instant death, almost. And he dreamed that the mamba swelled up and turned black and bursted, and a flower came out of it. And when he told me, my heart wilted. He thought because there was a flower in it, it was something good for a change, and I just broke down. I almost cried. I said, "Punkin, that is terrible. I wish you wouldn't go to church for two or three weekends. Just stay home." He said, "Why?" And I didn't want to tell him. I said, "Punkin, it's death. That mamba is a deadly thing, and that flower popping out of it, it's nothing but a funeral-arrangement flower." You know, you read the Scriptures about flowers fading and things of that nature, but you can't go into that because [people] don't understand the interpretation of dreams, and they think you're psycho anyway. And Punkin said, "Good God, I thought I'd had a good dream," and I said, "No, Punkin, that's terrible, and I wish you wouldn't go down to that home-coming [in Middlesboro]." He said, "I've got to go. I promised them I'd come." And I said, "Punkin, just don't go and apologize to them and ask the Lord to forgive you for making a promise you couldn't keep." And he said, "I can't do that."

And the next day, he rounded [up] the serpents—we'd caught most of them—and he headed on to the homecoming. The day [after that], Melinda was bitten. I wasn't there when it happened. But it was not one of Punkin's snakes that bit her. Now, Punkin had that dream three or four days before Melinda died. We talked about the dream dozens of times. I don't know if he would have listened, because Punkin believed that everybody has a certain time to go. The Book of

Revelations says that Jesus has the keys of death and hell. And it's my personal belief that He has the say-so when you leave here. And if He don't say so and He don't turn the key, I believe you're not gonna die, no matter what happens to you. It is my opinion that Satan is the death angel because [the Bible] says he comes to kill, steal, and destroy. But I don't think he can take anybody without the Lord letting him take 'em.

I [also] had a vision about Punkin going down to Alabama, but I didn't know where it was at. I just saw it was the inside of a building. I saw a type of sack that certain products come in, such as potatoes and whatnot—an old rough-made sack. Some people call 'em burlap; some people call 'em sackcloth. But I seen me and him in this church, and there was half of one of those old burlap sacks, and it was tied at the top. And I reached over and felt the sack, and I felt a jar of strychnine in it, and I felt over here, and there was a rattlesnake in it. And it was tied at the top. And I looked, and there were two Baptist ministers there, but they never spoke. And I'm not speaking ill of the Baptists, but they didn't want that sack in there, or Punkin. And Punkin reached in and got the serpent out, and it was a yellow rattlesnake, and it bit him right here on the left hand. And he shook it out, and it didn't bother him. Well, all of a sudden, from nowhere, this very, very huge yellow-orangey-looking oversized house cat just leaped and latched on his hand, and when it did, the blood just started gushing everywheres. And he finally got that cat flung out, and all that blood was spurting, and all of a sudden, I saw all the people that we know in the Church of Jesus Christ that handle serpents and a lot of the other Holiness churches that don't believe like we do. I saw all of us in the back praying. And I saw Punkin standing in the middle of them, and his body began to swell, and he looked at me and said, "Tell 'em they ain't no use praying. I'm going on."

And that's just the way the vision looked. I think that cat was from him having a stroke or a heart attack. I don't believe that the snake killed him.

I told Punkin [about] this dream. He was quiet for a few minutes. Then he asked me, "How do you interpret that cat?" And I said, "Punkin, I don't know, but you gonna go somewheres, I think, where people don't want you or serpents, and all that blood is either emotional hurt or death. When you dream of blood, it's just no good at all."

From my understanding, as soon as he was bit, he started swelling. Well, that's just not the way a snake reacts. Snakebites don't do that. I had an uncle who died of a stroke, and I knew that [Punkin] had had a stroke or a heart attack, and the snake got into the arrangement for some reason that only God knows. Now, it's my understanding from the autopsy reports that they found a small trace of poison in his system, but it was not even enough for a forensic lab to measure.

I've seen him bitten several times, and I've never seen the man get afraid when he got bit, although I have seen him worried two or three hours later. Some [people think] that he got afraid and had a heart attack, but I don't buy that. I've even seen him get bit and laugh. We were in the mountains hunting one day, and he couldn't stand them [snakes] getting away from him. There's one started up under a rock, and he went and grabbed it by the tail, and it turned and bit him on the finger. And he looked at me and said, "Cameron, why did I do that?" And I said, "Punkin, you just can't help it." And he just laughed for a minute, and he said, "Oh, it's starting to burn. I know I'm gonna suffer. Just pray it don't last too long." And we got down that old mining road. I got down and prayed with him awhile, and it started hurting, and I seen that praying wasn't gonna work that round, so I just got him on out of the mountain. He suffered pretty bad with it for about four or five days. [It was] extremely painful, hollering painful. He was groaning and hollering.

[He wouldn't have had a heart attack from fear.] He *wanted* to die. He didn't want to commit suicide, but he didn't want to stay here. He told me if it wasn't for his kids, he would go and be with the Lord right then. He just saw the world for what it was. It was not the pretty picture it was painted up to be in the Creation. Creation was intended [to be] a paradise for God's humans, but Satan turned that around. And then Punkin saw through a lot of things in this world. He was not an educated man—I'm not either—but he knew that sooner or later, he was gonna have to do a lot of suffering and suffer a lot of sorrow. That, compounded with the fact of losing his wife, and they took his disability income from him, and a whole lot of other things.

I knew something was wrong. Punkin didn't complain. I'd seen him in pain so bad it would show on his face. They give him medicine, but he didn't like to take it. He had a couple of blown disks in his back, and one removed. He asked me what they did to me when I had angioplasty, and he was holding his chest, and he said, "You have to promise not to tell Mom or Dad or Mark, but for about a month, my chest has been just about to kill me. It hurts so bad I can't get my breath." I said, "Punkin, you ought to do a lot of praying. You should go to a doctor. You might have a blockage or something that they can do something with."

He said, "No, I'll trust the Lord with this. If he takes me out of here, I'll be in a better world. I don't want to leave my kids, but if I have to continue living the way it is, without an income, sick, and no wife"—although people helped him some financially when he got out and traveled—"I'd just as soon die and go and be with the Lord, because I know God will take care of my children. If God wants to heal me, He can, and if He don't, it's not 'cause He's not able. If He don't, it's all right."

That was a couple, three months before he died. I think he had a heart attack the day Melinda died. I came over to Tennessee as soon as I heard that she was dead, and he was laying back on the couch holding his chest, groaning, really loud, loud enough to really make you hurt inside. It was from grief, but I knew there was something there besides grief, and I asked him was he all right. He wouldn't talk to anybody too much, but he said, "I'll be all right. Just pray." So he did that for about three days, but I think he had a heart attack then from the shock of what happened, because they told me he had slumped down when she was bitten.

That book [Dennis Covington's *Salvation on Sand Mountain*] done a lot of damage. [The part about Punkin's affair with someone else's wife] was not the least bit true. [Covington] got it from this lady's husband that Punkin was accused of having an affair with. I know for a fact it's not right. This man was deathly jealous over Punkin and other men. He thought his wife was interested in Punkin, so he started to beat the daylights out of her.

When the book came out, it was just like hitting a sandcastle with a bowling ball. Punkin had come up in there to preach funerals and help people, and then people tell stuff like that on him. And the worst part was, the people were supposed to be spiritual. They was some that knew how bad that man hated Punkin. They were people who knew what was going on before it started. God can tell people things. But nobody said anything, and Punkin was devastated with it. It really almost destroyed him. It got gossiped all over the country, and it caused him a lot of problems. And there are a lot of people up there in that part of the country respected Punkin a lot, 'cause they knew the truth. And there are a lot of people up there that are going to have a lot of answering to do. But he had some bitterness that the book had put a strain on his marriage, and he had a hurt inside him about some of the things people had said, but he forgave them. He forgave his mother-in-law for taking his children, which is something I could never comprehend, because I would never have let her see them again when I got them back the first time. He told me that she was his mother-in-law even though his wife was dead, and she and her husband were the grandparents of his children, and it was not right in the eyes of God to not let them see the children, no matter what they had done to him.

He was just a man, just like everybody else, but in my opinion, he was a man that loved everybody. And he taught his children to love God and their neighbors, no matter what color people were, no matter where they come from, if they were rich or they were poor. He was a man on a mission for Jesus Christ, and sometimes we didn't agree on things, spiritual and Biblical things, but it never put any ill feelings between us.

He made his mistakes along the way, but he never tried to hide his mistakes. Before Melinda died, Punkin started going over to the church where they wouldn't have the Christ [the Signs Following church in Jolo, which baptizes in the name of Jesus only, while others baptize in the name of Jesus Christ]. He and I had a bad argument over it. They was a big smoke got raised up about that. Before his death, he thought about getting married again, and a lot of them started smoke over that, too. I don't know the girl. She was from that church over in [Jolo] West Virginia. Some of them said that if Punkin married her, because she had a living [divorced] husband, that they wouldn't let him preach anymore. But some of the very ones who were saying that had problems of their own with God.

Punkin had got himself in a couple messes, as we all do. There's not many that walks the walk of God that don't fail. Almost every king or prophet in that Bible fell into a snare along the way, other than Enoch, Noah, Job, Daniel, and Jesus Christ. Punkin got ensnared a couple of times, and it took a while to get straightened out, but most people didn't show him the same kind of love that he showed everybody else. When he more or less got off the ladder, they wanted to kick him in the mud instead of pick him back up.

He was a good man to be around, and he was a man you could trust in dangerous places. He was made, in general, of a real jolly personality, but he had his other side, and a lot of people didn't like him because he would tell things the way they were. He preached what God gave him to preach. When he was in the pulpit, if [the Word] hit him, or if it hit his family, or if it hit the preacher of his own church, that was just tough. Or if it hit me. It hit me a couple times. One day, I lost my temper pretty bad, and I got mad at Punkin. I was in a bad mood. And he gave me a good rebuke, and I just kept my mouth closed because

I was guilty. If it was bad enough, he was going to give you a flogging. If it was bad enough. And the Bible says to rebuke before all what others might fear. But it had to be something fierce before he would say anything in front of everybody.

There are some things [about Punkin] that the truth needs to be set straight on. With that woman in Kentucky, it was just a Satan-built lie. [People] won't confront me to my face about it. And Punkin got damaged up there real bad from that, terrible bad from that. And he told me the week before he died, he said, "What really hurts me, I know I've done things wrong just like everybody else has, but what hurts me so much is that I don't know what I have done to make people hate me so bad."

Punkin could be derisive and make you mad. A lot of times, he'd hide behind the house and laugh at you after he got you mad. He just had that mischievous streak in him. He'd [hide from me up there] in the mountains, and I'd get real quiet and listen. He'd be behind a bunch of trees laughing after he'd got you angry. And he would do the pastor that way a bunch of times, too.

People are under the assumption that serpent handlers are heathen people and that we *teach* our children to handle serpents. They are under the assumption that our children are not educated. And they are under a whole lot of other assumptions that are not true. Now, when I was a child, I was in a serpent-handling church, but when I got older, I didn't believe. It wasn't forced on me. When I started going to church [again], it was because I found myself in [a bad] condition, and I started praying because I knew I had to find God or die. But after I got in the church and was baptized in the name of Jesus Christ and started fasting and praying, then the anointing started coming in my hands that I was to handle [serpents]. And I started handling. But prior to that, I told [my] church that I would probably not be handling any snakes, and I was *sure* not going to be drinking any strychnine. But I have been doing it ever since.

I've never seen a child endangered, and I've been around serpent handling off and on for forty-four years. I've never seen serpents crawling around in the church house. [Early in my life,] it was not in my mind to handle serpents. You have to find it yourself. When I was a child, I was still in [the church], and I knew the nature of snakes, because I'd seen a cat that had got bitten by a copperhead and seen a close family friend die of snakebite. I knew when I was a child that people had to have something [spiritual] in their lives before they could handle serpents without getting bit. But after I got older, you know, in teenage years, and started fooling with drugs and stuff, I departed from all of it. And I was more or less a heathen [until I came back to the church].

We tell our children to respect the law, to respect other people. We urge them to be educated. I have a stepson that I raised. He's a senior crew chief in the U.S. Air Force, and he's stationed in Japan right now. I have a daughter who lives in another state and is married to a deputy sheriff, and at this time, she is a housewife, but [she] is planning to be a mortician. She does not believe in snake handling, but she don't give me a hard time about it, although I did lose her for five years on account of it. Her mother wouldn't let me see her. But we have a good relationship [now]. And I have a niece who's from a family that practices serpent handling, that the navy tried to enlist as a lieutenant in atomic science due to her IQ. Her brother is a math major, and he attends serpent-handling churches. He's twenty-five years old.

We believe in the Constitution of the United States as long as it does not infringe on our constitutional rights of religion. Many of us have been in the military and fought for the rights that everybody else has enjoyed.

Our children are not *forced* to handle serpents. That's something that is widely misunderstood that I would like to get straight. They are taught to love Jesus Christ and to love their neighbors and to treat people right, but they're not forced to handle serpents. I would advise people never to pick up serpents unless the anointing is on you to do it. They will bite, and if you're not anointed, you could die.

Photo by Fred Brown

THE HOUSE OF
PRAYER IN THE NAME OF
JESUS CHRIST

MARSHALL, NORTH CAROLINA

*"If you want to look at
the church of tomorrow,
look at these children setting here."*

FROM PARROTTSVILLE, TENNESSEE, where Preacher John Brown and his family live, it is a fifty-minute drive to their church in Marshall, North Carolina, a trip that combines the grandeur of nature with the ingenuity of man. The narrow, two-lane road eventually broadens to a new, four-lane highway that cuts through seemingly impenetrable mountains, flies over the majestic French Broad River, and, around every bend, rises to heartbreakingly beautiful vistas. This rolling road, which runs alongside the Appalachian Trail, is unspoiled except for two hand-painted signs on the mountainside: *Milkshakes* and *Mayfield's Ice Cream*. The two placards, possibly left over from an early roadside store or gas station, promise much but lead nowhere. Since no other signs appear and no landmarks differentiate one mountain from another, once you leave the main road, you have to remember the way to the church: *Right at the stop sign, left at the barn, left by the wrecked house.*

In the washed yellow light of a cool spring evening, the little church looks idyllic with the mountain towering behind it and a lush green valley spilling out below. The air is fragrant with blooming honeysuckle and roses. The white frame building with its simple steeple sits back from the highway at the end of a long cinder road. A section of split-rail fence leads the way to the church steps. Along the fence, church member Katie Allen has planted rose bushes and spring bulbs. Sister Katie is a serenely beautiful woman formerly married to Buford Pack, who died after drinking strychnine in a serpent-handling service. The mother of seven handsome children and the church's unofficial florist, Katie is now married to church member Charles Allen. Each weekend in the spring and summer, she brings flowers from her own mountaintop garden to place on the piano in the sanctuary. This week, she has gathered pink roses, yellow, white, and purple irises, white peonies, lilies, and ivy. Years ago, Sister Katie's father donated the land on which the church now stands, and members paid for the construction of the building.

The small interior is dominated by a big wooden cross that reads *Jesus Christ is Lord.* A lace cloth covers the top of the pulpit, on which is centered a white ceramic sculpture depicting hands in prayer. Beside that are a bottle of olive oil for anointing penitents and a box of tissues. Above the altar are two signs, one listing the Ten Commandments and the other showing the Model Prayer (the Lord's Prayer).

Before the service, there are greetings all around. The congregation is made up of friends, family, and a few faithful members who have traveled long distances to be here. Cameron Short has driven down from Evarts, Kentucky, because it is a special occasion: Mark Brown, John's son, and Steve Frazier, John's nephew, are to be ordained as ministers this evening. The two cousins have been close friends since childhood and often go out together hunting snakes to be used in church services.

About twenty people show up. Of those twenty, there are five small children, four of them belonging to Mark and Shell Brown. The women hand the children back and forth, snuggling them as if each were their own. The one missing element is the energetic presence of John's other son, Punkin.

Glenn Dukes, a Signs Following minister from Chattanooga with a voice as powerful as a crashing wave, conducts the ceremony. He reads from Numbers: "Children of Israel must execute the service of the Lord." He entreats the two young men to "do the work of evangelists" and to "preach the straight Word of God, straight out of the Bible."

Then Dukes says, "These two ministers have spoke up somewhere, saying they would like to be ordained. What I want to know, who will stand good for them?"

John Brown steps forward. "Brother Glenn, I will reference them unto the Lord."

Dukes reads a verse from Second Timothy, fourth chapter. "Preach the Word," he tells the young ministers. "I want to say here and now, I'm charging you as an elder in the Church of the Living God [the church Dukes pastors] that you walk the life, walk the walk, talk the talk. *Do not preach your theories, ideas or opinions.* You preach strictly the *straight Word of God.* You teach what God taught, and don't be ashamed of who you are. If you can stand before that on the outside, let Jesus Christ be your guide. If you do this and you stick to the Word of God through this, and if you'll study this, you'll put a stop to a lot of ridiculousness in the church. There's a lot of tradition of men that's been in the church all these years that need to be stopped. I charge you to preach the Word in the name of Jesus Christ of Nazareth. I charge you two to uphold the faith. Uphold the faith and give your life for that faith. I'm talking about when God moves on you. Don't be swayed; don't be deterred; do not [express] *your* opinions or *your* thoughts. You don't have to think when you preach. *God* will put that in you and give you what He wants you to say."

During Dukes's remarks, children run back and forth among the pews, climb on the laps of adults, occasionally bang tambourines. Except for an infrequent shushing from grownups, the youngsters are rarely admonished. From the time they are born, they are carried to services, and it becomes a regular part of their weekly routine. But when they become old enough, they are allowed to make their own decisions about attending or not attending services.

Dukes then calls for the wives of the two men to come forward and stand with their husbands. Shell's children stare as their mother goes up. Diane Frazier, who is pregnant with her second child, hands her toddler to another woman.

"You know what's going to happen," says Dukes. "When they call to ask the brother a question and he ain't there, they ain't going to call back. They are going to ask the wife." The women nod.

Dukes continues, "In the name of Jesus Christ of Nazareth, God, the Lord, king and master of us all, guide these two men. Guide them, Lord." He shouts above the rising hum of voices filling the church.

"Thank you, Jesus."

"Praise His mighty name."

"Amen."

"Church, this is a serious thing," Dukes says as the praises fade into silence. "You young brothers, this is a serious thing. It's your job to straighten us up," he challenges.

Then John Brown, whose serpent-handling history dates back to the 1960s, gets up to speak. "These two young men know the qualifications of what it takes to be a minister," he says. "Mark has been taught from his youth on up [and] Steve for five or six years."

Then Brown fires up a sermon based on Acts 20 and 28. "There will be times when the heavens open up and blessings pour out. And there will be times when it seems like heaven is iron and the earth is brass. But there should be no compromise on the Word of God. You have to be in a position of where you speak the truth. Let me encourage you to be led of the spirit of God in all things. If you are an evangelist, speak the Word of God."

Dukes asks the congregation for questions. "I want the church, male and female, whoever the Lord moves, [to ask questions]. We are going to anoint these two brothers. We need to have respect. When they move out to preach, we will sit and listen to that Word. All brothers, let's pray for them."

He pours oil into his palm, rubs his hands together, then anoints the heads of the young men. He reminds them that there is "only one doctrine. Jesus Christ was crucified on the cross. And you must walk as an example." He raises his arms and looks toward the ceiling, then sits down with the other elders.

Cameron Short, seated behind the pulpit, has been silent so far, but now he comes forward and tells the two ministers that he has a good piece of advice for them. "I saw a vision on my way here," Short says. "My advice to you is to wait on the anointing of the Lord. When you are anointed, you won't make a mistake."

John Brown nods. "If your heart is not right, then hell is your home." He speaks almost in a whisper, as if his voice might break.

Glenn Dukes rests his hand on his right knee and bounces his foot unconsciously.

"Jesus Christ is God!" John shouts. "There is none before Him, and there is none after Him. Preach that which is sound doctrine, which you can depend on. He'll take care of you in good times and in bad times."

Then he asks the two young ministers to say a few words.

Steve Frazier climbs to the stage and stands behind the pulpit. He seems humbled by what is now expected of him. Pulling on his right ear, he circles the floor, moving constantly. "I thank Him for where He has brought me from and where He is leading me to. He had mercy on me when there was no mercy. I was on my way to hell." The elders listen expectantly. In the congregation, Peggy Brown leans over to pick up a restless grandchild.

Then Mark Brown, dressed in tan slacks and a long-sleeved blue shirt, gets up to say a few words about his commitment to the ministry.

After that, the ordination segues into the regular service. Peggy goes to the stage, Shell sits at the piano, and Mark and Cameron Short tune their guitars for an old Primitive Baptist song, "Had a Little Talk with Jesus." Children and adults pick up tambourines from benches around the church and begin to beat out an accompaniment to the music.

As the service progresses, the normally reticent Shell becomes more and more agitated. Abruptly, she leaves her piano bench and begins to walk slowly around the pulpit. She walks as if in a dream, appearing to become more and more focused on something only she understands, something only she hears. Then she begins to speak in tongues. Her voice grows deeper and louder. She walks down the aisle, lays hands on a member of the congregation, and shouts "Yea, I say yea." She continues in an ancient-sounding language that is unintelligible to those present. Formally, this condition is known as glossolalia, manifested in sounds made during a deeply religious experience. The Signs Followers call it the gift of tongues, but whatever its label, Shell knows only that it is a gift she cannot deny. She walks across the stage, lays her hand on the head of Cameron Short, and continues her liturgy, which even she, the messenger, does not understand. Occasionally, a word of English comes through. Somehow, a message is delivered to the person being addressed by God.

While Shell is still moving through the church, speaking in tongues, Peggy Brown, seated next to one of her grandsons on the second row, begins to rock and mumble beneath her breath. Her voice grows louder and more distinct, and she, too, rises, approaches a member of the congregation, and lays her hands on his head. Among the confusion of words that spills from her throat, a single comprehensible phrase emerges: "Nay, I say nay." It seems to be a message cautioning the person addressed either to stop behaving in an unacceptable way or to stop fearing something. Only the person to whom God speaks knows the entire message. Peggy's voice grows in volume and power. "Thou aren't a disobedient child," she says before lapsing back into tongues. "I have called thee unto my house. This is my house, and you will obey me!" she shouts. "Without Him on this earth, there is no rest. He is my breath and my heart of the everlasting heart."

Still shouting, she moves to the front of the church and turns toward the congregation. "If you rebel, He'll take you out of here. To honor Him—for no other purpose are you walking on this earth. He has been good to me, and I've been weak. But He is the only hope that we've got. You choose. You got your own will. I thank God for my son and my nephew, who is like my son. Be sure it is God. Put Him first in everything you do in life."

Now, she begins to wind down from her spiritual high. Her voice softens, grows fainter. "I love the Lord, and I'll praise Him for using me. He is real. I love Him tonight." She slips back into her bench and, still standing, grasps the back of the pew in front of her. She leans forward, head bowed. "I needed this tonight," she says, her voice vibrating. "It's been a long time."

Shell sings "Jesus Met a Woman One Day." Mark accompanies himself on the guitar as he sings "Power in the Blood." Then, after the prayer circle, in which several missing members are prayed for, Mark ends the service with one of the serpent handlers' favorite songs, "Some Call It Heaven, But I Call It Home." At one point, the word *shalom* bounces out over the heads of the congregation. It is the traditional Jewish greeting or farewell. Five-year-old Nathan Brown comes to the stage and sings with his father as his mother plays the piano. The hymn is "I Wonder What They're Doing in Heaven Today." The service ends with applause for Nathan, who grins broadly and skips down the aisle. Although the snake boxes sit close to the pulpit, not one believer has been prompted to handle serpents this evening.

At the end of the service, members embrace each other and congratulate the new ministers. John and Peggy Brown seem pleased that their son has chosen to preach the Word. If they feel apprehension, considering that Punkin's death in October 1998 is still a fresh wound in their hearts, they don't show it.

A few weeks later, at another Saturday-night service, John Brown looks down at the congregation, where his five grandchildren by Punkin and Melinda sit beside their cousins, the four sons of Mark and Shell. There are no snakes this night, not even in unopened boxes, because of the juvenile-court injunction that Punkin's children not be allowed to attend services in which dangerous animals are present.

"If you want to look at the church of tomorrow," says Preacher John Brown, "look at these children setting here." He pauses. He smiles. He might be remembering twelve-year-old Punkin, hands curling in anticipation of the time he would be old enough to take up serpents. He might be thinking of nine-year-old Jacob, who has said he wants to handle snakes like his daddy, Punkin. Or he might have in mind any of his other grandsons—Jonathan, Jeremiah, Daniel, Nathan, Steven, Samuel, Andrew—who could follow in their fathers' and grandfather's footsteps. Or Sarah, the only girl. He might be thinking about her and her future children and whether she will rear them to be Signs Followers. He might be thinking of his own grandfather, Pa Hance, and those long-ago days when the old man took him to so many different churches. Baptist, Holiness, Church of God—it didn't matter, because all Pa wanted was to live the kind of life that would get him to heaven, and all he talked about was what a good time he was going to have there.

Whatever John Brown is thinking is hidden behind his piercing blue eyes, from which he now blinks a few tears. His eyes get misty a lot these days, remembering his son Punkin and how he died in the prime of his life, or thinking of his own struggle to do the best he can for his orphaned grandchildren.

John Brown is tired, but he has too much at stake now to give up, and too much faith that God will eventually work His will, so he turns away from the children and walks back to the pulpit to get on with the service. "Praise God," he says. "Amen."

THE
COOTS
FAMILY

MIDDLESBORO, KENTUCKY

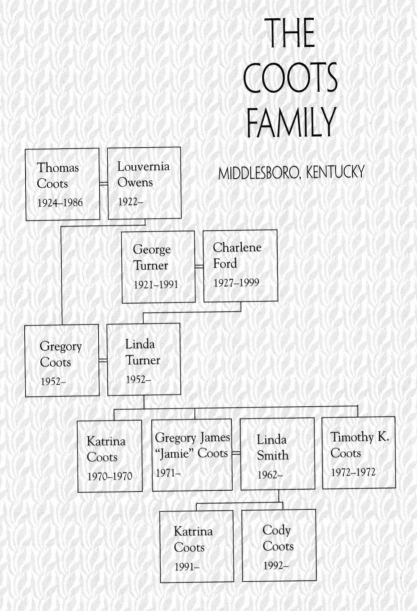

Thomas Coots 1924–1986

Louvernia Owens 1922–

George Turner 1921–1991

Charlene Ford 1927–1999

Gregory Coots 1952–

Linda Turner 1952–

Katrina Coots 1970–1970

Gregory James "Jamie" Coots 1971–

Linda Smith 1962–

Timothy K. Coots 1972–1972

Katrina Coots 1991–

Cody Coots 1992–

MIDDLESBORO, KENTUCKY

> *The first settlers found*
> *opportunities for shipping on the*
> *Mississippi and Ohio Rivers, farming*
> *on the fertile bottom land, and mining*
> *for coal deep beneath the earth.*

THE "DARK AND BLOODY GROUND." That was the name given to Kentucky by Indians who roamed the land during America's westward movement early in the nineteenth century. Whether prophecy or epithet, that label describes the violence the state has endured for over two hundred years now–skirmishes with Indians, brother fighting brother during the area's conflicted allegiance in the Civil War, bloody confrontations between coal miners and the federal government in the 1930s, and, more recently, unruly clashes between coal company officials and environmental-rights activists.

Ironically, in a land rich in minerals, the people who live in Kentucky have been victims, rather than beneficiaries, of its natural bounty. It is a state where money rolls in and rolls out again, mostly in boxcars loaded with coal. When times are good, towns prosper. When prices drop, coal becomes the black dragon of despair. The companies win. The people lose.

Kentucky is framed by West Virginia and Virginia to the east, Tennessee to the south, Missouri to the southwest, and Illinois, Indiana, and Ohio to the west and north. Middlesboro is in the Tri-State Area, where Tennessee, Kentucky, and Virginia meet.

The first settlers found opportunities for shipping on the Mississippi and Ohio Rivers, farming on the fertile bottom land, and mining for coal deep beneath the earth. By the latter part of the nineteenth century, coal mining was a profitable industry, though the miners themselves were never to receive many personal benefits from their labors. Sometimes, as in the case of Middlesboro, coal companies came in and established an entire town. When the coal ran out, they departed, leaving behind a raped and ravaged countryside and an abandoned people broken by unemployment and black lung, a debilitating disease caused by the inhalation of coal dust.

Named for its counterpart in the coal fields of northern England, Middlesboro was founded by Alexander Alan Arthur in 1889. Arthur established the American Association Ltd. of London for the distinct purpose of coal mining. Within a few years, the little town mushroomed from a few families to more than five thousand people. Industry flocked to this "Magic City of the South." Tent cities, banks, iron forges, tanneries, churches, and saloons were erected. In the town's earliest days, a portion of the revenues generated from deep-mining operations went to the queen's treasury in England, since Arthur's company was partially owned by Her Majesty.

The industry declined in the 1930s after being rocked by deadly labor battles, particularly in Harlan County, where the United Mine Workers tried to unionize the workers. Safety, adequate pay, and better living conditions were the issues promoted by the UMW under the guidance of its fearless leader, John L. Lewis. For years, coal wars raged between union workers and company management. Ragged armies of miners fought with shotguns, which they had previously used only for hunting, against the Tommy guns of federal troops and management. When the federal troops withdrew, they left behind death, injury, broken spirits, poverty, and a generation of men whose futures promised little beyond a monthly disability check and a miserable hardscrabble existence.

During the energy crisis of the 1970s, the industry experienced a resurgence. Eventually, it dropped off again, and today in Middlesboro, only 247 people are employed in mining. But hundreds of former mine workers and victims of black lung disease and other work-related illnesses and injuries are among the 3,000-plus Middlesboro citizens who fall below the poverty line. And that's among a population of about 11,000 in the city proper. The median income, as determined by the last census, is $14,821.

Failed by their employers and their government, faced with financial and educational deficits, the people have only one place to turn for a better life—and they have to die to get there. Seeking solace for their earthly travails, they turn to the church, where on Saturday nights and Sunday mornings and sometimes in between, they find hope in the Word of God and the promise of dwelling in ivory palaces. *Peace. Love. Rest.*

But getting to heaven is no easy road. Fundamentalist churches spring up like mushrooms in eastern Kentucky, but they don't offer their members empty promises. Worshipers have to work hard to get to see God. They have to live exemplary lives, obey the Ten Commandments, and adhere strictly to the Word, which in the case of Signs Following churches means taking up serpents, as interpreted in Jesus' remarks to his disciples at the Last Supper.

Some of the first services in Kentucky to attract converts were the old camp meetings. Around 1800, a preacher named James McGready organized outdoor religious events lasting for several days, at which people were saved, healed, and spiritually uplifted. The revival movement spread to other areas. Organized by evangelical sects, camp meetings served as both social and religious events where people could find comfort, company, and an escape from their hopeless lives.

Today, Middlesboro is home to scores of Fundamentalist churches based on hard-shell religious philosophies. The town has given rise to Pentecostal evangelists like the late Harrison Hayes, God's own messenger. A former Kentucky coal miner whose nickname was "High Weed," Hayes was a holy rolling man who rambled the landscape, pausing just long enough to leave behind his gigantic calling cards—large cement crosses and red-and-white signs that read, "Prepare to Meet God," "Jesus Is Coming Soon," and "Get Right with God." A man whose tank of religious energy was always full, Hayes would dig a hole, then, using a pulley system rigged on his pickup truck, lower the cross or sign, fill up the hole, and go on to another site. From 1940 until he died in 1986 at the age of eighty-eight, he erected crosses and signs in forty-four states.

Many such crosses, some erected by Hayes himself, can still be seen along Highway 25E on the last leg of the road from Knoxville, Tennessee, to Middlesboro. In late summer, velvety green fields with yellow patches of ripening tobacco and neat, cylindrical rolls of harvested hay border the highway. In the distance, so beautiful that they seem like an artificial backdrop, are the Cumberland Mountains, a part of the western Appalachians extending from southwestern Virginia to northern Alabama. It was through these mountains that Daniel Boone helped open the Wilderness Road, across which came settlers primarily of English, German, and Irish ancestry.

People born in Middlesboro tend to stay there. About four-fifths of its inhabitants were born in the state; if they move around at all, it is usually within Kentucky's borders. Currently, the future of Middlesboro, the largest city in southeastern Kentucky, looks brighter. These days, tourism is becoming an important element in the economic base, thanks to the widespread promotion of mountain scenery, hiking, boating, camping, and watersports. Cumberland Gap National Park draws more than a million visitors each year. And since twenty-five to thirty-four-year-olds make up the largest age group in the population, there will be opportunities for more change. Presently, most of the available job opportunities are in manufacturing. Real estate is also a growing industry in an area of gorgeous vistas and cheap housing. The median value of an owner-occupied housing unit is $42,400.

One day, the hillside scars scratched out by strip mining will be reforested, and more economic opportunities will be available. But until then, in the little churches tucked away among mountain knobs and back roads, the people will praise God in their old ways, still waiting to get on to a better place.

THE
SERPENT DIED

LOUVERNIA CHRISTINE OWENS COOTS
B. 1922

"Honey, just as soon as the Lord's through with me, I'll be there."

HER CHRISTIAN NAME IS LOUVERNIA CHRISTINE, but the serpent-handling believers all know her as Mamaw Coots. She has the face of an angel, and the aura that hovers around her suggests that she has one foot in this world and one in the next—a head start to heaven, she's that spotless. Often sought out by younger church members for advice and for interpretations of prophecies, Lou Coots is a calm, leveling influence as she sits on a bench behind the pulpit in her church, fingers laced together, hazel-colored eyes closed in concentration. Her gray hair is pulled into a neat bun at her neck, and she wears a bright printed dress.

Lou Coots is a fixture in the Full Gospel Tabernacle in Jesus Name in Middlesboro, Kentucky, a church she helped her husband establish in 1978. She still stands and sings the hymns vigorously, but she rarely performs solo, as she did in the days when she and her husband, Signs preacher Tommy Coots, made gospel albums together.

Except for her black puppy, Mr. Tom, which her grandson Jamie found caught in a wire fence behind the church, Mamaw Coots lives alone. But she is never lonely. She says she still talks to her husband, though he's been dead for thirteen years. "He comes to me sometimes," she says. "He came to me one night in a dream or something. It was so plain. He put his arms around me. He said,

'How much longer is it going to be?' And I said, 'Honey, just as soon as the Lord's through with me, I'll be there.' "

And God. She talks to Him, too. "His voice is real soft and low," she says. "Oh, Lord, yeah, it's a comforting voice."

Mamaw Coots says that if, as some people believe, the new millennium will signal the end of the world, she wants to be here when Jesus walks on the earth. And she wants to see Tommy again.

In the meantime, there is plenty of family around. Most of her children still live in Middlesboro—son Greg and his wife, Linda, and sons Ronnie, Mike, Bennie, and Alan. Her grandson Jamie and his wife, also named Linda, recently helped Mamaw move into a duplex a mile from their own house. It has two bedrooms, a carport, a patio, and a chain-link fence to keep Mr. Tom from straying. "And two bathrooms," exults Linda Smith Coots, Jamie's wife, who has only a single small bathroom that frequently has to accommodate out-of-town guests in addition to her family of four. Linda melts when she talks about Mamaw Coots. "There's no better person alive. And if you need something from God, she's the best person to ask to pray for you."

Mamaw Coots starts her days by reading the Bible. Then she fixes a breakfast of fried apples, biscuits, fried eggs, and bacon. If no one is there to eat it by the time she's through cooking, she starts calling relatives, but usually her sons Mike, Benny, and Alan show up unannounced. On Sunday mornings, the whole family meets at Mamaw's house.

Mamaw still has enough energy to do a once-a-week washing for her son Ronnie, who lives on a houseboat, and to clean house and wash clothes for church member Nedith Morrisey, eighty-six, and her husband, Doyle, ninety-two. And that's not all. On summer Thursdays, one of the sisters from the church brings corn, tomatoes, cabbages, beans, and cucumbers—anything left over from the vegetable stand where she sells her produce—and Mamaw starts canning. "She won't let nothing go to waste," says Linda. Until she moved, Mamaw had her own vegetable garden, but even without it, she still has plenty to do.

It's been a hard year for her since her best friend, Sister Charlene Turner, passed away. "They both took me under their wing when I married Jamie," says Linda. "I think Mamaw Coots is still grieving for Mamaw Turner. They walked this way together for twenty or thirty years. They were real close friends."

But Lou Coots's life continues to be enriched. Jamie is following in the footsteps of his grandfather. Even when he was a toddler, says Mamaw, Jamie showed an interest in music. "Tommy would take him to church and set him up on the Bible stand and let him sing," she remembers. "He was little—two or three years old. He's sung all his life, ever since he's been big enough to sing, and that would tickle Tom to death. Oh, Lord, I wish Tommy could have lived to see Jamie handle serpents." Even Jamie's daughter, Katrina, carries the family's musical gene. At seven, she plays the piano and organ and sings in church. Trina pushes her long, honey-colored hair over her shoulders and dismisses her talent with a smile and a shrug. "The Lord has just blessed me."

Lou Coots has seven children, all born at home, all still living. She has made record albums with her husband. She has sung on the radio. She has traveled around the Southeast singing and helping her husband spread the Word of God. And she's not finished yet, nor is God finished with her. Only recently, she says, He healed her of a broken arm. "I was out in the backyard [and] went to give the dog some food and water. Dog got in front of me, and I tripped over him and fell. I looked at my arm, and I said, 'Lord, my arm's broke.' I seen the bone pushed out against the skin, right above the elbow. I said, 'Lord, you gotta put it back together.' And so He did. I felt it go right back in place. Yeah, sure did. Then I told Him, 'Nobody here but You and me, Lord. You got to help me up.' And I put out my hand, and He helped me get to my feet. Never had any pain, never did lose a night's sleep. In two or three days, now, it swelled up and got real blue—bruised, you know—but it's better now."

Of Mamaw's seven children, only two are presently in the church—Sissy, who lives in Ohio, and Greg, who a few years ago handed over the pastorship of the Full Gospel Tabernacle in Jesus Name to twenty-seven-year-old Jamie. As for the others—Ronnie, Alan, Ray, Kathy, Bennie, and Mike—their mother believes the Lord will bring them back. "I may not live to see it, but I think they will [come back]," she says. "We read the Bible at home, always took them to church. They've heard the Word. They know what it is.

"I never drank strychnine or handled fire," Mamaw Coots says, although she has lived her life by the Signs. "I feel like I could do it, but the Lord don't tell me to, so I don't. The Lord spoke to me once and told me I would speak in tongues before I died. He said he would give me the Greek tongue."

Long ago, she stopped taking up serpents when the one she was handling died in her hand. "It went just limp as a rag, and I dropped it in the box. It was just like dropping a shoestring down in there. It was dead as four o'clock. I tell you, God does wonderful things for you, children, if you let Him. I haven't handled since then. I don't want to kill their snakes, and I'm afraid they'll die. Maybe they wouldn't, I don't know, but they think a lot of their snakes, now, they do."

IN HER OWN WORDS
LOUVERNIA COOTS

My dad's name was Thomas Owens, and my mother was Roxie. They weren't in the Signs Church. Mom would go to a Holiness church sometimes. Daddy wouldn't. He'd go to the Baptist. I had nine sisters and brothers. Even with all the children, it was a good life. This was in Wasioto, Kentucky, in Bell County. We always had plenty to eat, Lord have mercy, yeah. Daddy worked for the railroad, laying them old crossties. Now, they got machinery to do all that, but Daddy had to work hard. He had to put them ties in [by hand]. Many a time, I'd see him coming home with that old creosote on his arms from those ties, burned up to his elbows. *Burned up*. He was sixty-eight when he died. My mother lived till she was ninety.

I was twenty, almost twenty-one, when I met Tommy. He was born in Dorton Branch, Kentucky, up above Pineville. He was nineteen, two years younger than me. Lord, I thought he was all there was. I don't remember how he proposed. He just asked me would I marry him. I said yeah. We married after three months and stayed married forty-some years. We got married in Pineville, Kentucky, September of 1943. I turned twenty-one in November. We had seven children, all born at home. Never been to a doctor except to get a blood test when I's married. Well, though, when I was about thirteen years old, Daddy made me go to a doctor. Mama and Daddy was going to milk the cow, and I stayed by myself at the house, and I wanted to learn to sew on the sewing machine. And Daddy said, "Don't be bothering that sewing machine." So I got the old Singer out and started sewing on it and sewed the needle through [my index] finger. And it broke off in there. I took my teeth and pulled what I could out, and the eye of it stayed under my nail there. It swelled up, and Daddy made me go have that took out. And that's the only time I ever been to the doctor.

Punkin Brown cured me of the flu. I'd get it every month, and a lot of times, I'd have pneumonia, have to sit up on the side of the bed and pray all night. Couldn't breathe. I had this twelve or fifteen years, every month of my life. I'd take it, and Brother Coots would say, "I don't know what makes you so sick." I'd get sick and couldn't go to church with him or nothing. I'd say, "Well, honey, I just can't make it." And if I even so much as got my arm wet, next day, I'd take a cold. But now, it don't bother me. I was sitting in church, and Punkin was having church for the homecoming [in] 1995, and I wasn't sick or nothing that day. And he was preaching, anointment was so heavy, and he just passed by me—I think he was speaking in tongues—and I felt something come down, hit me in the head and go out my toes. It just felt like *power*—almost like a bolt—and just went plumb through my body. I told Punkin he give me a good over-hauling job, and he did. It's been four years [and I've not been sick since]. And [all he did was] just walk right by me. He was a wonderful man. We miss him today. Yeah, Lord, yeah.

The Lord would heal people through Tommy [and] cast out devils. But at the time Tommy and me got married, he wasn't even a Christian. He worked in a filling station for a while, then worked in a box factory out in Ohio. I went to church, but I wasn't what you'd call a Christian. We went to Baptist [churches], all of them. Ever which one we lived close to, that's the one I went to. But we weren't in the Signs Church yet. Then the Lord called Tommy to preach, and that's all he did after that.

We'd been married a few years when he was called to preach, and we'd been married six years before we had children. Once we got started, we couldn't quit. We ended up with seven. The children never went to a doctor, neither. We just prayed for them, and God healed them.

Oh, Lord, we had a happy family life. We had miracles, too. Oh, yeah, the miracle milk story. Now, let me tell it like it is. [When my daughter Kathy was] three weeks, my milk went bad. I raised every one of them on the breast. Never did have none on the bottle. So I had the church to pray for her. This was in Nicholasville, Kentucky. I had the church pray that the Lord would move— make [the milk] good, you know. Well, He did. And I let her nurse right on till she was nineteen months old. I thought I could wean her like I did the other children. See, I didn't know it was miracle milk. So when the church prayed, the Lord spoke to me. And I'd done tried to wean Kathy and had her off the breast nine days, tried my best to dry them up, and He'd come down every morning and every night [and fill my breasts again]. The milk wouldn't dry up. So I said to the church, "Well, you 'uns gonna have to pray again." And we prayed again, and the Lord spoke to me, and He said, "Touch not this that I've done." Said, "It's for her strength." And no doubt, that kid would have died if the Lord hadn't done that, see.

Well, she was standing there, pulling at my dress, wanting to nurse, and I picked her up and put her back to that breast. I'd had her off it *nine days*, now. I thought it would make her sick if I put her back on it, but I put her right back to that breast, and she nursed every day till she was five years old. And then God took the milk away from her. And she'd *fight* you over it, too. You could kid her about her breast, honey, and she would fight you, now. She had to have that milk. It kept her healthy, and I don't believe she'd of lived if the Lord hadn't moved that way. She wasn't sickly, but God spoke it, said, "This is her strength." See, if she hadn't got that miracle milk, she wouldn't have lived. And she's thirty-seven now.

He's good. The Lord's good.

Another miracle happened with Ronnie, my oldest. He got hit with a truck. Semi truck. Hit him in the back and knocked him about a hundred feet. He was going across the road, going to the store, and his daddy done told him *not* to go

Rev. Tommy Coots (right), and Louvernia Coots (second from left), at their baptism c. 1930s
Family photo

Tommy and Louvernia Coots, c. 1950
Family photo

to the store. We lived in Corbin then. He was eight or nine, maybe ten years old. He started to cross the road, and this big semi truck hit him right in the back, knocked him a hundred foot over the embankment. We lived down in the holler, away from the road, and these people that lived down there brought him up in the road. Another woman up on the hill, she come down and checked him out. She wanted him to go to a doctor, you know. And that woman said, "Well, let's call a ambulance and get him took to a doctor," and when [she said] that, Ronnie jerked away from 'em. He run all the way down that holler and run home. He had stone bruises on his feet. He wasn't going to go to no doctor, so he run home. And when he got home, we asked him what happened, and he told us. And in about thirty minutes, here come two policemen down there to check him out, see if he's hurt. They's gonna take him to the doctor. And they looked him over and said, "Boy, you're a lucky boy." That's all he had on him was some brier scratches.

Now, down in Nicholasville, where Kathy was born, the people didn't know anything about living by faith. That's when they put Brother Coots in jail. They's a bunch of neighbors, and they didn't live close to me, never was in my house. Fifteen of them swore a bunch of lies [and got a warrant for Tommy's arrest]. *Fifteen.*

[In court,] they said Tommy deserted his family, 'cause he went off [preaching] in revivals and I stayed home with seven kids. They couldn't understand that. They didn't know how we lived. And we trusted the Lord, you know, for everything. We had plenty, and they said we didn't have nothin' to eat, said the kids was hungry and cold. And when they got through, the judge said, "Brother Coots, call your witness." So Tom called me up there, and they didn't want me there, 'cause I was the only one could defend him, see? I was the only one he'd spoke to since he got that warrant, 'cause he was gone [to a revival]. The neighbors gathered in the courthouse, and I got on that witness stand, and God began to bless me, and I told them some things. I testified to them and told them what *they* needed. The Lord had moved through us, and we lived by faith, you know, and [I told] how God had healed us and take care of us. And that old judge said, "Is all your witnesses like this?" Tom said, "Yeah, I guess they are, 'cause they's all of the church down there." And [the judge] said, "Well, we don't want to hear any more. We'll let you go for now."

Then they tried to catch him hunting serpents, but see, they couldn't. The old judge sent a deputy up there to the house to watch him, and if he got caught hunting serpents, they was going to take him to jail. But the deputy was sitting out in the field watching, and the chiggers like to ate him up. He went back and told that judge, said, "Now, if you want to catch that man hunting snakes, you gonna have to go get him yourself." So they never did give us no more trouble after that trial.

First time I handled [serpents] was up in Harlan. Probably around the '80s. Brother Pete Rowe's church. The serpent died. The first time, he didn't die, but it did go limp. That happened every time I handled. [The serpent] didn't move around, *couldn't* move. When you're anointed, you can't express how it feels. It's a good feeling. They don't feel like snakes. They feel more like velvet. They don't feel rough when you're anointed. And you feel like you're plumb out of the world. Oh, yeah, it's joy, yeah. You'd have to handle one to know what I'm talking about. [I] stopped when it died in my hand.

When Brother Coots would handle serpents, they'd just go limp in his hand, too. Yeah, limp. Limber. Well, he waited on the anointing. See, the anointing will do that. If you don't wait on that, [the serpents will] try to get away from you. Yeah, if you ain't anointed heavy, they'll try to get away from you. I think they ought to put 'em up when they get wild, I sure do. When Brother Coots picked 'em up, they'd go limp, just like a string.

Tommy wasn't no quiet preacher, now, 'cause the power of God made him loud. He handled a lot of serpents. He'd hold them, and they couldn't do nothing. I never did put 'em around my neck. Lord never did move on me that way. But Tommy, he put 'em around his neck sometimes. One time, he put his foot down in a box on two big rattlers. He pulled his shoes off. We was in a service way up in Harlan somewheres—I can't remember where it was at—and he said, "Well, Lord, Lou, I'm gonna do something I ain't ever done since I been a Christian." And everybody was wondering what it was going to be, because he's always doing something. The Lord [always] moved on him to do something, you know. And we's wondering what it was. And he went over there and got a serpent box and two big black rattlers in it. He opened that lid, pulled his shoes and socks off, and put both his feet right in on top of them black rattlers. He sure did. It didn't scare me. I didn't feel no fear whenever he handled them.

After most of the children was all married, we made record albums, Tommy and me. We made a big one and a little 'un, too—them small records, 45s, and them big albums, 78s. First time, we made five hundred copies of the big album. The name of it was *Coots Duet*. Tommy's been dead thirteen years now, and we had them out quite a while before he died. Might have been twenty, twenty-five years ago. Hymns, spirituals. Most of them were songs that God give Tommy. He never did write a song. The Lord just give 'em to him. He never wrote one down. Lots of times, the Lord would give him one during the altar call, and he'd sing that song just that one time, and he'd never sing it no more. He couldn't remember it. God gave him hundreds of songs.

We traveled around and sang in a radio station in Harlan. We sang several times—station WHLN, Harlan, yeah. We sung in Middlesboro off and on for years and years. Sundays. Sunday mornings. Live. We'd go in the studio and sing, and Tommy'd preach. We'd get thirty minutes, but last time he was in there, we's on a hour. We'd all go down there and sing. The children were small then. If Tommy's mother didn't keep the children, we'd take them with us. My granddaughters used to sing, too, but they don't go to church now.

Another thing he did, Tommy cast out a lot of devils. I was right down by the side of 'em, praying for 'em. I wasn't afraid of 'em. I just wanted to see people delivered, and I knowed God could do it.

Lady in Nicholasville, we prayed for her about three times before God delivered her. We was having church one Sunday, and she was there, and she got to acting funny. Tom was preaching. Oh, the anointing was so heavy [that day]. But you could tell the devil was working on this sister. Tom knew the devil was in her, because every time he'd get anointed to preach, it would act up. She'd move around and act funny, and God let Tommy know what was going on. Trying to get her to leave the church—that's what that devil was trying to do. Well, she got up and went to the church door and tried to get out. Devil told her, said, "If you get out of here, you'll be all right." Well, she got back to the door and put her hand on the door, and the Lord let Tom know what she was doing, so he just pointed his finger from the pulpit to the door. Her back was to Tom when he pointed, and he just said, "In the name of Jesus," and she hit the floor, fell down. As far as she got was the door. And Tom said, "Pick her up and bring her up here."

So two brothers went back there and got her, brought her up in front, and he prayed for her. And that sister cried and begged Tom—but it was the devil in her talking—to not make that devil go out. The devil said, "I got a palace here, and I'm not leaving." And Tom commanded him to leave. [The devil] spoke through [this sister], but it was a man's voice, real strong, deep, and she spoke real strong, and said, "You can't make me go out." And Tom said, "This is one time you're going out, devil." And he did. He went out. And that woman fell in the floor like a dead person, laid there a few minutes, and she got up praising God, said, "He's gone! He's gone!" She got delivered that day. The devil can go out into another body or just in the air, you know. Spirits can go out in the air and go where they want to go. We got plenty of them out here today. Oh, yeah, we have. Well, that woman stayed in the church. She was all right from then on.

Yeah, and they was a little baby, two years old, going to church down there [who] set in her mother's lap. And Tom would get anointed to preach, and that baby would tell him to hush, and it weren't but two years old. Would tell him, "Hush, hush." And Tom told its mommy, "You bring that baby up here. I want to rebuke the devil out of it." And honey, he prayed for that baby and rebuked the devil out of that baby. The devil didn't want [Tom's] message to come forth, didn't want anybody to hear what Tom was preaching, see? The baby had a deep voice like a man. This was in Nicholasville, too. We were there 1962 to 1967. He preached [in Middlesboro] from 1967 to 1986.

I don't believe you have to handle serpents to go to heaven. I don't believe that. But it's the Word. And if you believe it, you'll do it. If the Lord moves on you to do the Signs, you'd better do it. But if the Lord don't open it up to you and let you understand it, you can't do it no way. You can still be in the church and go to heaven if you believe it. But if God tells you to move and you don't move, you're gonna get in trouble. You'll be a disobedient servant. We have to mind the spirit of God when it moves, and you know when it moves. If you don't mind Him, you could get sick or anything. Trouble'll start hitting you on every hand. You'll get punished, now, if you don't obey Him, 'cause he chastises them He loves.

GOD-GIVEN SONGS SUNG BY TOMMY COOTS

During the years he was a Signs preacher, Pastor Tommy Coots sang hundreds of hymns extemporaneously. He said that God put the words in his mouth. After he sang those words, he forgot them, but his wife, Lou, and Valerie Rowe began to write down many of the songs, and the congregation at the Full Gospel Tabernacle in Jesus Name continues to sing them today.

The Wrath of God

I've traveled over this county,
I've been from town to town.
I can see the end is now nearing
And the wrath of God pouring down.

Now, there's many souls God's calling,
He's calling, "Come unto Me,"
So don't wait till death overtakes you,
Come now, He'll set you free.

Now, we read in Revelation,
It tells of that great day
when the sinners they will be running,
From His face, they'll hide away.

Chorus

Oh, the wrath of God is soon coming,
To be poured out upon the unsaved.
So get ready while you're living,
From the cradle to the grave.

In the Beautiful City Somewhere

This world is too wicked to make it my home,
I've started to heaven on high.
When my work is done, my life's race is run,
I will move to a mansion on high.

There's many dear loved ones that have traveled this road,
Their life on this earth is no more.

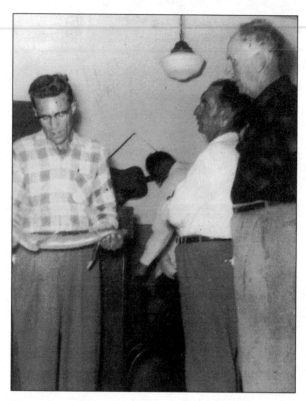

Tommy Coots (left) with snake that went limp in his hands, c. 1950
Family photo

They finished their journey, they've fought a good fight,
Now they're resting on God's peaceful shore.

When my work is done, my life's race is run,
And you come to look your last time,
Tell my friends down here to meet me up there,
In that beautiful city somewhere.

Chorus

In the beautiful city somewhere,
To reach is someday my prayer.
I'll say good-bye here, good morning up there,
In that beautiful city somewhere.

A LITTLE
YELLER RATTLER

GREGORY JAMES "JAMIE" COOTS
B. 1971

*"I knowed I was gonna have to suffer,
but I knowed I wasn't going to die."*

JAMIE COOTS IS A BIG MAN—260 pounds by his own estimate—and shaped like a linebacker. At five feet, seven inches, he looks as solid as a steel ball, and his closely shaved head adds to the effect of mass in motion. All this bulk gives the impression that Jamie Coots would be a formidable opponent for wrestling with the devil. If you had to bet on who would win the match, you'd probably put your money on Jamie.

During the week, he drives a rock truck the size of a boxcar for a Kentucky strip-mining operation. On the weekend, he is a considerable presence in his own church or the other Signs Following houses of worship he visits regularly, preaching, singing, and handling snakes nearly as long as he is tall.

Jamie Coots has religion in his genes, both from his grandparents and his father. Gregory Coots reared his son in the church, and when Jamie strayed temporarily, Greg literally prayed him back to God. The conversion was so thorough that soon afterward, Greg handed over to Jamie the ministry of the Full Gospel Tabernacle in Jesus Name. It is the same church founded in 1978 by Jamie's legendary grandfather, Tommy Coots, preacher, radio personality, and gospel singer.

Another influential person in Jamie's life, both spiritually and personally, was Punkin Brown. Punkin was a kindred spirit, the brother Jamie never had.

The two traveled the serpent-handling circuit together. They were a good pair—personable, young, handsome, and enthusiastic. Sometimes, the services where they preached didn't really get going until Punkin and Jamie arrived, and then the two friends warmed things up in a hurry. Now, since Punkin's death, one insider who understands the politics of the religion says that Jamie has become the man most sought after to preach at other churches and to minister to Signs believers throughout the Southeast. Jamie learned a lot about snakes from Punkin. One of the changes he has made in the Full Gospel Tabernacle is to bring in more serpents for services—big ones, dangerous ones, all potentially fatal. The meaner the snakes, the better the victory. If they aren't lethal, he says, they belong in the forest.

He keeps his serpents in a barnlike shed next to his house, heavily padlocked for the safety of family and neighbors. The shed is heated in cool weather. Jamie feeds and cares for the serpents daily, cleaning their boxes, washing the snakes, making sure they are healthy, ready, and in their prime. When they strike, they are as lethal as a bullet, and just about as fast.

Jamie is a devoted husband to his wife, Linda, and a good father to his daughter, Katrina, and son, Cody. But before this family chapter of his life was written, he had a wild streak. The title of a song by one of his country-music heroes, Hank Williams, Jr., described Jamie perfectly: "Whiskey Bent and Hell Bound." Whiskey, music, and women are the combustible combination he now views as a formula for sin in "the world," where he was lost for a time, singing sometimes for money, sometimes for adulation. These days, though, he performs only in church, using his talent and energy to do God's business, preaching the Word in a fiery storm of sermonizing and singing his heart out for God.

Like his grandfather before him, Jamie was cast in the mold of the old-fashioned fire-and-brimstone messengers, a spiritual man of steel. When he lets loose with a sermon, the words set the place on fire, often driving the faithful out of their pews and to the front of the church, where they dance, shout, and take up serpents. He follows all of the Signs—taking up serpents, handling fire, drinking deadly poisons, and healing the sick—although he has not yet been called upon to cast out devils. "Oh, you will know it" when he is anointed, says Linda. "His eyes turn plumb black, and his face gets real red, and he gets to breathing hard. And his shoulders shake. The Lord just shakes him all over. Oh, Lord, it's beautiful."

Jamie has faced death twice from the bites of poisonous reptiles—both rattlers—and he was once bitten by a copperhead. The worst bite came in December 1998, just a couple of weeks before Christmas, when Jamie was struck by a rattlesnake on the middle finger of the right hand—his guitar-strumming finger. The bite was not so much life threatening as it was painful. The swelling puffed his hand and finger into a throbbing balloon of brutal agony. For a month, he got no more than an hour's sleep a night. The first week after the bite, he walked the floor all night howling, crying, suffering the worst physical hurt he has ever

Jamie Coots handles a rattlesnake at the Middlesboro church
Photo by Scott Schwartz

endured in his life. When the pain ebbed, the rotting began. The flesh began to darken and pull away from the bone. The finger eventually shriveled into a leathery, black appendage that appeared to be mummified. The white bone was exposed from the finger's first digit to the red, swollen knuckle.

"It happened at a Sunday meeting at the church, a regular Sunday meeting," Jamie remembers. "The meeting was going pretty good, and I was handling a little yeller rattler. I still got it. It was a little yeller timber rattler, about two and a half foot long. I'd been handling him for several minutes, and he was handling good. I was just rubbing his head [with] my hand, just handling him and feeling real good. One of the sisters came and got it and handled it. It was the best victory I've ever seen her have handling serpents. And she don't handle them a lot. She's probably took 'em from me more than anybody. So she came and got it and handled it, and Linda was standing there behind me. After that sister gave it back to me, I was just standing there rubbing its head, and Linda was praising the Lord, and I thought, 'Well, [Linda] is going to come and get it and handle it.' She usually handles 'em when the other sister does. They work together real good in church. They pray together and prophesy. I thought, 'Well, she is going to come handle it, too.' [Later,] she said she wanted to and kind of felt like it, but she hadn't been praying like she should have been.

"I just kept on handling it, didn't feel like putting it up or nothing. All of a sudden, I rubbed that hand across that last time. He never kinked; he never struck; he just opened his mouth and grabbed my finger and held on." When Jamie unfastened the serpent's fangs from his finger, the snake dropped down and got him with one fang in the fatty part of the finger as well. "Well, I handled him maybe a minute or two more and put him up. I thought the Lord was just warning me. I didn't think the bite was going to hurt me. I testified for about fifteen minutes, and another brother preached about forty-five minutes. We had an altar call, and I sung the altar call song. A man come and prayed, and I got in and shouted and danced before the Lord. I've not danced in probably a year. I got in and danced and felt real good.

"It was over an hour before I started swelling. It just all of a sudden started swelling, moving up my finger. I could feel the pressure. I thought, 'Well, maybe it is going to hurt a little bit.' I'd of never [believed] everything that it done. I got to hurting pretty bad. Service was over, so I came on home. Lot of 'em came up here with me. I pulled off my long-sleeve dress shirt and put on a T-shirt, laid up in my waterbed, and figured we might as well get comfortable. *Here we go.*

"Then it got to hurting awful. The bed just didn't get it no more. I walked a path from the living room all the way through and around the house. This is in December. The only relief I could get was [to] set that air conditioner on high, sticking my hand up there and numbing that finger. I'd feel good for about forty-five minutes and go to aching again. The first night, I never slept a wink. Second night, I slept for fifteen minutes. Third night, I slept about forty-five minutes. Fourth night, I slept about twenty minutes. And I went for two months before I slept a full night. I'd get up hurting every night. I didn't think it was ever going to go away."

Jamie understood that the toxin from the bite was eating away everything—flesh, muscles, nerves, bone. He was going to lose the finger, maybe all the way down to the hand. And then something else struck him: He is right-handed. What if he couldn't play his guitar? As the finger grew worse, he'd look at it and cry. But after a while, it occurred to him that it could have been worse. It could have been his left hand, the one he needed to finger the frets. With his injured hand, he could still hold a guitar pick, could still pick the strings with another finger, although those who watched him play during that time saw him wince every time he accidently struck the end of his injured finger on the strings.

As that small part of him was dying off, Jamie tried to put things in perspective, but it wasn't easy. "On Christmas Eve, we always fix dinner here, because both my grandmothers fix it on Christmas," he says. "We invite everybody from church and some of the family. I was setting in here in the first bedroom, and that old dead skin was still on the finger. It stunk so bad. It had been close to three weeks, and it stunk so bad I'd keep it wrapped up. That heat would get to it where it was wrapped in that gauze bandage, and it would just smell. Out in a public place, I could smell it. I wasn't ashamed of being bit, but I was ashamed of that odor, it smelled so bad. So I decided I'm going to pull that old dead skin off there. It wasn't no good no way. It was blistered, dead skin. I could just move it every way, but I didn't know it had already rotted out. That black was all there was. And it was still all infected. That bone didn't start showing till later. So I pulled all that skin off, and all that was there was that black and that fingernail. I set on that bed, and I cried. I couldn't stand it. It wasn't the pain. It was just looking at it. I seen a lot of people bit, but that's the worst bite that I've seen. I thought at first, 'Well, it is because it is *my* finger,'

Jamie with his snake-bitten finger, before it fell off in 1999
Photo by Fred Brown

but then I got to asking everybody, and not many people have completely lost a finger to a bite. So it did hurt bad all the time.

"I was off work three weeks total. I went and tried to work one day on a Wednesday—not the Wednesday after I got bit, but the next Wednesday. I went in and worked about an hour and a half, and jarring that truck hurt so bad, I told Dad I had to go home. Took the rest of that week off, and took off the rest of my vacation. I told my boss I'd be back after Christmas vacation. I figured that'd give it enough time to ease off. My boss, he don't believe like I do, but he's a good boss, very understanding. He gave me twenty hours both weeks that I was off, and I worked one hour in two weeks. He gave me forty hours. Sent me a check home with Dad. That's how good he is to me. So then after Christmas vacation, I went back, and it still hurt. I'm heavy anyway, and I got to pull myself up in that truck, climb up that ladder. It would hurt, putting pressure on that hand and finger. But I'd put olive oil on it every morning and wrap it with gauze bandage. Well, I finally realized it wasn't getting no air, and it was just staying infected all the time. One Friday, I just decided, 'I ain't going to wrap it no more. I'm going to let it get all the air it can get.' And that's when it all dried out and the bone started showing [and] the fingernail fell off.

"It was connected down here [in the second digit of the middle finger], and then it pulled loose all the way out to there [the end of the finger]. But I just got to where I was used to it. After four months, I accepted the fact that if God didn't see fit to do a miracle, eventually [that part] right there is all I'm going to have.

"But I always said I wouldn't never go to a hospital for a bite. I said, 'Lord, if I ever go to a hospital, I'll quit handling.' But I don't fight nobody that does. I know people that go to the hospital. My own wife told me that if she ever got bit, she was going to the hospital. That's every individual's choice. They's been people ask me, 'Why don't you go have that finger cut off?' I couldn't. One of the brothers told me, said, 'Jamie, you done suffered the serpent bite.' I said, 'Yeah, but really, if I go to the hospital, I still have to fight that battle of the devil telling me, "You said you never would go, [and] here you went." ' "

But Jamie Coots doesn't give in to the devil that easily.

Jamie's sister-in-law, a nurse, told him that getting the infected area cut off would not solve his problem anyway. She said the knuckle was destroyed, too, so the physician would have to amputate the entire finger all the way to the first knuckle. "I figured I'd rather have half a finger than no finger," Jamie says.

"So I didn't go. And when people asked me, 'Why don't you cut it off?' I said, 'I ain't going to cut it off. If God wants it to fall off, it'll fall off. I don't know what it's going to do.'"

By the end of April 1999, Jamie's snake-struck finger finally did come off. "He was out working on the Jeep," says Linda, "and when he pressed down on the fender, the finger fell off. It didn't hurt so much as it was a shock. It bled a little bit, but not bad. But it scared Jamie. I was in the house ironing, and I heard him yell, 'Linda!' But you have to look at the humor of it. We got it in the house in a jar now."

The loss of his finger was a terrible ordeal, says Jamie, but it could have been worse. He won't reveal just what he did, but he believes the snakebite was God's way of punishing him. "It was my fault. Prior to going to church, I had done something that I knowed I shouldn't do. I didn't have any business handling [that day]. Even though I felt good, subconsciously I knowed what I was doing was wrong. Nobody knows [what it was] but my wife. I didn't backslide or anything, but I knew it was wrong, and then after I got bit, for some foolish reason, I decided to do it again. It was about a week later, and the pain was starting to ease off a little, and I went and done that same stupid thing again, and it started back to hurting and just did not let up.

"This has been my roughest bite, because with all the rest of them, they healed up. [Another] one left a scar [on my hand], but this finger I have to face every day. I have to look at it, and I have to think [about what caused it] every day. That's what a mistake cost me. I won't do it again, definitely not."

To make things worse, his longtime friend Punkin Brown was not there to help him through the bite, as he had been for previous ones. Jamie was on his own, but he remembered what Punkin had told him: He had to return to the serpent that bit him. He had to handle that snake before he could go on with his life and his ministry. So he determined that was exactly what he would do—handle the snake that had taken his finger off at the knuckle.

"I was getting kind of discouraged on it," he says. "I went about three months there and hadn't handled none. I went out here one Saturday night, out to the snake room, took a rattler out, and put it in the box. Its eyes was hazed over. He was shedding and was real touchy. Got him out on the hook, reached, and touched him, and he turned around. I dropped him back down in the box. I thought, 'Well, I ain't taking *you* nowhere.' So I got another one out there. I slid the den box and opened the lid up on him. Reached down there with the hook and touched him, and *he* turned around on me. Put *him* back down. Turned around to the canebrake [rattler]. His eyes was hazed over. I thought, 'Well, *he* might be all right.' I got him out and touched him, and he come around on me.

"I looked over, and all there was left to take was the one that bit me. I said, 'Lord God, ain't they something else I can take besides that?' But that was the Lord letting me know that it was time to get over that fear, you know. If I was going to handle anything, it was going to be the one that bit me. I took him to church Saturday night, and the Lord never moved on me to handle him. Sunday, I went back to church, and Brother Cameron Short brought a rattler down. And the Lord got to moving pretty good on one of the brothers, and he went and got Cameron's rattler out and handled it. Well, he was standing there offering it to me, and I hadn't handled nothing much. I thought, 'Aaaahhhh, I don't believe I want to,' you know. I looked at that finger and thought, 'Uuuuhhhh, I don't want it bit again.'

"Finally, the Lord moved on me real strong, and I reached and took it. Well, when I did and handled it, then the Lord let me know it was all right to get the one out that bit me. I had a copperhead in there with him. I got the one out that bit me and handled it. The Lord give me real good victory. So from then on, I begin to get over it, a little bit at a time. But I had to get over the fear of that one snake. He had me in such a shape, and the Lord let me know that I had to handle him first. I had to get over that.

"And the Lord blessed me," he says.

IN HIS OWN WORDS
JAMIE COOTS

I was born up here in Middlesboro, November 17, 1971. Of course, they took me to church all of my life. My grandfather didn't build the [current] church until 1978, [so] we was having house meetings at my grandmother's house [Mamaw Charlene Turner's], which is right up the road, where we always have the dinner at homecoming. Then my great-aunt, she had a house down there where the church is now, and she owned the property. She got sickly, and before she passed away, she deeded the property to the people for a church. And so we tore her old house down, which was about to fall down anyway. They tore it down and built the church. And from 1978 on, we had our own building.

I don't know the year my grandfather started those house meetings. I've got some of the old reel-to-reel tapes from back in the '60s where he was preaching on radio broadcasts. He was preaching long before the house meetings. See, they lived in Nicholasville, in Jasmine County. They moved around a lot, him being a preacher, just wherever they'd feel led to go for a church or whatever. And then they moved down here. When Mom and Dad met—I think that was in '67—my mom didn't believe like Grandpaw and Mamaw Coots did. So they got to explaining to her how they believed, and she got to praying for the Lord to open it up to her, [and] they just started having meetings in her mom's house. And they had house meetings up there until they built the church.

As far back as I can remember, there's always been serpents there, always serpent-handling meetings, just whenever the Lord moved. But I can always remember being around them. Dad used to keep 'em. He doesn't anymore. I keep all of 'em now. He used to keep 'em under the floor at home, under the house in boxes, locked. He had a little door that he hung a padlock on where nobody could get around them. He'd only keep 'em during the summer and [then] turn 'em loose, because they are so hard to keep during the winter. I keep mine all year long out there in the building, where it is heated.

Serpents has always been a big part of my life. My grandpaw, he kindly wanted to push me out to make me sing. He would take me to churches. I think the first time I sung, I was only three or four year old, it seems like. He set me up on the Bible stand, and I helped him sing "I'll Fly Away." Seems like it was a funeral, because I remember it being a big crowd. From then on, I always had an interest in church as a child. I stayed with Grandmaw and Papaw Coots a lot when I was little. They would keep me before I started to school and during the summer. I would stay with them and go to church wherever they'd go.

At home, Dad made me go. And he literally *made* me go until I was going on sixteen. And then I got so rebellious that I just refused to go, and I got into drinking and running with the wrong crowd. He made me go as long as he could keep that threat on me of making me go, and I thank God now that he did.

You know, the Bible says [to] train up a child in the way it should go, and when it grows old, it won't depart from it. The Signs Church says, well, you make a kid go until they are eleven, twelve, thirteen year old, and then when they say they don't want to go, you ought not make them go no more. But I don't see it that way. From the age of eleven or twelve on up is when they really begin to comprehend what church is about. I know that my daughter, she's seven year old, and there's no doubt she knows a lot of right from wrong. Not all of it. She knows a lot of it. She participates in the service now. She plays the organ and sings. She doesn't participate in the Signs or anything like that, but she participates in the singing. And I tell her, now, if she does something she knows is wrong, she is not allowed to sing [that week]. I give her that choice: "If you make the wrong choices, then you no longer participate in the service." But I feel like at her age, she don't really fully comprehend what living right is about, what church is about. So I feel like the years between twelve and fifteen, although I was sort of rebellious and didn't want to go, still yet, that's when I got most of my learning.

I got out for a couple of years. Just before me and Linda got married in early 1990 is the first time I ever prayed and decided I was going to try to be sincere about the church. I had already quit drinking. Well, not *quit* drinking, but I made a vow to the Lord as a sinner that I'd never get drunk anymore. That was an experience where I had to learn a hard lesson [that made me decide] I wasn't going to get drunk anymore.

On December 31, 1987, I was at a New Year's Eve party, and I consumed a considerable amount of alcohol. I drunk sixteen big Budweiser head-busters. Me and another man drunk a half-fifth of Vodka straight before they could get it away from us, and they mixed the other half in orange juice, and we drunk all of it. Then he told me, "I got just what you need at the house." I went to his house and bought two pints of Old Rocking Chair Red Liquor. I drunk one pint of that.

Well, this was down on Evans Drive down below the church. We were the party. I don't even remember walking home. But I know when I got home, Mom said she asked me if I had been drinking, and I said no, trying to deny it. We lived in a small house that I was raised in, a little two-bedroom house—my room and Mom and Dad's room. And the walls are real thin. All Dad done, he walked in and he just dropped his head in shame. Seem like maybe he told me he couldn't believe I'd done that or something. All that night or early morning, whenever it was that I got home, I laid there in the bed and was tormented by listening to him cry and pray. He would just weep. He said, "God, I didn't raise him that way." It hurt me that I'd hurt him. He'd always raised me better.

So I told the Lord that night, I said, "Lord, if you'll let me get through this," I said, "I'll never get drunk again." I would drink occasionally [after that night], but I would never get drunk. I was not only afraid of what would happen, but I thought, "Well, if I could drink a little bit, it won't show." I knowed if I got drunk, it would show, and I never wanted to disappoint him like that again.

But I still got out and run around, done things I ought not to have done. Then, seem like maybe March of 1990 was the first time I prayed. I was at a point then [that] I didn't even want to be around my dad, because I knew how he lived. And that spirit that was in me just didn't connect up with that spirit that was in him. I would get up and leave on the weekends when he was home, before he got out of bed.

But the night I went to the altar and prayed, a man was holding a revival at church, and I got down and prayed. I thought I was sincere then, but I still was like all young people—in part of the time and out part of the time. Wanted to go to church and yet wanted to do other things, too.

When I got up from the altar, out of the whole crowd, seem like the only one I could really see was Dad. He just came in my mind all the time. He'd pray for me. The life that he had always lived had shown a light in front of me. He was just bawling. It was what he wanted. I went back and hugged his neck and kissed him and told him I loved him. I went to the church then for a while. I was still dating and doing things I ought not do.

I didn't really start to live right until me and Linda got married. That's when I really decided it was time to try to live right. And I still didn't live like I do now. I still thought a little bit of this and a little bit of that would be all right. I never did drink, but I would fly off the handle and cuss. Get mad and cuss. That was about the worst thing.

Then when Katrina was born premature and had to stay in the hospital, that's when we decided it was time to really pray and seek God and live right. When we came back home and left her up there in the hospital, knowing that all we could do was pray and ask God to send her home, that's when I really started trying my best to live right. That's when I realized how serious it was. We would go up and see her every chance we could. I wasn't working at the time. It was hard to get means of going up there every weekend. They put so many IVs in her, all of her veins collapsed. I went in one day, and she wasn't in the [usual] place. I just panicked. The first thing I thought was, "She's dead." The nurse come to me. She'd seen I'd panicked. She said, "No, no, no, she's doing better." As they recovered, she said, they start here on this side of the door, and they move them all the way around the room. They get closer back to the door as they get better. So we went around, and she was doing better, but all of her veins had collapsed, and they had an IV in the side of her head. I just broke down then. I was already thinking she was gone, and then just seeing that . . . But God really moved for her.

We would go up every other week or so when we could. They treated us like dirt, 'cause they thought we were just neglecting the baby. Then we finally talked to [the hospital officials], and they moved her to Corbin [Kentucky], where it was a little closer. We could get there in less than an hour. And finally, she come home.

This was 1991. Trina was born in July, and I handled my first serpent in June at Bruce Helton's church in Shields, Kentucky. That was a month before Trina was born. I know I was trying to live right, or I wouldn't [have] even attempted to handle a serpent.

Right after I met Linda, I just simply told God, I said, "God, I can't live right unless I get married." I was doing things I knowed was wrong, and I knowed I couldn't correct it until I got married. So that next day, on Sunday service, I was up playing the guitar in the pulpit, which I didn't have no business in the pulpit at the time, but nevertheless, I was there. Linda was sitting in the back half of the church. Raford Dunn and Glenn Dukes used to come up just about every weekend for service. They was up that Sunday, and Brother Raford gave an altar call. I was standing there with my eyes closed, playing. I was telling the Lord, "I need a wife. If I'm going to live right, that's all there is to it." I said, "If Linda's the one meant for me, I'd like for You to show me a sign." I wanted to settle down. I didn't want to waste time like a lot of people do, with a two-, three-, four-year relationship and not get married. I was standing about the same place where I always set down, on the right side of the pulpit when you walk in. The Lord just told me to open my eyes, and I looked down, and Linda was at the altar praying.

So from then on, we tried to do a little better, which we still messed up, and we done things we ought not do. That was the weekend after Labor Day of 1990. Linda got baptized in November, and we married first of December. We had dated about three months.

It's been a wonderful marriage. A lot of people talk about their wives and things, and a lot probably don't believe me, but in eight years, we've had three major arguments—major where one of us was ready to pack up and leave. In eight years, I figure that's doing pretty good, you know. But the Lord has helped us. We always try to go to church and live right. That's been a big help.

I always looked at how my dad lived and how much he prayed. When I was at home, before I left and got married, he would go in the bedroom about an hour to an hour and a half before he went to sleep and lay on the bed and read the Bible and pray. Not many people do that anymore. Shame to say, I don't do that. And as far as I know, he still does that. We leave for work, now, five o'clock in the morning. He gets up at quarter to four and reads and prays every morning. He done that the whole time I's home. That meant a lot to me. That's something I didn't see out of anybody else. As far as I know, he still does that, in the morning and at night.

Fast? That's something I can't hardly do. Dad works out in the weather, in all kinds. He does the blasting, loading the holes with plastic, and I've seen him fast two and three days a week in dead summer working outside. Wringing wet with sweat, up on top of that mountain, without a drink of water. No nothing touching his lips. No water, nothing. That has had a great influence on me. Just that will power. I don't have that will power. I fast one day, and I've had the lick.

I look at Dad, and he doesn't participate in the service a whole lot, like others do. He is just one of the kinds that sits back and doesn't do much or say much. But yet I think to myself, "I know how good he lives. I know what he could do if he would." But yet he doesn't step out and do very much. He never has handled serpents very much. Still doesn't. He handled when I was growing up, but not much. He would handle them just every several year, it seem like. Not at every service. I think the last time he handled one is back before I got bit, maybe after Punkin died.

But now, my grandpaw, his life had more of an influence on me after he was already gone. Then I realized everything that he had done. Before I got in church, I didn't really realize, but his preaching, everything [he did], really had a big influence on me. I don't guess there is really anybody that I looked up to before I got into church. Just with Dad, the way he prayed and read the Bible really meant a lot to me, and still does to this day, because I still have not made myself get willing to do that.

But my grandfather was pretty well known throughout the churches. The main thing was, the Lord moved on him to cast out devils. That's something I've not seen since he died. I was so young, I don't really remember, but I've got a audio of him casting out a devil. It is a man's voice speaking out of a woman. It is a hair-raising experience. It really is. So I'd say that is the most thing he was known for. But he's been known throughout churches for his singing. He wrote, I'd be safe to say, close to a hundred songs. He played the guitar. Back in 1967 to '69, him and my grandmother made an album of his songs. So that was a lot of what he was known for, for his singing and playing.

Dad plays and sings along. He sits right behind the Bible stand. He's so little you can't see him. He's played the guitar for several years now and sang. Dad's probably wrote twenty to twenty-five songs. I've written three, maybe. The singing I just picked up from following along in church. The playing I picked up on my own. I'd watch my grandpaw and Dad play, and I would get a guitar out when nobody was around and try to make chords. A lot I learned when I first started out. I didn't play gospel. Course, I got jumped on pretty heavy for that. I played mostly country, and what I would do, I would turn on the radio or a record and play the guitar along with that. And that's where I learned to change chords and all like that. I would play country music in school and talent shows. I won money singing and playing music. But before I got in church, my grandmother, Mamaw Coots, she kindly stoutly rebuked me one time. She said, "Now, Jamie, the talent you got to be able to play and sing, everybody doesn't have it. God gave you that talent. And if you don't use it for God, God can take it away from you, too." That scared me. I thought, "Hey, now, I enjoy doing this, gospel or not. Let's not talk that way." But that put a lot of fear in me. I truly worried.

I was probably fifteen or sixteen year old [when she told me that]. I always thought about that, no matter where I was at. Playing or singing, I always thought, "This is a special talent. What would I do if God took it away?" I know the three times I been serpent-bit and hurt, when my hand and arm swelled so bad I couldn't play a guitar, I'd sit back, and it just grieved me. I couldn't stand it. I love to play the guitar. I'd still sing, but I couldn't play. A lot of people either sing or play, but it is something to me that goes together. It is extremely hard for me to sing and not play for myself.

I never did sing in joints. I went to vocational school, and we would have a competition day. They would come from different schools and participate in the competition. Well, I entered in the talent-show competition, and I beat two people at my vocational school. The principal of the vocational school told me that I couldn't sing anything with profanity. Hank Williams, Jr., was my hero. I've got a picture, if I can ever find it, where people has asked me and Linda both, "[Is] that Hank Williams, Jr.?" I was dressed up, always had long hair, full beard and mustache, sunglasses, cowboy hat. At the talent show, I sung a song. I hardly remember what it was now. It was one of his slow [ones], kind of like a love song, and, well, they gave me a standing ovation. They asked me to sing another. The first thing that rolled off my tongue is Hank Williams, Jr.'s, "Whiskey Bent and Hell Bound." So I sung that, and the principal, he's standing over here big-eyed. But then, when everybody got in it, he just got in and clapped his hands, you know. I won thirty dollars in that talent show.

Me and a friend of mine I taught to play guitar, we would go downtown on the parking lot and just sit around and play music and sing till four, five, and six o'clock in the morning. Now, we'd draw a crowd down there. People just come by, driving by, and stop. Police stopped, listened. We got brave one night. Somebody come by just joking, thrown some change out. The boy I was there with, he said, "Well." He opened up his guitar case and thrown that change in there. So about everybody come by, they started throwing money. But we just played more for the joy of playing.

I guess at one time, like anybody else, I probably had a dream of going to Nashville. I knowed I wasn't going to go far. I learned early in playing to take criticism. That is something I'm trying to teach that one over there [Katrina]. She don't take it well at all. I told her, "When you play and sing, you got to learn to be criticized." But a man told me one time. I thought I could sing pretty good back then, and I just kindly mentioned me and this boy I taught to play, [how] we was talking about going to Nashville. This man told me, he said, "Son, they's people down there that can sing you under a table [who are] starving to death. You just don't go down there 'cause you can sing and [end up making it]." Well, that broke my heart. But it was true. It takes more than just being able to play and sing.

[When I handled my first serpent, at Shields,] I had wanted to handle one for a long time. I went to church that night and prayed—prayed the whole night. And I fleeced the Lord for Bruce Helton to bring it to me. That was the only way I knowed to fleece the Lord, for Bruce to bring it to me. Well, it got all the way up to the end of the meeting, and I hadn't got to handle one. So I was real discouraged. I thought, "I know this is right. Why can't I do it?" The Lord hadn't seen fit to move, and I was getting real aggravated, and then the service ended. So I was mad. I was thinking, "This ain't right. I ought to have handled one."

Well, somebody had brought Bruce two big Southern copperheads, and after church, he was switching 'em out. He reached and got the first one with a hook and got it out of one box and put it in the other one, and then he laid his hook down. I was standing there all this time meditating, [telling] the Lord I'd like to handle one. That is all I had on my mind. I wanted to handle one. Bruce reached down and got it out of the box and handled it. He just turned around and offered it to me. I handled it. Course, he stood there and watched over me, to make sure that it didn't act up or anything, knowing that it was my first time. This is after church. That's when the Lord seen fit to move. Why, I don't know, unless it was where Bruce could stand and watch me closer. Because somebody first handling one, or doesn't handle them much, [the experienced handlers] like to watch 'em, just to make sure it don't act up. Being the first time, if one was to flinch a certain way, they'd like to get scared and squeeze it or something, you know, and get bit. Bruce watched me real close. And that kept me on a natural high for weeks. The Lord finally moved in what I wanted ever so bad.

I don't remember much from there, because within the next couple of weeks, Trina was born, and then we had all that hard time with her for a couple of months. So at that time, I was going through so much [that] I wasn't going to stick my hand in no snake box. I thought, "Well, I got enough sense to know not to do that." Of course, I got a little more ignorant as the years went along, and I got a few bites.

I guess I didn't start handling regularly until 1993. The first time I went to Georgia, they were taping that show *Beyond Bizarre*, on the Discovery Channel. That's when I started running around with Punkin. If you go run with Punkin, you going to handle serpents. Punkin was the one that helped me big time in serpent handling. He was always pushing me out to handle them, and so was [Carl] Porter [the former minister of a Signs church in Kingston, Georgia].

The first time I went down there to Porter's, I didn't know much about the cameras and the media, and I didn't care much for them even being there. I thought, "Church ain't no place for them." I told Punkin, "I'm not going to handle them serpents. I'm not going to fool with any and get on TV."

We went down, I think it was on Friday or Saturday night, and I was up singing. Porter would always get me to sing first. He loved to hear me sing. I was up singing, and they was handling serpents, and I had my eyes closed and [was] singing. I was saying to myself that I didn't want to handle any serpents. I couldn't get to feel the anointing I wanted to feel because I was worried about the cameras. Had my eyes closed, and I opened my eyes, and there stood Porter in front of me with three big rattlers. He just had 'em like this, offering them to me. As soon as I opened my eyes, son, I closed my eyes again. I said [to myself], "I'm going to ignore you, old man, and you'll go away." So I closed my eyes [like] it's just a bad dream. I opened them back up, and he's still there. I thought, "He's not going to go away." He was just kind of nodding his head, letting me know it was all right. But I didn't feel anything. I thought, "Aaaahhh . . ." But I reached out and took them anyway. When I did, *then* I felt the anointing, and I felt everything was all right.

At your own church, it's like in the Bible where it said that Jesus talks about a prophet being without honor in his own country. It's hard to get into it sometimes in your own church, because you know everybody's problems, you know everything going on, whereas if you go to a church where you don't know nobody, you don't know their troubles. [Then] you don't have those troubles to think about, and you can get [the spirit]. And that's what helped me a lot.

But Punkin always helped me in serpent handling, always encouraged me to handle them. When I got bit the first time, he was still pushing me to handle them, because he didn't want me to get to a place [where] fear overtook me. He pushed me out there, and he said, "You still got to go on. They going to bite. You going to get laid up sometimes, but you still got to go on."

The first time I got bit, it didn't hurt me. It was in the first of October of '93, is all I can remember. I had on a blue printed silk shirt. After it bit me, I handled it a few minutes longer and put it up, and I went outside. It was the first time I'd been bit, so I was pretty scared. I rolled up my shirt sleeve, and there was four holes running blood. I thought, "Oh, son, you've had the lick this time."

My wife came out the door just right behind me. She don't even remember it to this day. She came out the door and said, "God said they'd be no harm." I turned around and went right back in church, right back in the meeting. But the Lord spoke to me and told me there was some people there that didn't believe. They thought we'd pulled [the serpents'] teeth. Some people think they are milked or their fangs are pulled. So God let me know that. There was a man and a woman there that hadn't been coming very much, and they didn't much believe in serpent handling. So I unbuttoned my shirt sleeve, and I said, "There's people here that think these serpents ain't got teeth." I pulled my shirt sleeve up, and blood was coming out four holes. I said, "They got teeth, and they will bite." I just buttoned my shirt back up. From then on, those people were regular members until they both passed away. I preached at both their funerals.

Then I got bit two weeks later, October 22, 1993. I remember that one. I had just ran a week's revival up at [a church in Putney, Kentucky]. I run a week's revival there, and I had the flu the whole week before that. I hadn't been able to eat hardly anything and was real sick. We had a wonderful revival. But it was my first time ever holding a revival, and I was inexperienced. I closed out the meeting before I should have. It was just from inexperience. To this day, I think it was a stupid thing to do. I had fleeced the Lord that night that if somebody came and prayed, I would go on with the revival. Well, I don't know why I done it, but I got up when I started to preach and I told everybody I had fleeced the Lord [that] if somebody prayed, I would go on, but I said I want to go ahead and close out [the service]. Well, there hadn't even been an altar call give. I hadn't even preached yet. I don't know why to this day I done that. But I closed out on Friday night.

I came back to our church on Saturday night. The meeting hadn't been going very long, and there was two sisters there from Virginia. They'd not been around much serpent handling. So I got this rattler out and handled it. He got to squirming a little bit, and the Lord told me to put him up. But now, I wanted these two sisters to see me handling a serpent, since they hadn't seen it much. In my mind, I said, "God, I'll put it up when I get done." Well, right then, I decided I was going to play God. "I'll put it up when I get done."

I was testifying. Serpent's head [was] laying in my hand. Good victory. The Lord said, "Put him up," while I was testifying. I wasn't paying a bit more attention. I was testifying. [That serpent] rolled off my hand and come around [and] hit me right there with one fang. Hit me so hard it knocked my arm against my chest. Dad was setting directly behind me and couldn't see the bite, but he seen it jar me. It hit my arm so hard it jarred my body. I still handled it until I got done. I didn't put it up until I got done testifying. I done knowed I's ruined anyway. Soon as he bit me, my fingers went to rolling. He hit nerves. I thought, "Ole boy, this 'un ain't like the last one. You are going to suffer." I went and put him up. He never acted up no more after he bit me. He calmed right back down. I went and put him in the box after I got done testifying and sit down there on the bench.

I started getting kindly lightheaded. I thought, "Well, I'm going to go outside on the porch, get me some fresh air. I might be all right." I went outside and just stepped out the door, and my knees—both of them—buckled. I grabbed hold the door, and Carl Turner come out. I said, "Brother," I said, "take me in there and get people to pray for me." And I said, "[And then] take me up the road [to Mamaw Turner's house]. I'm going to suffer." He said, "How do you know?" And I said, "The Lord done let me know I'm going to suffer this time."

So he took me in the church, and they prayed for me, and then they took me on up the road right after they prayed for me. Course, the meeting broke, and everybody come up and was praying for me. Soon as I walked through the door [and] went in through the hallway at Mamaw Turner's and all the way down the hallway to the kitchen, I used the phone. Called Brother Brown and told Steve—[Steve] Frazier answered the phone, 'cause he was staying there; Punkin didn't have a phone then—I said, "Go tell Punkin that I'm bit." He said, "What bit you?." And I said, "A black timber rattler."

He went straight down [to Punkin's house], and Punkin came straight back up and called me back. I was scared. I was feeling things I never felt before. I thought, "Oh, I just don't know if I can stand this or not." I felt like if I could talk to Punkin and found out what these [symptoms] was, then I might feel a little better. So the first thing he asked me [was], "Are you hurting bad?" I said no. He said, "Are you numb and tingling?" I said, "Yeah, I feel like there's bugs under my skin." I could feel my skin moving in places, them nerves jerking and jingling. I could feel it. The whole time I was bit, right here in my arm, I could watch them nerves jerk and jump in my arm. He said, "I'll be right there."

[At that time,] before they fixed the road, it was about an hour and twenty minutes from Newport, Tennessee, to here. Seem to me like he made it in less than an hour. He had just come in from deer hunting. So he come through the door and come into the living room. You go straight across the living room and turn up the hall to the left, and I was the first door on the left, in the bedroom. Everybody was praying, and I'd done thrown up twice, all this black-looking stuff. It was getting pretty rough. And they had just laid me back down, and I heard him come up the hall speaking in tongues. He come through the door and touched me on top of my head and rubbed all the way down that leg, and I felt something go through me. I knowed then I was all right. I knowed I was gonna have to suffer, but I knowed I wasn't going to die. I had no more fear once I felt that. He stayed with me.

About three o'clock that morning, I decided I wanted to go [to my own house]. Punkin said, "Son, you don't need to move. You just stay here until you get to feel a little better." Well, I was stubborn. I thought I was feeling good enough. I wanted to go home. "I can't rest up here," I said. "I can rest better at my house." He threw me a couple of pillows, and I propped that arm up, and Linda drove me home, plumb on the other side of town.

After I got home, I told her, "I feel like I need to use the bathroom." Well, every time I'd sit down on the commode to use the bathroom, I'd feel like I was going to throw up. They got me a garbage can right in front of me. Well, she set me down on the commode and turned around to get the garbage can. That's all I remember. My head hit her back. And she just flung me back against the commode, scared to death. She said all she seen was the whites of my eyes. My eyes'd done set. She just thrown me back and screamed and went out. And the only thing I remember when I come to is that Punkin was right in my face, smacking me in the face, screaming at me. I came to. During that time, he was telling everybody, "Well, he's all right," but he told me after that, he said, "Jamie, you had a bad bite. I ain't never had a bite that bad."

When they set me down on the commode, my whole body drawn up and my eyes set in my head and I went, "Uuuuuuuuhhhhhh." That was it. And that is the exact same way that one of the brothers died. They set him on the commode, and he didn't come out of it. He stiffened up and died. Punkin told me, "Son, you done the same thing he done, but God took mercy on you." So I realized then just what a bad bite it was.

I went from October '93 till November of '97, the Sunday before Thanksgiving, when that copperhead bit me. I went four good years without a bite. That was four good years. But when that copperhead bit me, I had three copperheads and a rattler, handling them [all at once]. When I handle copperheads, I like to handle 'em at least three or more. I have handled thirteen. That's the way I like to handle them, just a big bundle of them. Sit 'em up on top of my head, that's the way I like to handle them when the Lord moves.

But I put that rattler in the box and shut the lid down quick, 'cause he went right into the back of the box and was coming back out, so I had to shut the lid quick. Well, when I did, the copperhead on top of the pile of the three fell down, right in the box, and I slammed that lid on him. Well, I didn't think very much about it. I just opened the lid and picked him back up and shut the lid back down, thrown him up there and went to shouting with him, feeling real good. Well, I just felt something just reach over and just dog-bite the snot out of me. I thought, "Here we go again." He bit me.

It was on a Sunday, and I testified a few minutes, and I got to hurting bad.

I told one of the brothers, I said, "Take me to the house." He put me in the car, and we pulled out of the church parking lot and down to just where you cross the railroad crossing, and I went to throwing up. I said, "Lord, I can't stand this throwing up. Please don't let me get so sick." As far as I remember, that's the only time I threw up, but I threw up four times and strained real hard. Well, we come across the tracks [and] around the road [to] a curve to the left going down the hill. They was a car in front of us, and I've always been pretty good on being able to look at a car from a distance and tell what kind it was. All I could see was a white blur. I couldn't see what kind of car it was, how big it was. And I thought, "This is bad. This is worse than what that rattler done to me." So I started praying. I said, "Lord, don't let it be this."

Linda didn't go to church that day. When we pulled into the driveway, she knowed what it was. I went in the house. She asked what bit me, and I said, "Copperhead." I came in, and I didn't get sick anymore. I didn't have that dizziness, but it was just a dead, aching pain. I mean hurting.

I called Punkin. I said, "I'm copperhead-bit." He said, "I'll be on up there." He come up, and he set right there in that chair all night. [He'd] doze off and go to sleep. And pain hit me, and I'd scream. He'd just raise up and look at me and grin, say, "Son, you going to have to tough it out," and lay that head right back and go to sleep. And I'd think to myself, "Don't you be telling me what I got to do, and you lay down there and go to sleep." I was a-hurtin' bad.

Well, the next night, there was all these people from the church in here, singing and praying. Punkin was sitting right here on this table and singing a song, the song I sing a lot, "God Has Been Good to Me." He was singing it, and Punkin was the type, if he didn't know the words to a song, it wasn't hard for him to add words. He'd just put his own in there. So he's adding words to it. That aggravates me. I want to learn a song just like it is, and that's how I want to sing it. I'm kicked back here on this couch, swelled up, turned blue, my arm a-hurting. He's just setting there getting on my nerves, adding all these words. It just bothered me. I said, "Well, that ain't the way it goes."

I seen a break. He quit singing, and Brother Cameron was over here playing the lead. Then I started singing. Well, when I started singing, I started feeling pretty good then. I looked around, and Punkin was gone. I thought, "Where is he went to?" He went out in the snake building, boxed up a black rattler, and brought it in here. Now, this room was full of people here, praying and singing.

Well, I started singing "Little David," and he just flipped that lid back and come shouting across the floor handling that big black rattler, and this room full of people. Which it was all church people, you know. That's just the way he was, and that's the way I am. I don't believe you have to be in church to handle them.

He got to handling that big rattler, and then one of the brothers that was there, *he* got to handling it. I was sitting here, and all I could do was cry. I wanted to handle it. He knew that. But that's what he was there for. He was there to push me on. So I was sitting here crying, wanting to handle it, and he was standing right over there, and I was singing, and Punkin just looked over at me. I think maybe I nodded my head or something. He just walked over and laid it in my hand.

I laid that big black rattler up there on that big swelled-up hand, where the copperhead bit me. I just laid it up there, and I said, "Now, bite me." I was feeling good then. I was *feeling good*. I didn't care.

Anytime you get bit, you are going to have a certain amount of fear. And if you got somebody like Punkin that will push through, [it helps you get over your fear]. Because he had been bit about seventeen times. A lot of the bites was at a young age. He just got bit simply because he wanted to handle them [when he wasn't anointed].

I got over that one. It left a mark there. It done a little bit, but not very much. That arm swelled up all the way across into my chest.

Punkin lost Melinda, buried her, lost his kids for six months. I never seen anybody go through what Punkin went through. As far as a human being fighting battles, I never seen nobody go through that. Then that kindly makes me worry about myself. What am I going to have to face?

It was Punkin's call to be an evangelist. My call is a pastor, pastor of this one church. I'll always travel. I told Dad that, when he asked me to take pastorship. See, he was over the church. It was just sort of dumped in his lap [after his father died]. He told me, "Jamie, I don't feel like it's meant for me to pastor." So we prayed about it, fleeced the Lord, and the Lord moved in the fleecing, and they prayed and asked me to take pastorship. And I told Dad, I said, "Daddy, I'll take it, but there'll still be times when I'm going to travel [that] you are going to have it."

A pastor is that one to take responsibility. Like when something happens, that's who it all falls on. I know it's just the regular feeding [of] the flock, taking care of the people, but to me, the main thing is [that] when heat comes, you are the main target.

When Melinda died at our house, 'cause she'd been bit at our church, I had a sergeant of [the] Middlesboro Police force come to my house. And I didn't know, but he was fixing to get a promotion to lieutenant or whatever, and he took me outside, put me in the police car, read me my rights, and was more or less trying to scare me. Read me my rights and said, "This is all on you. You are the pastor." He was trying to shake me, but I just kindly grinned at him [and] went on my way.

See, they are harder on it now than they was ten, fifteen year ago. Everybody now that gets bit and dies, the [law] puts more pressure, more pressure. That's one of the things a pastor has to deal with. To handle serpents in church in this state is a misdemeanor. I think the only state that it's not against the law is in West Virginia. But they passed a law here in 1947.

I had Punkin tell me, "Jamie, I've talked to some people [who think] that if you had not been pastor when Melinda died, there probably wouldn't [have been] serpents there." Because I stood very hard with it, regardless. I didn't care what nobody said. They was some people [who], when Melinda died, went [and] turned their serpents loose, and I just refused to do that. I was going to stand with it, regardless.

GETTING
GOD'S ATTENTION

LINDA SMITH COOTS
B. 1962

"I was the best sinner that ever was. I will be the best Christian that ever was."

LINDA COOTS IS ON SUCH INTIMATE TERMS with God that she sometimes argues with Him. The dialogue is more in the form of a query than a confrontation—a point to debate. Linda says she has been given the gift of prophecy and that sometimes God entrusts her with a message she's not eager to deliver.

Her straightforward attitude is typical of a young woman who learned her coping skills out in the world—and, she claims, learned them as a sinner. Linda weighs and measures everything before making decisions—the important ones, anyway. But when it comes to people, she wades right into new friendships, no strings attached. If you need it, she will share her last dollar with you, her last bite of food.

Knock on her door and she welcomes you with a smile that's twice her height. She's only four feet, eleven and a half inches tall—Punkin Brown teasingly called her "Munchkin"—but what she lacks in height, she makes up for in personality. The dark-eyed woman with curly brown hair is the dynamic mother of Katrina and Dakota ("Cody") and the wife of Preacher Jamie Coots.

Although Linda became a Signs believer only after she met Jamie, she is now one of the church's staunchest members. Getting there has meant making dramatic changes in her life over the past eight years. "Now, I don't know any-body as low as I was," Linda says matter-of-factly. "I mean, I was just the hottest little rip in the world. And look what God has brought me out of. I played my part well, and I thought to myself, 'I was the best sinner that ever was. I will be the best Christian that ever was.' If I could serve the Lord half as good as I served the devil, I'd be doing good." And that's what Linda has been doing ever since she married Jamie—and, figuratively, the church—back in 1990.

The Cootses' small frame house, the first Linda and Jamie have owned in their marriage, is one of their many blessings from God, say Linda. When money was scarce, the family lived in public housing. They left there after pressure from neighbors when Melinda Brown died in their apartment following a snake-bite at Jamie's Full Gospel Tabernacle in Jesus Name in 1995. Prayer and pa-tience, claims Linda, got them their present place on a side street in Middlesboro. The house, surrounded by a chain-link fence, is pale yellow with black shutters and has a swing on the front porch. A padlocked, heated shed in the backyard is home for the snakes Jamie keeps for use in church services.

Inside, the house is immaculately clean. On this day, it is fragrant with the aroma of the dinner to be eaten before the Saturday-night church service—chicken, cornbread, and beans. Family photographs hang on the walls next to pictures of Jamie and his father, Greg, snapped while they were handling ser-pents. It's a comfortable, homey place—flowered cushions on the sofa, hanging plants, soft easy chairs.

Punkin Brown used to sit in one of those chairs in the den far into the night, trading religious philosophy with Jamie, talking about the Word, com-forting Jamie when he was snakebitten or concerned about events in the church. Anytime Punkin visited, that room became his headquarters. "Punkin had the den, and we had the rest of the house," says Linda. Now, his absence is sorely felt. Linda tells how one night after Punkin's death, Jamie was restlessly twisting the dial on the television set when he hit on something that made him laugh. "I ought to call Punkin and tell him to turn the TV on," he told Linda. And then he remembered that Punkin was dead. Jamie's memory lapse illustrates how of-ten Punkin visited on his evangelical trips and how much a part of the family he became. In fact, Linda has already decided that she wants her daughter, Trina, born in 1991, to marry Punkin's son Jeremiah, who is two years older.

"Now, the Bible does tell you to marry your own faith rather than an out-sider," Linda admits, even though she herself was an outsider when she met

*Linda Coots in church with her children, Cody (left),
and Katrina (right), c. 1994*
Photo by Scott Schwartz

Jamie. Of their relationship, she says, "The Lord's just worked it out, but if you marry an outsider who don't believe this way, they're eventually going to pull you out of the church or you're going to pull them in. Most of the time, they pull you out. The Lord just blessed us right off, and I think that if anybody was worried about our marriage, it's because I wasn't in this faith. But the Lord, He molded me how He wanted me. He knew I would accept this. And as for Jamie being a good husband, take your list of what you want in a man and add ten more good things to it, and that's Jamie."

Linda's account of the first time she saw Jamie is a typical love-at-first-sight story. She laughs about how she has changed since that hot September day in 1990 when she and her sister Joan went for a walk and stopped at a little store to get something cold to drink. Joan recognized a man she knew, and the two sisters sat in a booth with him. That was just about the time that Jamie came in and sat at the counter. Jamie was then in the home-improvement business, but he wanted to get into mining, because that's where his father had always worked. He later told Linda that he came into the store that day because he had seen a man inside who might help him get a job. When Linda turned around and noticed him, she was hooked. "Prettiest thing I ever saw in this whole wide world," she says. "He had his beard, had his mustache, and his hair was kindly long. He looked over at me, and I said to Joan, 'Turn around and look. See if you can find a wedding band.' "

Linda did not look bad herself that day. Her short hair was bleached blond, she had a dark suntan, and she was wearing short shorts. "We always had to walk to stay pretty," says Linda with one of her broad grins. "When you was my age [twenty-eight], you wanted to look good if you wanted to find you a man to marry. And I always heard blondes had more fun, and they was the ones usually got the man, so I went all out to do this. See, I was married before, for twelve years. I got married at fifteen, when I first went into freshman year. I did finish high school. I married [someone] already out of school. Jamie and I get a lot of static over that, but once you repent and you're baptized, the Lord forgives you everything. There's no sin He keeps on. The only sin you're not forgiven is blasphemy. And, see, I didn't know this holy way. I wasn't raised that way."

Joan looked over at Jamie that day and reported that she didn't see a wedding band. "And when I turned around and looked, he winked at me," Linda recalls. "I said, 'Oh, he winked at me, Joan. Why don't he come over here?' And I turned around again, and he waved. Here he is, doing all this flirty stuff, and he wouldn't come over and talk to me. Anyways, we had to leave, and I said to Joan, 'Maybe he'll talk to me as I go out the door,' because I had to pass right by him. I wrote my name and number down on a napkin and gave it to Joan's friend, Eugene. I said, 'If he don't talk to me when we go out of here, you give that to him. I mean, you *give* that to him.' I started out the door, and he just grinned real big at me, and it broke my heart. I said, 'Why didn't he talk to me? He's married, that's what it is. He's flirting, but he's married.' "

That night, Joan called Linda to tell her about Eugene's discovery. The good news was that Jamie was not married. The bad news was that he was eighteen years old.

Eighteen or not, Jamie was hooked, too. When Eugene handed him that napkin with Linda's name and number on it, Jamie said, "No, I can't date her. She's just fifteen years old. I went to school with her." He had mistaken Linda for another girl.

Linda was distraught about the age difference. When Joan told her, she thought, "Oh, my God. He's eighteen years old, and I'm twenty-eight, going on twenty-nine."

It turned out that it didn't matter to Jamie. He called Linda the next night—

a Wednesday—and set up a date for Thursday. "And we went out Thursday night, and we went out every night then until December, and we got married," says Linda.

"When I first saw him, I didn't even know he went to church, much less a serpent-handling church. But we fleeced the Lord on our marriage. At the time, I had been praying, and I was lonely. I had my own trailer, and I lived miles and miles from Middlesboro, past the state park, and I worked at Cowden's, a Levi factory. I'd been working there nine years. I had several different jobs. I did attach facing, I did watch pockets, I done the leather labels, and I did set flies, the zippers. When Jamie and I met, I had been asking the Lord to give me knowledge of the Bible. I had never read the Bible. Didn't even have one except for a little-bitty one at home that I think Mom had given me. I would talk to God in my way, and I still talk to Him in the same way as I did then.

"There was this little girl sit beside me at work. We done set flies together. She had the long hair and the long dresses. She didn't wear makeup or pants, and she was pretty knowledgeable about the Bible. Sadly but true, she's backslid, but during that time, she was so faithful. It didn't really turn me off, but I thought, 'What's wrong with these people? Why don't they try to fix theirself up—do something, fix their hair?'

"Well, during work, we'd sit and talk about the Bible as we sewed. And she would learn me a lot of things about the Bible. This was before I met Jamie. And then maybe two weeks into me meeting Jamie, this girl and me had talked at work about the twelve disciples, but she couldn't name them right off. So when me and Jamie went on a date that night, I asked him about them, and sure enough, he knew it right off, honey. Until then, we hadn't talked about no Bible or church or anything spiritual, so I said, 'How do you know so much?' 'Well,' he said, 'my daddy's pastor of a church.' 'Really?' I said. 'So why haven't you asked me to go to church with you?' 'Well,' he said, 'I was raised in church, but I don't go steady, and I don't serve the Lord like we're taught to do.' "

Linda shrugs. At the time, she didn't know about all the strictures of the serpent-handling religion. In fact, she didn't even know that Jamie was a serpent handler. "Because, you know, in my religion—first Baptist and then Methodist—you go to church on Sunday, you wear what you want to during the week, you still love God, and you say, 'Lord, forgive me of everything.' You don't have to get down and cry about it. And you figure, 'Well, I'm all right.' But what he done, he took me to his mom and dad's house one night. I bonded immediately with them, and his mother told Jamie, 'I think you done good this time. This one sits and talks to me.'

"Anyway, after we come in from work that afternoon, he told me he had a video he wanted me to see. 'Now, we don't handle snakes at the church right now,' he said, 'but we do believe in handling serpents.' I said, 'You *do?*' But it never did shock me. So we sit down, and we put the video on, me and him and his mom, and I'm watching these people, and I'm amazed that you can handle a snake, that—*wow*—you can pick it up and *handle* it. I wouldn't. That's what I said. I'd be too scared to do it. And I'd be watching them handle that fire, and I was amazed. I never was scared, never did criticize it, but I just thought, 'I don't believe I'd do it.' But I didn't have the Holy Ghost then, either.

"So after that, we started going to church. First night at church, here I come into this church house. I have my beautiful little blond hair all kicked up and curled up, sprayed up, my beautiful makeup set perfect, my double rows of earrings, a ring on every finger, two or three necklaces, my little short dress, [skin] black from the tanning bed, smelling out of this world, my little high heels—had to have them high heels to make that short dress look good. Walked into that church, and these women turned around and looked at me—long hair, no makeup, dresses down to here—and I went, 'What have I got into? These people gonna think I'm a Jezebel.' I mean, here was Jamie with his mustache and his gold necklace and his rings and his tight jeans and shorts, and I never suspected he was a Holy Roller. Later, I had no trouble getting rid of my pants, but my makeup? I hated to get rid of my makeup. When you look in the mirror, you feel plain-looking, but then it grows on you. You think, 'Well, I look all right, but it would be fun to look a little bit better.'"

The worldly things she gave up no longer tempt Linda. There's a joyful spirit in her house—love, generosity, an underlying trust. In the living room sits a piano, a gift from Jamie's parents, who promised Trina they'd buy her a good one when she learned to play. Before that, says Linda, "Sister Gail Stewart gave us a old, banged-up black piano, real ugly, and some of the keys didn't work."

The first time Trina sat down to play, she discovered a gift no one knew she had. Seven years old, she had never had a lesson and couldn't read notes, but she was suddenly playing by ear. "Sister Gail brought the piano in May, and by August, Trina was running chords," says Linda. "We were sitting watching TV one night, and Jamie muted [the sound]. He said, 'Listen. Trina's running chords.'

Katrina Coots, age seven, playing the organ and singing in church, 1999
Photo by Fred Brown

So he grabs his guitar, and he runs in here real quick. 'Trina,' he says, 'do that again.' And she would do it. He sit down and said, 'Turn your back to me,' and she turned her back. He would strum a chord, and she'd tell him what chord it was and play it on the piano. Now, she don't know nothing about a guitar. So they got to where they would sit and he would tell her when to change chords, and she just played by ear. She's really blessed."

Now, Trina plays the electric organ in services, shouting an occasional "Praise God!" and belting out hymns at the microphone with a volume that Brenda Lee might envy.

While Linda talks, the children run in and out of the room, asking questions, wanting Linda's help with one thing or another. Linda stops her conversation and gives her children the same polite attention that she affords guests. Trina, who has fixed herself a snack of pickles and bananas, sits down on the sofa to listen to the grownups. Cody cleans his room.

"Our children have a very good, active life as children," says Linda. "We're more protective of our children than the world is. We get out and play baseball with them. Their life consists of Mommy and Daddy being there all the time. We don't drop them off anywhere, because you don't never know what other people are doing or showing them. They're young yet, but when they get older,

I'll still have a say over what they're allowed to see and not see, what they're allowed to listen to and not listen to. I feel like it's a responsibility to God for us to insist on that right in this home. God wants us to walk in a way that the children can watch how we walk and desire to live like that. We're always laughing and cutting up. We don't tell lies or talk dirty, but we do laugh a lot.

"When we go out in the Jeep, we'll buckle them in the back. Me and Jamie get in the front and at the same time scout for places to snake hunt. Now, he won't do no snake hunting with us in there. Sometimes, I'll go with him, I'll ride the roads. He scares me because he goes up some of the awfulest hills. I'm not as scared of the snakes as I am of him flipping the Jeep.

"As far as the kids are concerned, I'm bringing them up in this religion, and I would love for them to stay in this faith. I'm bringing them up in a way that once they decide to settle down and raise their own family, they'll not be unmoved. I'm home-schooling them this year, too. That way, I don't have to worry about them learning worldly things.

"A few months ago, I fleeced the Lord and said, 'Lord, if you want me to teach these children at home, send me a desk.' Because I was going to go to college. I'd registered and everything. So my sister Rita owns a house here in Middlesboro, and I was helping her clean it up after these people had moved, and they had left a desk. Well, I didn't think nothing about it, but I brought it home. And I was talking about going to college, and Jamie said, 'Linda, did you forget? The Lord answered your prayer.' And I said, 'What do you mean?' And he said, 'Well, He sent you a desk.' See, it's a little desk, and when I fleeced the Lord, I'd been thinking *big* desk, so, see, when you ask the Lord for something, you need to be *specific*. Anyway, the other obstacle to our home-schooling was that we'd been calling the Bell County home-schooling supervisor all summer, and we never could reach her. So I fleeced the Lord again, and I said, 'Lord, if it's all right for me to teach these children at home, let me get that woman today.' And Lord, if I didn't get her right off that day. Next problem was, how am I going to pay for the books? And the Lord made the way for money for the books. It's wonderful how things has opened up to us.

"If you bring up your children right, they'll know the right way, and they'll be steadfast. We've had people tell us [since] we was in church [that] we [shouldn't] drink coffee and we [shouldn't] watch TV. Well, I feel like, live the best you can live, and try not to make yourself miserable. I'm not here to please men. I want to serve the Lord and please Him. I love living like this. I *love* it.

It's peaceful, you're not tormented, you're not fighting and scratching with some-body all the time. There's love everywhere you go. They's more things in this life than just money and the material world—things that come from the heart."

IN HER OWN WORDS
LINDA SMITH COOTS

As far as my family, we had no religion. I was never in a church house with Mom until I was probably twenty-eight years old. I took her down to a Baptist church below where she lived. I was born in 1962 in Wooten, Kentucky. It's a coal-mining camp way up above Hazard. My dad's name was Eugene Smith, and my mother is Athalene. I have three sisters and three brothers. I was the baby of the girls.

My dad was a deep-mine coal miner. He was a good dad. He was always home with us when he wasn't working. He died in 1986 of a heart attack. [Even with seven children,] we always had nice furniture, always had a good car, al-ways had food to eat. Now, Mom worked us. Before we went to school, every-body had their own job to do in the morning. By the time we left that house, her house was clean, and she had nothing to do but cook supper and wash clothes. I'm thirty-seven, thirty-eight in July. Michael will be thirty-six in June. Wade's thirty-nine. Rita is the oldest—forty-five in August. That's how close all the children were.

[Dad] and Mom weren't religious people. They weren't *bad* people, but they never had time for church, really never did discuss church doctrine in any way. My mom won't discuss it now. My oldest sister and my brothers are Apostolic, which is basically the same thing we are, except they don't do the Signs, and they believe in Rapture. Now, you can't find the word *rapture* in the Bible, but what they mean is, God's gonna come back and take all of them home and leave the rest of us here. They don't believe they're gonna go through tribula-tions. And they believe that only the ones that's in the name of Jesus Christ is gonna make it.

Me and my sister Rita's very comfortable together. She teases me about my serpent handling sometime, and I tease her about her Rapture. But my brother, you can't speak to him about serpent handling at all, and you can't say anything about Rapture. He's just set in his ways. I have found that the people who's willing to bend a little, with an open mind, are ones you can work with. Rita does not cut my religion, and I do not cut hers. Rita lives really good. I admire the way she lives. And she's very smart. She's my oldest sister. She's the prettiest, but she's the oldest. She's an inspiration to me, and we do a lot of Bible study together, talking together, some praying. We don't really disagree on things. She knows that serpent handling's in the Bible, and I understand what she's saying, too, about the Rapture.

Mom was a housewife. She was a good mother. She kept a spotless house. She fed us good. We had a good family life. Until we moved to Middlesboro, she never did wear a pair of pants. Mom told me when she was a girl and she went to church, she remembers them opening the door of the coal stove and sticking their hands in and getting hot coals out. When my brother Michael Ray was born, Mom's hair was plumb down to here. That was her seventh child. And then when she moved to Middlesboro, she got her hair whacked off and started wearing pants and shorts and stuff.

My mother won't talk a whole lot about this, and now she shuns me to the world. She's ashamed of me [and] she's ashamed of Jamie, because we handle serpents, because we've been on TV [handling serpents], and because when Melinda died, it was in our house. She thinks it's the awfulest thing in the world that I got myself into this. The first time she seen me in my long dress and my long hair after I had joined church, she said, 'Why don't you go get you some clothes on and get them granny-ripping dresses off and do something with that long, stringy hair?' That was her first comment to me. Very disappointing. I talk to Mom, send her a Mother's Day card and birthday card. On Christmas, I took her some presents up there, and she didn't want me to stay. She wanted me to hurry and leave because she was afraid some people around there would recognize me or Jamie as the people on TV handling snakes. She don't want anybody to know that we're related.

She lives maybe five miles away. She's been [to this house] a couple times. We were very close until me and Jamie got married, and she liked Jamie till she found out that I started going up there at that church and I stopped wearing makeup and those short skirts and quit bleaching my hair, 'cause she was the one that done the roots, you know. According to Mom, if Dad knew about it, he'd roll over in his grave if he could see [me] now.

The Bible says, "If your brother sins against you seven times seven, how many times do you forgive him?" You forgive him forty-nine times. And if he sins against you seven times seventy, you forgive him four hundred and ninety times that day. If my husband goes out and sins against me, how can I claim to love God if I won't forgive him? And how can *he* claim to love God if he don't forgive *me* of it? We are people like everybody else. We make mistakes like everybody else. The devil is out after the ones trying to do the best they can do. It's not happened in this house, but I have seen houses it's happened in. The man or the woman, they can love one another and still mess up. But just because you mess up doesn't mean you have to pay for it all your life. We can forgive and forget and go on. I can't tell you how I would feel if it happened. I'm assuming it would be very, very bad. This is a thing that we've not faced, but things like this can happen to us, 'cause we're not better than anybody else. The only difference is that we've got God with us. And being close to God, I believe that a lot of times, we're harder on ourselves than what [other] people would be on us. And we beat ourselves down so bad.

But God's a forgiving God. If He wasn't so full of mercy, Lord, where would I be at right now? I'm not perfect, and I may say some things that hurt somebody, and I might not be aware of it, and sometimes I *might* be aware of it. But that's the difference. God lets me know if it's right or wrong, and if it's wrong, I'm going to pay for it. He's gonna chasten me some way or another. See, that's the difference in His people and sinners. We can get forgiveness, which a sinner can, too, if they repent—come to the altar and start serving the Lord.

When I was growing up and somebody in church did something bad, I remember Mom and Dad saying, "Lord, who'd have thought they would have done something like that?" You'd of thought [the sinners] was angels that fell, but they're just human beings, just like we are. You're no better, except you claim the blood of Jesus Christ. That's why the Bible tells you to be spotless, unspotted from the world. And there is some people out there in this lost and dying world that's watching, [thinking,] "I'm gonna see if they're trying to live as good as they say, or if they're just a hypocrite, playing along."

That first night I come into the church [with Jamie], it was amazing. The [people] didn't look at me. They didn't care about my makeup or nothing. They said, "Glad to see you here," and Jamie would introduce me to them— Mamaw Coots, Mamaw Turner, Sister Sharon, Uncle Carl, Sister Trina. But they never did look upon what I had on, never did say nothing about it, and I felt comfortable coming to church that way. Eventually, I would lose one of the earrings, and I would lose one of the necklaces, and the dresses would get just a little bit longer, and the makeup would be toned down, but Mom would still bleach my roots for me.

I went on that way for a couple months, and then I'll tell you what scared me so bad. I'd been there maybe three times. See, I was always used to quiet churches where everything appears to be in order. Honey, the music went to *going* that night. Jamie played guitar. He'd sit with me down on the chairs, and then he'd go up there and play guitar. I would be by myself during the music. Son, they's one night I's sitting there by myself, and Jamie's two little cousins were sitting aside me, and Jamie's up there singing. If the music's going on, there are no distractions. You can get your mind on God, and you can focus. And honest to God, here come a three-hundred-pound woman shouting up that middle aisle. *Bounce.* My seat would *bounce, bounce.* See, I didn't weigh but a hundred and twelve then. *Bounce, bounce.* I turned around to see what was going on. I see this woman *bouncing.* I'd never been so scared in my life. I didn't know what was going on. I'd never seen the Holy Ghost move at all in any way in my life. She was anointed, shouting up the aisle, speaking in tongues. And it scared me. I'd been going there maybe about a month. I'd heard her speak in tongues when she was singing or testifying, but I'd never seen her shout for the Lord. And it scared me.

They weren't handling serpents at the church at that time, and if I'd seen a snake, I'd probably laid down and died. The whole time I was going to church, I don't think they had any serpents in the church maybe up until maybe five or six months after me and Jamie were married. Nobody kept snakes. Mamaw Turner wouldn't keep them because of all the grandkids. Mamaw Coots won't keep 'em because of all the grandkids. We lived in an apartment, in public housing, and you're not allowed to have serpents, so there was nobody to keep serpents. So once me and Jamie were married, during that summer, him and a few of the brothers would go out serpent hunting, and they would bring 'em back, and they had 'em in a great big old box like a den box at the church. Nobody wanted them in the house 'cause of little children running around. And it would paranoid me. It's a scary idea. Lock and key.

It was right around June. We got married in January, and in June, I was six months pregnant with Trina. I was very toxic. My feet were swelling. My blood pressure was very high. They were suggesting bed rest. We'd go up Bruce's [Bruce

Helton's church in Evarts, Kentucky] a lot. And see, there wasn't a lot of action around our church. If you go up Bruce's, sometimes you seen action. You seen all these women speaking in tongues, falling out with the spirit, men handling serpents. Our church, you'd go, you'd sing, sometimes you'd see somebody shout. And looking back, I believe it's because we didn't have any Signs in the church. We believed in it, but we didn't have any [serpents] to put in there. And to explain Bruce's church, it was like it was on fire. You could go in [and] you could feel it.

And believe it or not, I got the desire. I wanted to handle a snake. I was pregnant with Trina, and I thought, "I'd love to handle one. I don't understand it, and I don't know how to do it, but I have a desire to do it." I felt something churning, and I wanted to do it. I said, "Now, Lord." And I'd heard them talk about when you wanted to do something for God and you weren't sure, you could fleece Him. And when you're young and you don't know His voice just yet, you fleece Him. And I said, "Now, Lord, if it's You, and it's all right for me to handle a serpent, You let Brother Sherman look back here at me." He went one further than that. Brother Sherman looked right at me and *handed* it to me. And he prophesied. He said, "The Lord says, 'Tonight, I lock their jaws. There'll be no harm.'" All kinds of people were going up there that night and taking serpents up, and when he looked at me and held it up to me, he said, "This is for you." I dropped down on my knees. I didn't have the courage to go do it. And I said, "Lord, if I go handle that serpent and me pregnant, it'd kill my baby if I was to get bit. I just can't do it. I'm afraid to do it. I ain't gonna do it." So I didn't do it. And needless to say, I desired it, but I was scared to do it.

And when Trina was four months old, I was pregnant with Cody. But with Trina, I was very toxic. They wanted to send me to the hospital in Lexington. When I was married, I weighed 112, and when they weighed me in Lexington, I was 202. My face was so swollen. My hands were swollen. I didn't even look like me. I couldn't even bend my fingers. They had heart monitors and everything in this world [on me]. There were so many things [connected to me] that they taught Jamie how to push them buttons, because he was sitting by my bedside. The doctor told Jamie, said, "Your wife has a fifty-fifty chance. We've got to get the baby out because it's working against her body, and the baby will not live."

They sent me down there on a Sunday night, and then the following Friday, they went ahead and took Trina. And when Trina was born, she was so tiny, she wasn't supposed to live. She weighed two pounds, eight and a half ounces when she was born. See how the Lord worked that miracle? She was in Lexington for a month, and then she was in Corbin for a month, and then she came home. To look at her now, you'd never know. And they kept telling us about birth defects she might have and different things that might be wrong with her, and for a long time, I was so scared.

And they put her on a breathing monitor. But she was so active. At three months, she was all over, turning over, and her legs flipping. So we brought her home on the monitor, and every night when that monitor would go off, it would scare me, and I'd run in there and shake her [to see if she was breathing], and she'd start crying. And then I would be shaking so hard [that] I didn't have no energy. And one night, Jamie said, "Linda, you're going to have to get rid of that thing. That's just the devil tormenting you. You're gonna have to put your faith in God that He is going to take care of this child. That thing right there [the monitor] is not gonna save her if God wants to take her out of here. You're going to have a nervous breakdown, or you're going to give my baby the shaken-baby syndrome. Something's going to have to stop." Jamie told me I was the one had to make the decision. So we took it off that night, and that was it. She slept with me most of the time after that because I breast-fed her, and she never did have no breathing problems. All of us had to learn CPR before we brought her home from the hospital, but we never did have no problems with her.

Cody was born in August, and it was sometime during that next winter [that] I still had the desire to handle serpents. I was into it like I never had been into it. Trina would be in the playpen asleep, and I'd be sitting at the kitchen table reading the Bible. It was nothing for me to read four and five hours a day. I'd get down and pray five or six times during what time I was reading. And God fed me. He talked me through it.

I still had that burning desire to take up serpents. But I had been taught in the church that not [just] anybody can take them up. It's not something that you can just walk in off the street and do. You've got to live holy. You've got to be clean. You better not have no sin on you at all when you do it. And you'd better obey God's voice when He says, "Take it up." And when he says, "Put it back," you put it back. Because you can move too fast, or you can move too slow, or you can have sin and get hurt. The only way I've ever took a serpent up, I'll check myself. I'll say, "Now, Lord, you're moving on me." Once you feel that anointing, what is it wanting you to do? Is it wanting you to shout? Is it wanting you to go over there and pray for a brother or sister? Is it wanting you to speak in tongues or prophesy? Or is it for you to go take a serpent up? There's different gifts for different things. And so when I feel the anointing, now I know, but then I didn't.

But I could just feel that burning inside me to take up a serpent. And I said, "Now, Lord, if this is You, let Jamie turn around and look at me." Now, Jamie's got the same Holy Ghost moving on him that I've got moving on me. So he turned around, and he looked right at me. And then he mocked [motioned] it to me. And I was still scared. I was right there in front. And I stepped out. And when I took hold of it, I'll never forget the first time I handled one. It was like silk. I expected it to be rough and real nasty feeling. It was like cold silk. All that could go through my mind was how smooth and silky it was. It was a rattle-snake, a big one. Anyways, I handled the serpent, and I just handed it back to Jamie.

I've been blessed several times to handle them since then. I've only handled a copperhead maybe one time. See, a copperhead is more apt to bite, and [the bitten place will] rot, but nine times out of ten, you don't have to fear death. Now, a rattlesnake, you fear death every time [you're bitten], until you pass through [the danger]. Brother Punkin always used to say that the first forty-eight hours were the toughest. After [that], the possibility of living is better. And when Melinda died in 1995, it went on for forty-eight hours. She was talk-ing. She never did really go plumb out. Steve and Diane Frazier was in there, and we was all gathered around the bed talking, and Diane said, "I don't know what's wrong with it," talking about her car. Honey, Melinda just raised up from the bed and tells her, "Diane, all you have to do is open that hood, find this little switch, and do something to the battery, and that'll take care of it right there." Mechanic from the bed. And she died the next day.

She would join in on the conversation. Punkin, when he went up there and asked her to go to the hospital, he cried. What he told Jamie was, he said, "Jamie, I can do it for myself, but I can't stand to see her laying there suffering like that. I don't know what to do. If I make her go, and she gets over it, she'll never forgive me for making her go and not letting her trust in the Lord. But you don't know how bad I want to go grab her and just make her go." He was wor-ried from the beginning, it had hurt her so bad. He said, "I know that the times she's seen me laying, suffering, I just never did think she would ever worry as bad as I worry about her right now, but now that I've set here and watched her suffer through it, I see all that I've put her through the times that I've been bit."

Melinda had been handling serpents since she was fourteen or fifteen, and once her mom and dad backslid, they gave her a hard time about it. They wanted Melinda out of it, and Melinda said, "No, I lived this way when I was at home. I believed it then, and I believe it now. You or Punkin, nobody's going to change the way I feel about God. Ain't nobody *makes* me do this. I *believe* it this way." And I know what she's talking about now.

The first time Jamie got snakebit was about 1993. It was a rattlesnake that bit him, on the forearm. I'd never seen nobody bit before. I was so scared that I called Punkin to come up here [to Middlesboro]. Jamie got bit two o'clock Sunday, and Punkin was gone deer hunting. He later told Jamie he had dreamed that he'd walked in the door [of his house], still had his deer-hunting outfit on, and Melinda said, "You gotta go to Middlesboro. Jamie's bit." And that's exactly how it happened.

Punkin got here that same day before it got dark, and he came up, and he checked Jamie out, and once Punkin was there, we started making decisions. We had Jamie up to Mamaw Turner's, but Jamie just couldn't get comfortable in that bed. He said, "I've got to go home. I can't stand it here. There's no air conditioning." And Punkin said, "Okay, we'll take you home." So Punkin helps Jamie out the door, and they lay the seat of his car back and put Jamie's arm on the armrest with pillows. And I'm driving Jamie, and Punkin's behind me, and [Jamie's] mom and dad are driving behind him, so we haul him home. The babies stayed with Jamie's mom and dad. It's not something you want your children to see you go through. I know children need to know there's death in serpents and there's harm, and my children will tell you quick how Daddy hollered and went on because he was in agony, how it hurt. But they are scared, and it's best to shield them. It was the best thing in the world when Punkin sent his children home with Sister Shell when Melinda was bit.

When we got home, Punkin said, "Here's what we're gonna do. Let's put a fan over here in the window," because, you know, a rattler usually affects the breathing. He said, "Get me some ice water. We'll keep wet rags on the bite." Just like Jamie said, it's easy for men when they get snakebit. They've got all these men around the temple to take care of them. I mean, we usually have a houseful. Brother Punkin was always here, and when Jamie got that copperhead bite last time, Punkin was sitting there in that rocking chair in the den. Punkin didn't do nothing but sit there and sleep, and every time Jamie would holler, Punkin would laugh and say, "Tough it out, son. That's all you can do." He'd sit there and laugh and go back to sleep. Oh, we could have wrung his neck.

When Jamie has been bit by a rattlesnake, three times it's hurt him. And he's been bit once or twice [when] it didn't even swell or hurt him. And he's been bit once by a copperhead. This last one was a rattlesnake bite. Yeah. The copperhead bit him in the palm of his hand, and it didn't even leave a scar. Well, Jamie don't see nothing wrong with going to the doctor if you get bit, but to himself, he feels if he can handle them, he needs to have faith in the Lord to help him. But in the event that I got bit, he said he'd probably grab me out of here before my head would spin and take me on to the emergency room. Would I let him take me? I'd have to experience it to know what I'd do. On the one hand, I'd like to have the faith in the Lord to move, because it would be His will whether I live or die, hospital or at home, either one. And on the other hand, it's just according to how scared I get. And my children. Not only my younguns—that's a lot—but Jamie also.

But I'll tell you the reason that some people that handle serpents and get bit don't go to the hospital. We get a bad rap, and we get talked real bad about. [If you're a serpent handler and] you go to the hospital, [you'll] see how they talk to you. They treat you like dirt. They talk to you like a dog because you were handling serpents. You can take the meanest, hatefulest person in the world that's against serpent handling and put them in a hospital room with somebody's been serpent handling, and how do you think they're going to treat them? They treat them like dirt. And me and my sister Rita, who's a nurse, we talked about that, because they's a lot of women up there [at the hospital] don't believe in snake handling, and all I can say is, I hope I get somebody like Rita, who's open-minded and [will] say, "God bless you, and let's take care of you, lady." And professionally, they have no right treating you [badly]. But what are you going to do? It's your word against theirs, against the hospital.

And when Melinda died, and they took her body up there to the hospital, and they talked to Peggy [Brown], they weren't very nice at all. And the police treated us like dogs. They came out there and told Jamie that if he didn't tell whose serpent it was [that bit her], who it belonged to, they would arrest him and take him to jail. And Jamie pleaded confidentiality, as pastor. They read him his rights and put him in the backseat of the [patrol] car. They couldn't arrest him for anything, 'cause it was just a misdemeanor. But that's how dirty they get us.

And they was a girl up there where we lived in public housing. She's Trinity [a subgroup of the Holiness faith], but she goes to a serpent-handling church. Do you know she is the very one went and took up a petition to have us kicked out of the project, out of public housing, because Melinda died up there? Our landlord loved us, and she did tell Jamie, "Now, Jamie, if somebody else gets bit, don't bring 'em up here. It's a lot of publicity, her dying—a big commotion. So don't bring nobody else up here."

Jamie is a pastor. [If] somebody gets snakebit, where are they supposed to go? Take somebody from Alabama. [You can't say,] "I'm sorry. You can't come to my house." And that's when Jamie prayed to God and said, "I want out of this place. This is one of my requirements of being a pastor, taking care of people that come to my church." And the Lord blessed us [with] this house. We lived here, rented it two year, and bought it. Now, the Lord's good, ain't He? My mom said, "Why didn't you make [Melinda] go to the hospital?" I said, "Mom, Punkin asked her. Punkin asked her several times." Actually, he *begged* her once. I was in there, and he was crying. He said, "Melinda, we got them kids." She said, "Punkin, I trust in the Lord." And that was her wishes.

We were there that night when Punkin died, too. I didn't realize he was bit until everybody gathered around and started praying for him, and then he raised his hand, and I seen blood, and I just fell to my knees and went to praying, but I couldn't get no relief from my prayer. A lot of times, you can get relief and comfort from praying. But I couldn't get it. And I knew. I knew *he's not gonna make it.* I did not feel the comfort and reassurance I needed. [I said,] "God, you're not giving me something. Something's wrong, isn't it? He's gonna die." And he did.

Jamie and I got there late that night. We had a terrible trip. It had rained, and at the restaurant, we had to wait to be seated, and by the time we got there [to Alabama], we was probably forty-five minutes late. Well, Punkin was standing on the porch when we got there. It was real dark, and I heard Punkin say, "It's about time you get here," and Jamie laughed and got up there on the porch, and they shook hands and hugged. And Punkin said, "I see you brought Munchkin with you," talking about me. And we went on into the church, and him and Jamie went up there to the pulpit and sat down. And they lowered their heads and got to whispering the way they always did. Punkin would let Jamie know what was going on and what was happening and who's doing what wherever, or if they'd caught any fresh rattlers while they been down here. And while somebody'd be singing, he'd catch Jamie up on anything he needed to be caught up on.

When Punkin got up to sing, I felt the Lord so good. I stood up, and I was singing. Then he went to preaching, and his preaching was so good, I didn't even know he was bit. I know that when he raised his hand up, I seen blood come down, so it had to be on the finger. I didn't realize he was bit until a bunch of people started gathering around praying for him. Well, son, he didn't last I believe it was five minutes.

I disapprove of that videotape [that recorded his death]. It should have been cut off immediately, pulled out, and cut all to pieces. That way, the police couldn't confiscate it. This is personal, private stuff. To me, it's putting the state and religion back together, because the police can come in and do what they want to with your religion. They took the tape. All they want to show is the bad part. All they want to talk about is when people get killed [by serpents], not how many times they handled them with victory.

We don't set Punkin up as a god, but I'm here to tell you, he was a good man. He went to all churches. Everybody welcomed him and loved having him. He come to our house, and he'd stay here. Jamie would get up in the morning and go to work, and we'd lock that door in there. The den was Punkin's. He didn't want them kids in there when he was sleeping. Punkin would hunt all day long. He'd come home, we'd eat supper, we'd go to church, and him and Jamie sat up till two or three in the morning, talking. He was like an uncle to my children. He pulled both of Trina's first teeth. Or we'd all go down to see him as a family thing, then Melinda would come up here. And after Melinda died, he would come up here in the summer, and he would bring the kids. Hopefully, Jeremiah will be my son-in-law someday. We encourage it. Trina thinks he's wonderful, and he likes her, too.

Punkin's family was always there [for him]. That's all Punkin could talk about—his mom. And his dad was just like Jamie's dad. He'd say, "Do you need any money? What are you going to drive?" If they didn't have no money, Carl Porter would call up and say, "You boys coming down [to Georgia] this weekend? We gonna have some reporters." He always liked them to come down there. And they'd say, "We ain't got no money to get down there." And Carl would say, "Go pawn something. I'll give you the money when you get here." So they'd pawn whatever they needed to pawn, 'cause neither one of them was working at the time. And when they get to Georgia, Porter takes a big offering up, and Porter gives it to Jamie, and Jamie gives Punkin whatever they needed, and Jamie would bring home with him whatever we needed. If Jamie didn't have no money and Punkin wanted to go to Alabama or wherever, I never did worry, because I knew Punkin would take care of Jamie if he got bit or something. I relied a whole lot on Punkin to take care of Jamie like an older brother.

Jamie says there will never, ever be nobody that'll have that place in his heart or take that place in his heart like Punkin. See, Jamie's an only child, and Punkin was the brother he never had. We don't say Punkin was perfect, but he always did the right thing. He never did wrong nobody in nothing. He was real easygoing. Real easy. And he taught Jamie a lot. [After Punkin's death, Jamie] went through a terrible time. He'd cry, bawl a lot. When he finally did break down, it was a bad breakdown. He said, "Linda, I don't have no best friend anymore." Punkin was Jamie's life, 'cause they went everywhere together, did everything together. They would talk to one another three and four times a week. We didn't realize until later that Punkin was here just as much as Jamie's mom and dad was here.

Just before he died, Punkin was thinking about getting married, but the woman's ex-husband was still alive. We didn't see no wrong in Punkin dating her, and he said she was really good to his kids, and she really helped Punkin's mom, but we worried that if he married her, a lot of people would turn against him because she was divorced. Some of our church members didn't want to hear him preach no more. We prayed about it, and we fasted, and the Lord spoke to Jamie one day when he was praying, and said, "As long as my spirit dwells with him, you will dwell with him." We knew God would take care of it, and He did. This has been a hard time for Jamie. It was our first homecoming without Punkin. He always used to be there.

A lot of times, we have to have patience and wait upon the Lord. That is so hard. When the Lord moves on you, when you're a sinner and you're in the congregation, you can feel a pulling love, pulling you to come into this place. And most of the time, He'll pull it into the altar. You'll feel this deep sensation of wanting to cry and give your life to God. And once you do that, you repent, and you get baptized, and it's a deeper sensation. It goes deeper. Oh, it's just like an overwhelming love, like the love of seeing a newborn baby, the love that swells up inside you, a happiness and a joy. And at the same time all these feelings is going on, you can hear His voice telling you what He's wanting you to do. You just have to sit back and take your time and see what He's wanting you to do. There's times when I'm feeling the anointing so good [that] I'll be singing, I'll have my eyes closed, and I'll be praying in the Lord, and God will speak to me: "Pray for Brother Carl" or "Pray for Sister Coots." And you go do what God tells you to do, just like prophesying.

I keep my eyes closed. When my eyes are open, I'm focusing on everything, but when my eyes are closed, the Lord will say, "Speak to so-and-so," and sometimes I look to see where they're at. "Oh. Okay." And sometimes, I'll stand back, and I'll say, "Lord, what is it?" And the Lord will start telling me what I need to say to them. And I can't change it. I tried to change it one time, and it didn't work. The Lord wanted me to go to Greg, my father-in-law, and tell him, "Trouble is coming. Seek me fast, and seek me much." I didn't want to tell Greg trouble was coming, and I made something up in my mind, and I said, "Now, Lord, I'm not going to tell him trouble's coming, because if trouble don't come, then I'm a false prophet, and I missed it." But I know what I'm feeling, so I've *got* to be telling the truth, but I didn't want to tell him that. So I went up there with the intention of telling him something not as bad as "Trouble's coming," but maybe, "Watch out."

It didn't happen that way. God spoke through me what He wanted spoke. Honest, the next day when Greg went to work, they laid him off. And he was the backbone of the church, paid all the bills on the church. He kept me and Jamie up, and [his wife] Linda, and this was great trouble for him. It was great trouble for everybody, even the church. So he even made Linda fast, two or three days, and Linda said, "Oh, Lord, he's making me fast." And don't you know, [Greg] went Friday evening, said the Lord had spoke to him, said, "Fast and pray and seek me much, and I'll move." That Friday evening, he went up and talked to a man [about a job], and they hired him right off, said, "Come in Monday morning." See how fast God moves?

One time, Mamaw Turner told me, said, "Linda, if you can't prophesy something good to me, why don't you just not prophesy to me no more?" But the Lord spoke to me and told me to tell Mamaw, said, "There's great sickness on the way," and for her not to lean on an arm of flesh, but to lean on Him, and He would take care of her and bring her through it, and to give Him the praise and the glory, and not man. And I said, "Lord, I can't tell her that. It's too personal. Lord, I can't give something out like that." I do argue with the Lord, and that's a lot wrong with us these days. But I thought, "If something don't come to pass,

I'm in trouble. I will be known as a false prophet, big time." See? The devil's always fighting you, and people's all too ready to say, "Well, she prophesied that last week, and it didn't happen. She's a liar. She's not a god."

Now, men, they don't care. They just go right on, and they're constantly telling us women, "Now, you-all go in there, sit back, quit being disobedient, and get up when God speaks, and do what God tells, or say what God tells." But a lot of times, people will fight you. I mean, it's personal. You go up and say to anybody, "Yea, my child, I'm well pleased in you, and I love you, and I'm going to move"—anybody could give that kind of prophecy. But you go up to somebody and say, "There's gonna be a great sickness come upon you," and that's a little bit more personal.

But I went to her, and I prophesied it to her. So I waited about a week later, and then two weeks later, and I started worrying. So I went to church Sunday, and I knew I shouldn't do this, I knew it was wrong, but I said, "Greg, where's Mamaw?" [He said,] "She's feeling real bad. She's having chest pains." I was sad that she was sick but [was relieved that my prophesy was not false]. Then, the following week, they flew her to [the University of Tennessee Hospital], and she had to have open-heart surgery. I believe that God was telling her that she needed to get close enough to God that while she was going through this sickness, she could speak with Him and let man go about doing their business of taking care of her. And I feel like God gave her that prophecy.

I got down on my knees that day before I went to church that night, and I said, "God, I know You didn't lie. I know what I felt when You told me to speak to her, but I'm worried somebody's gonna start saying I'm a false prophet. What's going on?" And the Lord showed it to me. He let me know that He gave me that prophecy because He wanted her to know that she didn't need to worry through this. He told her He was going to bring her out of it, [that] she shouldn't worry [about being] sick. And she testified she didn't worry at all, because she held on to the prophecy. So when I went to church that night, I didn't rejoice at her being sick. I rejoiced that I didn't miss [the prophecy]. I knew what was moving on me, but they's still times you worry.

[One time] when I was praying for an elder sister, the Lord opened it up to me [and said], "Death is nigh." And I thought, "Oh, my God, you don't prophesy something like that. Ain't no way I'm prophesying that to her." Well, hit went on three months, and I prayed, "Lord, I don't understand. Why ain't she dead? You told me, 'Death is nigh.'" I know what was moving on me. I fleeced the Lord to let Mamaw Coots and another sister come and pray for me, and that sister come back there and prayed for me and said, "My child, I say obey me," and I still wouldn't go to tell her. I wouldn't do it, because that's something *stiff.* I could have told her and been called a false prophet, but old, wise Mamaw Coots—she's my confidante; she's the one I run to when I need things—I said, "Mamaw, I don't know what's going on, but I missed [the prophecy]." And you know what Mamaw Coots said? She said, "No, Linda, you didn't miss it, honey. You're thinking carnally minded. Think spiritual. She's not in church no more. She's quit. She's not coming here no more. *Spiritually,* she's dead."

Yeah, that's right! You're good, Mamaw, you're *good.* He didn't say "fleshly." He just said, "Death is nigh." And right after that, that sister started going to another church.

[When God speaks to you,] it's just something that comes into your mind. But I've heard His actual voice. One time, it was when I was saying something I shouldn't have been saying, telling something that should have been kept to myself. It was very fearsome. I mean, I felt fear in my stomach, and I heard Him say, "Linda." It wasn't in my head, neither. It sounded like it was beside that door. I looked to see if it was Jamie. I thought maybe Jamie had got out of bed and come in there and heard me saying [something], because they was a situation going on [in church]. And I called Rita, and I tell Rita everything. I know God didn't want me to say anything about it. He just wanted me to let it go, because He had done gave me a prophecy. He had done spoke through a sister at church that He was in this, and that He was going to move. And I was telling Rita about the situation and about the prophecy, and I believe in my heart the Lord was disappointed in me. I should never have been saying it to her. Not that it was gossip or anything bad, but it was God's business, nobody else's. I heard that voice, and an awful fear come on me, and I knew better than to think it was Jamie, 'cause I knowed I wouldn't be that scared of Jamie. And I knew then that I shouldn't talk about that situation, and I'm trying not to. I'm trying to be good.

[God is loving, but He's also] very strict. If we get out of the will of God— [if you say,] "I'm gonna do it, I don't care if it's right or wrong, I'm gonna say it"—you're gonna get in trouble for it. Somewhere, you're gonna suffer. And I pray to God that *I'm* gonna suffer, and not my children, because honest to God, when you come here and them kids are sick, you know Linda done something this week she shouldn't have done. Diarrhea and throwing up, that's how God whups me, either through my children getting sick or myself getting sick. Or when I am disobedient or when I sin, I go to church, and I sit there like I'm dead, and I hate that. I *hate* that. I don't get up and sing and shout and speak in tongues and prophesy and do as good as I normally do. You see me sitting there in the back, you know Linda done something this week, something wrong.

I had been going through a really bad trial, and God had sent a sister [Shell Brown] up here to stay the week with me. Shell come up, and me and her sit up half the night talking. I opened it up to her, and she said she felt God's center here, and she had been through the same thing that I'd went through, and she helped me, oh, so great. After she went back home, I was walking through the house one day. I was just a-bawling. I fasted more than I'd ever fasted in my life over that trial. But God moved in it. I fasted three whole days and nights—didn't eat a bite. I said, "God, You've got to move this. You've just *got* to move this. I'll get Your attention some way or another." Prayer? I'd get in the prayer line every time it was open. I come through the house that day, and God knowed it—He's so smart. I said, "Lord, please get me out of this, help me through this trial. I haven't sinned through it, but the devil's tormenting me. Help me, Lord. You see what I'm going through. Now, I'm begging You to help me." You know what He spoke? "The next one will be even worse."

And God knows my heart to this day. This has been going on three years, every other month. People can try you. You've got people in church looking for something to puff up and pout about. And you've got to show God, you've got to show love, say, "Oh, we miss you, we love you, please come back," 'cause you don't know. And although they go through their little petty disagreements, they're still your brothers and sisters.

But when He said, "The next one will be worse," He knew exactly what He was saying. It's worse. It's worse. It's an ongoing thing, been going on for three years. God knows all about it, and He'll move in His time. He said He would. But I've just got to hold up the faith and love God and love them people, no matter what we go through, and let God work it out. Because if I take it in my own hands, I'll mess it up.

But anyway, I had fasted for three days in that trial, and we went down to Georgia to church, and I was sitting in the back. I was bawling my eyes out, and I said, "Lord, I just don't feel right sitting in the back. I just don't believe the back of the church is where I belong. I need to be in front, in the service. That's where I belong. I'm your child. I shouldn't be sitting back here on the back bench like a scared-to-death sinner ready to run right out the door. Lord, I don't know, but I've asked You to move. I know I've not sinned during this trial, but I know it's driving me crazy, and I'm afraid I'm going to do wrong." And I was a-bawling and a-crying and praying.

So I got up, wiped my eyes out, stood up, started playing my tambourine, looked up front, and there's Brother Bill Pelfrey. He looked plumb up in the air, looked plumb back there at that back bench, shook his head no, and grinned. Well, I's sitting there. I thought, "God, I feel You all over me, but I's scared to do it." Because you check yourself. Have you sinned? Are you in shape to take a serpent up? Have you said something to somebody? Have you done anything? Have you screamed at the kids that you shouldn't have done? Have you done any little thing that God ain't forgive you for? And I felt clean. I said, "God, I'm not dirty." I started up that aisle, buddy, and when I did, the Lord moved so good [that] I got up there and I took that serpent up, and I just bawled and cried the whole time I was holding it, because to me it was renewing my relationship with God. He was showing me that He was pleased in me, and He was reassuring me He's going to move in this, [that he will] let me hang on, and that I've pleased Him.

The Lord used me one night. We had a brother in the church. He was down, real down, and it's the first time God ever opened somebody's heart up to me. It scared me. I didn't know the brother was going through something, because I'm not close to the brothers in church. And the Lord told me to go to him and prophesy to him. I went to him, laid my hands on his head. And you know, I'm gentle, but Lord, when I put my hands on his head, God moved my hands, just jerking. I said, "I say, 'Nay, nay,' I say, 'Nay!' This I think: I say, 'Nay!'" And it's real hateful coming out of me. And just as soon as I took my hand down and turned around to walk off, *suicide* came out in my mind.

In the car on the way home, I said, "Jamie, I'm not saying this is God, 'cause I don't know, but it scares me," 'cause God had never opened a heart up to me like that. I said, "Jamie, that brother, the thought that came to my mind was suicide."

Well, me and Jamie and this man went up to Bruce Helton's church the following week, and they was in the front of the van, and me and the kids was in the back, and Jamie asked him, said, "When Linda prophesied [to] you on Sunday, was suicide on your mind?" He broke down and cried. He said, "Yeah," said it was, said, "I've already tried it." Said, "I was sitting there during church service thinking I was wasting my time being there, that I needed to try it again. Then Linda come and spoke to me, and the Lord told me no three times." He said, "I knowed it was God when she came over and laid her hands on me and by the anger in her voice God was using." He said, "There was no way she'd know what I was thinking."

I knew he'd been having trouble and hadn't been coming to church as much as he usually did. I don't remember how his face looked when I touched him. All I remember is, my hand was moving hard and the voice was coming out hateful. Very hateful.

The anointing is something you feel when you're right with God. [When I think about my own children handling serpents,] I feel terrified. After Jamie got bit the first time, it was months and months and months before I'd take up another serpent, and every time he'd take up another serpent, I would run to the bathroom. I couldn't bear to watch it, it scared me so bad. And where there's fear, there's torment, and there's not perfect love.

So on one Sunday, we was getting ready to get up and leave, and Jamie was up there handling serpents, and I turned around to walk on out the door. Church was over, but they was still feeling pretty good—some of the men was—and I started to walk out the door, and I said, "Lord God, I don't know. I just don't know if I can handle it, him handling snakes. They're scaring me so bad." And right at that minute, Jamie, in a very strong, loud, authoritative voice, started prophesying, speaking in tongues, and that's what made me turn around. He said, "Yea, my child, I say this is for you, and have no fear that I am in this." And honey, I turned around and shouted all the way up to the front of the church and took the serpent. When he prophesied that to me, Lord, the anointing just fell all over me, and I went up there to the front of the church, and I knew it was God. I *knew* it was God.

It's like last week. After we moved Mamaw Coots into her new house on Saturday, Jamie started limping. He didn't know what was wrong or how he hurt his foot. But Sunday when we went to church, he was limping. Well, the service was so good. The Lord shouted Jamie, and while he was shouting for the Lord, Brother Jimmy Turner—he has visions—he said he saw a vision of two hands clamping around Jamie's ankle, and after Jamie came out of the anointing, he didn't limp no more.

In serpent-handling churches, I believe that children should sit in the back. Sometimes, they will sit up front and rock if Mamaw or somebody's up there with them. The front seats. Not up on the pulpit. Trina will go up there and play the organ. And she watches. She knows to watch when the men head toward that serpent box. She knows to get down off that organ, get in the back of the church. And you witness this: We're not teaching them to be *scared* of the serpents, but always to be *cautious* [and to] watch. If Trina's wanting to participate in the singing and playing a musical instrument, she's gonna have to watch. The organ's on this side, and the serpent box is on the other, and a bunch of people in the middle, which shields her, but I don't want to take a chance. I mean, I love my kids just as good as anybody else loves theirs, and I don't want to take a chance of risk. Who knows what could happen? I mean, I know serpents don't get loose, and I know the handlers don't throw 'em in the floor, shake 'em out or nothing, but who's to say? Something might happen one of these days, and how would I feel if I didn't do my duty to protect my children? And I can understand why the law and the public is so interested in this. You cannot turn kids loose in a serpent-handling church. You cannot. If you do, you're stupid to begin with, and there's some of [the children] that just don't watch.

As far as Trina and Cody handling serpents, I won't say they won't when they get older. As long as they live in our house, you can tell they're close enough to God. If they're anointed, if they've got the Holy Ghost, then they can handle serpents [when they are old enough]. Trina wears dresses all the time, never pants. She plays piano. We don't listen to nothing but gospel music. We have a TV in the den, and Cody has TV in his room. We're particular about what we watch. The kids will tell you right now they're not allowed to watch *The Simpsons*, MTV, country TV, rock-'n'-roll, and nasty stuff, especially talk shows. They're brought up like regular children. They get to pick the toys they want. They pick their own clothes now. They go out. They got their bikes. There are places they don't get to go, but we take them to the movies. We don't go often, but we do go when something good comes on. They have an ordinary childhood.

I've seen people twenty or thirty years old who can't handle a serpent. They're not ready spiritually. Jamie's mom, Linda, she's *never* handled one. She lives good. She lives a real good life. But she's never handled one. I think it's up to the individual. And as far as my children, even if they get eighteen, I've got to have a whole lot more out of them before I'd let them do it.

Listening to the experience of Linda watching Jamie take 'em up, you know, it still frightens her. It's her kid, and of course you know what's gonna scare us.

It's our children. But serpent handling is wonderful. It's great. I desire it. I desire it [and] I love to do it, but I want my children to know serpent handling is not all of this faith. Trina and Cody go around acting like they're speaking in tongues, shouting, praying for the sick. And these children know that there's more to it than serpent handling.

There is times we can go three months, have great services, speak in tongues, pray for the sick, prophesy, have wonderful preaching, messages, wonderful singing, and never take a serpent out of the box. People don't understand. They think every time we go to meeting, it's about snake handling. If you go to Jolo, it is. But it's not like that everywhere you go. Jamie goes to his snake room; he puts them in a box; he locks them up; we take them to church. If the anointing don't move in that particular area, he brings them back home and puts them back outside in the snake room.

Jamie don't get to hunt too often. Spring is a great time to find them, but they're trying to get one of the Jeeps running, and he is off three days a week. Starting about a month from now, he'll be working six days a week, ten, eight hours a day. He works on a strip job. He's a rock-truck driver. He won't have time to do a whole lot of hunting, and he just gets one week vacation a year, which last year, the last of June, we went to Myrtle Beach.

See, we're normal people. We take vacations and do things that other people do. Sometimes, we may look different. I get out and get tan in the summertime. The only difference between me and other people is that in our church, women wear dresses at all times. Maybe some of my dresses are long, and some of my dresses aren't so long. You won't see jewelry on me, and makeup, and my hair's long. You'll not see makeup, but you'll see hair spray.

We've been talked about for [letting our children watch] TV. As far as the TV is concerned, it's got channels on it, and you can change them. You don't have to let them watch filth. Mamaw Coots don't watch TV; she brought her children up that way. Whatever condemns you, you'd better not do it. I don't eat chocolate. I don't drink pop. I don't chew gum. I don't trim my hair. I told the Lord that I wouldn't do it. And if I can just instill that in my kids' hearts when they get out and do whatever they want to do, [they'll do the right thing]. See, Jamie was like that. Linda will tell you. When they get a certain age, you can't make them go to church. And when Jamie got fifteen, he had no desire to go to church anymore. He wanted to be with the world. So you can't stay home and baby-sit. You go on to church, you turn them loose, and they're going to do what they're going to do. All you can do is pray that God keeps His hands on them. And Jamie went back to it. He didn't stray out of it too long—two years, maybe three years.

I love living like this. If you need anything, you call anybody in church. We have got the closest-knitted church of any of them I know. A lot of it's family, [and] a lot of it's not. And if you need anything in any way, they'll help you. It's there. And if I've got something where I can help somebody, I'll give it to them. I'll be there to help them. Now, we had a sister without groceries, and she didn't really have a lot of money to buy any, and I just got on the phone and dialed my good sisters, and I said, "Let's just bag some things up. If you ain't got nothing, clean that freezer out, refrigerator out, cabinets, and let's get on to church." I didn't go that night because I was very ill, but Jamie just had his mother collect the rest of it, and they piled them in that sister's car, and she was happy-go-lucky.

And if we've got extra money, we give them extra money. There's time people's had to do us that way. People's gave us groceries. They gave us gas money. This [church] ain't just a place to go and worship God. It *is* God. It is love. They are wonderful people. There ain't nobody like God's people. And I'm going to say, I don't care who don't like it, there are good people in every church. You'll hear some people say, "Well, now, there might be good in every church, but only this particular kind is going to make it." Well, that's up to God, right? If He picks this one here and this one here and says, "This one is the only one gonna make it in," [then] this one over there is going to have to come over here eventually. He's got children all over the world. And the Bible [says that] He has children of a different fold. I'm telling you what: God can use who He wants to use. You know what I mean? And people just judge too much. When you exalt yourself, you're nothing to God. It's the ones come on low, the ones God can use, that He loves.

Greg Coots handles a serpent in a revival. Bruce Helton stands in the background.
Photo by Scott Schwartz

LIVING
BY FAITH

GREGORY COOTS
B. 1952

"The devil goes to church, too."

IMAGINE THIS. You're sitting on a hard wooden pew in a little church in rural Kentucky. It's a cold winter night, but the service is getting warmer and warmer. There is music, singing, and shouting. Up by the altar, Tommy Coots, the preacher, flips open the snake box and pulls out a thick black timber rattler. He raises it high above his head and begins to shout. Suddenly, the serpent swings its muscular body down and around and sinks its fangs into the preacher's finger. But he ignores the bite, the blood, and whatever pain he is beginning to experience and continues to hold the snake aloft. *And he never stops preaching his sermon.* He keeps talking, reminding the congregation that reptiles are potent and dangerous. But, he adds, "with the power of God, anything is possible." The bitten arm swells, then miraculously recedes to its normal size while the preacher extols God's overwhelming power. In a few minutes, the snake goes limp and dies in the preacher's hands. He finishes the service.

Later that evening, after the preacher has gone home, the family tosses the rattler into the coal stove and burns it.

Amen.

Renowned serpent-handling evangelist Tommy Coots could make vengeful snakes wilt; he could convince lost sinners to sing the praises of God; and he could force stubborn devils to scramble away in fear.

Greg Coots, his son, used to love to hear his father tell this particular story. It happened when he was too small to join the church, but it made an unforgettable impression on him. Of the seven Coots children, only Greg has remained in the serpent-handling religion. He has never even considered straying from the church, nor has he ever forgotten his father's message: "With God, anything is possible." And through the years, Greg Coots has witnessed miracles and seen that message proved again and again.

A shy, handsome man with a slight build and wavy, graying hair, Greg likes to tell about the miracle that happened to him when he was six years old. As a child, he was always playing with bullets. He loved to hunt with his brothers in the woods, where they often shot squirrels and rabbits for the dinner table. On this particular day, he wanted to show his brother how he could make a .22-caliber shell fire without using a rifle. He had done it before, by squeezing the shell with a pair of pliers until the bullet blasted away. But during this demonstration, all he could manage to do was mangle the bullet. So he put the shell on a rock and smacked it with a hammer.

"Mom and Dad, they went to town to be in church that day," Greg recalls. "It was on a Sunday, and me and my brother come back from hunting, and he wanted me to show him how I shot those shells. When I hit [the shell], it went off, and about a third of the hull buried [itself] right underneath my right eyeball. Somebody got hold of Mom and Dad, and they come home. I had my eye covered up where it had been a-bleeding.

"They started praying, and after that shell buried underneath my eye, I started going to church, serving the Lord. They brought me all the way from Nicholasville, Kentucky, fifteen or twenty miles on this side of Lexington, all the way up here to Pineville over there behind my grandpaw's to baptize me in the Cumberland River. Dad brought me up here on that Sunday—the first Sunday after this went in my eye. And they'd been people took me home, took tweezers, tried to pull it out and everything. You could see it. But all the time it was in there, it never did hurt. My eyes would water and kind of cover over of a night, and in the morning, I'd get up [and] I'd have to wash it out with warm water. But the whole nine days in there, it never did hurt. After I got saved and they baptized me in the name of Jesus Christ, we went back home, and the following Tuesday, I woke up and that [shell fragment] was laying there on my pillow. That piece of copper shell. It was nine days. That shell was half as big as your little nail. It was a copper hull, buried right down underneath my eyeball there. It never got into the eyeball itself.

"Never did go to the doctor with it, nor anything. The whole time us kids was growing up, we was never to a doctor. Mom and Dad, if we got sick, anything happened, they prayed for us, and the Lord healed us. I never did go to a doctor until I was up and married and I was twenty-one year old. I got hurt on a job, and they took me to the hospital. That's the only time I ever seen one. I've seen my brothers have broke arms, bone sticking through the skin. The Lord put [the bones] back. Wasn't raised to see a doctor, and never did go to one. Never did take no shots in school. Never did take no medicine. They used to give us them little sugar blocks [polio vaccine] that they give you in school. I'd always give mine to somebody else. Never did take it. I had one shot in my life, growing up. They had to give me a vaccination shot they used to give you when you start school. They give me that, and I went home and was on the couch, sick, swelled up for two or three days. I never did take another shot after that until I was grown and married.

"Mom was a strong believer in faith. We lived by faith, and God healed us of anything we had. I never did have the mumps. Mumps went all through my brothers. I remember them having them, jaws all swelled up. One or two it fell on, and yet they had children when they's married and growed up. I don't remember if I had the measles. If I did, I was small. Anything we had, we didn't take no medicine for. God took care of it, whatever it was."

As he grew older, Greg's faith became even stronger. He would fast three days a week for six or seven weeks at a time. His fasts were of the Old Testament kind, which means that he had nothing at all—no food, not a drop of water. He fed on the Lord, he said.

And he studied. Every morning, he rose before dawn and read the Bible for an hour or more. Every night, he read more Scripture and prayed for an hour or more before going to sleep. "Everything a body and soul needs can be found in the Bible," he says. Today, he continues to fast and pray. And when he preaches, handles serpents, or plays the guitar in the church his father began, his emotion is so great that he cannot keep from weeping.

"I believe you have to stay with the Word of God," Greg will tell you. "There's a lot of churches they won't have all the Word. There's not many that really tries to live to where they can really do the Word. To believe it. But I think you have to take it just as it is in the Bible, from lid to lid. What the Word says is that the spirit and the Word agree. If we got the spirit of God dwelling within us, there is no way that spirit that wrote the Word in the beginning is going to reject it. If you got a spirit that don't agree with the Word of God, then that spirit ain't God. It's the spirit of the devil."

IN HIS OWN WORDS
GREGORY COOTS

I have been taking up serpents since I was nineteen years old. I've never been bitten. It is all in the Lord's hands, is all I know. I don't handle them a whole lot. I don't like to handle them just because somebody else is. I want to really be sure the Lord wants me to do it before I go and do that. I know there is danger in it. I know there is death in it. Myself, I don't want to fool with 'em— not myself, I don't. I won't pick them up by faith. I want the Lord to really be a-moving to do that.

It wasn't too long after I was married [when I took up the first one]. It was in 1970 or '71. They had a meeting that night, preaching, and Dad got a big rattlesnake out. I was standing behind the stove. It was kind of wintertime. The Lord sent him over to me with that big rattlesnake, and he handed it to me, and the Lord prophesied to me and said, "Many times thou hast desired this, and, yea, I was with thee." And Dad give me that rattlesnake. That was the first time.

Before the church was built, we was having a house meeting at [my mother-in-law's] house. One Sunday, the Lord let me handle a cottonmouth. That was my second time. It didn't cause me any problems. I just let it crawl up in my hands.

Then we was in church one day after we got it built. Dad laid a copperhead in the floor and told me to get it. That was the third time.

My dad and mom used to go around to a lot of churches and sing. People loved to hear them. Dad started out in Church of God churches. They ordained him to be a deacon, and the Lord began to move and call him to preach, and he started preaching from then on. Then he started going to Pentecostal churches that took up serpents. He was at church one night singing, and he knowed they had [serpents] there, but he was just singing. It might have been Lee Valentine had two [serpents] and [was] handling them, and Dad said the brothers come to him crying and told him, "They'll not hurt you." Dad said that was the last thing he remembered. When he come to, he had [a serpent] in each hand [and was] shouting across the floor. From then on, he took up serpents.

We moved close to the church [in Middlesboro] in 1967 or '68. We got acquainted with [my future wife] Linda's mom and dad. They started going to church with us.

After Dad got to preaching, he was in the Signs. He practiced the Signs, and he could cast out devils. I remember one in particular I heard him talk about. I wasn't with him, you know, when it happened, when he experienced it. That's the one he made an album of, Dad did. He's got talking on it about it. He used to tape his services so that people could listen to it later. I think it's about seven minutes long on his album. He didn't record the event itself—just what happened. That woman, when that devil took hold of her, she was probably seven or eight times stronger than normal. She slang them off, a grown man, just slang him off. It wasn't her a-doing it, [it was the devil inside her,] and he cast out that devil from her.

Now, there is a gift [mentioned] in the Bible, the gift of discerning. That's when the spirit begins to move. In that gift, the Lord [works] through you. The Lord moves that way. I've never seen it, but it can be done. [Some people] can discern those spirits, because the devil goes to church, too. If you are walking down the street, some people say they can tell if [another] person has the devil in them. I can't do that. In the church, the pastors and the preachers and overseers like that of the church—now, they's some of them that can do it in the church. Now, Dad, there's a lot of times when the Lord would use him in a discerning spirit. The devil will work in any way that he can, through anybody, to try to hinder or tear down. So, yeah, the devil goes to church, too.

When a body goes places or hears the preacher, when they are reading the Word, they need to follow it with them. Because there's a lot of people who want to add a little here and there, take something out of here and there. If you don't know the Word, then you don't know if they are right or not. So a body needs to study the Word and know what the Word says. Then when somebody quotes it, you can say, "That's right. It's in there."

I'm a licensed blaster for coal strip mines. I put in the dynamite. The company I was working for when I got hurt, they sent me and another boy to school to learn us to do all that and get our license in 1978. I been doing it ever since. It is outside work, and you have to work in the rain and snow, it don't matter. But I've always enjoyed it. It is really about the only work I like to do. You got to know what you are doing. It is a lot safer now than it used to be. Technology and things they use, it is a lot safer. Jamie works for the same company. He drives a rock truck. I get up at 3:30, fix my coffee and stuff I take to work. Get [Linda] up at 4 A.M., and we sit around and talk until 5 A.M. I want to be wide awake and not sleepy. It takes about forty-five minutes to drive to work. I never was one to just get up and put clothes on and go to work.

We got married in 1969. I got hurt on a job up here in 1973. I got covered up. A high wall covered me up in 1973, June. I was cleaning coal with a small loader on a strip mine, and about a thirty- or forty-foot-high wall come in, covered the loader up. Dirt and rock. It fell in on the loader and filled the cab full up to my knees and brought the top of it and mashed it down on me and had my chest pressed against the steering wheel. Had my breath cut off. I couldn't breathe. The people that was working with me, they brought in another loader and hooked the end of the cab and lifted the cab up off of me so I could breathe and took me to the hospital.

I went back to work in '75. [The accident] didn't do nothing. It like to cut my thumb off. Just a piece of skin holding it. Broke my wrist, and that was all it done. It bruised my chest and back up real bad. It injured my spine. They was two vertebras in my back way up high. I went to the doctor in Knoxville during that time I was off for that, and he looked at the x-rays, and he said, "I don't see how you are walking. I don't see why you don't have paralysis." I didn't know what paralysis was, but [I found out it meant] being paralyzed. He said they was two bones in my spine, one mashed together 50 percent and the other 30 percent. And it never did bother me. I never did have no back problems other than just maybe working hard or something like that. It'd hurt a little bit. Other than that, it don't ever bother me.

It went from '73 to 1982, I never was sick much. Didn't have anything happen or anything. Didn't take no medicine or nothing. Then in 1982, I got real bad sick working, and the job shut down. I got real bad off. I was having real bad headaches. Didn't take nothing. There was a time or two I went to the emergency room to get a shot for the headache to ease it off. I started going to the doctor then in '82, trying to find out what my problem was.

They found a spot on my lungs. Got pneumonia, double pneumonia. They first thought it was cancer at worst. So the doctor down here in Middlesboro, she did all she could, so she sent me to Knoxville. They figured out through a lot of tests and stuff the problem I had—that spot on my lungs—was some kind of fungus, and it got in my bloodstream and went to my brain and caused a big abscess on my brain. On my right side, a big abscess in there. Well, I couldn't tell it [at first], you know, [but] at the last, before I went to Knoxville, I got to where I couldn't hardly walk. Start walking, take two or three steps, and come back two or three, like a drunk.

They found out what it was, and they went in on a Sunday to do emergency surgery on it. They come in and shaved my head and went in and done the surgery, cut my head open. Went in there on Sunday, took me down on Monday to do x-rays, and when they done the x-rays, they found that they'd missed it. They didn't get a thing after going in there. So they took me back down on a Tuesday and went back in the same way, going to get it that way. And the second time, they got in there, and some way or another, they put a tap on it to drain it, and they run a tube out the top of my head all the way down the side of the bed. And stuff drained out of that for two or three days into a bag on the bed. After all that was done and all that healed up, they took the tube out and all sewed up and everything, took all the stitches out, got all that took care of. They sent me home.

They first told me in the hospital over there [that] they's this doctor that all he done was internal medicine. He was working on all the medication I was taking. He said what I had was a fungus that was slow growing. They put me on Septra DS, taking three a day for one solid year. That was in '83. For one solid year, they put me on that. They said, "[It] just don't matter if you get to feeling better, think you are feeling good. Don't quit taking it. You take it for one year." So I took it for one year, and they put me on Dilantin for the seizures. They said, "Anytime you've had a head injury or brain surgery or anything, it causes you to have seizures." I didn't know what seizures was or [how] they affected me or nothing. So they put me on a hundred milligrams Dilantin a day. [The doctor] told me, said, "You will have to take this for life, that Dilantin, because you'll have seizures."

So I come back home. I was taking all the medication they give me. Took that Septra DS for one year, and the Dilantin. I was at work one day and had a seizure. Me and a buddy of mine was working together, and after dinner, we started going 'bout our jobs, and he asked me, "What's the matter with you?" I said, "I don't know. I don't know where I'm at or what I'm doing." I'd had a seizure, blacked out, and they took me to the hospital. They increased my dosages up. After that, I had two [seizures] at home and another one at work. And they upped my dosages to four hundred milligram a day of Dilantin.

In 1987, I was still taking that, [and] we was having a house meeting at Linda's mom's house one Monday night, I believe it was, before her daddy died. And before church, I was reading the Bible, and I felt one of them seizures coming. I was reading, and everything started going together, and people talking started fading off. I sat there and read, and I just talked to the Lord. I said, "Lord, would You heal me of this? I can't take medicine and pray for people and have faith for them, and me take medicine myself." That's the way I talked to the Lord, setting right there.

Well, that just went away. Church got started. Preacher started preaching. I asked the Lord while he was preaching, I said, "Lord, if You've healed me of this, You let the preacher come over, put his arm around me." I hadn't much more than thought it to the Lord, and the preacher come over and put his arm around me and give me a big hug. And from that time to this, I've never took another Dilantin. Lord healed me of that then, that night I asked Him. He healed me that night, and I've not took no more medicine since then and never had a seizure since then. That was '89. If I get sick [now], I just wait on the Lord to move it. Get a bad headache, I just go to bed and go to sleep and get up next morning, [and] it's gone. So I don't take nothin'. I'd rather trust the Lord to take care of it than take medicine. I don't take no aspirin or nothing like that, not a thing. I take vitamins.

Now, Mama has never went to a doctor. She went to a doctor to get a blood test. That was back [when], before you could get married, you had to go to a doctor to get a blood test. That was the only time she was ever at a doctor at all. She had seven kids at home. My brother before me weighed fourteen pounds. The Lord took care of us. The Lord has done so much for her.

The Lord has [also] taken care of Jamie. The times he got bit, I never really had no fear or worry about him. I didn't worry about him even after Melinda and Punkin got bit and died. I believe God can take care of you.

We don't know when that time is that we are going to die, but God does. I believe God saw the end before the beginning. Before He even created anything, He knew what the end was going to be, and when. Man don't, but God does. They's a few in the Bible born to do just what they did, just for that purpose, like Judas when he betrayed Jesus. He was born for that purpose. That's what he was there to do. The Bible says, "It is once appointed unto every man to die," so when our appointment comes, there ain't no doctors that can keep you here, no matter what's the matter with us or what they may try to do. When our appointed time comes, we are gone. That's our end. We all have an appointed time.

Only God can give life and take life. Punkin had an appointed time. The serpent was the way for him to go. That was his appointed time. It didn't matter how many doctors, or who was there. That was his appointed time right then. He went through many a bite, so if that hadn't been his appointed time right then, he'd still be here today. Whenever your appointed time comes, that's the end.

Linda Turner Coots, left, in church with husband Greg and mother-in-law
Louvernia Coots, 1999
Photo by Fred Brown

STREETS OF GOLD, GATES OF PEARL, WALLS OF JASPER

LINDA TURNER COOTS
B. 1952

"Love. That's the most important thing, to have that love."

HARD TIMES. That's the way it was in the 1930s, when George Washington Turner dropped out of school and went to work in the mines at the age of thirteen, because there were seven mouths to feed in his family. Those were difficult years for the whole country, the years of the Great Depression, when everybody had to pitch in and do his part. Consequently, Linda Turner Coots's father never learned to read. And even though his luck changed when he got a job in the Middlesboro Tannery after his marriage to Charlene Campbell, he came out of the mines with black lung, trading bad for worse. He relied on his wife to read the Bible to him regularly. George Turner knew that every word in it was true, because it was God's Word. That's all he needed to get him through.

Charlene had an interesting background of her own. Her mother, Susie, was descended from the Campbells who founded Campbell County. Susie's father, Charlie Mars, had a less distinguished history. He "got into trouble," was the way the family phrased it, which meant that he had killed a man and gone to prison. When he was released, he changed his name to Charlie Ford in order to make a new beginning. Linda can't remember much else about her grandfather except that he was a ladies' man. "Anyway, that's what Mama told me," she says.

"Now, my mama was bold. She'd speak her mind. They was a woman in the church wouldn't talk to Mama when they passed on the street. So one day in church, this woman came up and put her arms around Mama, and Mama rebuked her. She said, 'If you can't speak to me on the street, don't you hug me in church.' That's the way she was."

Things were pretty much centered around family life for the Turners. Then they met the Cootses, who moved into a log house over the hill. Greg Coots, who was later to become Linda Turner's husband, wasn't even around the first time Linda met the family. He had remained behind with friends in Nicholasville when the family returned to Middlesboro. "His oldest sister, Lucinda, the one they called Sandy, came over to our house with her brother Michael, and we got to talking," says Linda. "And then we went up to their house, and I met his mother. We were all just kids at the time."

When she finally got a look at Greg, Linda was smitten. "I had a crush on him," she remembers fondly. Handsome and thin, with reddish brown hair, Greg was not much of a talker. "One time, my sister and I saw Greg walking into town," says Linda. "My sister wanted me to follow him. I said, 'I'm not going to chase him. He'll have to chase me.' " But Greg never made a move, so Linda had to change her strategy. "I was never backward about talking to boys. Well, now, Alan, Greg's brother, he would come over to my house all the time, talk to me, and tell me about other girls he went out with. Then I started going up there to his house, and that's when I met Greg. I guess the reason I liked him was because he was real shy and backward. There was something special about him. So I made the first move. We were talking, and I just walked over to him and kissed him. It kind of embarrassed him, but after that, we started dating.

"My daddy never wanted me to get married and leave home, 'cause I was his pick. I was the oldest girl, and he was real strict on me. He wouldn't let me go nowhere. When I was dating Greg, he made him leave at eight o'clock on weeknights and at ten or eleven on weekends."

Her father's curfews didn't deter Gregory Coots, who might have been shy but was determined as well. Linda and Greg have been married now for almost thirty years. "We were both fifteen when we met and seventeen when we got married," says Linda. "That was in 1969. Dad didn't want me to get married, and Greg's mom didn't want him to get married, because Greg was the one she kind of depended on. She called him her special child. Her husband was an evangelist, and he had to depend on whatever money people gave him. So when we went to get married, just my mother and Greg's dad went with us. But afterwards, Dad called him his 'Greggy Boy,' and all my family loved him. My sisters and brothers told me that if anything ever happened to our marriage, they'd never speak to *me* again. And then Mamaw Coots got to realizing eventually that I wasn't going to keep Greg from helping her. I never did say nothing when he helped her out. She had a hard time sometimes, 'cause all the money they had was what people in the church would give them.

"When we got married, Greg was working at Ray Stapleton's filling station, making fifty dollars a week. Our first apartment was seventy-eight a month, everything furnished, even cable TV."

Linda and Greg reside in Middlesboro close to their only living child, Jamie, and to Greg's mother, Louvernia. Ever since Jamie was three years old, the couple has lived in the same one-story, two-bedroom house with green vinyl siding and a creek-rock foundation. There is one big tree in the front yard, but Greg cut down the other trees because they were chestnuts—too messy, he said. Linda is close enough to walk to her mother-in-law's house and to Jamie's house, where she likes to see her two grandchildren, Cody and Trina. Trina was named after Linda's first child, Katrina, who died at the age of two weeks.

Linda has worked part-time in a used furniture store and a used clothing store. But after Jamie was born, she stayed at home, which is what her husband wanted. Today, when she has some extra time, she likes to work with wood, especially building dollhouses.

Linda has long, wavy brown hair that falls to the middle of her back. Her speech is sprinkled with frequent "honey"s; her deep, husky voice translates well into singing in church. During services at the Full Gospel Tabernacle in Jesus Name, she closes her eyes in concentration as she sings. Usually, she sits on the stage near her husband, who plays guitar. Jamie, who is the preacher now, also plays guitar, and Jamie's wife sings.

"Most of us know the key the hymns are played in, and Jamie starts with the chords," says Linda. "Or Gregory. Now, I'm odd, because no matter how many guitars are playing, if Gregory's not playing a guitar, I can't sing, because I've always sung with him playing.

"A lot of these songs are handed down, through songs we've heard growing up in church, and a lot of the songs now, like [the ones] Jamie sings, were songs that we sung back when I started going to church, but they 'upbeat' them. They've got more rhythm. They're faster. There's a lot of them in the church that's written down on paper, out of notebooks, where people wrote them down. Greg's dad, we got a lot of his old songs wrote down. Gregory's got a songbook that someone published, and there's a picture of Greg's dad on the cover. We've got some that's typed. Greg's dad got a lot of songs from God, and Greg's mom wrote them down. Her or Valerie Rowe. Those songs, he got from God. Some, he just sang that one time, at that moment, and then he'd forget the song. God would give it to him. He'd sing it one time and no more. That'd be it. And Greg, he's made a lot of God's songs, too. Trina likes to listen to them on tape."

For the Cootses, church is a family affair. Greg's mother sits behind the pulpit and participates in the singing, and granddaughter Katrina plays the electric organ and sings as well. Services are held in the very building where, in 1978, Tommy Coots founded the ministry that has since passed to son Greg and then from Greg to Jamie. Linda's aunt, Gracie Turner, deeded the land to the church when her husband died. "They tore the house down to build the church," says Linda. "It was falling down anyway, but when I was little, I used to go up there all the time. I'd sit and listen to my uncle telling stories about the old days. He'd been bedridden about fourteen years. He just got sick one day and went to bed and never did get back up. So when he died, Aunt Gracie gave the land to the church." Before that, Tommy Coots held worship services in the Turners' house, located a couple of hundred yards down the road. Also recently burned is the log cabin the Cootses lived in when they came to Middlesboro from Nicholasville, where Tommy had a pastorship.

After the Turners and Cootses became friends, Tommy began telling the Turners about the Signs. They weren't going to church at the time. Charlene Turner believed in the Father, Son, and Holy Ghost and was reluctant to accept Tommy's philosophy of Jesus and God as one. Eventually, though, Tommy convinced her so thoroughly that she allowed services to be held in her house.

Considering all the children—fourteen altogether, counting both families—and the four adults, they had the makings of a church. After Tommy's death, however, some of the children fell away. "Now, Greg's brother Alan went to church *one time*," says Linda. "And the first time he was praying at the altar, somebody came up and laid hands on him, and he said it was like somebody poured ice water on him. That's what happens when people are not fully anointed and they lay hands on you. So that was the first time and the last time Alan went to the altar, and he hasn't been in church since.

"The one time Greg quit going to church was when he got real disheartened because people wouldn't come to his dad's church. His dad was disheartened, too. I was pregnant with my first baby—that was Katrina. [Right after she was born,] we were over at Greg's mother's house. We went over there and spent the night, and the baby died in bed with us. They said it was crib death. You can't explain it. People ask you how you feel, and the only way I can explain it is that when you lose a child, it's like a part of *you* that's died. That was my first baby. Then I lost my last baby, Timothy Keith. He died in the hospital. They said his lungs weren't developed. He was just five pounds. He was born before his time. Right before he was born, they found I was having some kind of problems. The doctor examined me, and the baby must have been in some stress, because they had to do a C-section. They took him early, and his lungs wasn't developed. He only lived two or three hours. I never got to see him. But Jamie was my middle child. And I guess that's why I've always been so protective of him.

"We think God took Katrina away because we had quit going to church. And when God whips you, you know it.

"My mom died in June of 1999. She'd had heart trouble, but she just died in her sleep, which is the way she wanted to go. And my dad died of an aneurism to his brain on March 8, 1991. I've lost both of them, but that just gives me that much more reason to go to heaven for."

IN HER OWN WORDS
LINDA TURNER COOTS

I was born right up above the church on Evans Drive—that's where my mom lived at—right here in Middlesboro. I had five brothers and three sisters. There were nine of us children. I was the oldest girl. I guess you could say we had a normal childhood. It wasn't real exciting.

My dad worked at the tannery. He had black lung disease, but what he died of was an aneurism to his brain. He had a lot of little strokes, and he smoked a lot, but after he stopped smoking, his cough cleared up. One day—this was about ten years before he died—he was standing in the hallway at home, talking to my mother. He was real agitated, like he was running on his nerves, couldn't quit talking, couldn't quit walking. Mama said he just turned white as a sheet, and where he stood was a puddle of water, so much fluid come out of his body. Then he just quit talking. After that, he got worse and worse. Lost his eyesight, too. But he already had trouble with that, 'cause one time, he had a fight with my uncle, and my uncle threw a bottle of Clorox in his eyes. He was so afraid of doctors, so afraid of being put to sleep, he wouldn't go to the doctor, and he lost most of his sight. After his stroke, he was like an invalid. He was completely dependent on Mom, and when he finally went to the hospital, he said to Mama, "I won't be back." He was in the hospital in Knoxville about three weeks. My brother Carl stayed with him the whole time, and we'd drive in to see him two or three times a week. And Carl was with him when he died. He was the one called us when Daddy died, and he was the one called us when Mama died.

She had hypertension, too, and so does Carl, and so do I. One time, I started bleeding from the nose and mouth, and the doctor said a blood vessel breaking did that, but what I think happened was, I ate some pure honey and had a allergic reaction. I was taking blood-pressure medicine for a long time, until right up before Mama died. But I stopped because I figured Mama was taking all that medicine, and she had surgery, and it didn't help her. God's the only one that can cure you. He's helped me, and I feel all right.

Greg was shy—real backward. Me and him was the same age, born the same month. I was born March 9, and he's born March 15, 1952.

Then my aunt Gracie donated the property to the church, and at her death, Greg's dad started building the church. Just before we got married, we was having church, I guess it was downtown. And there was a man—Royce Moore, from out of Cincinnati, Ohio—and he was having a revival, and that's when I got saved. I was seventeen. There were no serpents there. But I got saved when I was seventeen and was baptized. It's almost thirty years now.

We started going to a church over on Eleventh Street here in Middlesboro. It was Ben Laws's church. He's dead now. He was a serpent handler. That was the first time I ever seen Gregory handle a serpent, was over there. He hadn't handled before, not that I know of. His dad was handling serpents, and he just walked up, and Greg was standing there a-crying, and he laid the serpent in Greg's hand—a rattlesnake. I was standing next to him. It was what we call the serpent being dead under the anointment. The serpent *wasn't* dead, though. It was just laying there.

Greg's always had the desire to handle serpents. It never did frighten me. I've been around it, but I've never handled a serpent. I would love to, and I have no fear of them. Jamie, when he started preaching, the way he brought it out was, it was the Sign of all the believers. If you believed it, you would do it. And I told my husband, "I guess really I never had enough faith to go and flip the lid back and take one out of the box." For the past few years, though, I've had the desire. I would like to feel that anointing. If you say you believe it, somewhere down the road, you'll do it.

Greg doesn't handle a whole lot. Just recently, we were in church, and we were with Brother Punkin. I've seen [Greg handle] twice lately. I think the first time was when Punkin handed him one, and the second time was our last home-coming. He don't handle them very often. He really has to be covered up with the spirit of God before he'll move, because when he handles them, they just lay across his hand. They don't move or nothing.

My father-in-law cast out devils in demon-possessed people. He would talk to them. He enjoyed talking to people that the devil would speak out of and tell him what their names were. I guess he loved that as much as he loved handling serpents.

We was having church at my mama's before the church was built, and my ex-sister-in-law—the one who married my brother Carl—she prayed and repented. And she was up, and the house was full. They were handling serpents. My brother-in-law was handling fire. And Joyce leaps up shouting, speaking in tongues, and Greg's dad, he held up his hand and wanted everybody to listen. And he said, "There's something that just don't sound right." Joyce was speaking in tongues, but it wasn't God. And when he pointed his finger at her, she just fell on the floor. And then he begin to pray for her, and that devil was talking, and it was saying that Jesus was the devil. And he cast the devil off her. Joyce repented of her sins, but somewhere, that devil took over, and she didn't know how to resist him.

And there were two or three more—Hayden Becknol out of Lexington, Ann Watson from Williamsburg.

Hayden, Greg's dad prayed for him one night at my mom's and cast the devil out of him. He told the devil to go into the dog that was outside. And when he done that, the dog howled, made the awfulest, pitiful sound. It went mad a few days after that, and my uncle had to kill it. He had to destroy the dog.

Then Ann, she was a friend of mine, and she left her husband and come up here, and she started going to church. And I don't know how it come about.

Greg's dad just was praying for her one day at my mom's, and the devil began to act up in her, and talk, say things. Greg's dad told us, "When you cast out a devil, you have to keep your mind on God and keep calling on Jesus, saying his name," because, he said, "when that devil comes out, it's gotta go somewhere." And that name of Jesus is the only thing that devil doesn't want nothing to do with. So as long as you're calling on His name, that name, *Jesus*, has power over the devil. You can call on *Father*, and you can call on *Lord*, it don't bother the devil. It's when you speak that name of *Jesus* that you see him begin to act up.

Greg's mom and dad would always come and get Jamie when he was real little, take him over there to their house, and keep him awhile, then bring him back home. When Jamie was two years old, he wanted to dress up like his papaw. He wanted to wear western boots. He wanted to wear suits and ties. And Greg's dad started taking him to church with him.

That same year, Greg's dad was over in Dorton Branch at a revival. He took Jamie to a funeral over there and set him on the Bible stand, and Jamie sung. I don't remember what it was he sung. It probably wasn't a complete song, but he sung. He was talking good, though. Jamie is my doll baby. He started talking early, Jamie did. Everyone says he takes after me. He's one that loves to talk. His papaw was always proud of Jamie. I just wish he could have lived to see him now. Jamie wasn't even in church when his grandpa died. Now, he would sing in church, but he wasn't serving God. He wasn't saved. He had been going to church, but he really wasn't into it. I think he went more or less because of the girls that were going to church. When him and Linda started dating, I remember the night that she repented. And him and her, I think they were baptized the same time.

The first time I saw him handle a serpent, I was proud of him. It didn't frighten me. No, I've always been proud of him, proud to see that he's carrying on where his grandpa left off.

Papaw's church was started about 1978, and it's still there. The Full Gospel Tabernacle of Jesus Christ. For a little while after Gregory's dad died, Brother Pete Rowe was coming from Baxter [to preach], and they wanted to change the name to the Church of Jesus Christ, because that was what his church was over in Baxter, so the church went under that name for a little while.

Greg's dad had wanted it based on the full Gospel. There's a lot of people turned against him because of serpent handling, and they wouldn't come to church. But he believed just as strong. He was just telling them that it was the

Word of God. Either you believed or you didn't, and hell was going to be your home. He said, "I wouldn't deny it for my mother." His mother was dead, and he said, "If my mother walked through that door and said, 'Son, if you will deny this, I can come back,'" he said he wouldn't deny it for her. Some people hated him. They called him up, called him all kinds of names, and he was really criticized. One, because he preached Jesus to be God so strong. When he was put in jail that time, a lot of people were against him, a lot of people who lived around Nicholasville, Kentucky. Said he had deserted his family. And they died. Some of those people [who had him arrested] died [soon afterward]. And [people said he didn't send his children to] school or [to doctors either].

Greg was hardly ever sick, and growing up, Jamie was hardly ever sick. When he was a teenager, he got hurt. I can't remember. One time, he had a problem with his leg. He got so he could hardly walk, and he hadn't had an injury. I thought he had growing pains. Gregory took him to a man [who] had a tent revival one morning, and they prayed for him, and God healed him. Greg has always prayed for him. We didn't take him to no doctors. If you get bit, you trust God to deliver you.

It's sad, it's sad, Punkin Brown being bit. He was a precious person. He was a big help. He would come and have church with us when there was hardly no one there. There was a lot of people against Jamie, too, because he always stood by Punkin.

It's hard to count the number of serpent handlers, because some of them are [secretive about it]. They don't care to do it as long as [others may find out]. Jamie says they don't want publicity and don't want to be persecuted, but I think they are ashamed if they don't tell it. There's some Pentecostals around Pineville, Kentucky, that still handle. It's hard to know how many there is. And a lot of churches don't really tell when someone is serpent-bit. They will call you and say, "Pray for so-and-so. He's in trouble."

When Greg's daddy was real sick, him and Greg's mom made the decision that Joe Law would take over the pastorship. So it went real good for a while. And [then] there was a sister who got serpent-bit and got hurt, and her daughter come to church and threw a fit and took her to the doctor. Well, then, after that, they made a decision not to have serpents in the church for a while. My brother Carl never did agree to it. He wouldn't agree to taking the serpents out, but he didn't have no say-so in the church. But Brother Joe was the pastor, and they was a lot of people there influencing him. So they took the serpents out for almost a year. And then, one time, a sister got up and told them that our church was founded on the full Gospel. We believe in taking up serpents. We believe in Signs Following. So the people who were there left, and we brought the serpents back.

Greg, well, he never did claim to be a preacher, but he more or less took care of the church [after that]. And when Jamie and Linda got in the church and Jamie got saved, Greg prayed about it, and he felt like Jamie was more qualified to take over the pastorship than he was. Jamie was about twenty-two. He had been raised in serpent handling, and he's always believed in it all his life, ever since he'd been old enough to know what church was all about. Financially, the church doesn't have many bills. We have the light bill and a small payment that Gregory financed to buy a van for the church. Greg paid tithes out of his check, and Jamie helps. Gregory has more or less carried the financial things ever since the church has been built. He's always paid tithes, ever since we've been married. For a while, he paid them to his mom, and then when the church was built, he paid them to the church. Ten percent of whatever he makes.

Greg has two sisters and four brothers. Well, see, when Greg's dad was living, they all went to church, all except for Alan. Ronnie, Greg's oldest brother, he was going to church. And Bennie, Michael, and Ron's wife. Ronnie and his wife, they got saved. And Bennie got saved, and that's where he met his wife at, in the church. And Sissy and her husband, they got saved, and [Greg's] baby sister [Kathy]. My brother Jimmy, my brother Carl and his wife, Joyce, my sister Frances and her husband, my baby sister, Kathy—they were all going to church at that time. And after Greg's dad died, I don't know, something happened. All his brothers and sisters, you could hardly get them back in the church after that.

I've never seen Greg's mom handle serpents. Now, they said she did one time, and that was up at Baxter, at Pete Rose's church, and the serpent died, and they said they wouldn't let her handle their serpents no more. She's one, she don't get up and do a lot of shouting, and she sings some. But first time I've seen her dance in the spirit of God was in Barbourville at a revival. I got to see her dance that night. You don't see her move unless she gets covered up with the spirit of God. Then she'll move.

We used to baptize in Canaan Creek, Indian River, over on the belt line. It's a pretty good-sized creek, a real pretty place. It's growed up real bad now. People don't baptize there anymore because of all the water snakes. What you see me wear, this is what I wear when I go to church—blue-jean dresses—and that's what you wear to be baptized. Pin the skirt between your legs, so your dress won't come up.

Yeah, I been to a lot of baptizings. I've seen the Lord baptize Greg's dad one Sunday. They was about fifteen people being baptized that Sunday, and he baptized every one of 'em, and then he was just standing in the water after everybody else walked out, and it was just like something just laid him down in the water and brought him back up. It was beautiful. He never said anything [about that experience]. We watched it. It was amazing. Trina loves those stories. She used to go to sleep listening to tapes of her papaw.

I just know that the Word of God is the truth. They say that speaking in tongues is evidence of the Holy Ghost, but I believe the real gift of God is eternal life. I wish everybody could see heaven, but they can't. It's not for everybody. It's only for a chosen few. Everyone's not going to see Him. I have friends who say they're Christians, but the way I feel about it, they don't believe in the full Gospel, and they're not gonna make it. They're not gonna go where Jesus is.

In heaven, it's gonna be beautiful. Streets of gold, gates of pearl, walls of jasper. I don't know [exactly] what it's going to be like. I just want to make it.

Love. That's the most important thing, to have that love.

Photo by Fred Brown

THE FULL GOSPEL TABERNACLE IN JESUS NAME

MIDDLESBORO, KENTUCKY

> *"This thing I'm a-talking about will handle fire; it will take up serpents; it will cast the devil out; it'll do all the signs."*

ON THIS WARM APRIL NIGHT in Middlesboro, Kentucky, the Full Gospel Tabernacle in Jesus Name is holding a revival to try to build up its thinning membership. Since the recent deaths of Punkin and Melinda Brown, a few members, says Pastor Jamie Coots, have set free the serpents they kept for handling at services. But fear of being bitten accounts for only part of the problem. It is more likely the legal consequences of serpent handling that are keeping away some of the former members. Parents worry about the precedent that was set when Punkin's five children were removed from his home because a Tennessee juvenile-court judge ruled that their presence in church constituted a danger to their safety. Tonight, preachers from several serpent-handling churches have come together to help Jamie Coots spread the Word and convince people to return to the fold.

But at its core, the Full Gospel Tabernacle in Jesus Name is a family-run operation that is not likely to change, regardless of outside threats. There's too much history in it, and too much faith. Tommy and Louvernia Coots, Jamie's paternal grandparents, started the church in 1978. His maternal grandparents, Charlene and George Washington Turner, were stalwart members.

The little white church is only a few blocks from the main street that runs through the beginning of the Middlesboro suburbs. Turn right, cross the railroad tracks, take another right into the gravel driveway, and you're there. You have to look for it, since the line of trees on the right side of the driveway and a hill on the left almost obscure it from view of the casual passerby. On the road below the church is the bright blue house with white trim where Charlene and George Turner brought up their family and where Tommy Coots held some of his first services in the community. On the right of the church is the former site of the Cootses' log house, which recently burned to the ground.

The church is a simple one-story building with white siding. Four brick-and-cement steps lead to the entry landing; there is a black wrought-iron hand railing on the left side. A ramp for wheelchairs is on one side of the entrance. On the other is a bench where early-comers—mostly men—gather to talk before services. At the peak of the roof is a handmade cross. Beneath that, a hand-lettered sign reads, "Full Gospel Tabernacle in Jesus Name. Serv. Wed. P.M. 7:00. Sat. 7 P.M. Sun. 1 P.M. Pastor Jamie Coots."

Inside, the building has red indoor-outdoor carpeting except for the area in front of the altar, where there is a smooth parquet floor. Seating consists of a few wooden pews and some theater seats welded together. A sign on the pulpit reads, "Jesus Made the World," and a placard on the wall says, "For there is one God, and one mediator between God and men—the man Jesus Christ." There is also a mandate that all serpent-handling churches believe: "To preach in the church you must PREACH THE WORD."

It doesn't matter, though, what the church looks like, how simple or unprepossessing it is. It's what happens inside that counts. The history inside this small building includes people saved, fire and serpents handled, poison swallowed, devils cast out, prophecies spoken, songs delivered directly from God, and lost souls won over to the Lord, all through the Word. This is the building where God moved through Tommy Coots to deliver miracles, and where Jamie

Coots first brought Linda to see what his family believed in. This is the place where Gregory Coots and his wife, Linda, sing together and watch grandchildren Katrina and Cody grow up as they raised their only living child, Jamie—in the Word, in the spirit. This is the building where Louvernia Coots, who has lived spotlessly, sits on a bench on the rostrum every service and waits to see what else the Lord wants her to do in this life.

On this spring evening, Jamie preaches and plays the guitar, his wife and mother sing, his father plays the electric guitar, and his daughter plays the organ. So far, Cody, born in 1992, doesn't take part in services, but he knows what the church stands for.

Trina has a remarkable stage presence. "God gave her piano lessons," says her father. "The other night, she got a CD that is a recorded professional, Ricky Skaggs. She can play along with it, just like they do. She still amazes me to be seven years old. And she amazes people in church. Most people that's in church that's been singing a couple of years, they don't know what chord they sing in, because they don't play. See, that is the advantage of playing with yourself as you sing. So she'll get up and sing, and she'll tell them D chord. And they will just look at me and grin. No doubt, what's going through their mind is, 'How did she know what she sings in?'

"Dad was going to pay for music lessons for her. Linda wanted her to learn to read music, because she took band in high school. She knows how to read music, and she figured that may be an advantage to Trina somewhere down the road. We took her [to lessons] for two weeks, and for one thing, they wanted her to play little folk songs, and all she wanted to play was gospel. That's all we listen to, so that's all she wants to play. She come home after the second lesson and told her mom that she just didn't want to take lessons anymore. And Linda said, 'Jamie, I'm afraid if we give her lessons, if somebody were to ask who gave her lessons, and she was to tell them, they would give that person all the credit for what she knew. I don't want it to be that way. I want God to get all the credit.' So she quit. I told her that was up to her. If she wanted to learn it, fine, but she just said she wasn't interested."

Tonight, Trina wears a pale blue dress. She is so small that she is nearly hidden behind the large electric organ. Her legs dangle from the bench, too short to reach the floor. Her long, silky, light brown hair is pulled up into a ponytail, making her look as fresh and crisp as a new morning.

The musicians are tuning their electric and six-string guitars. A small crowd has gathered for the service. Some of the members are fanning themselves. Those just arriving embrace their friends and shake hands with visitors. Children squirm on the theater chairs, and a couple of babies crawl on the floor.

Trina looks at her father to indicate that she is ready. He smiles and nods, and the music erupts, filling every corner of the Full Gospel Tabernacle, Trina in the lead singing "Everyone's Talking about a Man Like Jesus." Jamie and Greg provide the rhythm for the gospel hymn, a favorite among the serpent handlers. Cameron Short's electric guitar peels off layers of sound as he runs country riffs.

"Praise God!" somebody shouts.

Jamie starts in with "I Wonder What They Are Doing in Heaven Today." Beneath his powerful voice, Trina gives a throaty shout as her hands work furiously on the organ. Sometimes, she plays with one hand, raises the other, and waves it quickly. Sometimes, she tosses back her head and sings with her eyes shut.

Cameron Short runs his fingers up and down the electric guitar like wildfire. The congregation is now in the spirit, singing, swaying, raising their hands and shouting "Praise God!" and "Oh, Jesus!" Some stand to clap and sing and dance in front of their seats.

Next, Jamie begins a bluesy gospel song. He is venturing down into the deep, deep blues when, all of a sudden, the floor begins to shake. The entire congregation is stamping like a small army on the march.

Trina hollers, "Aaaaah, Looorddddd!"

Linda, who has the gift of tongues and prophecy, begins to shout, "Ohhhhh, God. Help me, Jesus. Oh, God. Save me, Jesus. Hallelujah. Oh, I praise You, Jesus. Thank You, my God. Ohhhhh."

Cameron Short continues his hot country-guitar licks.

The sound is joyful and uninhibited, but occasionally, Jamie grimaces from the pain in his strumming hand. It was the previous December when he suffered the serious bite on the middle finger of his right hand. The end of the finger, which he will eventually lose, is shrunken and black—mummified—though the nail remains intact on the leathery flesh. From the knuckle down, bare bone shows. It's been five months now, and Jamie's wound is still agonizingly painful, his hand still swollen and inflamed. But he's learned to live with the pain. He's waiting to see if the finger will drop off of its own accord, because he has put his faith in the Lord to heal him.

Jamie segues into another song as Cameron Short's hands flash up and down the strings of his instrument so smoothly that his guitar hisses like the rattle-snakes in the boxes on the rostrum. Then Trina begins to sing. She grabs the microphone and pulls the cord out so that she has plenty of room to move around. Her performance is energetic and uninhibited. She sings "Jesus Said It, I Believe It." Before the song is over, Linda begins to speak in tongues. The music stops momentarily, then begins again, Trina picking up the melody in midsong without missing a beat.

Jamie tells the congregation that he has just returned from Macedonia, Alabama, and the Rock House Holiness Church of God, the place where his best friend, Punkin Brown, died half a year earlier. He has had only a few hours of sleep, because he has driven all night to get back in time for the revival at his own church.

He begins to preach about a ship that went down at sea. "They were fearful, and it went down to the bottom. People ask me how I feel about going back, how I feel about Punkin. I feel good. He's a good God. He's merciful, full of love and kindness. Lot of people not very kind today, not merciful. God's merciful. I appreciate the Lord. He's a good God. I appreciate what He has done for me. He's always been there. I'm so appreciative that I know who He is. Lot of people today, they worship they know not what. I'm glad I know the name. I'm glad I don't have to get down to pray to this or that, but I can get down and call on His name."

From the back of the church, someone shouts an amen.

"I love the Lord, love His name," Jamie continues. "When I pray and begin to seek the Lord a little more and get over my troubles and trials in my life, I talk to Him. He's always there. He's always ready to give a holy hand. No matter what we may go through, He's still God. I appreciate Him, and I love Him. It was kindly hard down there [in Macedonia] last night. First time I been back since Brother Punkin got bit. It was all I could do to sit and watch the floor. But God is still God."

"Yes, He is," Brother Cameron Short says.

"One of these days, I'm going to fight my last battle."

"Amen."

"You are going to fight yours, and I'm going to fight mine. Scripture says it is once appointed for a man to die. You can't put it off. We can't skip it. We are going to face it, brother. Just pray to be ready to go. That's the main thing. We got to fight our fight."

"Yes, we do."

"When we die, we better die in the Lord. When we lay down our life, we need to be ready. Scripture says we are not promised a tomorrow. We need to live every day like it is our last and be ready to go."

"Amen."

"Praise the Lord. Praise the Lord."

"Thank You, Jesus."

When Jamie sits down, Greg strides to the pulpit. Whenever Greg Coots is moved by the spirit, he begins to weep, and he is moved tonight. Tears stream down his face.

"The Lord has been there when I was sick," he says. "He was there every time when I called on Him. He heard and answered my prayers. I thank Him. I was thinking about some things. I want to talk about the Lord's will. Sometimes, I do a lot of things on my job—sit and read, talk to the Lord. Things may come to my mind. I want to start with one verse in I Peter, third chapter, nineteenth verse: 'By which also he went and preached unto the spirits in prison.' *Speaking of Jesus*. I begin to think in my mind, when He got there and He was preaching in this prison, maybe some of them didn't know what was going on. The Lord was preaching Scripture. And somebody said, 'That's Him. That's the Lord. That I know.' He said, 'How do you know?' He said, 'I heard His voice.' He said, 'Yeah, yeah, that's Him. That's the Lord. I remember. That's Him. That's the Lord.'"

"Ohhhhh, glory."

"Yeaahhhhhh."

"I began to think in my mind what they were doing in that prison. Oh, the Lord is good. 'Yeah,' he said. 'I know that is the Lord. That's what I know.'"

"Yeeeeaaaaaaahhhhh."

Some in the congregation begin to stamp their feet. Some hop up and down.

"Praise Jesus."

"Ahhh," says Greg. "So many, so many knew who He was. They begin to tell, 'That's Him. That's the Lord.' Ahhh, but how many, how many really knows the Lord?"

"Come *on*! Tell it like it is."

Glenn Dukes, a preacher from Chattanooga, takes up the cause behind the pulpit. He is a big man with a big voice.

"We need to put all we can into this," he intones. "This may be the last night we have here, see. So we need to put everything we got into praising the Lord tonight, while we are alive and while we can. So let's everybody come together. We are all one body. There's just one body. So let's everybody do what you can. Put a little effort into it, and when somebody sits down, don't worry about them sitting down. *They probably tired.* Shout on! You get the fire in the Holiness, we won't be tired no more, will we?"

The resounding chorus of shouts sounds like a wind in the forest, lifting and falling in intensity.

"In Your mighty name," says Dukes over the din.

And then Brother Raford Dunn from Chattanooga jumps up. Immediately, he falls to his knees and shouts, "You have to humble yourself before the Lord!"

He picks up a bottle of kerosene, lights the wick, and begins to dance with the fire bottle in his hand. Flames lap at his shirt sleeve and ignite. He slaps them out and puts the bottle down.

"Now, we know that the church is a-backing up," he shouts. "Maybe not the church, but the people. You might as well think about this, because the Bible says we need to come back and walk and talk to God every day. *Hallelujah.* Ole Daniel, he prayed three times a day. He walked with God. *Hallelujah.* We can have more than what we got. I'm not saying you ain't got enough to go to heaven. We have to take it all, every bit of it. We can't take out what we want and leave the rest of it. You have to take it all. He told me to love my brother, and if I don't love my brother, then I've left the spirit of the Lord, because God is love. *Hallelujah.* Glory to God. He loves the praises of His people. *Hallelujah.*

"He said, 'These things I do. Even greater can *you* be.' *Hallelujah.* If He walked on the water, then *you* can walk on it, too, if you walk in the spirit of the Lord. Is that right? Haaaa? Glory to God. You going to have to be willing to accept what God gives you. Huuuh? Huuuh? I didn't come up here to see what this church was going to do. I didn't come up here to see what *this* sister was going to do and *that* brother's going to do. I come up here to *obey the Lord.* Is that all right? *Glory to God.* I didn't drive all the way from Chattanooga up here, *Glory to God,* to make a fool of myself."

He asks Jamie Coots to open his Bible to the Book of Romans, from which he intends to preach. For the next forty-five minutes, Raford and Jamie do a call-and-response from Romans.

Finally, Dunn says, "I'm getting short winded, but I still like to do this. *Read.*"

Jamie reads another verse, and Dunn says, "God sent Jesus in the likeness of sinful flesh. Jesus walked this earth just like me and you are walking today. *Hallelujah. Glory to God.* They crucified Him, *glory to God.* Somebody comes along and just hurts your feelings, hurt your feelings just a little bit. 'Ahhh, I'm just going to quit. *I'm a-going to quit.*' Haaaa? Well, God bless you. They *hung* Jesus Christ. They hung Him for what He believed. *Hallelujah. Glory to God.* And we walk around all the time *with our feelings in our hands.* Haaaa? *Hallelujah.* We say, 'I'm not going back to that church. The pastor *hurt my feelings.*' The pastor may a-*not* hurt your feelings. All you're doing is trying to find an *excuse to quit. Hallelujah. Glory to God.* You are not walking in the spirit of God. Ain't no way. There ain't no way that the spirit is going to hurt your feelings, *glory to God.* If you got your feelings hurt, then you wasn't walking in the spirit."

Dunn dances across the floor and begins to breathe hard. His chest is heaving. Sweat is pouring from his matted hair. He shouts unintelligible verses of Scripture. Coming to a stop in front of the pulpit, he folds his arms around his bone-thin frame and narrows his lips. He looks back at Jamie. "For the carnal mind is sin. The carnal mind is huge. Huuuh?" He pauses. "Read some more."

Jamie reads some more, and Dunn gets his second wind. "You take a field of cows. You fix the field where they can't get out. But just as soon as you open that gate, some of them cows is going to get out, ain't they? Or all of them. That's what we done. We've let down the sanctity of Holiness. We've opened up the gates, and the devil moved in and destroyed everything there is in the house. I believe tonight that God can do anything, except fail. I can see Him every day. Every morning, you wake up, you look out for the church, you see God. You see trees, fields of green—that's the work of the Lord. See it rain, whatever the weather may be, God did it. We ought to be pleased with it, because God made it." He looks at Jamie. "Read some more."

Jamie reads another verse, to which Dunn replies, "Where is the Holy Ghost? It is Jesus Christ Himself, walking among us. Church, what are we doing? *What are we doing?* Church, why haven't we gotten fat working in the church? What are we doing? *We are not obeying God.* This thing I'm a-talking about will handle fire; it will take up serpents; it will cast the devil out; it'll do all the Signs. You hear me? We need to lay the flesh down and take up the cause and follow God, just like it's written in the Word. *Just like it's written in the Word.* This right here will never leave you. It'll never lead you wrong, *glory to God.* But there's one thing about it. You going to have to live according to this. *Hallelujah, hallelujah.*"

Now, Preacher John Brown stands and begins to shout over the *amens* and *praise Gods* that have filled the church from floor to ceiling. "Bless His name tonight. He is a worthy God, *amen,* and worthy of all praise. I praise Him tonight. He said, 'I'll never leave you, *amen.* I'll never forsake you.' I believe that tonight. I believe He'll go all the way with you. I was thinking tonight about the Signs of the Gospel, *amen,* how the apostles worked, *amen,* when the Holy Ghost moved on them. I believe God's Word will take care of you. [People] leave this world in car wrecks every day, *amen.* I think we are predestinated. I am worried about life tonight. I am not talking about this life, *amen,* but the life eternal."

John Brown skips across the floor behind the pulpit, and the service erupts into a roar of sound.

"Tell it like it is!" somebody shouts.

"Praise the Lord."

"Hallelujah!"

"Amen."

Amen.

THE ELKINS FAMILY

JOLO, WEST VIRGINIA

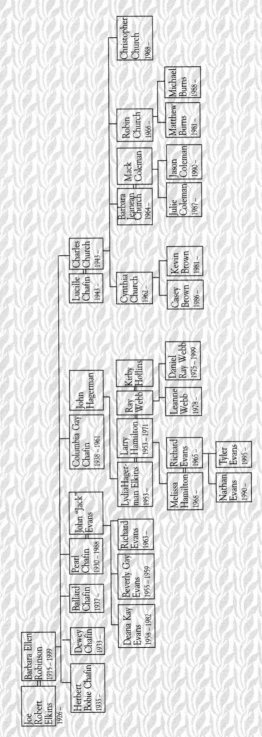

Joe Robert Elkins 1926–

Barbara Ellen Robinson 1915–1999

Herbert Bobie Chafin 1935–

Dewey Chafin 1933–

Ballard Chafin 1937–

Pearl Chafin 1930–1988

John "Jack" Evans

Deana Kay Evans 1958–1982

Beverly Gay Evans 1955–1959

Richard Evans 1963–

Columbia Gay Chafin 1938–1961

John Hagerman

Lydia Hagerman Elkins 1953–

Larry Hamilton 1953–1971

Ray Webb

Kirby Hollins

Melissa Hamilton 1968–

Richard Evans 1965–

Leanne Webb 1978–

Daniel Ray Webb 1975–1999

Nathan Evans 1990–

Tyler Evans 1995–

Lucille Chafin 1943–

Charles Church 1943–

Cynthia Church 1962–

Casey Brown 1986–

Kevin Brown 1981–

Barbara Jeanean Church 1964–

Mack Coleman

Julie Coleman 1987–

Jason Coleman 1990–

Robin Church 1966–

Matthew Burns 1981–

Michael Burns 1988–

Christopher Church 1968–

JOLO,
WEST VIRGINIA

> The church becomes a refuge
> in places where life is hard.

JOLO, WEST VIRGINIA, POPULATION FIVE HUNDRED, is so small that it has no courthouse or city hall—only a tiny post office to mark its official presence east of Grundy, Virginia. The mountainous terrain leaves Jolo's inhabitants little choice but to work in the coal mines in and around McDowell County, where their fathers and grandfathers worked before them. Since 1883, the industry has been both the bane and the bounty of the area. Figures from the 1992 economic census show that in McDowell County alone, there are sixty-five mining establishments that provide a total of nine hundred jobs. But statistics don't reveal the real truth: The companies prosper, not the miners, who almost inevitably end up on disability with black lung or emphysema.

The two-lane road that leads into Jolo from Grundy climbs Bradshaw Mountain, where houses and trailers perch precariously on the steep hillsides. In this isolated section of the Appalachian Mountains, Virginia and West Virginia share joint custody of some of the most beautiful scenery in the country—and some of the most heartbreaking poverty.

Descending from the mountain, which is resplendent with green pines and hemlocks, you get your first sight of Jolo in the valley below. Except for the rutted scars left by strip mining, the natural background is breathtaking. But proof of hardscrabble lives dominates the roadsides—cinder-block houses, trailers, makeshift structures covered with insulation sheets, rusty skeletons of abandoned automobiles, and random piles of litter. Some yards are lined with cages of fighting cocks, while others boast neat flower beds and porch swings. The accouterments of the properties reflect the difference between those residents who still hope and those who have given up.

Three Forks Road, part of Route 83, the two-lane highway that winds through Jolo, is sprinkled with fine grit from the coal trucks that drive through daily. This is an unforgiving land. Rocks rise from the earth as ubiquitously as weeds. Parts of the area are shadowed for almost half the day by the surrounding mountains. Tug Fork River meanders alongside the winding road, but it, too, suffers from man-made pollution. The river emanates from Dry Fork, then runs into the Big Sandy, which eventually winds its way into the Ohio and Mississippi Rivers.

In Jolo's tiny business section, most enterprises—beauty shops, thrift stores, video dealers, a tanning salon—are housed in trailers and decrepit buildings. Here, too, you see incongruous combinations. The yard of one house is littered with trash, yet beside its white picket fence, hundreds of daffodils have been lovingly planted. Nothing, it seems, is ever thrown away in Jolo. An abandoned school bus sits in one yard, and rusting automobile fenders, hoods, and trunks are used for riprap along the banks of the creek, dry now from the long summer drought.

Clothes hang on lines in almost every yard or are strung across front porches, but there are few people outside except on Saturdays, when nearly every family hauls out clothing and household items for unadvertised yard sales. Periodically, makeshift crosses decorated with plastic flowers mark the sites of fatal accidents along the steep, winding roads. A sign points the way to a place called War, West Virginia. A cinder-block car wash called Niki's Buggy Bath bears the tongue-in-cheek warning, "Enter at own risk."

Off Three Forks Road is a monument to the coal miners who have lived, worked, and died in McDowell County. Beneath the imposing sculpted figure of a miner, the inscription reads, "Out of the tunnels walks a blacken[ed] man clean with the courage it took to go in."

If it is lunchtime, visitors to Jolo quickly learn that there are only two restaurants in town. One serves takeout food, to be eaten at its single roadside picnic table. The other is a small, homey place mysteriously named the Hemlock. Nobody who works there seems to remember why the restaurant has that name or appreciates the irony of it. It's a neighborly place with artificial flowers in vases, puffy curtains gathered at the windows, and a simple, straightforward menu. Its eight small tables are almost always in use, and the parking lot is a gathering place for the town's young people.

No fast-food franchises or steakhouses are to be found in Jolo, but the town has an abundance of churches. In this part of the country, the soul is hungrier than the body, and there are plenty of places that provide that kind of sustenance. Along the streets of Jolo, houses of worship—Community Church of God, Primitive Baptist Church, Community House of God, Living Word Outreach, Hale Creek Pentecostal Holiness—are wedged haphazardly among residences and businesses. The church becomes a refuge in places where life is hard, and Jesus represents a promise and an escape. Weekend services are a reprieve from bone-breaking work and an uncertain future. The church offers comfort, friendship, music, and entertainment. An innocent kind of joy—sometimes even ecstasy and rapture—pervades the services and provides transcendence from everyday hardships. Worshipers can count on a good, old-fashioned sermon served up with fire and spirit. They can also count on music that is moving and energetic enough to rival any local rock concert. It is easy to see why so many people here have turned to God: Church is one of the most fulfilling aspects of their lives.

Women marry young in this part of the country, some as early as fourteen or fifteen. The West Virginia Census says that women under twenty account for 27 percent of the births in the state. Education is another area where poverty and geography play a part. Fewer than half the citizens of McDowell County—42 percent—have a high-school education, and only 5 percent are college graduates. The 13 percent unemployment exceeds the national average, and per capita income is $12,537. According to February 1999 estimates by the United States Census Bureau, almost twelve thousand people in the county—over a third of the population—live in poverty.

There are other factors that keep the area mired in indigence. Of the 32,662 inhabitants of the county, 10,000 are Social Security recipients, 3,000 are retired workers, and 3,258 are Supplemental Security Income recipients, which means that a good percentage of the citizens are on some sort of assistance. Few people migrate to the county, and many who are born within its boundaries leave to seek better educational and financial opportunities.

It was in the latter part of the 1800s that the railroad made it possible to transport coal from the rich mines in southwestern West Virginia. McDowell County swelled almost overnight with new towns and inhabitants. Thousands of European immigrants came to work in the coal fields. By 1910, the black population had expanded from 0.1 percent to almost 31 percent.

But although wages were adequate and housing was cheap, get-rich-quick dreams turned out to be delusional, because it was the companies that controlled the destinies of the miners. Workers were required to lease company tools and equipment, and costs for company-owned housing and goods from the company store were deducted from workers' pay. Scrip, a monetary system developed by the companies, was the form of payment used, and it was redeemable only at the company store. When the miners received pay raises, prices at the company stores were simultaneously inflated. Miners were also cheated through a practice known as cribbing, a method used by the companies to alter the weight of the coal brought in by miners so that they were paid for less than they had actually extracted.

Ever since their Scots-Irish ancestors were stopped in their journey west by the rugged and unforgiving mountains, the land has been holding West Virginians hostage to its buried treasure and a never-ending cycle of hard work and deprivation. Through more than a century, this cycle has continued, but so has the spirit of a people whose toughness and forbearance have long represented the very essence of endurance.

A SOLDIER
OF GOD

On Friday, February 5, 1999, Barbara Elkins, eighty-
three-year-old matriarch of the Church of the Lord Jesus in Jolo, West Virginia, died
peacefully in her sleep. At her funeral, held the following Tuesday in chilly, rainy weather
at the little church she and her husband, Bob, founded, family and friends turned out
to commemorate her life. Her family—composed of her husband, four living children,
thirty-five grandchildren, and six great-grandchildren—mourned her death, as did church
members and friends, many from other Signs Following churches in the Southeast.
Ironically, Barbara, who had handled serpents for almost fifty years, requested beforehand that no snakes be taken up at her funeral. "The little ones might get hurt," she
said.

ON THE DAY OF BARBARA ELKINS'S FUNERAL, the February sky is overcast, and
rain falls intermittently. Outside the small, white-frame Church of the Lord Jesus,
mourners skirt the muddy pools that have collected in the gravel parking lot
and huddle in small groups, talking quietly, their shoulders hunched against the
weather. Friends greet each other solemnly, shake their heads, tell stories about
how Barbara inspired them. Here and there, women weep on the shoulders of
husbands or acquaintances. One by one, the people slowly make their way into
the church, reluctant to say good-bye to an old friend.

Inside the church, Barbara's body, surrounded by sprays of pink flowers, lies in her gold-and-white casket by the altar, dominating this building for the last time. Grief is palpable among the mourners. The church has lost its founder, mother, wife, sister, friend.

In contrast to its usual robust music and energetic preaching, the church is quiet while the mourners file in. There is faint whispering, ragged weeping, a baby's cry. Even the children are subdued. Barbara's many grandchildren and great-grandchildren all called her Mamaw or Mom. Many of them have already experienced the death of loved ones, but for Mamaw to pass on is unthinkable. Nobody knows quite how to proceed without her, especially her husband, Bob Elkins, preacher of the church and Barbara's partner for nearly fifty years. He sits in the front row surrounded by his family. Gone are his usual stamina and vibrant personality. On this day, he is overcome with grief and stunned disbelief.

A black choir from Spirit and Truth Ministries in Alabaster, Alabama, comes in to pay tribute to Barbara. Barbara's granddaughter Lydia has attended their church since her husband, Kirby, was transferred to Alabama. The choir members sit together on the third row of the church, praising God and occasionally speaking in tongues.

Family members and church members, many carrying babies or leading children by the hands, take their seats. Friends from out of state, neighbors, and scholars who have studied the serpent-handling religion greet the family and nod at each other. A reporter is politely but firmly requested not to take pictures or make notes during the service.

When at last the music begins—piano, organ, and guitar—emotions run high. This is the final opportunity to celebrate Barbara Elkins's life as she lived it—with dedication and dignity and enthusiasm. It is a time to play her favorite hymns and to tell stories about her accomplishments and her miracles. Her life was the church, and the church was her life. Everyone agrees she is better off in heaven, free of the pain for which she refused to seek medical attention, but they mourn for themselves. There is singing, preaching, crying, clapping, and exultation.

"She was the makings of me," testifies a mourner. "I used to dance for other people, [but] since I met Barbara, I've been dancing for God."

Carl Porter tells about a dream of Barbara's that Bob Elkins related to him before the funeral service. "Barb said she dreamed she was on a trip," says Carl,

Barbara Elkins handles a serpent during a Jolo church service, c. 1995
Photo by Verlin Short

"and she'd been traveling all night. 'I barely made it home,' she told her husband." Porter says that if a saint like Barbara Elkins barely made it home to heaven, he can't imagine how hard it will be for the rest of us. Then he talks about how hard it is to follow the road that leads to glory. "It's difficult, but it's good for the old, and it's good for the young, and it makes you speak in an unknown tongue."

After two hours during which Barbara's friends recount her good deeds and remember her as a prayer warrior, a soldier of God, and a saint, the family asks friends to come forward to view the body before the casket is carried to the grave site a few hundred feet away on the mountain. Several crumple with grief. Lydia starts up the aisle toward her children and collapses. Two granddaughters lean into the casket and weep inconsolably.

At the back of the church, just before the casket is closed, a small boy tries to get the attention of his cousins. "Nana is sick," he says, looking toward the front of the church. Nobody pays any attention. "Nana is sick," he says again, and sits down in his chair, confused. He seems to absorb, perhaps for the first time, the enormity of what has happened. Barbara Elkins, matriarch of the Elkins family, is making her final appearance in the Church of the Lord Jesus. For the Elkins family and the Jolo church, it is the end of an era.

Outside, it is raining harder. The crowd begins to thin out to start the muddy walk up to the burial site. The mourners file by the casket one last time, then step through the side door and out into the rain.

Barbara Elkins was the mother and grandmother of a long line of serpent-handling believers. She saw her mission on earth as building a church, living a rigid Christian life, and believing in God. In January 1998, she fell and hurt her knee. She was bedridden for a while and was confined to a wheelchair after that. For as long as most people could remember, Barbara Elkins had stood in front of the pulpit, fully participating in services, but toward the end, she sat on a bench behind the pulpit, often bouncing a grandchild on her lap, always watching those who handled serpents. But her spirit remained indomitable. For a while, she handled serpents from her wheelchair, but in time, she grew too frail to continue the practice she so firmly believed in.

Until the church was recently remodeled, two long pews sat on the small stage behind the pulpit. One had a long, flowered pillow and a smaller pillow. This is where Barbara always sat during services. Her granddaughter and namesake, Barbara Coleman, wipes away a tear as she describes how it always makes her sad to see those pillows. She can't help it, but she resents it when somebody else sits there now. "When I come in, I automatically look for her, and I get sad," says Barbie. "I know that after Punkin died, and after Mamaw died, every time I went to church, they would sing a song. And I couldn't hear [the music] because it would remind me of Punkin, or now, when you come in the church and you don't see Mamaw . . ." She stops for a moment to regain her composure. "Mamaw had been gone from services for a long time, and I had been gone for a long time, but when I used to come on a regular basis, my mamaw was here. You always look in that corner, and to me, if somebody is sitting in her seat, I don't like it. I want them to get up, because it was just Mamaw's seat."

Over the years, Barbara Elkins lost one child and many friends to serpent bites and other tragedies, but her faith in God never wavered nor did her conviction that the reward for a life well lived would come only after death. Her long black dresses and the thick white hair she had left uncut since her twenty-first birthday made her a dramatic presence in the Church of the Lord Jesus. Even though her husband was the preacher, there was never any doubt that Barbara was the real foundation of the church. She could be fierce when she thought people were breaking God's laws, but she had a beauty that came from within. "I hate to say this," she said modestly in the last interview she granted, three weeks before she died, "but they say I'm just like my mother. She was real pretty." Still, it was the strength of conviction inside Barbara Elkins that people admired. A college student who sat in on her last interview commented that during that hour, Barbara's blue eyes seemed to be seeing something far off. It was "as if she was having a conversation with the angels," the student said.

Barbara seemed to draw light and strength from her conviction that she was following God's mandate. Once she picked up a serpent, she assumed a fierce determination that commanded respect even from nonbelievers. "When the spirit moves on me to handle a serpent, He will take care of me," she said. "I have read the Bible, but most of the time, I get it from the Lord. I'm by myself all day, and I meditate in my heart all day. I've had my mind on the Lord for more than fifty-three years."

She was born in Kentucky's coal-mining country, where the land is so steep and jagged that it seems impossible that people could carve out even a ragged existence. Her parents, Jerry and Serece Branham Robinson, were Old Regular Baptists, members of a mountain religion whose roots were planted by the pioneers who came to Appalachia from Ulster, Ireland. They were Scots-Irish people already accustomed to hardship and deprivation. Her mother died when Barbara was about seven, after which she was raised by a stepmother and her grandmother, who was the most influential person in her life. "Her grandmother was a Cherokee Indian, and she was a hard woman, from what Mom told and from stories I picked up from cousins," says Barbara's daughter Lucille.

When Barbara left Kentucky, she was probably thirteen or fourteen, says Lucille. "Back in those days, it wasn't that uncommon [for girls to leave home at such a young age]. She was about fourteen when she got married the first time."

It was not until her twenty-sixth year that Barbara became convinced of the power of serpent handling, when George Went Hensley handed her a snake at a church meeting in Virginia. "I remember I was just getting a good blessing, and he just walked over and handed me the rattler," Barbara said. "Oh, yeah, I was scared, but when the power of God gets on you, you are not afraid. For fifty-three years since, I have been handling them, and I have been bitten sixteen times, by both copperheads and rattlers. I'll tell you, the copperhead hurts me the worst. But I got a hornet's sting once that a serpent never did do me like that. I got heavy around my heart and numb all over. It lasted about twenty-four hours."

Barbara not only handled serpents—she drank poison, spoke in tongues, and laid hands on the sick as well.

When she was twenty years old, she experienced her first great miracle. In suffering a relapse of the tuberculosis she had contracted as a child, she hemorrhaged. Her family gave up hope for her recovery, convinced that she was spiraling toward death. Then she sent a prayer handkerchief to the Holiness church where Hensley was preaching. That evening, a child knocked on her door and handed back the handkerchief, which had been prayed over by Hensley and the congregation. "I would have pinned it on me, but I was healed," she said. "My room was about seven or eight steps up from my porch. I walked down them steps and walked to the bus stop and walked from the bus stop across town and up about three flights of stairs, where they had the service. I went to church that night. Yeah. That just done something to me. I knowed it was God. I was in bad shape. I had hemorrhaged. They anointed the handkerchief with oil and prayed over it. On Monday morning, I went to washing my kitchen walls down. And my daughter said, 'Are you better?' She didn't know. She looked up and clapped her hands and said, 'Praise the Lord!'"

Barbara never stopped mourning the death of her daughter Columbia to snakebite at the age of twenty-three, but she remained steadfast in her religion. She adopted Columbia's daughter Lydia, then nine, and took care of her until Lydia married.

And she always fretted about her son Dewey Chafin, child of her first marriage, and one of the best-known handlers among the Signs Followers. Dewey, born in 1933, has a penchant for fearlessly handling exotic snakes. He has been bitten 133 times. At the Kingston, Georgia, homecoming just before Barbara took to a wheelchair, Dewey picked up four large rattlers, two in each hand, his signature move. Earlier that day, a young woman had been bitten when she was handed a snake by her husband. and Barbara Elkins felt ill at ease. Somehow, the air seemed different. The sky outside was black with an approaching storm. The barometer was falling. Occasionally, the church lights blinked off and then on again. Suddenly, a vicious thunderstorm flashed across the Georgia Piedmont, and the lights flickered and went out, leaving the tiny church in darkness. The congregation, which had been singing, fell silent. After each crash of thunder, the buzzing of rattlesnakes could be heard above the rain.

Dewey Chafin was a victim of the elements. He could not see to put the snakes into the boxes, and to put them down would have placed the congregation at risk. So he stood in the dark holding four venomous snakes. When the lightning flashed again, Barbara Elkins could be seen at his side, her hand on his shoulder. It was a ghostlike image. For fifteen minutes, Dewey held the writhing snakes in the darkened church, and for fifteen minutes, Barbara remained by his side, her hand on his arm.

When the lightning and thunder receded into the distance and the lights came on, Dewey stood before the pulpit with glassy eyes. He seemed disoriented. But there was no mistaking the emotion of Barbara Elkins. She was angry. She was angry at Dewey for having held the snakes throughout the storm and angry at the other men for not coming forward to help him. Most of all, she had feared that Dewey was not fully anointed when he took up those serpents, that he was handling on faith, and Barbara always warned her children not to handle unless they were anointed, because that is the time when God gives His permission for the Sign Followers to handle serpents.

She watched as Dewey stuffed the rattlers back inside their boxes and, still dazed, walked down the aisle and out of the church. When he returned, it was with an Eastern diamondback rattler, a much larger and angrier snake than the ones he had held in the dark. This one was shedding its skin, a time when snakes become nervous and ill tempered and constitute an even greater threat than usual.

Barbara put a hand to her mouth and began to pray. Nothing felt right to her. She had a sense that things were out of control, so she called the Jolo people together and insisted that they leave the homecoming service. She could not be coaxed to stay even for the picnic that was being laid out on tables on the lawn. Her granddaughter Lydia followed her. Outside, they passed tables laden with fried chicken, gravy, biscuits, coleslaw, corn, potatoes, pudding, iced tea, cakes, pies, and vegetables.

Barbara Elkins, undaunted, majestic in her determination, walked by the tables without a glance. "The Jolo people," she said, "are going home."

IN HER OWN WORDS
BARBARA ELKINS

Taped three weeks before her death, this was the last interview Barbara Elkins granted, and the only one she gave in the last ten years of her life.

I'm from Kentucky, Greasy Creek, in the mountains in Pike County. Where I was born was a coal town in Jenkins, Kentucky. My father was a coal miner, worked around the mines. He didn't go into the mines. Well, maybe. I hate to tell it like that, but he was more like a flunky. He did a little bit of everything. The name of the mine was McKenny Field Company, as far back as I can remember. Greasy Creek was a little ways out of the camp. McKenny Field Company owned it. The house in Greasy Creek was a nice place. It was about six rooms. It was not a company house. It was a family house. The fireplace was in the living room. That is where everyone gathered around. They had big fire screens then. They had an old hearth. We didn't cook there. We just kept the house warm. We burned both coal and wood.

Jerry Robinson, that was my father's name. Cere is my mother's name. It is not a family name, but an old name. It was a good, moral home. They was loving parents, especially my mother. I didn't have but one brother and one sister living. My brother's name was Mallie. He has been dead five or six year now. Sister Isunty, now, she died when she was twelve years old. Frankie Robinson and Platt Robinson and Bruck Robinson and Marydell Robinson, they were my uncles and married aunt.

We was Baptist, Old Regular Baptist. It was something like Primitive Baptist. My mother read the Bible. She didn't read it to me, but she taught me like a mother would. She'd tell us things about the Lord. My mother was churchgoing. She took me to the Baptist church. I don't remember how old I was.

I was a normal child. I was shy. I don't remember what made me shy. I was just that way. I hate to say this, but I was awful pretty. They say I'm just like my mother. She was real pretty. I didn't get to play with dolls, didn't have any. The time I spent outdoors was in a cornfield. I worked hoeing corn.

My mother died of tuberculosis when I was seven years old. Then I went to live with my grandmother Margaret Branham. That was at Greasy Creek also. I was raised as an orphan, and I didn't have much schooling. I went to the third grade. I lived with my grandmother until I was a teenager. We had a pretty hard time. We had plenty to eat. We raised what we had to eat, raised everything that we could raise. But coffee and flour, we had to buy.

It was in Clendennon, Virginia. That was the first time I ever seen George Hensley. I was living in Cinderella, West Virginia, and I was married at the time. It was not a revival meeting, but a monthly meeting. Our pastor was Effie Gilmer, and Hensley was at church. It was during the day, and it was a real good service. They were really clean people. Hensley didn't preach that day. He just danced and shouted the power of God. I was over in the congregation, with the women. And he come and sang me out. He brought me a black rattler. I never will forget it. I had never handled any before. I was in my twenties. I'm eighty-three now. That's about sixty years of handling serpents.

I never thought I would handle serpents. No. You couldn't get me in a barn or a crib in dead wintertime. I was afraid of them. And I'm still scared of them without the Lord. Without the anointing of God, I don't fool with them. No. Once, I had a nervous breakdown by finding one in my dining room. It was before one of my children was born. I got in awful shape. It scared me to death, and it was just a little old house snake.

If I didn't feel protected by God that first time, oh, yeah, I wouldn't have done it. My hands was a little cold and numb, was all. It didn't excite me or scare me no way. It just made me feel big. I was not afraid. No. That snake was just kind of cold. I'd heard my hands would feel cold. [The snakes] are firm and as solid feeling as they look.

I have been bitten sixteen times, but I want to make this clear: I was under the anointing every time I was ever bit. That protected me. I never felt afraid I was going to die, never did. I hadn't been in serpent handling but about a year— I was about twenty-six or twenty-seven—and it was a copperhead that bit me. In fact, the first time I was ever bit, I was dead for about forty minutes, from what they told me. My heart stopped. They was a-praying about me. They wasn't any pain about me. It seemed like I went to sleep. And that is as much as I know until I sort of come at myself. I don't remember anything. The people around me said I had died. I didn't realize where I was at and what was going on. [Some of the brothers] and Sister Jenny McCoy were sitting right up in the bed with me, praying. And I did realize a little something, but my eyes had glassed over. But when I was going, I had two little girls, my two youngest ones, Columbia Gay and Lucille. I seen the curls around their faces, and I hated to leave them so bad. But God brought me through it. That was my first time. Now, I've been bitten in different places since then.

When I got the Holy Ghost, I got the fire with it. During a church service, my hands was laying in a gas stove. You know how hot they can get. It was the old-time kind. I had my hands back like that in the stove in the church. I didn't stick them there. I didn't realize where they were. But I couldn't feel. Some of the members went to cut the stove off to remove my hands, [and] another sister standing there said, "Don't do that." She said, "That's the Lord." She wouldn't let them move me. I have seen that before. The older saints, seem like they just believed more, had more faith or something. They could hold fire. To me, it didn't make any difference. I've took people's white shirts and held a torch under them, and it wouldn't even blacken them. I have used handkerchiefs, set them afire, and then when I put them out, they wouldn't even be stained. I explain it that it is the power of God.

[When I handled serpents,] my daddy, he wouldn't criticize me or put me down, but he'd tell me—he called me Bobby—he'd say, "Bobby, I worry about you at night. I wake up, and I wake up thinking about you getting snakebit. Or you drink that poison." They talked funny back then. He'd say, "You drink that *pisen*." He said he would lay and wait for somebody to come tell him I was dead and gone. I was bit one time, and I went to see him. He didn't have nothing to say bad. He never did. He never condemned me for it. No. He just worried about me. He didn't tell me not to do it.

My first husband, he wasn't nothing. He was in the first church where I handled serpents. He made me promise I wouldn't get up where they was. Well, I didn't. Well, maybe an hour. My husband was not a serpent handler, and he was not a churchgoing fellow. He went to church twice with me in the nineteen years we were married. He let on like if he ever got into it, it would be Holiness. Was he a good man? He was a good worker. He was a good provider. He was a good stomper, too. That means beatin' on me at home. That's right. There was a lot of it at home. Most of the time, I took a whippin' from him before I went to church, and one when I come back. He beat on me with his fist. Knock me down, kick me. When he was beating on me, I prayed. Yeah. Prayed for my life. But before I was going to church, I fought back. I couldn't say nothing.

He was a drinking man, but he didn't have to drink alcohol to be bad. I remember one time in particular. Our kitchen was right out in the living room. He was sitting in the living room, and I was cleaning the kitchen after supper. Everything was just as smooth. He picked up an alarm clock. He picked up that alarm clock and thrown it at me and hit me on the side of the head. I don't know why. It didn't knock me out. It just kind of touched it, like. Another time I remember, the kids was out playing, and I cooked him up three or four plates of food. And he just up and poured it out in the bed. He'd tell me to go back and get him some more. After a while, I turned around. I knowed better, but I was trying to be obedient. Dewey came in. He was just a big ole boy, about thirteen or fourteen. He came in the home, and he knowed I'd been praying. He just fell into him [beat up his father]. He asked if [his father] understood.

That man was a coward. Me and my children had to help him. He'd get in a fight where we'd see people beat him half to death. We'd jump in and take his part and take him to the house.

He did beat on the children. My boy next to Dewey, he thrown him out in the yard one time, and it hurt him a little bit. He had thrown him by his head. And now, the next to the baby girl, she was just crawling around. He turned around, picked her up, and thrown her out. She was just a-crawling. I put up with it nineteen year. I just couldn't take it no more. That time, I went up to his first cousin and told him I wanted to borrow a gun to kill a rat with. And he knowed what I had taken to do. I aimed to kill [my husband]. My oldest girl slipped around and told him. My oldest child, she was protective of all of us.

That was Pearl. [My husband's cousin] begin to laugh, and he told one of the boys to go in and get the gun for me. They didn't know no better. They went ahead and got it. They brought it out, and he just looked at it, and he told them to take it and put it back.

But after me and Bob [Elkins] was married, the children just loved to come home. They'd have a good time. Me and Bob went to Grundy once. When we come back, they was just dancing and listening to Elvis. When me and Bob come in, it was like dropping a match. They'd have fun. We didn't tighten down on them. We didn't like them dancing, but we didn't say anything. Me and Bob been married since 1949. Married the thirteenth day of October 1949.

I had six children—Pearl, then Dewey, Herbert, Ballard, Columbia, and Lucille. All [are] alive but Pearl and Columbia. I never did explain serpent handling to my children. They didn't ask me. They just thought everything I done was fine. I taught them anything I could think of that was good. They read the

Bob and Barbara Elkins, c. 1970
Family photo

Bible themselves. I encouraged them to. But now, the reason I didn't [read the Bible to them was] I couldn't read too good. I took them to the serpent-handling church. Oh, yeah, I took them all the time. They knew about the religion. They loved to go to church with me.

When they first took up serpents, now, they was of age. I believe Dewey must of been about twenty, maybe twenty-five. Herbert and Ballard handled serpents. Pearl didn't. Columbia was about twenty. She handled two years. Lucille was about the same age. Columbia [was bitten by a serpent and] died in 1961. She was twenty-three years old. She had one child—that was Lydia. We raised Lydia after that. We adopted her. And now, Lydia takes up serpents. Now, I got great-grandchildren that handle serpents.

[Columbia's death] was the only time we were discriminated against because of our belief. There were some neighbor problems. Some people called on the phone and said Columbia's child was a snake orphan. We had a lot of things done to us. People wrote us letters. Oh, mercy, we had a stack of letters—over a thousand letters, from every state in the Union. They didn't know what they was doing. They didn't know nothing about us. It wasn't just close to home. People around our neighborhood treated us good. We just lived through it and tightened down and took it. We just didn't answer. When people wrote those letters, we did not feel angry. No. We just felt sorry for them. We don't have anything against them. We was with a real good friend in church, and they was a man got up and said that Columbia had gone to hell right after she died, and there was no repenting. You know, now, that grieved us in our heart. But we didn't get mad. We couldn't afford to, and leave our soul when we knowed he couldn't hurt her. We was treated awful bad that night, not by our church members, but others. Our church members stood like the Rock of Gibraltar.

We had never worried about Columbia handling serpents. No. Never did. She lived four days after she was bitten. We was praying for her. Every one of the children was praying and stood right by us. She was sitting up in bed, talking in tongues with the Holy Ghost. I knew it was the Holy Ghost talking to her. I'm sure it was. She was a mommy's girl.

Bob tried to get her to go [to the hospital]. We asked her, and she rebuked us and asked us if we had lost our faith. I never lose my faith, but she was my youngun. I'd of took her if she had wanted to went. But I couldn't afford to turn against her, and her fighting, and putting unbelief in her. I just went along. We live what we put out. What we put out, we live it, we practice it. Anyone who

*Columbia Gaye in 1960, the year before her
death by snakebite*
Family photo

puts it out ought to be able to do it before he starts putting it on somebody else.

The same power that takes up [a] serpent through a man takes it up through a woman. People used to laugh at me. I was into everything, and so people would say I would be a tomboy. You know what I'd tell them? "We are serving the same God, and there is one Spirit, and the same God that deals with the man deals with me." I'd say that anything a man can do, I can do.

Outside of the services, nobody handles snakes at home. No. Nothing but cleaning and washing them. Maybe we use a hook. I was bit one time using a hook. I said I wouldn't do that no more. I was washing them, and I'm not anointed when I wash them.

When you are anointed, you feel it from the inside. It is just a good, light feeling. Yeah. You just feel like inside, you can do anything.

I used to be awful bad to pray at home and take up serpents by myself. One day, I was praying [at home by myself]. We had a big cobra. Boy, when that anointing hit me, I hit that box. But that was my last time ever hitting it with the cobra. Bob and Dewey took the keys to the boxes. But that thing, I got it. As much as we handled serpents, we didn't know they could bite backwards. That thing come back on me, and it didn't miss me *that far* on my arm. Well, I told Dewey and Bob about it when they come to the house. They went right then and got the key and locked it up. They said, "Old woman, they's no more for you." I wasn't allowed none of them by myself. But there wasn't no more, and they wouldn't have been nohow, 'cause I didn't know that thing could bite backwards. We have handled cobras here when they bring them to us, but we don't hunt for 'em. None of us have been bitten by the cobra.

When you are anointed, God gives you wisdom, and you know how dangerous they are. I don't think any of the women in our church ever handled them but me. They used to be a sister come and handle them a lot—Sister Gracie Hollins from Kentucky. She could handle them real good and have good victory, but I don't know about now. Columbia's daughter Lydia is married to Gracie's son Kirby.

I would never consider giving up serpent handling. No. Never. There is no way you can take hold of the reins and then look back. Now, I want more of the Lord.

We believe you can raise the dead. I've actually seen it. Now, there was a boy. He is grown now. Ray Mullins is his name. When he was a baby, I lived in one of the houses [nearby], and a woman came hollering at me to come over there, that the baby was dead. I went over there. The color had changed. He was black. The women who had [the baby] put [him] over my arms. I never was in that house before. I didn't know a thing about where nothing sit. I was praying for its mother. I was asking God to comfort her, she was carrying on so. You know, the Lord spoke to me. He said, "You go in the bedroom and stand by the dresser." I went into the bedroom, and I stood by that dresser. They was a mirror there. I was not looking at the mirror. I was looking at the end of the dresser, and I was walking the baby. And that baby cried. He'd been dead for a while, and it yelled out good. And he lives back out on the mountain now. I'd never been in that house before. I didn't know too much about the people. And I walked straight to that dresser.

Serpent handling has caused me a lot of heartache—a lot of it. But it hasn't changed my life, only brought me closer [to God]. Dewey has been bit so much, and [he] got so low when he was bit by that Eastern diamondback rattler. Two year after that, he was bit by a rattler [between his eyes], and that knot come up there, right out there where he was bit. He was bit on the hand, and that knot came out on his head, too. There's been a lot of things about the Lord that we couldn't really honestly explain it. You have to experience it. But despite the heartache, I feel blessed.

There have been some rough goings, but we didn't quit. Once, this boy [had been coming to our] church, and his family's brother come and decided they weren't going to have [the boy] coming here. They were raised Baptists. They come in and took some serpents out and killed them. They come in with sticks and masks on and pushed some of the people around. They took some of the serpents and thrown them out the church window and poured the [strychnine] out and took one of the serpents out and shot it. They took some out and burned them. They did that three or four times. This was about five or six years ago. They come one night [and] we welcomed them to the church. They come in, sat down in the aisle, and they all had canes. When somebody came by, they would stick that cane out and try to trip them. They brought the canes to hit people with. But that boy never did quit the church. He goes to another church now, but he is still handling serpents, and they don't bother us anymore. He even preaches for us some at our church.

None of our children has ever questioned our faith. No. Not a time. But when someone dies, it hurts. I just feel bewildered. A few months ago, we had a brother to die that we thought a lot of. That was Punkin Brown. It really went deep in us. But the serpent-handling religion will go on until the end.

It's been sixty years or longer that I went to see a doctor. That's right. The Lord has healed me of TB, and just as soon as he healed me, I've been told I had cancer, but I couldn't say that I have. I know I've done a lot of suffering, and people tell me what it was. But I can't say for sure. I never took an aspirin. I drank herbal tea.

We welcome outsiders to come to our church. Some people call us crazy. They say that we have low self-esteem and we do it to build ourselves up. But that don't bother us a bit. We know what we got. You see, in the Word, you are justified.

PRAY
WITHOUT CEASING

"I DIED," SAYS BROTHER BOB ELKINS. "I was bit, and I
died. If I could have told the people who were praying [to] just leave me alone,
I would have. But it was the most beautifulest place I ever seen. I can't express
it, the place I was in. It was clean. It was beautiful. It looked like a big white
valley. You could see castles like they draw on paper and things, and there seemed
to be people around them castles. It was the most settled peace I ever felt in my
life. I was at rest. I don't know how long I was dead. My heart stopped. But the
people kept praying and praying, and God honored their prayers, and I come
back to life."

The Reverend Joe Robert Elkins is an old-fashioned Holiness pastor whose
big hands seem to swallow a microphone when he preaches at the Church of
the Lord Jesus in Jolo. Age has altered his formerly muscular coal miner's body.
His hair has turned silver, and his eyes are magnified behind bottle-thick glasses
he has worn most of his life. Yet time has not diminished his powerful, one-man
campaign against evil.

"The devil, he's talking to you all the time," warns Brother Bob. "He's pol-
luting your mind. He's telling you every lie that he can think of to tell you. And
after a while, you just keep believing that lie. And after a while, he's *got you.*
But if you got God within you, and the devil comes along and tries to pull you

*Bob Elkins with
step-granddaughter Barbara
Coleman, in the prayer line
at Jolo, 1999*
Photo by Fred Brown

away, there is something within you will *stay* that devil. If he tries to pull something over on you, there is something that will talk to you, and that *something* is
the spirit of God."

Bob Elkins's sermons are part song, part shout, part dance, and all soul.
When he cranks up that fire and begins to preach, the Jolo church is trans-
formed. It's a lively place anyway. Sermons and hymns are punctuated by frequent shouts and exclamations, and the music, captured by four microphones,
fairly shakes the walls. But when Brother Bob stirs the pot, worshipers are virtu-
ally snatched from their seats by the spirit and pulled to the front of the church,
where they dance, spin, and shout. Serpents are quickly removed from boxes
when he begins to roll the Word down the aisles like a bowling ball, shouting
into his microphone. He bobs and weaves like a prizefighter, and there's no doubt
who his opponent is.

Brother Bob is blessed with an uncommon sense of timing and rhythm. His
sermons are tough Old Testament lessons shouted in thunderous tones, then
electronically magnified as well, so it is impossible to miss the point. If you were
to attempt to mold the quintessential Holiness preacher, you would begin with

Bob Elkins. When this tell-it-like-it-is pastor starts preaching to his flock, he doesn't stop until he has beaten the devil into submission. His weapons are the words he claims he gets directly from God, no rehearsal necessary.

God always tells him what to say, just as He did back in 1962 following the death by snakebite of his wife's twenty-three-year-old daughter, Columbia, when public furor erupted over the handling of snakes in religious services. Bob and his wife, Barbara, spoke before members of the West Virginia legislature to defend their religious right to handle serpents. They came away victorious.

"We didn't think beforehand what we was going to say," says Bob. "God just put the words in our mouth, and those people said we knew more about the Bible than they could ever hope to know." Bob smiles whenever he repeats that story. "They passed it in the House, but it died in the Senate. Never got out of the Senate. I figure me and Barb and Dewey [Chafin, his stepson] saved the church. I met with some of the lawmakers in Welch, West Virginia. They'd have these meetings, and I would know when they were going to have them, and I was informed of what was going to go on. The legislators were nice to me, and the governor, he was nice. That was Governor Cecil Underwood. He informed us that as long as he was governor, he didn't think there would be a law against [serpent handling]. He felt like people ought to have the freedom to worship the Lord in the way they wanted to."

It hasn't been easy, though. Brother Bob has faced hatred and prejudice from all sorts of groups. "This front door," he says, pointing to the solid wood door through which he entered the church, "used to be glass." And then he tells the story of the time an outsider forced his way into a service, tried to dance with the women, punched a member in the nose, and dragged Brother Bob across the floor by his hair. To finish things off, the intruder smashed his fist through the glass door, gashing his arm from wrist to shoulder. "A few months later, that man died," recounts Brother Bob. He makes no outward judgment, but the expression on his face assures you that, eventually, God will punish those who persecute His obedient children.

The Signs believers leave vengeance to the Lord. They never hold grudges, always forgive the interloper.

Another time, at an outdoor service in Tennessee, where serpent handling is a misdemeanor, Brother Bob was arrested along with twelve other people. The policeman who arrested them smashed Brother Bob in the ribs with his stick. "Don't do that," said Brother Bob.

The policeman pulled back his jacket lapel and showed his badge. "I can do anything I want," he declared.

Another officer shook out the snake boxes and shot the serpents.

Brother Bob wasn't detained, because he had not been handling snakes at the moment of the raid, but some of the other participants in the service were jailed. Bob is a man so gentle and sincere that it is difficult to doubt anything he says, and when he tells you that the two policemen and the judge who sentenced the serpent handlers soon all met their ends, you are inclined to believe him. When God asserted that vengeance was His, He was serious.

Bob Elkins the preacher is a fierce warrior in church, a figure to be reckoned with, but Bob Elkins the father is a comforter and counselor to the family he adopted when he married Barbara Robinson Chafin. To his congregation and the community of serpent handlers across the Southeast, he is Popaw or Brother Bob. Even people outside the church call him Popaw. All six children he adopted consider him their father and call him Dad, and the offspring of those adopted children call him Popaw.

"They wouldn't be able to tell any difference between him and a real dad," says Charles Church, who is married to Bob's adopted daughter Lucille. "He's really been good to them—not only to [Barbara's] children and the children he raised, but his grandchildren and great-grandchildren. Even the children in the church, there's not a child come up here that don't call him Popaw. He never had no [biological] children, but he's got more grandchildren that call him Popaw than anybody I know of. Even some of the younger people, like Bootie [church member Bootie Christian], who is twenty-seven years old, call him that."

Despite the support of his large extended family, Brother Bob was devastated by his wife's death in February 1999. No one knows the exact nature of Barbara's illness, since she never went to a doctor in her eighty-three years, relying on God to heal her, but her family believes it was cancer that killed her.

From the day of their marriage—October 13, 1949—the couple stood side by side on every issue, fighting together for what they believed in, working to raise Barbara's six children from her first marriage and the grandchildren who eventually came into their care.

At Barbara's funeral, Bob was so weak and disheartened that he had to be helped from his seat by family members. For a while, he seemed too depressed and too frail to continue his ministry. Much of the time, he could do little more than sit and cry. But now, he has called up the spirit inside him, knowing he has to carry on by himself the long battle he and Barbara won years ago in the West Virginia legislature.

"This old body is going to go back to the dust of the earth," said Bob in a recent sermon. "It is going to be done away with. These old bones is goin' to decay. But this on the inside, this spirit within you that controls your body, it's going to live on somewhere, too."

The Church of the Lord Jesus, founded by the couple in 1956, is one of the best-known churches within the serpent-handling religion simply because the family has generously allowed the outside world to witness services. Rarely is any member of the media turned down upon asking permission to film, record, or write about serpent handlers, despite occasional broken promises and misinformation released by those who have slanted their stories toward sensationalism.

As for Barbara, Bob says he still talks to her every day. She is buried on a hillside across the street from the church, on a plot of land the Elkins family bought years ago. Bob's stepson Dewey says that any serpent-handling believer can be buried there, even if they aren't related to the Elkinses, because, in the end, all Signs Followers are part of the same family.

IN HIS OWN WORDS
JOE ROBERT ELKINS

Bob Elkins, eight years old
Family photo

I met Barb in church in Williamson, West Virginia, 1948. We went to church together a lot for a long time. She had come there, and she usually stayed with my mom and dad and helped take care of them. None of Barb's children were mine. There were six of them. I can't tell no difference in it, just as if the kids were mine. When we got married, Dewey, he was in the army, but I raised Ballard, Herbert, Columbia, and Ceil [Lucille]. Pearl, she was already married. And then when Dewey got out of the army, he came and stayed with us. About everybody calls me Popaw. I try to

Barbara and Bob Elkins with grandchildren, c. 1950
Family photo

be good to people and show them good spirits and do what I can for them. The kids come into the church as they felt repentance move upon them. We didn't pressure them or nothing.

I'm from Kentucky. I was born in Greasy Creek, Kentucky. My parents moved [to Jolo] when I was real little, [and] I been here mostly ever since. I must have been about four or five years old. I really don't know. I can't remember that far back. My daddy came here to work in the mines [because] the mines had worked out [been depleted] in Greasy Creek. He went to truck mining then to make a living. Just a little ole dog coal, I call [it]. Let's see, he was sixty-two when he died. He had a stroke. I was just a small boy when he had the stroke. I must have been about twelve years old.

My dad was a member of the church, and he preached. Rell Elkins was his name. He handled serpents. I was raised into the church. I started with the Church of God. [As] just a small boy, I'd go places, and I'd play music in churches. I played the guitar all around Jolo and over in Virginia, but I was about twenty years when I really started praying.

I didn't start a church until 1950. It was of this faith. Way it started, people would ask me to come to their houses and have prayer meetings. I didn't call myself a preacher at that time. I'd just go. We'd sing and pray, and everybody [would] get up and have a good time in the Lord, you know. As I grew older, the Lord began to give me the Word, and I preached to people. They called me Preacher, but I just conducted the service, more or less. People would pray, and it just kept adding on to the [membership], and we finally built a church down here above the road in 1956. The name was the Church of the Lord Jesus. It was down at Jolo, just at the mouth of this hollow after you go out on the main road. It was just five hundred, six hundred feet below in that hollow. Me and Barb were married at the time we started that first church, but we lived up here. I owned all of this [land] at one time, this whole thing up and down through here.

I was a coal miner. I worked in the deep mines, mostly. I bossed about all my life, but I [also] worked operating machinery. I operated miners, scoops, tractors. The last ten years, I was superintendent for No. 10 coal mine. I was down in the mines for about forty-two years. When you are superintendent, you don't stay outside all the time. You got to make your rounds to make sure you know what's going on inside. I also worked in Virginia.

About 1960, I got my back broke in a big kettle bottom. It comes up like a

Christmas tree, and it is just real slick. It's called soapstone. You take the coal out from under it, why, it'll just sit down. Back then, they didn't have miners [cutting machines] and things like they have today. [When] you cut the coal, you stood a chance of cutting across the face with a machine. I went to take the jack down, [and] the top was smooth. When I pulled [it] out, the kettle bottom came down. I was in the Signs Church at the time, [but] I had to have medical help on that injury. I was two years on crutches. I got to where I could get around. I worked in a store, picking up light things. Then I got to where I could go back in the mines. I retired from the mines in 1991.

The first church me and Barb had was small, real small. It was only twenty-eight foot long, and the building was too small. It was a two-story building, but we just owned the top of it. And the people who built it, they owned the bottom of it. They'd let *anybody* move in there [on the bottom floor]. They'd drink and carry on downstairs while we was trying to have service. So we tried to build one. We built it right beside the road. The crowds we have now are not nothing to what we had then, and the state police had to direct traffic. We had big crowds back then because it was something different to people. It was something new, you know, handling serpents, handling fire, drinking poison. People come to see, come to watch.

But then we started this church, Church of the Lord Jesus. This building was built about 1980 or '81. But the church goes back a long time. Not this building. This church, well, it means everything to me. It means I can come in here and I can preach the Word of God just like it is. I don't have to worry about it. I don't have to worry about what people are going to say. Ain't nobody going to put me out, because we built it, and that is what we built it for, to preach the Word, [so] that people could worship the Lord in the way that they wanted to. It ain't everywhere you go. You can't go in and preach and put in action what we believe. Here, nobody tells us what we can do and what we can't do. We do what the spirit leads us to do in service, and what the Word backs up. We don't want to do anything that is not in the Word. We just want to do what the Word says do. I'm talking about what the Word in the Bible says.

There are other churches that don't practice serpent handling that are partly in and partly out of the Word. They are doing what they want to do, but they don't want to do this part. When they told John, in the Book of John, to eat the book, [Jesus] said, "In your mouth it will be sweet, but in your belly it will be bitter." This [serpent handling] is the bitter part. The [other churches] all lay hands on the sick, speak in tongues, and go through the motions of casting out a devil, but you don't see them jump on the strychnine jar, and you don't see them getting no serpents. But the same man said it all in the sixteenth chapter of Mark. He said *these* Signs. Not *a* Sign. *These* Signs. All five will follow them that believe. We take up the serpent, literally. And for those who don't believe and who criticize us, I just pray for them. That's all I can do. They are still blinded to the truth. The Bible says to know the truth, and the truth will set you free. They are not being set free from the yoke of bondage yet. The scales have not peeled from their eyes to see the Word.

I been called just about anything you could think of. Been called Tarzan. But the Bible says they'd speak all manner of evil against you. I *know* that I'm in the Word when they do that. It really don't bother me what people think.

We preach against sin. I guess we preach harder against sin than any church I know of. A lot of people, they preach. They say, "If you sin, you can't go to heaven," but they don't never tell the people what the sin is. You got to tell people what they are doing that is wrong. A sin is professing it and not possessing it—not living in the Word. If you are not a doer of the Word, you are deceiving yourself, and you are going to be lost in the end. You have deprived yourself of the pleasures of the world, and you are going to miss heaven, too. A lot of people does the signs up there [abide by the rules posted on the wall of the Jolo church], but they don't feel like it is a sin. But it *is* a sin, because you got Bible verse there [to prove it]. Smoking and chewing tobacco is a sin. You crave that thing. The Holy Ghost is the comforter. Cigarettes is not the comforter. Smoke is not your comforter. The Holy Ghost will comfort you. People will go buy cigarettes and things other than food, and I've seen it happen. I worked at a store. They'd buy the tobacco before they'd buy food for their children. They were satisfying their lust, you see. It is hard, but you got to keep freed up. It's like a woman's hair. She shouldn't cut it. In Corinthians, long hair was give to a woman for her glory, for her cover, the covering of her head. And if they cut it off, they cut their glory off.

The Bible says [that] no man is to see God at any time. God is a spirit. The spirit dwells in Jesus. Jesus was a man, just like we are. He was born of a woman, just like we are. I don't believe He had a long beard, because He wouldn't teach me to use a razor and not use one Himself. He said to be like Him. To be like Him, we have to do the things that He done. That's the way I see it. And he picked up serpents, just like us. That was the last message that He preached, the last message that Jesus preached. Sixteenth chapter of Mark. He told His disciples to go into all the world and to preach the Gospel to every creature. "He that believeth and is baptized shall be saved; but he that believeth not shall be damned. And these signs shall follow them that believe; In my name shall they cast out devils; they shall speak with new tongues; They shall take up serpents; and if they drink any deadly thing, it shall not hurt them; they shall lay hands on the sick, and they shall recover." And the Lord had spoke these words unto them, and they went forth confirming the Word. *Confirm* is something you have to do. With Signs following. And he sealed it with an amen. That's just like a notary public putting a seal on paper today. That was His last sermon, and He was ascended.

Sometimes, we handle serpents on faith alone. When you are handling them by faith, you are waiting on the anointing. You are believing that God is going to meet you and take care of you. But the anointing will take care of it. If He moves upon you to handle it, His anointing will take care of you. If you move by faith, you are moving out on the promises of God. You got to keep the faith, believing that He's going to meet you. He said, "I'll never leave you. I'll never forsake you." He won't forsake you if you believe Him strong enough. And if you are bit while handling on faith, you are just bit. We are just bit, and we have to trust God to heal us. Faith is the substance of things that are hoped for that's not seen. It is not more dangerous to take up serpents on faith alone and not waiting on the anointing. The anointing is faith in action. And I can't explain the feeling of the anointing.

I was bitten on faith once. I was right there beside the electric organ. I died! That was '94. Just immediately after I was bit, they had to carry me out and take me to the house. It was a rattler. It was a canebrake rattler. My heart stopped. Jesus said He'd give you power to heal the sick, cleanse the leprosy, and raise the dead. The same power that heals the sick will raise the dead. You just have to believe it more. I believe that God hears our prayers and brings the dead back to life. I believe you can be prayed back from the dead. I don't know how long I was out. They was in there with me. I know if I could have talked, where I was at, I would have told them [to] just leave me alone.

In the works of God, He allows things to happen that His Word might be made manifest. See, there is an appointed time for everybody. They's a time that we are going to go, that all the praying we can do, it's not going to save us, because that is God's appointed time. I believe that if the right people is there and they got the faith and the Word, if we are where we ought to be in God, see, they can pray you back. At that time, He would restore that person in order to let me know that He was with me, that He had given me the power that I could do these things. But there comes a time that you are going to go, regardless, when that appointed time comes.

I don't think Punkin Brown died by a serpent bite. I believe the man had a heart attack. That's my personal belief. I've never known nobody to die [in] that period of time from a serpent bite, that fast. I've known people to die from a serpent bite, you know, but not that quick. I have been bitten nineteen times.

But I'd like for the world to know that we don't just handle the serpents. A lot of people have the wrong impression. They call it "going up there to that snake church." But we don't *worship* serpents, because they are of the devil. We only practice the Word of God and let God's power be made manifest over the devil. He has all power over the devil. I'd like for the world to know that. Lot of people think all we do is handle serpents. We pray for the sick. They's some sick people that's healed here. We drink the strychnine. We don't deny none of the five Signs. We do our best to put all five in action, because He said *these* Signs. We don't just pick out praying for the sick or speaking with tongues, but *all five* Signs is going to be made manifest in God's church.

You are either a believer or an unbeliever, and the unbeliever is going to hell. I believe they are going to burn. I believe they are going to be tormented in those flames. Now, the grave is hell, but the Bible said there is a lake of fire prepared for the devil and his angels. That's where the rich man went. He was tormented in that flame. People that don't serve God's going to be tormented in that flame for ever and ever, "where the worm dieth not, and the fire is not quenched." No end. That lake of fire is going to be as long as heaven is long.

The Bible says to pray without ceasing. See, you go with a prayer in your mind all the time, lest you enter in the temptations. Prayer is what keeps the temptation away. When you are approached by the devil, you pray. God moves that thing. He said to resist the devil, and [the devil] would flee from you.

And we cast out devils. I have seen that happen. See, the devil is a spirit, just like God was a spirit. That spirit works in the being, in the flesh, in the mind, and in the heart of a person. God gives you power to pray for that thing, and it has to leave that body. That spirit has to leave that body in order for you to be made whole. God's spirit comes in and cleanses that soul. That spirit of the devil has to go out, and then that body don't do the things that the spirit before had it a-doing. It minds the things of God.

You know [when] a person is possessed because in some cases, the devil will talk to you. The spirit that is in a person will naturally speak out against you. It'll tell you, wide open, right in plain talk, that it don't *want* to leave. But still, God will give you power over that. The devil will talk back to you. He'll cuss you, right in church. I've seen that happen. It'll say, "I don't *want* out." They'll use profane language. Yeah, I've seen that.

A lot of times, people will come to prayer that has a devil. They want rid of it, and yet they don't want rid of it. But when the power of God begins to move on that thing, it don't want to leave that soul, because it's *got* it. It don't have to work somewhere else. It wants to stay there. That's its home. Until [the devil] comes out, it'll talk back to you. It'll tell you what it *don't* want to do, because he's already got that person. That's why the Bible says, "Greater is He that's in you." If you've got God within you, then you've got what it takes to cast that devil out. You can feel the presence of the deliverance when the devil leaves a body.

God talks to people, if they would just slow down and listen. God talks. I hear Him. He speaks to you through the heart. It is a small, still voice. It is real quiet. [It] speaks within you. You hear it. It is a spirit of God [that] talks to you, 'cause God is a spirit, and that spirit talks to you. When it tells you something, you can mark it down. It'll happen. But it ain't every spirit that talks to you that is God.

Sometimes, when you speak in tongues, the Bible says you are speaking unto God, and not to man. It is not something that we understand, not in an unknown tongue. I'm just glorifying God, magnifying God. When I am speaking in an unknown tongue, I speak unto His people. Other tongues is more than one tongue. Other tongues is different nationalities. That's the way they spoke on the day of Pentecost. That's the way the Lord speaks today. If the Lord wants me to know something that wouldn't edify the sinner back there, but it would edify the church, why, He would speak in other tongues. They'd be somebody to interpret it to the church. God doesn't speak to no effect. It is for a *purpose*. Lot of times, let's say there would be a German back there, and the Lord speaks to somebody back here. He knows what [God is] saying. It might be talking right direct to him. It could be Italian or Greek or whatever. The Lord could speak in that language to this person here, and they would know what it [meant].

People think we are crazy, but it is a wise man who fears the Lord and keeps His Commandments.

Barbara Coleman dancing in the spirit at Jolo Church, 1999
Photo by Fred Brown

NOBODY CAN
STOP ME NOW

BARBARA JEANEAN CHURCH
COLEMAN
B. 1964

*"If you're blessed to handle serpents . . .
[and] the snake goes limp like a shoestring, common sense will tell you that
you can't do that yourself. You have to
have that love inside."*

LOVE STORIES ARE ALWAYS COMPLICATED, but in the
Signs Following churches, restrictions for marriage and divorce are even more
complex than in many other religions–so complex and so narrowly defined, in
fact, that in order to marry, members of the sect often have to defy the very
rules they have lived by for years. Believers can marry nonbelievers if they continue to follow the Signs outlined in Mark 16, but if they divorce and remarry,
they are considered "double-married" as long as the ex-husband or ex-wife is
alive. And those who are double-married are considered unfit to preach the
Word.

It is a difficult, soul-searching choice—physical, earthly love versus godly,
spiritual love. Barbie Coleman and Punkin Brown, who fell in love two years
after the death of Punkin's wife, Melinda, ultimately decided to give each other
up for the laws of the church that had formed their lifelong religious and personal philosophies.

In the Signs Following Church, members are not even allowed to divorce unless their spouses are unbelievers or are unfaithful. Although Barbie's

divorce in March 1998 was approved in the eyes of the church, she would have been considered double-married had she taken another husband. And that was a situation Punkin Brown could not reconcile with his own inflexible counsel against adultery.

When Barbie talks about Punkin, it is with a break in her voice and tears in her eyes. "I had seen Punkin at different times through the years," she recalls. "We never said more than hello. Then, after I was separated, something just clicked. He was the kindest man and the strongest man I've ever known. The more we talked about religion, [the more] we realized we seen a lot of things eye to eye. But then, too, we had our differences.

"He's been portrayed as a really hard man. He was. He believed [his religion] hard. His convictions were very deep. But he wasn't a hard man [personally]. He loved his children, and he was good to other people's children. When we lived in Tennessee, he used to tease my son, Jason, about a rat-tail haircut he had. Punkin used to pull it. Once, when Punkin was taking all the boys to get a haircut, I told him to try and talk Jason into getting the rat-tail cut off. Well, Punkin wouldn't do it. He said, 'You know what your mom wants, but it's up to you, and I'm not going to be the bad guy. Keep it if you want.' Well, after Punkin died, Jason, Jacob, and Jeremiah [Barbie's son and Punkin's twin sons] asked me for a pair of scissors. I didn't want to give them the scissors, but they said it was important, so I did. I give them just a few seconds and went to see what they were cutting, and by that time, they had already cut his rat-tail and were writing on an envelope: 'To Punkin. I cut my rat-tail off for you. I miss you and love you. Love, Jason.'

"And when Punkin died, my daughter, Julie, just started crying so hard," Barbie adds. "She loved him because he had done so much for her. [Punkin] loved both [my children], but I think that Julie held a very special place in his heart.

"Even after we had agreed not to date anymore, he looked out for me and my kids. He wanted me to stay in Tennessee because he told me once that he was afraid no one would take care of me like he tried to. I know there was a time when maybe if he hadn't of been here, I don't think I'd be the person I am now. I was really in a mess at one time. That's one of the reasons why I went back to church. But we decided to put all [our feelings] aside for God.

"Punkin's mother and daddy are like my own parents. I tell people that I have a mom and a dad [Lucille and Charles Church]. I also have a mommy and daddy in Peggy and John Brown. They all took care of me when I had no place to go. They took me and my children in and made us feel a love that was truly a gift from God.

"To John, I was a free woman, and he didn't feel like it was wrong for us to get married."

John Brown confirms Barbie's story. "Punkin and Barbara did talk about getting married," he says. "She moved down here, and Punkin moved out of his trailer and moved in with Peggy and me and give her his house, but they never did live together or anything like that. She'll tell you right today that when Punkin died, he was the same man he was when he was married to Melinda. They was a lot of talk going around, but in fact, I was hoping they *would* get married. But this is the way Punkin saw it. He saw where the Bible says in I Timothy, chapter 3, 'A bishop then must be blameless, the husband of one wife, vigilant, sober, of good behaviour, given to hospitality, apt to teach. . . . And let these also first be proved; and let them use the office of a deacon, being found blameless.'

"Okay, now. Punkin thought because Barbie had been married before, and her husband was still living, he shouldn't marry her. That was the reason he said he wouldn't be able to preach. But now, I see it a little bit different than what they do. In one place, I find where the Bible says [that] if a woman is married to an unbeliever, if they depart, a brother or sister is not under bondage." The Scripture John is referring to is I Corinthians 7:15, which reads, "But if the unbeliever depart, let him depart. A brother or a sister is not under bondage in such cases; but God has called us to peace."

"So that is the way I see it," says John. "But that is not the way Punkin saw it. He believed that if he married her, then he would be committing adultery. If it hadn't been for that, they probably would have married. That was a big hurdle. Barbie's husband was an unbeliever, and Punkin thought the world of Barbie, but he wouldn't go against the Word of God. He thought that if he married her, he wouldn't have been able to preach the Word.

"At the time Punkin died, they weren't seeing each other. Barbie lived in the house below us for a while, and then she moved back to Jolo, West Virginia, again."

The time Barbie spent living near Punkin and his family was one of her happiest periods in recent years. "I was at a terrible time in my life when he came along and gave me laughter and helped me to be a stronger person, to be able to trust and love. And I only hope that in some small way, I brought some sort of help and happiness to him.

"I moved down there to Tennessee with my kids right before my divorce was final, and we lived in the house next to the Browns, and I got a job working at Spring Arbor, a Christian warehouse.

"I helped take care of Punkin's kids. I'll love them till the day I die. I still talk to them. And even when Punkin and I talked about getting married, I never said I would try to take their mother's place. Sarah [Punkin's daughter] asked me if she should call me Mommy. I said, 'Sarah, if you want to call me Mommy, that's fine. You can call me whatever you want, but you had a mommy that loved you. And I know I could never take the place of your mommy.'

"You know, there are some people that want to look into other people's lives so they don't have to look into their own. I always try to look at things from my heart and wonder how I would feel in the other person's place. If I judge somebody, I have to meet double that standard, be twice as good as the person I judge. And I don't want to go to hell, so I don't want to put anyone else there. You have to stand before God for yourself.

"Punkin and I really cared about each other, but he did the right thing. He preached against adultery and fornication, and he believed that if he married me, with an ex-husband still living, he would be committing adultery and would no longer be able to preach. I agreed with anything that he said, because all along, I had doubts of my own, too, and I told him that I knew he would make the right decision. And no matter how much you love somebody, you want to do the right thing. At the time he died, we weren't seeing each other. We decided to wait and see what the Lord wanted for us."

Punkin's death was a shock to the entire serpent-handling community, but for Barbara Coleman, it was the most devastating news of her life to that point. She is still trying to understand her personal loss in relation to God's greater plan, but she is generous and optimistic when rationalizing the tragedy. "Punkin's with Melinda now, which is where he belongs," she says. "He's next to her in heaven. She was his wife. He loved her."

But Barbie's heartache didn't end there. Four months after Punkin's death, and four days after Barbie returned to Jolo, her beloved grandmother Barbara Elkins, matriarch of the family, died at the age of eighty-three. Barbie had been out of the church since her marriage in 1985. But she says that "no matter what was going on, I could tell my mamaw, and while we were talking, she would reach over and touch me—pick at my clothes, hold my hand.

"[The] only two people that Mamaw would let clean her up was me and my cousin Melissa. I was at the church when Melissa got bit one night, but I wasn't *in* church. I had backslid, and I was still in sin, so I was standing in the back. But that night, seeing my best friend and my cousin hurt, and knowing that if I had prayed a prayer, the Lord would not have heard me, and the closeness that comes when there's any suffering in the church, that closeness and love, [the way] people unite—it was painful to me. And I knew then that, in my life, I had went all that I could go without God. Oh, yeah, I had my friends [outside the church]. Last week, the son of an old friend passed away, and I went to see her, and we sat and talked and laughed, but I thought, 'I'm not like this anymore.'

"I've always been a plain and simple person, never put on a lot of makeup or dressed up very much. I believe you should be pretty on the inside, and I wanted someone to love me for the way I am on the inside. Punkin did. He always told me that I have a good heart."

Barbara Coleman is a pretty woman with dark eyes and long, dark hair that she has not cut since her return to the church. She is tall and slender and has a heart-shaped face and small, dainty hands. Born in Iaeger, West Virginia, in 1964, she is the second daughter of Lucille Chafin Church and Charles Church. Both her parents and her sister Cynthia are members of the serpent-handling religion. Her younger sister, Robin, is not currently in the church. "It is really heartbreaking for me," says Barbie. "Robin used to belong to the church and do all the Signs, and she has a gift of music and was healed from very bad allergies by God. She used to sing and praise the Lord so much." Her brother Christopher has never been an active member of the church, "but he believes in the Signs," says Barbie. "I feel like that if he should ever give his life to God, he will be a Signs believer. He is planning on getting married soon to a girl he met in Japan, and it is my understanding that he told her that [what] he believes is something he would not change."

Barbie looks too young to be the mother of two children, but her daughter, Julia, born in 1987, has already been baptized and has the Holy Ghost. Jason, born in 1990, whom Barbie calls her baby, will decide about the church when he's ready to make that decision for himself.

For a mother in the Signs Following religion, there are conflicting emotions about children handling serpents. Generally, eighteen is the age when the Signs Followers allow their children to take up serpents in church, although there

*Barbara Coleman
with her son Jason during a Jolo
service, 1999*
Photo by Fred Brown

have been some exceptions. Punkin Brown, for example, first handled in church at seventeen, but his parents were not present that evening. Opponents of the practice cite accounts of young children handling; George Went Hensley supposedly allowed children as young as eight to pick up snakes. But many of the stories are apocryphal. Present-day Signs Followers are highly protective of their sons and daughters and generally send children to the back of the church when snake boxes are opened on the rostrum. Although a few churches allow children to roam freely during services, the adults usher them back to the pews as soon as snakes are taken out.

"When my kids are old enough to handle serpents, I will probably be terrified," says Barbie. "As a mother, I don't want them to. You look at your kids and you think, 'What if something were to happen to them?' You think, 'How would they grow up without me?' When the anointing comes, you don't think about it. With the flesh, though, it is always there. You think, 'If I get bit, how would I cook for my kids? How would I clean for my kids?' You always think about them, whether it is thinking about yourself or protecting them. A daddy is good, but a daddy is not a mommy. Nobody can replace a mother. You can't. That's where you have to trust in the Lord. Sometimes, that does get hard.

"I believe that if the Lord was to take me out tomorrow, I've got enough faith that I'll get to see my kids, because I have taught them the right way. I'll see them on the other side. You are not going to miss them if you die and go to heaven. I know that I would be happy [in heaven], but while I'm on this earth, I just couldn't bear the thought of not having my kids.

"Julie is so kind hearted, and she is just so smart. She has big black eyes and dark hair. Jason, my baby, is a mama's boy. He has blond hair and blue eyes and is skinny and tall like me. Julie's birth was easy, but the doctors gave me very little hope with Jason. When he was born, I wasn't in the church. And once, when he was about two and took a real bad spell, they had brought me a prayer cloth from the church, and I pinned it on my baby's clothes, and he got better. When Julie was about a year old, she had a really high fever—a hundred and four degrees—and even as a sinner, I knew that God was the only one who could heal her. So before I took her to the hospital, I called my grandmother and asked her to pray, and she did, and Julie was starting to feel better by the time I got her to the hospital.

"Right now, my kids know to go to the back of the church when the serpents come out. I know, for example, that Julia has her whole heart in it, but I don't let her around the area where the serpents are out. John Brown baptized her. It was not something I made her do. I let her read both Scriptures about baptism, and I let her make her own mind up, because I didn't want her to have any doubts.

"You have to believe [the Signs] yourself and laying on hands and everything else. I will not *make* my children go to a serpent-handling church. They go to a Christian school that doesn't believe in serpent handling. I want them to see all sides. I want them to make that decision for themselves."

IN HER OWN WORDS
BARBARA COLEMAN

Growing up, I was a tomboy. If the boys were playing football, they'd always come and get me to play. My best friend was a boy, and I would beat him up, and when the time came that he was able to beat me up, I decided I wouldn't fight boys no more.

When I was in high school, I wasn't going to church. I was a cheerleader, and I was allowed to go to dances, wear pants, be a regular teenager. I had a lot of friends in school—the fun people, the ones who would sneak behind the school building and smoke. I could sit down and laugh with a boy whether he was my boyfriend or not. I could never be mean to people in school. My parents didn't forbid me to do anything, except my daddy wouldn't allow me to walk on the road when I went to visit friends. He was worried about me, and he always drove me there. When Christian people came to our house, we respected them.

I prayed [joined the church] when I was sixteen. When I was younger, I didn't have as many cares of the world as I have now, and I could dedicate more of my time and energy to the Lord. And I remember thinking, "Nobody can stop me now." I've got it written down [in my journal]: "I'm going [to the serpent box] on my own." [The anointing] didn't come [right away], but when it did, I knew that Mom and Dad wouldn't panic. They would worry, but that's natural. I was old enough to make up my own mind, and that is what I wanted to do. I have it written down, the first time I went to the box by myself. It was September 11, 1982. I went in by myself and took up a serpent. It was a yellow rattler. I think that was after my cousin Deana had died. I can tell you the dress I had on. It was a burgundy dress. The Lord just really moved on me. The Lord let me do it.

When I handled at Marshall, Mark Brown and Steve Frazier had handled serpents and put them up. I don't like to take them from someone else, because if I got bit, whoever handed them to me would feel guilty. I like going in the serpent box myself. That way, you know it's not you but the God you have within you.

And sometimes, I step back from it. In church the other day, they had a black rattler, and it was mean, flipping backwards and trying to bite everybody. And I moved up to the rostrum. I was scared of it. Without the Lord, there is no way you can handle, and when you put them up, you know that God has been with you and kept you safe. I know I have to have my life in order to be worthy to handle serpents or pray for the sick. If not, I will stay out of the box. When I am anointed to handle, physically, I always feel peaceful and calm, and there is no fear about me. But when that fear hits, I put the serpents up.

My grandmother used to get angry when she thought we were handling serpents too much. But you can't feel what other people are feeling when they handle serpents. You can't understand. My hands shake when God is on me, but

I'm not scared. It's emotional. The Bible talks about not being able to contain the feeling. It's not fear. My legs have went weak, and I've fell to my knees with the emotion, and the best blessing is when I can just stand and cry. That's a peaceful and humble feeling. That's when it feels like it's just me and God and nobody else, even with a church full of people.

At Punkin's funeral, I handled serpents, and they were so limp, it was a blessing. I know he wanted serpents handled at his funeral, and I felt ready to handle. It was a joy. All the heartache I had felt [disappeared], and I felt the Lord with me, and I was calm. It was probably the most peaceful time I'd had since I had heard the news [of his death].

But if I were to walk in my yard and see something green, I'd run in the house. I'm not going to lie about it. I'm scared of a spider, snake, anything. When I'm in church, though, [the feeling] is just from the top of your head to the bottom of your feet, and there is no fear. You know if you were to get bit, and you got the anointing like that, and with the Holy Ghost moving in you, I believe you will be okay.

I know we should get to the point daily that if we come upon a serpent, we could pick it up, because we should live that clean of a life at all times and be able to take up serpents even when the anointing is not on us. We should be able to take them up by faith. I believe that, and yet I can't [do it]. But just because you are not anointed and you get bit does not mean you are going to die and go to hell. I remember one time when Mom got bit and she was dying. A rattler had bitten her. She got bit twice on both hands, [by] a pygmy rattler and a copperhead. This was 1982. I was sitting up in the bed with Mom, and I seen her eyes roll back in the top of her head, and she quit breathing. I just started screaming. Somebody picked me up and took me out of the room. I don't know who it was. They prayed, and when I went back in the room, she was okay. I mean, I seen her eyes roll back, and she quit breathing.

Some people think we are crazy to handle serpents. As children, we had a normal life, but people don't want to believe that. We are always portrayed as poor, dumb hillbillies. My little boy and my cousin Melissa's oldest boy are six months apart. They weren't but about two years old, and the television people [came to the church], and they wanted to ask the boys what they thought about serpent handling. They are *two years old*! What could they possibly think about it?

One night, my husband and I went out in another city, and people started talking about the church. My husband said, "That's my wife's people." The others said they heard that [we] go up there and throw snakes on people. It made me so mad. My ex-husband does not believe [the way I do], but he said, "No, I've been around them. They don't throw snakes on people." And I said, "They never *make* people handle them. Growing up, I was never told that I had to handle them."

People look at you like you are nasty. I wanted to put my children in a Christian school over the mountain in Buchanan County [Virginia]. They were testing children for entering. My children make A's and B's in school. The principal said, "Are you in any way affiliated with *that* church in Jolo?" I said, "Yes, that's my family's church. My grandparents'." He told me my kids couldn't go to his school because they attended this church. He said he could not teach them one thing and have me teach them another. I asked him, "Do you teach out of the Bible?" He said yes. And I said, "Okay, I teach my kids out of the Bible. I teach my children to love, accept, and respect people for who and what they are." He said, "Do you think I am being rude?" and I said, "Yes, I do. I teach my kids that there are sixty-six books in the Bible, and they have to live by all of them. But you're the one who has to lay down and sleep at night."

Imagine. I want my kids to get an education, but because we go to this church, they couldn't get it there. My little girl goes to church, and she wears dresses, and I don't let my children watch certain things on television. That's why I wanted them in private school. And this man, who was supposed to be a preacher and a man of God, told me my children could not come there. He told me that he would set me up on a home-schooling program. Why? We don't teach our children to go to school and talk about snakes. I had never come against anything like that. It blew my mind. Matthew 10:14 says, "And whosoever shall not receive you, nor hear your words, when ye depart out of that house or city, shake off the dust of your feet." So I went to pick up my kids from the school, and I said to them, "Knock the dust off your feet, because you will never be back here again."

Everybody has their own opinion. When I first got baptized in John Brown's church [which believes in the One God doctrine, meaning that there is only one God, not three individuals in the Godhead], the family had their own opinions as to why I did it. But it was something I had prayed on for a long time. There are differences in all churches. For example, the way I'm baptized is Acts 2:38: "Then Peter said unto them, Repent, and be baptized, every one of you, in the name of Jesus Christ for the remission of sins, and ye shall receive the gift of the Holy Ghost." And they did receive the Holy Ghost after the baptism of Jesus Christ. But in the Lord Jesus Church, they are baptized in the name of Lord Jesus [not Jesus Christ]. Anything you do in word or deed, you do in the name of Lord Jesus. But I'm not baptized that way.

Actually, I was baptized two times when I was living in Tennessee. The first time was by Punkin. It was back in the springtime when the days were beginning to warm up real good and it was sort of hot. Daniel, Punkin's son, and I were sitting on the steps, and Punkin had been working in the garden. He pulled up on the tractor and said, "It's a good day to hit the water." And so he baptized me that day. And later, John [Punkin's father] baptized me again.

I don't think anybody can keep you out of the church if you are divorced. If I were to ever remarry [and my ex-husband is still alive], some people would say I would go to hell, and others would say I could remarry because of the way my divorce come about. I don't know. Right now, I'm not looking to remarry. If that time ever comes, the Lord will let me know, so I don't worry about it.

You need to always be living right. I believe [the devil] can be in a room with you. I've woke up lots of nights with nightmares, and I just begin to pray and rebuke the devil and maybe anoint my room, and it leaves. I know my cousin Brenda [was spending the night with me] one time, [and she] was having a bad dream. We were both in church at the time. In her dream, the thing was moving to the bottom of the bed. We were in the same bed, so she said, "Well, good. If Barbie knows it's there, it'll leave." She said no sooner had she thought that [than] it came back to her side of the bed. And as it was coming back to her side of the bed, I just woke up. I shook her, and I said, "Are you okay?" And we prayed, and she went back to sleep. In her dream, she could see it. You could feel it. It was the devil.

You have to be strong, because the devil will try to torment you. But I believe he only has as much power as you'll let him have. And if you are ever around something like that when it is being cast out of someone, it's strong, and if you don't have the true Holy Ghost and what it takes, that devil can come into you. It has to find a new home. And if you are not living right, it could possibly enter you.

I prayed when I was sixteen, and I started dating my future husband when I was about nineteen. We dated for two years before we got married. Some members of his family were religious, and he went to church with me, but he just said he would never handle serpents and would never try to stop me from handling serpents unless I was pregnant with his child. When I went back to the Signs Church, he told me I could not take his children up there, but I did.

I was twenty-one when we got married, in July of 1985, and I was out of the church for about thirteen years. I went to a different church for about three years—Church of God, a non-serpent-handling church. My family talked to me about it, but nobody said anything mean. Dewey [Chafin] said, "As long as you are going *somewhere* . . ." Because they knew what I believed in my heart.

I wasn't completely satisfied, and I backslid. But anything I did when I was in sin, I got what-for from my mamaw [Barbara Elkins]. But I also knew I was still welcome and I was still loved. I knew when we weren't in church, Mamaw would worry. But I have a video of her telling how much she loved all her grandchildren, even the ones who weren't in the church.

When I was growing up, Mamaw would call Mom, and me and Mamaw could talk for ten or fifteen minutes before Mom could get on the phone. She used to say, "Is this Beulah?" And I'd say, "Is this Bertha?" I love my mommy, I got a good mommy, but I could go to Mamaw when I couldn't go to anybody else.

A couple of years ago, I had a bad car wreck. I was on my way to church in the van, and thirty feet from my house, a tie rod broke, and I lost control and veered into a ditch. I didn't have my seat belt on because I was having trouble getting it closed. I can remember praising the Lord because my kids weren't with me when it happened. My nose was smashed, my leg was cut, and I had what the doctor called an "optic floor blowout." After I had finally got to come home [from the hospital], Popaw come up to the house, and he sit down on the bed with me, and he looked at me, and he just started crying. It broke my heart, because he was hurting. That's the one thing about the love in this family. I was the one not able to walk or barely able to see. When I knew my popaw was crying, I couldn't stand the hurt that I had brought him—not intentionally, it was just an accident. But it broke my heart to sit and see him crying over me.

Mamaw continually worried about us. She was so strong and loved her family so much that when you hurt her or did something to disappoint her, *you* hurt. It made you feel bad. She had that way. It didn't matter. You were still loved.

I was thirty-four years old [when] I lived with her back during the winter in November and December of 1998. I wish now I hadn't left sometimes, because I was only back about four days before she died. But I remember she told me, "You got a bedroom in there. You come and go as you want." She'd sit and play with your hair when she was talking to you, or rub your hand. You knew that everything was okay.

Me and Dewey would laugh. Dewey is how old? Sixty-something? And he stayed up there [with Mamaw and Popaw]. I was thirty-four and living with Mamaw. At one time or another, every one of her grandkids stayed with her, and she took care of us. I can remember me and Melissa and my sister Robin setting up all night long playing church. When we'd come from Ohio, we'd stay two and three weeks during the summer. We'd play church all night long. We'd get in Mamaw's high heels and shout, and her and Popaw would get up, and we'd sneak and get in the bed, and they thought we were asleep. They'd go back to bed, and we'd get up and do it again. Mamaw would be getting ready to get Popaw off to work in the morning [when] we'd be going to bed. When we'd get up—ten or eleven or even one o'clock—she'd have our breakfast cooked, lunch on the stove, and Popaw's dinner on the back burner. Everything was always clean, never dirty.

We wanted to be like Mamaw because she was strong and she taught us to keep a clean house, to feed people, to be kind to people, and never miss church. She was hard in church, and I've heard people say that she let her family get away with more [than she did other people]. Oh, no, no.

When I was in sin, I know I was ornery, but better than some and worse than others. But I always wanted to hide it from Mamaw. I would have never let her know half the things that I did, and I hope to this day that she didn't know half the things. I mean, it wasn't any more than what most people do, but it was just the fact that it would be a disappointment to Mamaw. And I could not stand to disappoint her. That was [true of] all of us.

She was sick a couple of years ago. I wasn't in church. I had come back from Daytona. I remember, I would sit with her, and they'd call for me to come up there, and she had a high fever. I set up all night, and I kept them cold rags on her neck and head. I'd go to leave the room, and she'd take and throw them in the floor. I'd come in, and I'd see them, and I'd say, "Mamaw, did you put these off of you?" She'd say, "I'm fine." I'd say, "No, Mamaw, we've got to get your fever down." And so I'd wrap her up again, and if I had to leave the room, she'd throw them off of her. She said, "You are freezing me to death." Last summer when I was up there with her, she was [telling about it], and she'd say, "I'd go to sleep, and I would have nightmares of Barbie coming after me with those cold rags."

I believe that is the time when she had asked me to do her hair when she died. I walked in one time, and Bug [Barbie's cousin Lydia] said, "You know that Mom wants you to do her hair [when she dies]." I said, "I don't know if I can do that or not." Now, I have always fixed her hair a lot, but I didn't know if I could do it when she died. Bug said, "Before it is over with, she will ask you about it."

Last summer, I was laying in the bed with her, and we was talking, and she said, "If anything happens to me, I want you to fix my hair. Let me look like me. I don't want them to just pull it straight back. I want to look like me, Barbie." I just set there, and then I said, "Okay, I will. I promise." As hard as it was, I made her that promise.

I did it. I didn't think I could go alone [to fix her hair], but then that was a special time. There are certain people that Mamaw would let do certain things. She was a particular woman with her clothes, as far as being neat and clean. At first, I thought, "I can't go by myself. Somebody's got to go with me." But before the day came, I had got to the point that it was the last time I got to fix her hair, and I wanted to go alone. My sister said, "If you want me to go, call me and I'll meet you." Then Bug had thought about coming, but I told Bug that I wanted to do that [alone].

I went to the funeral home, and I put her perfume on her, and I fixed her hair, and I took my hair bow out of my hair and put it in hers, and I got to talk to her. It wasn't as hard as I thought it would be when I first went in. But I got to see her when they were leaving with her from the house. I got up there in time. At the funeral home, they had her on a table, you know. That wasn't so hard. And then it was hard to do her hair, because I remembered the way I would do it at the house. I would get up in the bed with her, and I would put my knees up, and I would say, "Mamaw, just lean on me, and I'll hold you up." I would be halfway leaning backward, doing her hair. But in the funeral home, it was hard because of the way she was laying. I couldn't raise her up. So the funeral home people said, "Well, we'll put her in her coffin and let you see it." Then I wished somebody had been there. That was the hard part. It was hard to see her on that table, but harder to see her in the casket. You know, when they first bring them in [for the funeral] and you hadn't seen them before that, it is a shock. But later, when they brought her into the church, I had already had that initial shock, and [I] was just watching everybody else go through it.

I'm glad I had that time alone with her. Even though she wasn't [alive], it was something that Mamaw and I did.

I can remember back during the winter, she was going Christmas shopping, and I had taken my kids to school and come back, and I did her hair. And I remember we'd cleaned her up, and she was laying there, and I put perfume on her stomach, and she just giggled like a baby. She just always smelled so good. [When I was] growing up, I remember she always smelled of powders. I've been around people that always smell good, always have perfume on, and then when they are gone, nobody thinks to put perfume on them. [When she died,] Mamaw had to smell like Mamaw, 'cause she always smelled so soft. So I put a little perfume on her. Yeah, I did. I told her, "Now you smell like Mamaw."

I'd like to go back to Tennessee, if it's the Lord's will. I want to go to school in Tazewell to get my licensed practical nurse's training.

To sum me up, I love kids, dogs, cats. When I was a little girl, I would pick up every stray dog. People would laugh at me.

There have been times when you pray so hard during the week, and you feel so good, and you want everybody to feel what you're feeling, and if you're blessed to handle serpents, or you see somebody healed, or if the snake goes limp like a shoestring, common sense will tell you that you can't do that yourself. You have to have that love inside. It's that God inside of you. There were times when things were going so bad in my life that I could have lost my mind, but I believe God kept His hand on me.

But you have to wait. There's a song that Punkin used to sing: "Wait on the Lord and Be of Good Courage."

*Dewey Chafin in the Jolo church in 1999
with his signature handful of serpents*
Photos by Fred Brown

STRAIGHT FROM
THE BIBLE

DEWEY CHAFIN
B. 1933

"I saw [that lawyer] awhile back, and he said I would have been a rich man now [if I'd sued]. I said, 'I am rich.'"

THE RUGGED WEST VIRGINIA COAL COUNTRY has produced a resilient brand of people, among them Dewey Chafin, a serpent handler who has worked as a butcher, an automobile production worker, a road builder, and a deep-coal miner. At eighteen, he fought in the Korean War until a mortar shell exploded next to him, leaving him partially deaf and afflicted with other physical problems that remain with him to this day. When Dewey Chafin looks at you with those sunken, transparent blue eyes, you feel as if you are staring into the depths of his soul. He's a quiet and solitary man who barely speaks above a mumble. When he comes to church, it's usually late, and after he greets friends and handles serpents, he slips away as mysteriously as he appeared.

There is something majestic about Dewey Chafin, born of an abusive coal-mining father and a devout serpent-handling mother. He is a tall and muscular man with hair so white it is almost diaphanous. His arms are as solid as pig iron. For a man who is in his late sixties and has been bitten by the deadliest of reptiles, he is in remarkably good shape. His hands, though, show battle scars from handling snakes in services at the Church of the Lord Jesus.

Dewey's generous and sweet-natured personality comes through in his constant beatific smile. But when it comes to picking up deadly reptiles, he is absolutely fearless. His trademark is holding aloft two large snakes in each of his oversized hands. Sometimes, he will even stack several snakes in one hand while holding another in the air above him. Though he appears to be entirely engrossed in his communication with the serpents, you can see that he is always watching the younger, less experienced handlers to see that they are safe. This made-in-the-hills superstar has been bitten more than any other handler in the Southeast—133 times, by his own count. The mere mention of his first name brings instant recognition.

And yet Dewey Chafin is a gentle man who instantly turns away from confrontation. Arguing is against his religion. Nor will he drink coffee or chew gum, for fear that doing so is against God's Word as he reads it. Even when he is working outside in ninety-degree weather, he wears long-sleeved shirts and will not uncover his arms, for he claims it is against the Bible. Curse words are also anathema. Dewey considers even seemingly innocent statements like "I'll bet you" to be defamatory, because, he says, they amount to lying.

The second son of Barbara Elkins, Dewey was given love and religion by his mother but little more than room, board, and physical abuse by his father, Garnet Chafin, who worked all day and drank all night. Barbara and her six children were lucky to make it to the company store to trade scrip for food before Garnet got there and drank up his paycheck. If they won the race, there was food on the table.

"Usually, he got paid Friday evening," says Dewey. "And if you weren't there Friday morning, he'd get [the paycheck]. We didn't get it all, but we got a lot of it. He probably made less than a dollar an hour."

By the time he was fifteen years old, Dewey had had enough. His mother had already fled the flying fists and taken the younger children with her. And even though Dewey was by then too large for Garnet to whip, he wanted out, so his father willingly signed papers saying his son was old enough to join the army.

"He lied and I lied" is the way Dewey puts it. "I had to get away from there."

Three years later, in 1951, the United States was heavily embroiled in the Korean War, a world away from Dewey's mountainous Mingo County, West Virginia. He trained at Fort Knox and then shipped overseas with an infantry outfit. He cannot recall the name of the unit or much about his combat experience, because his battle injury knocked out part of his memory. "I got the concussion from combat," says Dewey. "It was a mortar round. It is just something that happens. There was no sense in being scared. I guess everybody is scared at times, you know. I was almost on the border line at the Thirty-eighth Parallel. I got that mortar there. Wheeew. I had been in combat about three months."

A decade after his discharge, he was still suffering greatly from the injury. "In 1961, I went to the hospital in Bluefield, and they operated on my ear for constant infections caused by the combat incident. They put me to sleep, and I went into cardiac arrest. I died on the operating table. I was out, they told me, about forty-three minutes.

"I should be brain-dead, just like a vegetable. Know nothing. But when I got out, the people in the church prayed for me. They just kept praying. The saints prayed for me. They kept praying here and down at the old church. What I thank God for is that I know God. I give Him credit for everything.

"The doctor that did the operation wasn't the one who caused the problems. It was the anesthesia. They said they either gave me too much of it or it was something I was allergic to. I was talking to a lawyer. He told me we had a good lawsuit if I wanted to take it. I said, 'No, God done taken care of all this. No point in taking a lawsuit.'

"I saw [that lawyer] awhile back, and he said I would have been a rich man by now [if I'd sued]. I said, 'I *am* rich.'

"I got discharged from the army after two years, seven months, and fifteen days," says Dewey. Then he laughs and adds, "I don't know how I remember that.

"I wasn't completely in the church back then. I'd go occasionally. I never came up here [to Jolo]. I'd go to a revival. Effie Gilmer—I'm sure you've heard of her, the woman evangelist—she was holding service. She came here for quite a while. But she backed up on serpent handling, too. She got too old, or her mind went, they say.

"I was not saved at that revival, but they were handling serpents. I didn't know nothing then. I just went because it was something to do. But after I came back, I got in the church then, but not directly.

"I worked for General Motors. Worked on the road from Chillicothe [Ohio] to Lake Ohio when they were building that four-lane. I done a lot of work in Columbus, Ohio, for a while. I was a butcher for a while. I went to Virginia for a while and then came back to West Virginia. I always liked West Virginia. I came back here in 1956."

Dewey believes that his current chest pains and heart problems can also be traced to his war injury. "They got me down on paper as being 60 percent disabled for [my] heart," he says. Recently, he traveled to Richmond, Virginia, to see a heart specialist. After an examination, the doctor told Dewey that he needed a heart catheterization to remove plaque from the vessels around his heart and neck, but they gave him only a fifty-fifty chance of surviving the procedure. Dewey promptly turned his red pickup truck around and returned to Jolo. "I didn't like those odds," he says. "A fifty-fifty chance of dying. I said, 'I ain't going to do it.'"

Further complicating his health problems is diabetes. As Dewey phrases it, he "has the sugar." He gives himself shots of insulin each night.

Dewey's religious philosophy is cut straight from the Old Testament. He can spout a line from the Bible to back up any aspect of his daily routine. He is so attuned to the Bible that he sometimes lapses into Biblical phraseology in the middle of an ordinary conversation, using "hath" instead of "has," for example.

Although Dewey is clearly the beloved stepson and uncle of the Elkins clan, he is also the source of much amusement and concern in the family. Rarely will you find him where he's expected at any given hour. His stepfather, Bob Elkins, says, "Dewey has his own time frame." And if he does something unexpected, a relative will smile and say, "That's Dewey for you."

"I like to keep moving," Dewey says. His perpetual motion results from sheer energy more than anything else, but it is also true that his various illnesses have made him wary of lying down, because he's afraid he might not get back up. Consequently, he's always working at some chore or traveling around West Virginia, hauling and trading.

Like the fifty-dollar bear he once owned. His relatives laugh out loud about that one.

"This friend of mine had two bears, and he asked if I wanted one," Dewey says. "It was a little 'un. My friend lived right across the creek, and he hadn't seen me in a long time, and he said, 'You want a bear, don't you?' I said yeah, and he said, 'Well, I got one you can have for fifty dollars, and I got one you can have for a hundred dollars.' I took the fifty-dollar bear. It was mostly a brown bear.

"So I took that bear and put it up, and then I went to get a permit for it. And they wouldn't give me a permit. The county turned me down. So I went to Charleston to the Department of Natural Resources, and they said, 'We'll give you a permit, but where is the bear?' I said, 'Well, it's at the house.' They didn't say nothing.

"So I got back here about two, three hours later. I went up there to where I had the bear penned up, and there was the Department of Natural Resources. They wanted to know where the bear was. I showed them. He said, 'Well, you know you can't keep it.' I said, 'I don't know why. It's on my property, and I paid for it.' He said, 'Well, you can't keep it.' They said they'd be here in the morning to get it. And they said, 'It better be here when we get here.' I said, 'If somebody comes and steals it at night, it isn't my fault.' They said, 'Well, you'll still be responsible.' They always had an answer for me.

"They gave me a twenty-five-dollar fine, and next day, they told me to go get the bear and put it in the truck. I said, 'Well, it's your bear. It ain't mine.' I said, 'You go get it.' I didn't put it in there for them.

"They tranquilized it, and when they pulled the tranquilizer gun out and give it another shot, I said, 'There ain't no need to put it to sleep.' I said, 'I'll put it in there for you.' But it just fell over like it was dead."

"Dewey doesn't take care of hisself like he should," Bob Elkins says woefully. "He stays up late, gets maybe one or two hours sleep a night. He don't eat right, maybe a piece of toast or something. And then he's gone again. And he's got the sugar." After fifty years, Bob is still a loving father to his stepson. Dewey lives with him, even though he has a wife in Jolo. The two are separated, but Dewey still cuts her grass, drives her to the grocery store, and does all the repairs around her house.

When Dewey is gone, he is often out hunting snakes for church service. He also seeks out the exotic reptiles the church uses from time to time. Dewey says flatly that the church does not use endangered or protected reptiles in services. "There are dealers," he says. "And if they let [the snakes] come into the U.S. at the airports, then that makes it all right." In addition to practically every deadly American reptile, Dewey has bought mambas, king cobras, and Gaboon vipers. Some of the king cobras he has purchased have stretched more than twelve feet in length.

Ray McAllister, one of the church's regulars and a longtime friend of Dewey and Brother Bob, says the church is currently looking for a deadly sea snake to handle. If that sort of snake can be found anywhere near West Virginia, Dewey is the one most likely to turn it up.

For Dewey, it doesn't really matter what venomous creature is brought to services at Jolo. If it's there, he'll handle it. Usually, he's the first to go to the box, which he approaches with a fearless abandonment. Occasionally, he will simply pour a box full of reptiles out on the floor, then scoop them all up in one swipe of his massive hands.

Some nights when Bootie Christian—a church member with an extraordinary talent for playing the electric guitar—is making the church shake with gospel rock, Dewey's eyes will glaze over. When he is fully anointed, he seems to be in another place and time, a spiritual being holding a handful of serpents, wrapping them around his neck, tossing them toward the church's ceiling and catching them as if they are falling pieces of rope. Sometimes, he dresses in a shirt embroidered with patterns of snakes along the shoulders and chest. His eyes seem to blaze red, and his face is lit with a detached but tender smile. On some nights, there is a distinct aura about him.

"I trust God in all things," Dewey says.

He seems to establish a sort of understanding with the snakes he holds. He is both thrilling and terrifying to watch as a huge Southern copperhead climbs the air in front of his face and is met with his penetrating but almost friendly gaze. Every Saturday night and Sunday afternoon, this man can be found in church, calm in the eye of his own religious storm.

"I don't know what tomorrow may bring," Dewey says. "I may be dead. But tonight, I'm going to worship God, the Lord Jesus, who is a doer."

So is Dewey Chafin.

IN HIS OWN WORDS
DEWEY CHAFIN

I was born in Delbarton in Mingo County in 1933. It was a coal county. My daddy, Garnet, worked in the deep mines. He went to work in the mines when he was fifteen. He died in '54. Garnet was his first name. You spell it two ways, one for men and one for women, and I don't know how you spell it.

He beat my mother, Barb, for years. They got married when she was fourteen and Garnet was eighteen. He beat her all the time. Of a night, he'd start picking at her for something, and she'd have to go out and lay out in the mountains. He beat her more than anyone else, more than the children. No way to explain it all. He threw me into the wall. He would throw the babies against the wall, but I guess he never threw the babies with me around. He was just too mean or too crazy or something. He was an alcoholic. I would think that made him do that, but [even] when he wasn't drunk, he was a wicked man. But he was a good provider, I got to say that.

Barb just ran away [with the younger children]. She had took all she could, the beatings. My oldest sister, Pearl, was at work at the company store. She had got married. I was the only one staying there. There wasn't none around but me at that time. I stayed at the house with Garnet. The one below me, Kirby, he was over at my granddad and grandmother's. They partly raised me, too. Garnet didn't try to get Barb back. He just kept drinking.

I worked in the mines for a while. I went into the army at fifteen in 1948. So I was about seventeen years old when I went into the mines. I got sixteen years in. I hung brattice [cloth], ran a motor [to take in mine supplies]. I built stoppings. It had to do with ventilation. You got openings, and the brattice are up here. It keeps your air from circulating back out.

It was '55 when I went to church here. We didn't have the old church. The year after I started, we were right above there in an old building. We had a colored pastor, Wilfred Dickerson. He lived at Parham. Dickerson was a coal miner and worked at the No. 1 Barley. He lived at No. 1. He lived up toward War, West Virginia. He handled serpents. He was our first pastor and pastored three or four years. He was handling serpents before he was our pastor. He has been dead now eight years or so. He had churches in New York, Chicago. He died of natural causes and maybe old age, too. But that's natural.

I joined the church in 1956. I got started in September in the church, and maybe the next summer, I was handling serpents. Since then, I have never left the church or backslid.

Back then, we had a lot of people come to service. There were hundreds. They would be lined up by the old post office almost all the way back to the curve [a distance of a mile or so]. Some would get in church, and some just stood outside. I don't know how they could stand outside, but they would stand outside on the side of the road.

They'd bring snakes there, and they would say they poured liquor down them, hold 'em and burn 'em with cigarettes or something. People wanted us to handle them. They would get them good and mad. And naturally, [the snakes] were touchy. [The people] really were wanting you bit.

The first time I ever handled a serpent, [the anointing] felt just like it does now. It starts in my stomach, the feeling does. It works different in different people, but I get a little feeling right here [in the pit of my stomach], and it just gets bigger and bigger and bigger, and from there on up through my chest and my shoulders. It is a good feeling, a warm feeling. You can feel it.

I sometimes take serpents up on faith, 'cause the Lord lets me feel like it. This is without the anointing. You get a little feeling, but that's not a full anointing. You get a feel like a little pressure.

Over the years, I have been bitten 133 times. My last bite was a rattler at our last homecoming. If I ain't mistaken, it was a timber rattler. I was bit by two different rattlers. One was yellow and one was black. It don't make no difference. They bit me on the left thumb and forefinger. It was both at the same time. It was like they had talked it over. They both hit at the same time.

I had got bitten that week by a cottonmouth also. It was a Thursday night. I was watering them. I was checking some rattlers I had [in a box] with a copperhead. I had the copperhead with my right hand, and I reached back over to get a cottonmouth. I don't know what made me do it. I was just going to check him. I just pulled that lid up, and he popped it to me. He got me on the left hand. I knew right then when I got bit it was going to hurt. It started at my hand. I said, "Oh, yeah, I know this is going to hurt."

When they hit, you can tell. Well, I can. I can tell if there is going to be very much pain. When that venom hits, whether it is much venom or not, somehow or other, you can tell. About five minutes later, you can pretty well know how the venom is spreading. Sometimes, the venom will lay right there for a minute or so. I don't know how come or why. But it will lay there. Then it will start up and start spreading out.

My hand swelled bad. I try not to let them put me in bed. I like to stay on my feet. When you are laying down, it seems like [the serpent has] won half the battle.

Sometimes, when you get a bite, like on a finger, it will rot out. When I got bit that Thursday, and then in church, I couldn't tell much difference in my hand. It was more trouble with pain than anything. But anytime you are bit, it hurts. And you can't build up resistance.

I keep my own serpents. I've had as much as a hundred snakes at one time. Now, all I got is four. I don't keep as many now, because the more you got, the more you have to turn loose. After the homecoming, we take them back to the woods and try to take them back where we got 'em.

We get them from different places. Lot of times, you have to get them from under rocks. Sometimes, you just take your hook. If they are crawling off, you get them.

Sometimes, we get exotic snakes. We just get them from different places—Georgia, Florida, Alabama. It is not black market. I don't think you can have the California red rattlers. They are protected. Anything that is protected, you shouldn't use. The black mamba I had came from South America somewhere, I think. But then, you can get them from dealers.

I've handled mambas, cobras, the king cobra. The longest one of them was about five feet. The king cobra was twelve foot long. I brought him to church, and I handled him, and others did. If you bring them here, somebody is going to handle them.

I handled a Gaboon viper. I've handled yellow and black timber rattlers, canebrakes, Southern copperheads, rubber-banded copperheads, sidewinder rattlers, cottonmouths, Eastern and Western diamondbacks. The Eastern I had was sixty-two inches long. That Eastern bit me over the right eye, and I went blind from about 5 P.M. until 2 or 3 P.M. the next day. The Western diamondback bit me on the hand, and the Eastern bit me over the right eye. When the Eastern hit me, it was like you hit me with a fist. It sounded all the way [to the] back of the church. This one wasn't too big. I felt it, and they said they heard it. I stayed a little bit with the service, and then I left. We lived up on the hill then. I made it pretty good.

I have seen the spitting cobra, but I haven't handled it myself. I'm not afraid of it. You could wear glasses and pick it up. But they are dangerous around the public and around children in the church. You got to look out for the children. Some people handle cobras, but they could spit in your eye, and that is just the same as biting you on the hand. There is not a whole lot of difference in a snake biting and spitting in your eyes. And they tell me that they are accurate, too.

Sometimes, when people get bit, they drop the snakes, and somebody picks them right up. I wasn't bit too bad the last time, but I got bit eight times then. I threw one of them down on the floor, and another handler picked it up. They was rattlers, and one was [what we call] a mangrove. The mangrove got me, but they are not as toxic [as rattlers].

I handle them all alike. The cottonmouth is aggressive, but they aren't as aggressive as the Eastern and Westerns. I had two Easterns that weighed twenty-five pounds between them. One was a little bigger than the other. They are worse than a cottonmouth. And they are a whole lot worse if they bite you.

The most dangerous snake I have handled was the mamba. I didn't have any problems with it. It didn't bite me. I'm glad it didn't.

I've had coral snakes, too. Haven't had any in a while, but I had a long one once. It was a red one. It was [over a foot] long. You know, they don't get that big. No one wanted to handle it. I think everyone was scared of it. But I handled it.

The Gaboon viper was a really big snake. I was not bitten by it, or the cobra. But I have been bitten by copperheads—Southern copperheads, the Northern copperhead, canebrake rattlesnakes, Eastern diamondback and Western diamondback, red rattlers, Pacific rattlers.

I don't have any exotics now. Mostly just timber rattlers. And Richard [Evans, my niece Missy's husband] has two Southern copperheads. They are really big. He has one he calls Annie. She is about as big as I've seen. Arnold is the boy. He is about four foot long, maybe five. I don't name my snakes. Sometimes, I call them Hardheads or something. I've got a Western diamondback right now, but I don't know where it's at. He's not loose, I just gave him to somebody, and I can't remember where it is. I loaned it to somebody.

Some people don't understand our religion, but it determines everything I do in life. I don't drink coffee. I don't chew gum. I don't smoke cigarettes, argue, fight, cuss. If you start an argument with me, just start, and I'll be out of your way in less than a minute.

Cussing is definitely a no-no. People take cussing being just one thing, like using God's name in vain. But cussing is a lot more than that. There are a lot of ways you can cuss without using God's name in vain.

Barb didn't make a big deal about it, but she is where I got the biggest part of my Holiness. From Barb. She was a fine person.

This is a Lord Jesus church. There's a difference in churches. We all believe in one God. But when the Apostle Paul went to the water to baptize them, he did it in the name of the Lord Jesus. That is the word he used. Now, some baptize in the name of Jesus Christ for the remission of their sins. It's in the Bible, but there is nowhere in the Bible where it ever did say anybody is baptized any other way. Not the Father, the Son, or the Holy Ghost, or Jesus Christ. There is no other way. He did say they were baptized in the name of the Lord Jesus. We make that distinction between the two. It ain't no big deal. The only way to prove how they baptized in the Bible is Acts 8:17 and 19:5. They were baptized in the name of the Lord Jesus. But the Father, Son, and Holy Ghost are all one.

There's no steps in becoming baptized. There is not a procedure. They come to the altar, they pray and repent, and the Bible says you must be baptized. In my opinion, you've got to be baptized in water—immersed in it, not sprinkled or anything like that. You got to be in the deep water. That is our way of going to the water. They take them down to the water and then baptize them in the name of the Lord Jesus and put them under the water. We take them to the Tug River at Bradshaw. What we believe is, we are going to the water. We are going to a river, a creek, or something.

When someone joins the church, they pray for forgiveness. That's why they say they prayed. They have repented their sins. When they [talk about] the first time they prayed, that means that is the first time they became a member of the church.

I don't much believe in joining churches. The Bible says we are one spirit. We are all baptized into one body. It ain't but one God. If you are in that body of Christ and I'm in that body of Christ, we are the same body. There is no way in the world to get out of it. Because there is one spirit of God, and they's one spirit of the devil. Anything you can think of, there is one of. We got one body, we got one blood, one life, and that's it. Just one thing.

People who don't handle serpents have an opportunity to go to heaven, too. You don't have to be a Signs Follower. I believe that handling serpents is a calling. It is also a Sign. The Bible says, "These signs shall follow them that believe." And if we are believing, we are going to do it. That's why a lot of people say, "If you don't handle serpents, then you don't believe." But if somebody does not handle serpents but is a Christian in every other way, they have as much a chance of going to heaven as I do. Maybe better. I'm not saying that everybody has got to handle snakes. If I were to say that, I would be wrong.

I let God guide me. I hear His voice in my own sense. It is not just like me talking to you. I hear it in my mind, in my head. You hear a voice that's not a reach-out voice like a deep voice. It is like a ringing in your head, except it is a voice. Nobody can hear it but you. God tells me it is okay to handle serpents. Now, I have had Him say, "*Don't* do it." And I won't do it. [And sometimes,] He just says, "You are going to get bit." He doesn't say not to do it. He just says, "You are going to get bit."

There was a man once who was out in the center of the church there. He had a serpent, and he offered it to me, and the Lord just said, "Don't take them." I just shook my head. I know it is God's Word. You can't go wrong. But as far as taking them up, you can do it at the wrong time. You get in trouble. When that voice told me not to, I didn't.

One time, that voice told me to throw them down. So I throwed them down, and took it to be God. I throwed them down, and as soon as they hit the floor, I picked them right straight back up. But He just said, "Throw them down. They are going to bite you." Everything was all right. It worked, because they didn't bite me.

I always listen, because the devil can slip in there sometime. The devil can throw his voice and make it sound like God. The devil can slip inside the voice and make you think you hear God, and you don't hear God. If you don't know the feeling of God, there is a real distinction there. You can tell like if He's told you to do something, and you start to do it, and then if God wants you to do it, He'll let you know.

As far as casting out devils, I've seen them cast out. I don't say that I've cast them out. I've participated in the prayer of faith that got the devil out. Evidently, anybody that is praying, they got a hand in it. You got to give God credit, because He is the head of it. He is using you as a weapon, and you got to say, "We," meaning God. Or, "God used me." You still got to use that.

I've seen devils come out sometimes. They'll fight. You are casting them out, and they'll say, "Leave me alone." A person comes to you and says, "Pray for me. I need to get rid of this thing." Then you start praying for the individual. Then the devil that's in there, he is like a cigarette demon or any kind of devil. They don't want to come out. That's their home. You are running it off. They don't like it.

Sometimes, you hear the devil. It will say, "Get away from me." That is the devil inside that person talking. If it comes out of them, you can tell the difference. It is a different sound. The devil will argue with you. You just tell it flat out, "That God's got power over you, devil. You might as well come on. You might as well get gone now."

GETTING
YOUR HEART REPENTED

LYDIA ELKINS HOLLINS
B. 1952

"The fear of God that's the beginning of wisdom—that's the only fear of God that I want to have."

"I WAS NINE," SAYS LYDIA HOLLINS. "Old enough to understand she was dead."

Lydia sits in the cool shadows of the Church of the Lord Jesus, speaking quietly in her deep, intense voice, a voice that is often heard joyfully belting out hymns. But today, she is somber as she talks about her mother, Columbia Gay Hagerman, who died in 1961 of a snakebite.

Lydia is the granddaughter and adopted daughter of Preacher Bob Elkins and his late wife, Barbara. Since her teenage years, she has been active in the church her grandparents founded—so active that she is now a fixture there. Services wouldn't be the same without Lydia, who, with her exuberant singing and spirited organ playing, adds an element of drama and excitement to an already stirring event.

Lydia's mother was just twenty-three years old when she died. In a photograph taken just before her death, she looks into the camera with a mischievous grin, a pretty girl with her arms crossed in a teasing attitude. She appears to be dressed up to go somewhere. The collar of her pastel dress is turned up. Her belt has a gleaming silver buckle. She wears tiny star-shaped earrings. Her wavy, reddish brown hair is pulled back from her face and pinned behind her ears, where it falls in curls around her shoulders. In the background of the picture is the quintessential West Virginia countryside—a barn, a muddy yard rutted by tire tracks, fence posts strung with wire, and the ever-present mountains, which have determined not only the history but also the future of Lydia's West Virginia serpent-handling family.

Lydia is now twice as old as her mother was when that photo was taken. "My mom was very young when she died, and I remember she was a beautiful woman," she says. "We was more like sisters instead of mom and daughter, because she was so young. We lived in a holler, and when my mom and I would go out, we would walk up and down the holler. I was a little brat. If she didn't do things I would want her to do, I'd say, 'I'll tell Mamaw on you.' I kinda went between her and my [grandparents] so I could get my way. We used to go to church together, too. I remember her telling me about always staying in the faith. My dad, John Hagerman, would go to church with us, but he wasn't a member, and he never handled serpents. I was the only child of him and my mother.

"I had lived with Mamaw and Popaw my whole life, from the day I was born. When my mom died, my dad let them adopt me, because that was the only home I'd ever known. My father wasn't living with us at the time my mother died. He had been in the army, and he and my mom were divorced, and he had remarried and had children by his second marriage. He was living in Indiana, but he came in for the funeral and the wake. He always visited me when I was a child, though, and I'm on real good terms with him still. He lives in Anderson, Indiana, and I visit him once a year."

Lydia, nicknamed "Bug" because she weighed less than five pounds at birth, has Columbia's determined but shapely chin and small, dainty fingers. Her considerable presence in church makes her appear taller than her five feet, three inches. As she tells what she remembers of her mother, her blue eyes seem to darken. Most of what comes back to her from that terrible day are details—flashes of sound, smells, memories of women weeping, people praying.

"I remember I was kind of wandering through the house, and everyone was picking me up and showing me compassion. I knew my mother was serpent-bit, but that was nothing uncommon to me. It was just something I knew. We handle serpents. We get bit."

The people who prayed over Columbia continually asked her if she wanted medical help. She rebuked them, says Lydia, and asked them if they had lost their faith.

Lydia Elkins Hollins under the anointment in a Jolo service in 1999
Photo by Fred Brown

Columbia, called "Columby" by her family, was bitten in church on a Sunday. By Thursday, after five days of agonizing pain, she was unable to eat. One of the details of that day that Lydia sharply remembers is the soup. Someone made Columby some potato soup, hoping to strengthen her, but she was too sick and too weak to eat it. "I remember that she was off in a side room from the kitchen, and that potato soup was cooling," says Lydia. "After she died, there was no one left in that room, and I kind of wandered in by myself, and I got up on that little rollaway bed she was on, and I kissed her on the neck, and she was still warm.

"She was in awful pain, but she suffered it quietly. Even as a nine-year-old child, I accepted my mother's death as part of God's plan. I been born in Holiness. I been raised in Holiness."

As Lydia puts it, she hasn't always "been on the right road. Sometimes, I yielded my [body] to flesh, rather than spiritual things. I yielded to worldly things." But for the last eight years, she says, "God has had my life. I've devoted myself to the Lord. I started singing in the church when I was fourteen, when I gave my heart to God. And that's when I started handling serpents, when I was fourteen."

Lydia has faced numerous other losses in her life. She has seen family members and friends die from both snakebite and disease. She lost her first husband—Larry Hamilton, the father of her daughter Melissa—in an automobile accident after only two years of marriage, and lost her son, Daniel Ray, in December 1999. But one of the worst trials she has suffered occurred when her grandmother died in February 1999. For forty-six years, Lydia depended on Barbara Elkins for guidance, sustenance, and advice, and when Barbara's coffin was carried out of the church on the day of her funeral, her family seemed temporarily to have lost its very core. "My mom and dad [Barbara and Bob Elkins] will always be the biggest inspirations in my spiritual life," says Lydia.

In the long run, none of these sorrows has diminished Lydia's faith. She believes that God has a plan, no matter how circuitous, for everyone. She and her present husband, Kirby Hollins, a roof bolter in the Alabama coal mines, are two of the Jolo church's staunchest members. Kirby, whose mother, Gracie, is a well-known serpent handler in Kentucky, suffered a serious bite in July 1993, but he continues to handle serpents without hesitation. He is quiet and shy and has a boyish smile.

Though Kirby stays mostly in the background at church, Lydia's robust voice can be heard throughout the service, singing as she plays the organ. She has the timbre and style of a country-music singer, and had fate directed her elsewhere, she might have made a living in the musical field. Her talent is God-given. She had a few piano lessons as a child, but for the most part, she plays by ear, as does her daughter, Melissa Evans.

Following the Signs has been Lydia's desire almost all her life. She picks up serpents boldly. Unlike women in many other serpent-handling churches, the Jolo women go directly to the snake boxes to pick up serpents, instead of waiting to be handed them by male church members.

"When you're in the spirit, there's no fear," declares Lydia. "There's no fear 'cause God don't give us fear, because fear is torment, and God's not torment. Ain't no word in His vocabulary [for] fear and torment. Just the fear of God that's the beginning of wisdom—that's the only fear of God that I want to have."

IN HER OWN WORDS
LYDIA HOLLINS

I started praying and singing in the church when I was fourteen years old. Gave my heart to God. And that's when I started handling serpents, when I was fourteen. I haven't always been what I was supposed to be with the Lord. But we've all failed, come short of the glory of God. Since I prayed, though, I been trying to serve God and give Him my all, except when I was down and out.

The way I felt the first time [I handled serpents] is better felt than told. When I get the anointing, I get real weak in my stomach, and my hands get real cold. Now, when I'm not in the spirit, don't even come near me [with a snake]. I have a terrible fear of serpents when I'm not in the spirit.

I have been bitten five times—four times by copperheads and once by a rattler. There were times that I thought I might die.

My first bite was in 1978, May or June. I got a canebrake [rattler] bite, and I didn't hurt a whole lot, [but] I stayed unconscious a whole lot. I can't tell you how long. Every time I came to, [the people from the church] would be praying. They'd be in my face praying.

I got bit at the first Jolo church [which later burned down. The present

Lydia holding Barbara Church, 1965. In the background is Ray Webb, whom Lydia later married twice.
Elkins family photo

Lydia with Bob Elkins, c. 1963
Elkins family photo

church was constructed in 1980]. When we're young, we have to learn. There's a learning process. We'd just got a canebrake rattler for the service, and Dewey [Chafin, her uncle] told me, "You really need to know when the spirit moves on you. You need to know what you're doing in the spirit when you handle this." I said, "I know how to handle serpents. You don't have to tell me." So it wasn't too long into the service [when] I got bit. And the first person I looked at was Dewey, and he said, "I *told* you."

Brother Brady Dawson [a church member] took [the serpent] out of my hand, and I walked up on the pulpit, and I turned my back to the audience, and I told my dad, I said, "I can't breathe," and he carried me out. And I remember them carrying me into Mamaw's house, and they got me in the bathroom to change my clothes, and I sat down on the commode for them to change my clothes, and I [fainted]. And when I came to, I heard my mom [Barbara] say, "Not again. Not again, Lord." She was referring to my mom that had died. Then they carried me into the bedroom, and after that, I just went in and out a lot for a day and a half.

I never did have one pain with that rattler bite. It was on my right hand, right up from my little finger in the tender part of my right hand. It didn't bother me or nothing. But now, with my copperhead bites, it was a different story. I had *four* of them, and twice, I thought I was leaving here.

[When you're bitten,] the saints [church members] always stay with you until you're well enough on your own or till you can do things on your own. With my first copperhead bite, there was four or five of the saints that was around me, and I could just feel some spirit leaving me. They started praying, and I said, "I'm leaving here if y'all don't get victory." Life was leaving me. I remember Danny Ray, my only son—he was about two—looking through the windows, and then he would come in the bedroom to check on me. He was really too young to understand what was happening. There were four or five of the saints around the bed, and they started praying, and I felt my spirit come back. I felt life coming back into me. I didn't have pain one after that. I got up that evening and ate brown beans and kraut. It went as fast as it came.

Now, one copperhead bite I got—my last bite was April of '94—I went to Mom's and stayed two hours, then I went home [to Kentucky]. And on Tuesday, I went back to work, back to the computer and typing. I was a secretary for the Health Department.

The only bite that's left me maimed was on my left hand with a copperhead.

There was about a dozen copperheads that one of the brothers was handling, and I had come off [playing] the organ, and I reached, and he reached about the same time, and as soon as I got [the serpent] in my hand, that copperhead bit me. It hit me on the middle finger of the left hand, and it hurt me so bad that I turned my back to the audience, and I just started crying. That was the worst bite I ever had. It eat some of the meat out of my finger and twisted it, disfigured it. But it don't bother me playing the organ.

My first husband—Larry Hamilton, Melissa's dad—died in a car wreck, and Mamaw and Popaw raised Melissa. We were [living] in the house with them. Melissa stayed with them, and when I moved out, she could [have gone also], but she had always been with Mamaw and Popaw, and I wouldn't take her from them as long as she would always know I was her mother. We have a real good relationship. She knows that. I met my second husband through church. Ray Webb. He's the father of my [younger] kids, Leanna and Danny Ray. Me and Kirby have no children.

For eight years, I've been completely in the Lord. It has a lot to do with my marriage and growing into spiritual maturity. We have a praying home, and that's unity. You come together. I met Kirby through the Kentucky churches.

Of my children, Melissa is the only one that's praying at this time. That means she belongs to the church. She's got the Holy Ghost. But the other two hold to serpent handling and Holiness. My two [youngest] children haven't handled serpents. Leanna is twenty-one, married, and expecting a baby. Melissa is married to [church member] Richard Evans. Daniel Ray was killed in an accident in December 1999.

[I didn't have to explain serpent handling to my children because] all of them have been born into the Holiness Church and serpent handling, so it's just a way of life. If they decide to give their heart to God, that's where they'll give their heart to God at. It'll be at this church.

When I was in school, I only had one incident out of the whole time when a boy had made fun of serpent handling. My science teacher, Louie Wimmer, sent me out of the classroom, and he talked to the class and said, "I don't ever, *ever* want to ever hear nothing like that again." But only that one time when I went to school at Bradshaw and Iaeger, *one time*.

I moved to Kentucky because my husband Kirby got transferred in the mines. He worked at Harmon Branch. And [while] we lived [in Kentucky], we traveled back home every weekend. *Every weekend*. Ninety-one miles each way. A hundred eighty-two miles round trip. Snow, ice, rain, shine. Maybe out of all of those years [from 1989 to 1995], there may have been five weekends that we didn't make it, and that's pushing it.

Then when Kirby got transferred to Alabaster, Alabama, I couldn't find a serpent-handling church. So one day, I was in a laundromat, praying over my food. I had gone out and got me something to eat, and I was praying over my food. There was a black deacon there. I didn't know that he was a deacon at the time, but he said, "You're Holiness, aren't you?" And I said, "Yes, I am." I had been down there since December 2 and hadn't been to church but one time. And this was February. You know, you take a serpent handler out of church, and you don't know how they are going to survive. And I said, "I'm looking for a Holiness serpent-handling church." And he said, "Well, I can help you on one of them. I can help you on a Holiness church, but they don't handle serpents." "That's fine," I said. "I'll take that."

So he told me to call Elder Mack Harris, Jr., at the Spirit and Truth Ministries in Calera, Alabama. He gave me the phone number, and I called him up. Mom Harris answered the phone, and I said, "May I speak to Elder Harris?" And she said, "Yes, you may." I said to Elder Harris, "You don't know me, and I don't know you, but one of the brothers gave me your number. I need a church to go to." He said, "We'd be glad to have you." And I said, "I'd be glad to come, because I haven't been but once since December." He said, "We'll come by and pick you up. Tell us where you live." I said, "Well, first I have a question for you. I'm white. Does that matter?" And he said, "Sister, there's no color in God."

That was on Wednesday. They said they would pick me up at three o'clock on Sunday. Then they called back and said it would be five o'clock when they picked me up [because] they were going to visit a church. So we waited. My husband Kirby took me to meet them, and we waited till something like five-thirty. That's something I learned—they always run late. Kirby said, "They're not coming. Let's go home." I said, "No. Did you ever think this is the devil, trying to trick me out of getting to go to church?"

And they pulled up in that car, and I got out of my car, and my husband delivered me into their hands. I didn't know them people. *He* didn't know them people. He didn't know if they was going to bring me back dead or alive. But I got in that car with four black people and went to church. It was Elder Harris and his wife, Mom Harris, their son Eric, who's fifteen, and one of the sisters from the church. I was the only white face there. And God had to do it. When

I got in that car, Elder Harris said, "Praise God, sister. We're glad to have you." He was praising God, and he just started rejoicing, talking about the Lord, and then he started speaking in tongues, driving down the road, and it was just like the spirit joined us right then. And it's been that way ever since. I never felt out of place at that church because I was white. I never felt intimidated. I'm going there now again, because Kirby's got transferred back. I feel like I belonged there all my life. It's just like I'm family.

I haven't known a whole lot of the world. Put me out on the street, I probably wouldn't last an hour. My husband laughs at me. He says, "You couldn't make it out there." Elder Harris said, "You should consider yourself fortunate that you've always known the way."

People ask me the difference of being in [the black church in] Alabama and [the serpent-handling church in] West Virginia. Nothing. There's no difference. They just don't handle serpents. When I go there, they're at home with the world, and I take my Holy Ghost with me. I sing in the church there and play the keyboard. Even though a lot of black people don't know nothing about serpent handling or being around it, but still yet, Elder Harris knows it's the Word, and he's a man of God. [But] he don't care to be connected with serpent handling. Now, the first pastor of our church in Bartley, West Virginia, Bishop Winford Dickerson, he was black, and he handled serpents. And there are a few black people who belong to serpent-handling churches, and they handle, too, but they don't handle at Spirit and Truth Ministries. Now, they know I belong to a serpent-handling church. Elder Harris has preached twice at Jolo, and he didn't handle serpents, but they were handled by other people at that service.

In church services, there's a lot of spirit in the music, but it comes from being anointed. You get anointed to sing, same as when you handle serpents. I could go up there right now and sit down at that organ, and it probably wouldn't sound the same to you as it did when you was in church with me [during services]. You play [music] with that anointing that God gives you. And it's different from playing in the flesh. It's like a direct contact of God.

But the music in both churches is very spiritual. When Mamaw died, [the] Spirit and Truth Ministries choir came and sang at her funeral. It's wonderful when black and white folks can worship together. I'm the only white person in the church, but they accepted me as a child of God. My husband Kirby loves the Harrises, and we do a lot of things together. They went to a church in Biloxi last weekend, and we stayed with Eric while they were away. But Kirby won't go to church services there because they have women preachers, and he doesn't believe in that. Paul said, "I suffer not a woman to teach," and that's the way the men in the Jolo church believe. They believe that men should handle the business of the church. We socialize with the Harrises—Holiness people do socialize—but just because we socialize doesn't mean we sin. No. And once a week, I cook dinner for Elder Harris and Eric and Mom Harris, because she works full-time as a certified nurse's assistant. It's not a duty. It's a blessing for me and my husband.

Black churches usually have an administrative staff—fifteen to twenty people—and I am now Elder Harris's personal nurse. That means I'm his personal aide. He sweats a lot when he preaches, because he preaches so hard, and I wash and keep all his towels and handkerchiefs, his water and juice, his Gatorade, his breath mints. And I put his robe on him after he preaches.

Handling serpents is no different for women than for men. There is no extra feeling of responsibility because I'm a mother. When I handle serpents, I wouldn't think about my children, because they are flesh. When you're in the spirit, you have no flesh about you. Don't even enter my mind. That's why we teach our children the right way. When you love somebody, you tell them the truth.

We know that the Bible says [that] heaven does not appear to us or enter into the hearts of man. He's went away to prepare a home for us. We know it's a street of gold, because the Bible speaks of that. Gates of pearl, walls of jasper. All the things that we have given up—all the diamonds, all the sapphires, all the different things that we have sacrificed in our flesh down here—up there, we're going to be walking on a street of gold. We don't wear gold here, but we're going to be *walking* on it up there.

The main thing in any church—not just serpent-handling [churches] but any church—is a pure heart. Get your heart right. Live every day for God. Yield your [body] to God. And if I would have to speak words of wisdom or speak words of salvation or be a soul winner to anybody, I would say, "Get your heart repented." Because when that heart's right, everything else is going to clean up. *Everything* else. Jesus said He looked on the very intents of our hearts. That's why it's so important to get that heart right. Be repented, get the Holy Ghost, and be baptized in Lord Jesus' name. [That's] the only way for eternal life.

Melissa Evans with a handful of copperheads at a Jolo service in 1999.
Her great-aunt, Lucille Church, watches (right).
Photo by Fred Brown

WAITING TO SEE
THE LORD

MELISSA "MISSY" GAY
HAMILTON EVANS
B. 1968

*"The Lord's blessed me. He's give
me everything I have."*

ARNOLD AND ANNIE ARE REGULARS at the Church of
the Lord Jesus. They're not Elkins family members. They're Southern copperheads, and they show up at just about every service, sometimes in ill temper.
Melissa Evans found out just how ill a couple of years ago.

"We don't ordinarily name our snakes," says Melissa. "But somebody gave
my mommy this little ole copperhead, real skinny and half dead, and Mommy
gave him to my husband, Richard, and he started taking care of him and feeding him. That snake would eat thirty to forty mice a summer—even more'n
that, if you offered it to him. We named him Arnold, after that pig on the
television show *Green Acres*, because he ate like a pig.

"And that's the only snake that's ever bit me, Arnold. He's a big copperhead, about four feet long now, and kindly heavy. It was homecoming '97. Richard was holding Arnold, and Dewey [Chafin] and me reached for it at the same
time, and it was me that took it. I was holding Arnold and shouting with him,
and then he bit me. I didn't really get sick. I can handle pain fairly well, but I
don't like to feel nauseated. Right then, as soon as he bit me, I could feel it
swelling, and it burned just like I had my arm in a fire. He hit me right above
the elbow on the inside of my right arm. I flinched, but I continued to handle.

They asked me if I was bitten. I said yes, and I don't think Richard thought I was, because I was still anointed, still shouting. So Richard took him from me, and he pushed up the sleeve of my dress and looked at my arm. There was already a little bruise about the size of a dime—no blood—and it felt like someone had stabbed a needle into my arm, like a hypodermic needle.

"It didn't stop me. I went home and changed my dress, 'cause the one I had on had tight sleeves. Then I came back and finished the services and come home and finished cooking for the homecoming lunch the next day. And Sunday, I got up and went to church again. That copperhead was huge. It was real big. It could have really laid a hurting on me, but the Lord didn't see fit for it to, so it didn't. The Lord moved for me really good. He blessed my soul."

It takes more than a four-foot Southern copperhead to stop Melissa Evans, the mother of two boys—Nathan, born in 1990, and Tyler, five years younger. Small-boned and thin, Missy is much tougher than she appears. She's quiet, soft-spoken, and wiry and has long reddish brown hair.

Melissa has been in serpent handling almost half her young life. She was raised in the church by her grandmother, Barbara Elkins, since the day she was born. During that time, she has weathered enough trials—serious illness, the deaths of close relatives and friends, financial, family, and personal problems—to sorely test her faith. But she remains steadfast in her belief that following the Signs is the road to heaven. "She will tell you real quick what she stands for," says Lucille Church, her great-aunt. "Melissa is bold when it comes to her salvation."

Melissa has seen so much death and injury from snakebites that it makes her fear for the time when her sons will be old enough to handle. Even her grandmother—the mother of the church, who reared her family to follow the Signs—often warned family members to be careful when handling serpents. "Mamaw did not like for me to handle serpents," says Melissa. "She said, 'You have two kids. You do not need to handle. There are other things for you to do to follow the Signs.' Oh, she worried about me. But the Lord is going to take care of me. If I die, then He's going to take care of my kids. He's going to see that they're raised right.

"The same spirit that moves on a man moves on a woman. I can give you a good example. We were in church one night, and there was this copperhead that had bit Richard about a week before. I went to handle it, and he took the box away from me. I got it back. Well, he just skidded it across the pulpit. I scooted it back. He scooted it again on me. He didn't want me to go in there, because he was afraid I would get bit, because he'd been bit. But I got it, and I handled it, and the Lord blessed me. It didn't bite me. It didn't hurt me.

"The Lord blessed me with it, but Richard was scared for me [just like Mamaw was]. I'm the last of the children she raised, and when I left there, she started working on my two boys. She teased me. She said, 'You don't know how to raise them younguns. Why don't you give them to me?' I'd always lived with her before I got married, and she had tried to adopt me, but Mommy [Lydia Elkins Hollins, who herself was adopted by Barbara and Bob Elkins when her mother, Columbia Gay, died] said no. Every day, I look at Mamaw's picture and tell her I love her. What gives me comfort now is knowing that she don't suffer anymore. She don't have any pain. If I stand true to the Lord, I'm going to see her again. I haven't lost her forever. It's just for a little while. I think she looks down on us all the time.

"I've seen her perform miracles. Yeah, I've seen her handle fire a couple of times. And I was little when this happened, but I've heard the story. She prayed for Hershel Blankenship, one of the brothers in the church. And he had a brain tumor. He was supposed to go in for surgery. And my grandmother prayed for him in church, and the Lord cured him. When he went back to the doctor, they couldn't find the tumor. It didn't show up on the x-rays. It was gone. And he still comes to church today."

Melissa lives with her children and her husband, Richard Evans, a coal miner, in a new double-wide trailer they were able to buy after the Equal Employment Opportunity Commission represented Richard in a 1996 lawsuit against his employer, the Upper Mill Mining Company.

What happened to Richard is a classic case of adding insult to injury—in this case, adding snakebite to injury. A jury in the United States District Court for the Western District of Virginia found that the Grundy, Virginia, company had violated Title VII of the 1964 Civil Rights Act by firing Richard on the basis of his religion.

Richard, hired as a bridge operator in 1991, was constantly harassed by fellow workers because of his faith. "Richard was really persecuted for handling serpents," Melissa says. "They would write on his buggy, 'Copperhead,' or they called him 'Rattlesnake.' " Richard complained to his supervisors, but they failed to stop the harassment.

When he was bitten by a broad-banded copperhead during a church service

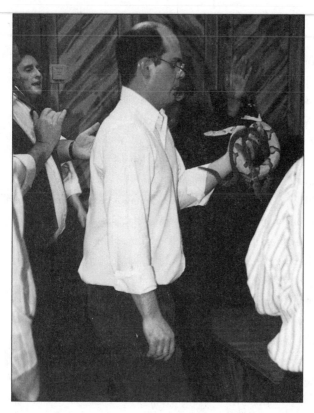

*Richard Evans handling
serpents at a 1999 Jolo
church service.*
Photo by Fred Brown

in July 1993, he asked his employer for a one-week leave of absence. His supervisor approved the leave but threatened that Richard might lose his job if a snakebite kept him out. In February 1994, Richard was bitten once more. He obtained a doctor's excuse but did not reveal that his illness resulted from a snakebite. Then, in March 1994, Richard was bitten again. When he called in sick the next two days, his supervisor, Elster McClanahan, told him he was obligated to return with a note saying he was under a doctor's care. Richard said that he was willing to get a note from his doctor confirming his injury, but that obtaining treatment was against his religion. McClanahan fired him.

Richard and Melissa then sought the aid of the EEOC. The case was settled in May 1997. In the meantime, Richard was rehired by the company in October 1994.

In its argument, the EEOC contended that Upper Mill "failed to accommodate Evans' religious beliefs and fired him because of those beliefs." The jury awarded him $20,475 in back pay but refused to impose punitive damages on the company. Victor M. Lawrence, the lead EEOC attorney in the case, says that the standard for awarding punitive damages is evidence of malice or reckless indifference. "I think that any company that is aware of this ruling [should] be more cautious in taking action against an employee in this type of circumstance," he says.

The Evanses' new home is only a few miles from the church where Melissa grew up seeing more drama unfold than most people see in an entire lifetime. She remains committed to the lifelong promise she has made to God, because she believes that, ultimately, she will be rewarded.

IN HER OWN WORDS
MELISSA GAY EVANS

I was born in Richlands, Virginia, in 1968 but have lived all my life in Jolo, West Virginia. My mommy was real young when she had me. She was about sixteen, and we lived with Mamaw and Popaw. And later, when Mommy went to Ohio for a couple of weeks, I stayed there with them, 'cause that was the only home I knew. My grandmother was a strong and independent woman. Seemed like she never did let her feelings show. She was always there for me. She loved me. I *knew* she loved me. She and Popaw wanted to adopt me. Mommy wouldn't let them, but she said I could live with them as long as I knew that she was really my mother. Later, Mommy lived in the house across the street from the church, up there on the hill next to where Dewey lived, but with Mamaw and Popaw was where I lived. Every once in a while, I would spend a week with [Mommy], but a lot of the time, she was gone. Mommy was everywhere, but I know she loves me. That's just the way it was.

My daddy was Larry Hamilton. I was eighteen months old when he died, so I don't remember much about him. He had been off in Vietnam, and he was on his way to get Mommy and me to take us back to live with him on the army base when he had an automobile accident and died. I don't know how it happened. I just know it was an accident. I *do* remember one thing about him. They used to have a restaurant down at the mouth of the hollow, a drive-in restaurant, and it was called the Blue Swan Drive-In. One day, Mommy and Daddy were racing each other in different cars, and I was in the car with him. He pulled into the Blue Swan and bought me a hamburger and a milk shake. I used to love milk shakes. And I don't remember this, but they say I used to love to talk to him on the telephone, too.

When Mommy married Ray Webb, they lived in Jolo across from the church. I stayed with my grandparents. Mommy had two more children. That was Leanne [born in 1978] and Daniel Ray [born in 1975]. Considering that we lived apart, I'm pretty close to my half-sister and half-brother.

I joined the church in Jolo when I was twelve, and I started playing the piano in church when I was thirteen. Never had a lesson. I started by playing chords on the piano and keyboard, and then I played the drums. I just knew how.

I went to church for about four years, and then I quit. That was about '84. When you get in high school, it gets really hard. People don't understand the way you dress. One day, I was waiting for the school bus, and me and my teacher got into [an argument]. She came up to me and said it was tempting the Lord to handle snakes. She said we were in a cult, and that if my grandpa told me to jump off a bridge, I probably would. I told her the Bible says that the Lord cannot be tempted in any way. But she kept on talking, and I just tried to ignore her. I just let it roll off me. It's hard to serve the Lord. If anyone tells you it's easy, they are lying to you.

When I was sixteen, I had to have my spleen removed. The doctors said it was the size of a football. I have congenital fibrosis of the liver, which makes your liver gradually deteriorate, but I have regular checkups, and right now, I'm doing good.

I married Richard in May of 1988. He's from Defiance, Ohio. Mamaw didn't come to the wedding, and when I left the house, she said, "You're leaving here an Elkins, and you'll be coming back as an Evans." Richard was kindly a party person, to put it mildly. He was on a downhill grade and into partying really bad. He was spending our money on drugs, and we couldn't pay our bills. We couldn't even afford groceries. Well, one night we were in bed, and he started praying. So I prayed with him. It was about ten o'clock at night, and Richard called Popaw and asked him to meet him down at the church. Popaw met him, and ever since then, our life has changed. Our marriage has changed.

I got back in church in March of 1993, when I was twenty-two. Evidently, these things had been on Richard's mind quite a bit. He worked in the coal mines at Grundy, and he'd been smoking about three packs of cigarettes a day. When he woke up the next morning after praying the night before, he saw his cigarettes laying there in the kitchen, and he put them on top of the refrigerator. When he came home from work, he saw the cigarettes on the refrigerator, and he said, "Why didn't you throw them away?" and I said, "This is for you to do. I can't do this for you." And the Lord moved on him [to break his smoking habit] and for a lot of other things.

Richard's a coal miner. He's a general laborer and a belt man. He was a bridge operator, where they do continuous hauling from the bridges on to the belts, but now where he works, they use a scoop. He's been bitten twenty-two times. In church, he does a little dance step when he's getting in the spirit that's sort of like a clog dance. I don't know what you call it. He just does it. When he first shouted, that's what the Lord give him.

When Richard was fired from the mines, he got unemployment for seven months, but that ran out, and we didn't have no money. I tried to get welfare, but I couldn't because we had two cars, and they said we'd have to sell one if we wanted it, or get an estimate on the truck. Finally, in 1997, we got Richard's back wages with interest, but the jury didn't award us punitive damages, because the mines had hired Richard back seven months after they fired him. They were supposed to give us a lump-sum settlement, but they claimed they were going bankrupt and could only afford to give us bimonthly payments until the settlement was paid off. So we had to agree to that.

But the Lord's blessed me. He's give me everything I have, including a new house. We used to live in a twelve-by-fifty-eight-foot trailer with two bedrooms and one bathroom, and that done us for ten years. Now, we have a new and bigger double-wide, and it's real nice.

Just a few months ago, I got bacterial meningitis and septicemia. We never did find out how I got it. I was in quarantine for four days. I had been sick Tuesday morning, and I got the shakes. We was in revival Tuesday night, and Wednesday morning when I woke up, I could hardly move my arms. But most of the pain was in my back. My spine had swelled and was infected. The doctors told Richard, said if I lived, I might not be able to walk again, and I might have seizures for the rest of my life.

During the time I was in the hospital, Richard was bitten by a black rattler. That night, he came to the hospital, and the nurse looked at him and said, "Are

you okay?" And he didn't want to say anything because he didn't want treatment. He stayed with me all that night and the next day, until he knew I was
going to be all right. I stayed in the hospital a week, and when I came home, I
was on an intravenous for five days. The doctors gave me antibiotics, but the
cure is all due to the Lord. I attribute that mostly to prayer.

Richard's hand is crippled from the last bite. There is no feeling in his left
hand or fingers. He will probably never get it back.

I don't like talking to reporters, because you never know how the story's
going to turn out. The first interview we ever gave was to *Dateline NBC*. They
were supposed to talk to Richard, but it was all about me, because I was pregnant with Tyler, and the night before, in church, I had handled a black rattler.
And they just tore me to pieces. They asked me, what if I got bit? Wasn't I
worried about my baby dying? How come I didn't care about my baby? We were
standing right out there in the yard of our house. After Tyler was born, they
called a couple of months later, so they could tell the people who'd seen the
show how I was. They called it an "update." I said, "Yes, he's fine, and he's
healthy."

I want my boys to grow up in the church, because I want them to go to
heaven. I've seen death in [snake handling], and those are my children. I'm
worried, but I love them, and I want them to be in church. Popaw says children
can handle serpents when they reach eighteen. I say twenty-one, because I worry
about them and I want to put off them handling as long as I can. But if the Lord
anoints them, then they have to do it.

Heaven is going to be remarkable, unreal. I picture it as a big old cloud.
And to see the Lord? I can't wait. The Bible says what the Lord looks like. He
has hair white as snow. His hair is not right in the pictures we see of Jesus. They
paint it brown. And his eyes ain't like that in the pictures. They give him a
colored eye. His eyes are balls of fire.

And I can't wait to see Mamaw and everybody that I know that has made
it, and to sit and sing and be able to talk to them. I can't imagine. I just can't
imagine. Happy are you if you die in the Lord.

LIVING THE HARD LIFE

CHARLES "JUNIOR" CHURCH
B. 1943

"When you serve God, it is a constant war, a constant battle."

WHEN CHARLES CHURCH WALKS into the Church of the Lord Jesus, he looks like a successful businessman. He's tall and stocky, with a receding hairline and a serious expression that conceals his kindhearted nature. He wears rimless glasses and snappy suits and ties, making him as nattily attired as the well-dressed preacher, Bob Elkins, who is Charles's father-in-law.

Charles Church has worked hard to get where he is today. Born in Pineville, West Virginia, in February 1943, he was the son of Blanche White, who came from a family of eighteen children, and Neute Church, a coal miner who had run his own mines in Buchanan County, Virginia. Neute, born in 1900, was widowed when he met Blanche, who agreed to be his wife even though she was twenty years younger. She lived on one side of the mountain, and Neute lived on the other. Somehow, they came together, married, and had children of their own. Charles, called "Junior," has three sisters from that union and three older half-sisters and a half-brother from his father's first marriage. Before he was born, his mother gave birth to twins—a boy and a girl, one of whom died at two months and one at three months, both from pneumonia.

His childhood, spent partly in Whitewood, Virginia, and partly in Bradshaw, West Virginia, was a mixture of work and play. As the only boy at home, he

Charles Church, seven years old
Family photo

Charles in Germany, 1961
Family photo

"had to carry in the coal and the wood," he says. "I fished and hunted with my friends, but my father and I never had a close relationship because he was so much older. He worked all the time. Before he was a miner, he was a lumberjack. I can remember them hauling him out of the woods in a truck after a big log rolled over on his leg and broke it. After that, he worked as a coal miner. He never had any schooling, but he could read and write. He retired once—in 1962—and just wandered around because he didn't know what to do with himself. So in 1964, he went back to the mines. [He] retired again at seventy-three. He died in 1996 at the age of ninety-five."

There wasn't much in the way of religion for Charles when he was growing up. "My mom would go to church here and there, but we didn't talk much about religion at home, didn't read the Bible or anything like that. My father never did go to church."

When he turned seventeen, Charles had the choice of going into the mines or joining the army. His father took him down to sign up for the service, and Charles left home. He was stationed in Germany for thirty-four months, from 1960 to June 1963. It was the first time he'd ever been away from home, aside from visiting relatives in the summertime.

While he was away, Charles's mother joined the Church of the Lord Jesus at Jolo, the place where Charles would eventually meet his wife and find solace in a faith he had previously ridiculed.

In 1961, while Charles was in Germany, his mother wrote to tell him about the death by snakebite of Columbia Gay Hagerman. "I wrote her back a real nasty letter," Charles recalls. "I can't remember exactly what I said, but it was real nasty, condemning serpent handling and saying people were wrong to practice it. I didn't know anything about the church then. I don't think I'd even read two chapters of the Bible."

Returning to Jolo after his discharge, Charles was reunited with his best friend, Charlie Kennedy, a boyhood schoolmate and a nephew of Bob Elkins. "Charlie and I went to school together and played football together, hung out in movies, drank. Charlie died last year of cirrhosis. He had been a big drinker, although he quit a few years ago. It hurt me when he died. He'd grown up in the serpent-handling church, and he was coming back a little before he got real sick."

Charles found himself in need of work. Bob Elkins's stepsons Dewey and Herbert Chafin operated a mine, and they gave him a job on a cutting machine. "That's where you cut coal on the bottom, about eight feet down, then drill it and put powder in and blast," Charles says. "Then the coal is broken up and shoveled up by hand. That was in the old days. They've got better ways to do it now. I'd been working at GM and got laid off and worked at the Ogle Mines in Coalwood, West Virginia, for ten months, then went back to Ohio. Then when I came back to West Virginia, I worked at Island Creek and the Beatrice Mines. Those were twelve hundred to fourteen hundred feet down underground."

The more Charles heard from Bob Elkins, the more he began to understand what the serpent-handling religion was all about. Sometimes after church, he and Charlie Kennedy would go to Bob's house. That's where Charles met Lucille "Ceil" Chafin, Bob's pretty stepdaughter, a saucy girl with a sense of humor and a sincere dedication to the Lord. He was attracted, Charles will tell you, chuckling, by the fact that Lucille was so little. He thinks a while longer. "She wasn't fat," he says. Then the real truth comes out: "She was real pretty."

Since Jolo had little to offer in the way of entertainment, their dates consisted mainly of going to church. One night, Charles had an epiphany. Sitting on the back row with some of his friends while Lucille participated in the service at the front of the church, Charles was laughing and making fun of the serpent handlers. Moments later, he was afflicted with the worst stomach pains he had ever experienced. Convinced that God was punishing him for his unbelief, he promised both Lucille and the Lord that night that he would never criticize the practice again.

Charles and Lucille Church, Easter 1997
Family photo

"Then Lorraine Street and her husband, Howard—that was Bob's sister and her husband—got to talking to me about it," Charles says. "And the more I hung around and got the Word and saw the old people that had lived it thirty and forty years, I learned from them. So my children have been raised in this religion. Now, I read the Bible, and I take it literally. There is nothing in there that you can change, not a thing."

Charles and Lucille were married in February 1961. "We took Bob's brother Dave and his girlfriend and went over to Grundy and got married."

It was the beginning of significant changes in Charles's life. The following summer, he prayed and joined the church, and shortly after that, he took up his first serpent. "Richard Kennedy handed it to me. It was a big red copperhead, and I took it on faith. I was up, sitting on the rostrum, and he laid it in my hand. That was the first time. Since then, I've been bitten four times. Only two really hurt me. One was a copperhead. They swell up, and they hurt real bad. The other time, I got bit in the woods by a rattler while we were hunting snakes for services. I wasn't trying to pick it up. My son-in-law Danny Brown had it looped with a hook, and it reared back and bit me, but it never hurt me. I felt it a little bit—weak in my knees, you know, and my legs for a couple of minutes.

But it didn't bother me. I just said, 'The Lord will take care of it.' It didn't even scare me. It's an example of the Lord making a liar out of the devil. It was said that if that serpent ever bites somebody, it's really going to put the hurt on them. Well, it didn't. You got to believe God. Let God be the truth, and everything else will be a lie."

Shortly after he and Lucille were married, Charles heard of a program for maintenance trainees at a GE foundry in Defiance, Ohio. He worked there for nearly ten years, except for a ten-month layoff, when he returned to the West Virginia mines. After ending his stint in Ohio as a journeyman millwright, he returned to Buchanan County and became a tipple foreman at a coal preparation plant, an operation where raw coal is prepared, cleaned, and shipped out.

Today, Charles owns fifty-two acres of land in Cedar Bluff, Virginia, a seventy-four-mile round trip from the Jolo church. He doesn't farm the land but runs cattle on it. He and Lucille have four children. Two of them—Cynthia and Barbara—are presently in the church. Robin, the mother of two boys, Matthew and Michael, used to play the organ in the church but is presently not attending. Christopher, a chief petty officer in the navy, is not in the church either, but, says Charles, "he believes." All three daughters are working toward careers in the medical field. Cynthia is pursuing a degree to become an LPN; Barbie is set to begin classes; and Robin will soon finish her clinicals for LPN certification.

Charles and Lucille brought their children up in a strict but loving home. "They were good children," says Charles. "They got good grades in school; they came inside the house when it got dark; they always played where we could see them. When they got old enough, we let them go out to parties and things, but not until then.

"When a child leaves the church, we try to talk to them about it, but if they're grown, all you can do is wait and pray that God will move in some way."

Sometimes, it is hard for parents in this religion to set aside fleshly emotions, especially where their children are concerned. "When my kids started handling serpents," Charles confesses, "I tried not to feel fear, because snakes can sense that fear. All animals can. But the joy in this belief is the supernatural part about it, the discernment and the prophecies that come to pass."

Now, every facet of Charles Church's life is affected by his religion. "It isn't something you just do on Sunday and then forget about it during the week," Charles says. "It is every day. It is literal. It is not *part* of my life, it *is* my life."

IN HIS OWN WORDS
CHARLES CHURCH

Outsiders make light of you when you are a serpent handler. They say the poison we drink isn't strong. They print photographs of kids close to the serpent boxes. They say Mark ended his book at the twelfth chapter. And they say the Bible really doesn't tell us to take up serpents. But in the Book of Acts, it shows the apostles did handle serpents and did the Signs and wonders with their hands.

This kind of life is hard. We try to live every day according to the Bible, and that is hard. When you meet these people in church, and then you go to their homes, they are the same. They won't be out here during the week a-drinking and swearing and then come in here in the church and act different. This religion is an everyday thing. We don't smoke or drink or curse. We try to control our tempers. I used to smoke four packs of cigarettes a day, but that is an addiction, and an addiction is lust. It is not the lust of the eye, it is the lust of the flesh, and the Bible speaks against it. Lust of the eye is covetousness. But lust of the flesh is whatsoever your flesh wants.

It is hard out there in the world. You go out there, and you are a working man, and you work around a bunch of people who drink and cuss. It's hard to close your ears to something that you hear or close your eyes to things that you see. That is why you have to keep a prayer in your heart: "Lord, I'm here, and I'm in this world, but I'm not of this world. Help me."

And the devil will work in your mind. The devil will even speak to you pretending to be God. He imitates God's voice, which is a still, small voice, but if you have experienced the spirit, you know that voice, and you can recognize the devil by what he tells you to do. [God's voice] is a constant prayer, and with that constant prayer, He helps you fight those spirits. We don't fight against flesh and blood. If flesh and blood were to fight, we'd just knock 'em out, get rid of them, but we fight against spirits that talk to us in our mind all the time.

I've been mean in my lifetime. I drank and I smoked, but I've never experienced anything greater than the spirit of the Lord. But when you serve God, it is a constant war, a constant battle. If you just serve the devil and don't serve God, then the devil's already got you, and it don't bother you. When you try to serve God, then you got a warfare there between the good spirit and the bad spirit. The good spirit is constantly trying to fight the devil so you can serve the Lord.

Miracles are performed every day in the church. Ceil's mother, Barbara, had the gift of fire. She had a great anointing to handle it. She used to dip her hands into a coal stove and carry out hot coals with her hands, and she was never burned. Ceil has that gift, too. She says the fire feels cool. Barbara would actually pour kerosene on the floor and set it on fire and dance barefooted in the fire and never be burned. Once, I saw her hold out a sinner man's tie and put that torch under it, keep it there for five minutes, and it didn't ever burn. She had a lot of power with it.

Several years ago at the old church down by the side of the road, there was a guy came. He was a sinner man. He came to church every weekend. He sat in the back. The Holy Ghost spoke through a sister in the church, and Bob got up and told the man, said, "The Holy Ghost spoke and said, 'You pray tonight, for tomorrow there will be no need.'" The sinner man said, "Well, Bob, there are some things I got to take care of first." And the next day, his wife killed him. That was God speaking through Bob to give that man a message. If he had prayed that night, he'd been alive the next day, but the next day at one o'clock— I will never forget it, because the Lord give me the message—his wife shot his brains out. The Bible tells us that God won't do anything until He reveals it first to His prophets.

These are miracles, supernatural things, mysteries. Shortly before Ceil's sister Columbia Gay died, a bird flew into the church during a service and lit on her shoulder for a long time, then flew out again. And when Brother Raford Dunn was bitten in Brother Carl Porter's church, we took him downstairs, and he was laying on a bed. Lydia was sitting next to him and praying for him, and she said she could actually feel his heart beating. And then she felt it *quit* beating. We prayed for him down there, and he came back to life.

God is everything, and we have dominion over everything, if we would just use it. That body nailed on the cross was the same body that God made in the beginning. It changed from flesh to spirit, but that fleshly body was named Jesus. It is complicated until you start praying and reading the Bible and understand what God is trying to tell you. There is nothing that God can't do.

You go out here and interview a thousand people who believe in God. You say, "Do you believe God parted the Red Sea for the people?" They say yes. You say, "Do you believe that Jesus walked on water?" Yeah. "Do you believe that

Elijah called fire down from heaven?" They'll say yes, they believe all that. You say, "Do you believe, 'They shall take up serpents?' " They'll say, "No, no, no, no, no." They don't want to suffer for the Lord like the Lord suffered for us. But we have to. He said, "Take up your cross and follow me." And in those days, the cross was a symbol of suffering and shame. That's the way the Romans made the people suffer and shamed, by nailing them on a cross. But Jesus suffered, and we have to suffer, too. We have to offer the same sacrifice that He offered, and that is our flesh. But when we offer it, it has to be acceptable to God, without spot or blemish, without sin, with nothing bad in our life.

When the spirit of the Lord is on you, you are not afraid of them serpents. There's no fear. There's no end. There's nothing. Now, we love our women. We love our wives as Christ loved the church. Naturally, when your wife takes up a serpent, there's flesh in the way. But the spirit helps you, like when your wife handles serpents. There is no fear. There is peace, joy, happiness, and love.

Long hair was given to a woman for her glory, for the covering of her head. Because of the angels, the women were given long hair. And if they cut it off, they cut their glory off. But Paul teaches that it is a shame for a man to have long hair. And facial hair—beards and mustaches—is long hair. In all the paintings of Jesus, he is portrayed with long hair, but that is an imaginary picture that somebody had of Jesus. In the old Bible [the Old Testament], Isaiah said, ["In the same day shall the Lord shave with a razor"]. We don't have any paintings of Jesus in our church, because it is hard to imagine. I see the Lord and God together, because they are just one, you see. We are in his likeness. Two arms, two legs.

Put your faith in Him, and whatever happens, happens. Because it is what He wants, not what I want. And what pleases the Lord is what I want.

THE RIGHT TIME, THE RIGHT PLACE

LUCILLE CHAFIN CHURCH
B. 1943

"You just show up, and God will show out."

IT'S EASY TO TELL WHEN LUCILLE "CEIL" CHURCH GETS ANOINTED during services at the Church of the Lord Jesus.

It's Labor Day weekend, the annual homecoming, and Lucille, stirred by the holy anointing of God, begins to circle the area in front of the pulpit, sometimes raising her arms, sometimes weaving and bumping into others. She seems blind to her surroundings, concentrating instead on some inner voice that only she can hear. On her pale face is an expression both pained and ecstatic. Watching her, you fear that she might stumble, but though she's unsteady, she continues to spin across the room, accelerating to a final dash to the altar.

And that's when she opens the snake box. Her fingers fumble at the lock, then she reaches in for the twisted mass of copperheads under the glass lid. It's hard to tell how many are wound together in a thick knot—eight, maybe ten. Their necks wind up and out, testing the air, and their tails writhe above and below the thick, muscled mass in Lucille's hand. She raises the clump of serpents above her head and walks a circle around the rostrum and back again, smiling broadly now and praising God. She shows no fear, only triumph, because once in the spirit, she forgets about the flesh, secure in the belief that God will protect her.

"When I handle them, that's the way I like to do it," says Lucille. "God really blessed me in this service. And the next day, on Sunday morning, they had a humongous canebrake rattler, a mean one that was moving around a lot. I felt like I should take up that rattler, and when I did, it just laid there in my hand and quieted right down. It was because I was obedient to God."

It's not that Lucille has never been bitten. She *has* been—twelve times in the thirty-six years she's been handling serpents.

On the first occasion, she was struck four times by two different copperheads—bitten on both hands—but she went on and handled them anyway. Serpent handlers claim that the copperhead delivers the most painful bite they've experienced. "Yes, it was bad," says Lucille. "Yeah, I was leaving this world. When I came out of it, when the life came back in me, Dewey had put my kids out of the room, and I just remember Brother Ray McAllister and Danny Hagerman, who was in the church at that time—he's passed on now—and Donnie Turner. And they were right up in the bed with me, praying. I was leaving this world. I had lost all my body functions—bowels, the whole nine yards. And that was the copperheads. I was bitten so many times, I guess."

The second time she was bitten, it was twice on the same hand by two different serpents—one a rattler, one a copperhead. "The rattler bit me on the thumb at the joint, and the copperhead got me on the same hand—the left one—at the joint of the forefinger." She never even got them out of the box before she was struck. "I went in with one hand and got bitten," she says. "But even after getting bitten, I reached for another one. Oh, yeah, because the joy is unspeakable. The fear doesn't take over. There's no fear in God. You just know that you're going to be all right.

"When I am anointed, I just get weak in my legs and my stomach, and my hands get cold. No matter how warm it is in the church, your hands will get cold. That feeling continues as you handle the serpents, and when that feeling starts to leave you, then it's time to put them up. I wouldn't say the protection is gone, but as long as you feel that, you know that it's ordained of God. You're in the right place at the right time, but once that starts to leave, the best thing to do is put them up.

"I was twenty when I joined the church. I was also twenty when I picked up my first serpent.

"One time, I was bitten at home, when I was bathing the serpents. Bitten by a pygmy rattler. They're called a ground rattler in Georgia. That's where they

Lucille Church, fourteen years old
Family photo

find them. They're smaller than an ordinary rattler, but they bite, trust me. That was in '84, maybe '85.

"The last time I got bitten, my niece Melissa had had a dream that I was bit, and she saw blood running down the palm of my left hand, but the Lord had told me, 'The left hand won't hurt, but the right hand will.' And it happened exactly the way Melissa had dreamed it. Some said I was bitten five times—that was on both hands. And I looked down, and blood was running down my palm. That was Wednesday. My hands stayed swollen for probably three weeks, but after the first three days, I begin to clean my house, washing down the walls, everything. And on Sunday after I was bitten on Wednesday, I went back and played my keyboard in church, even though I was still swollen. I didn't miss a key. God blessed me."

Lucille plays by ear. Occasionally, she sings as well. She has never had a music lesson. "It just happened, you know," she says. "God just blessed me. After Mom married Bob Elkins, Bob started me out on a guitar when I was about eight years old. Then he taught me the mandolin, then drums. And one day, I decided I wanted to play the piano. I'd never had any lessons, but I just started playing at church. The Lord gave it to me."

She is the mother of four grown children—Cynthia, Barbara, Robin, and Christopher—and the wife of Charles Church. "My son in the navy has never handled serpents," says Lucille. "When he was little—about ten years old—he prayed, and he will tell you real quick what he believes. He stands for it, but he's never done it. But yeah, my girls have, all three of them. None of the three have ever been bitten, thank God."

Lucille has wide-set hazel eyes and long, pale brown hair that is graying at the temples and forehead. In deference to the church's mandate that women must not cut their hair, she pulls hers back from her face and lets it hang down her back. She has a fair complexion and is shorter than her daughters, who get their height from their father.

The Charles Church family, c. 1975
Front row left to right: Charles, Lucille, Christopher
back row left to right: Cynthia, Barbara, Robin
Family photo

Despite the deaths of her mother, Barbara, her sisters Columbia and Pearl, and her beloved nieces Deana Kay and Beverly Gay, Lucille retains an unquenchable sense of humor, even in church. During the Labor Day weekend service, as she takes off her shoes to dance, she laughs and shows her daughter Barbara the pink footies she is wearing. With her children and husband, she plays the comic, making faces and joking. She banters good-naturedly with her grandchildren.

This doesn't mean she never has dark days. She is just beginning to come out of the depression she suffered when her mother died in February 1999. "Mom was a very strong woman emotionally," says Lucille. "When we came up against something, she would tell us, 'You can overcome this.' She would not get excited *until it was over.* And even then, she'd just say, 'You need to be careful, now. Know what you're doing.' She worried. I'm sure she worried, because I worry. I've got two girls that handle.

"I tell my children what my mother told me: If they're going to go to church—be in the church—to live that good, clean life. Abide by what the Bible tells them to do. Be obedient to the pastor. [Follow] the things that we were taught when we were growing up, such as [not] cutting [our] hair, [not wearing] the jewelry. All the things we had to give up, I've passed on to my kids."

IN HER OWN WORDS
LUCILLE CHAFIN CHURCH

I was born in Mingo County, in Delbarton, West Virginia. The first eight years of my life, we lived in a coal camp where my father worked. Of the children, Pearl was the oldest, then Dewey, Herbert, Ballard, Columbia Gay, then me. I was the youngest. Columbia was two years older than me. She died in September of 1961 of snakebite, and Pearl died of Alzheimer's in August of '88.

My father was brutal. He was a drinker, but even when he wasn't drinking, he was mean. He would beat on all of us, even the babies. One time, when Columbia Gay and I were around five or six years old, he took our heads and beat them together. The miners were paid in scrip on Friday mornings, and if my mother got to the company store before my father did, she could use his scrip to buy groceries, but if he got there first, the money went for booze. He would go into town and drink every weekend. Our house was built into a hill, and there was a balcony upstairs off one of the bedrooms, and when my father got mean, Mom would go upstairs with the kids to get away from him. And from that balcony, you could get on the hill behind the house and go up into the woods. That's what she would do. Sometimes, we slept in the woods. And one time, Mom and Dewey and Bobie [Herbert] had to sleep in a water-tank shed.

My best memories as far as family life are from the time Bob Elkins became my dad. Actually, he has always seemed like my real father, because I guess I have shut out a lot of memories about my actual father. Bob has always been there for us. After Mom married him, it was a normal life. When Bob would get in from work and we would get in from school, in the evening was the family meal. Prayer was said with the meal, and we were brought up to read the Bible, to read the Word. We were taught the right way to go, but they never forced serpent handling on us. We handle serpents by our own choice simply because we were taught to read the Word of God, and we know the right way. Of course, our parents had a big influence. I don't mean to belittle that, because they lived the life in front of us. But it was just normal—TV in the evenings, bedtime a certain time. We had a religious upbringing. Mom and Dad were strict on us, and there were a lot of things that other kids got to do that we weren't allowed to do. We had privileges, but not like a lot of the other kids. And in church, we knew that if we ever went to the altar and repented, we had to toe the mark. We had to live the life.

The first time my mother got bit in church one night, I was about five or six years old. I was asleep in the bed, and my sister Pearl came and told me Mom had been bit. I was worried, yes, but I guess I just always believed the Signs.

My sister and I loved to dance. Rock-'n'-roll. When Elvis first came out, I pretty much had him down pat. They would get me to do it—the other kids— or they would catch me mocking him, imitating him. Being the youngest, I was a little mischievous. One night, we were down in the basement, and we were really having a good time. We were having a ball. And Mom and Dad came home from church and found us dancing. They didn't say anything. We were normal teenagers, and there were a lot of things our parents kept us from, but I think they were just being good parents. It wasn't that we were being kept from a normal life. I think they were just more or less protecting us.

When Columbia and I were little girls, when we were still with my [biological] dad, there used to be an old trunk upstairs in the house, and she and I would sit at it and play like we were playing a piano in church. My dad didn't have any religious beliefs, so we would pick this up when we were able to go to church with my mother. We mostly played by ear. I fooled around with the piano, but my sister and I would pound on that trunk as if it was a piano, and we would just shout.

I remember my granddad—my real granddad—he was a carpenter, and he worked in the coal camp where we lived. And we would go over to the neighbors' house where he was working, and there were some little boys that were family friends, and we would just start shouting and dancing. I'm talking about little kids—five, six years old. Oh, Granddad would get so mad at us. I remember running from him, running from my grandfather to keep him from spanking us, because he didn't want us doing that.

So that's how long it's been. Even then, I guess I feel like the Lord's always been there, had something planned for me. And after Mom married Bob and our life became normal, they would go to church, and his mother would baby-sit us, and we and Bob's sister's boys would build this bonfire outside in a chicken lot. We'd dance around that fire, and I mean, we would actually have church. I was eight or nine. I was little.

Between me and Columbia, there was two years. We were very, very close. Different in a lot of ways, but very close. The neighbors used to say that where you seen one of us, you seen both. Her death is the hardest thing, other than Mom's death, that I've ever had to deal with. When I lost my older sister Pearl in '88, it hurt, trust me. It hurt, and it still hurts, but not like it did when Columbia died. There was almost eleven years between Pearl and me. And Columbia Gay and I were two years apart. We ran around together, we double-dated, everything. She was outgoing, and I was more reserved, quiet. But I was always a shoe freak and a clothes freak, and I remember Columbia kept her clothes clean, and she was really pretty, but I never wanted anybody to mess with my shoes. I was very meticulous. I was such a neatness freak. And she borrowed my shoestrings once, the ones for the black-and-white rock-'n'-roll shoes with the buckle on the back. My shoestrings were spotless. She got my shoestrings and put them in her shoes, and I knew they were mine, and I remember the biggest fight that she and I ever had was over those shoestrings.

I was twenty-one when Columbia died. She was twenty-three. I was with her when she got bit by a yellow timber rattler, and I was with her when she died. I was there when the police came. Some neighbor called the police because somebody had reported that we wouldn't let her have a doctor. Not true. Bob's brother-in-law Howard asked her, he said, "Do you want a doctor?" She said, "Have you lost your faith?" No, we always ask [anyone who is bitten if they want a doctor].

She had just died when the state police came to the door. They came in the house, and one of the policemen approached me. Now, listen to this one. He asked me would I uncover her and let them look at her. And I had to do this. It's one of the hardest things that I ever had to put in the back of my mind. I don't know what he was looking for. He never said. But the law became involved after that. It was Columbia's death that was directly responsible for that bill that was introduced into the legislature [to make snake handling illegal in West Virginia].

I never felt discriminated against in school or criticized for my beliefs, because I guess the Lord had his hand on all of us when we were going to school. [During those years,] we didn't have a church [of our own]. Mom and Dad were traveling around to different churches. Everybody knew we were serpent handlers, but it wasn't a big deal. So no particular incidents stand out [from my childhood].

But this Jolo church became nationally known when Columbia died. We were ostracized, and—oh, mercy—we got letters. People called us murderers. They called us anything and everything that you can imagine. And then we got some that commented on how much faith we had. We got good, and we got bad.

I was pregnant then with Barbie, about six or seven months pregnant. And one day in church, this preacher reached me a black rattler. And I turned sideways, and some way, there were some photographers there, and they got that picture, and it was in *Saturday Evening Post*. For a long, long time, I got letters about that, some critical, some okay. They were asking me a lot of questions, but I didn't bother to answer any of them, because I felt like if they wanted to know, let them come and see. Since then, the church has grown.

My mom and dad fought to keep the legislature from passing the law against serpent handling in the state of West Virginia. That was in 1962 and 1963. I remember sitting down for my mom and writing letters. Dewey fought it, too. Mom and Dad went before the legislators. They knew they were going to encounter professors and well-educated people. We're just common people. We're not stupid, but we're not into lawmaking. We just know God's law. And the Lord helped [Mom and Dad]. He took over, and when they would be asked a question, He gave them Scriptures to answer with. You know, it's the Book. Don't even think of what you're going to say. Just go, and He'll tell you what to say. When you come up against opposition of the devil, you don't have to worry about what you're going to say. You just show up, and God will show out. He said to open your mouth, and He would fill it. Mom and Dad were not afraid. The devil doesn't intimidate a true saint of God. When the spirit's upon you, you're not intimidated, because that would be flesh, and spirit and flesh don't well [up] at the same time.

I sat down and helped write letters. We wrote to Senator Robert Byrd and Elizabeth Key. She was one of the lawmakers. Senator Byrd had been one of West Virginia's senators for as long as I can remember.

Jack Christian was the sheriff of McDowell County that year. He never interfered with serpent handling. [It's] not that he was for it, but he never tried to help the lawmakers, and he never tried to stop services. We've never had the law come in and stop services. We've had the law come in and sit and *watch* us, now, lots of times. At the old church, we had services that were so big the state police had to come and direct traffic. The crowd was so huge that there were people standing out on the road, and the cars couldn't get through. People would just stand around outside and listen to what was going on inside.

[The legislators heard] one day of testimony, and I think they may have decided almost immediately that we could continue to handle serpents in church. But I know this: Serpent handling never was stopped at the Jolo church, law or no law.

There are other [serpent-handling] churches in Michigan and Indiana and Ohio, even Florida and California and Arizona. We've gotten letters from California, from people who are into this religion. I would say that if the truth was known, they're in every state in the Union, but they keep a low profile. They don't want to be preyed upon, because they don't want to have to fight the battle. Jolo's been through it. Jolo fought the battle and won. I don't mean to say that the other churches are cowardly about it. I'm just saying that they would rather not have the publicity. And it's against the law in most states, but they handle serpents in all kinds of churches in Kentucky.

My husband is strong in the church, and, oh, yes, he handles serpents. He's been bit. He's even handled a cobra at home. One time, Carl Porter from Georgia had a cobra. Nobody else had been able to get one, and he brought it out to our house in Richlands, Virginia. You could get near that thing, and it would be ready to bite. Carl was outside, and he called, "Junior Church, come out here." Junior walked out, picked the box up, poured it out, picked it up, and the serpent went limp. That's what God does. My grandchildren saw it happen. And that cobra never struck at anybody else. As a matter of fact, it died in a couple of days. See, the power of God is so strong and so real, I can't sit here and tell you what it's like. It's something you have to experience.

When my husband picked up the cobra that day, he felt the faith, and then the Lord met him. It was the right time, the right place. And the Lord just met him. The anointing is within us, and all we have to do is pray and get it stirred up inside of us.

Our children are not deprived. My grandchildren have got computers. They've got TVs. They got bicycles. They've got Play Stations, VCRs. You name it, they've got it. These kids play my keyboard and Popaw's guitar. But you ask them what they believe, you know what they'll tell you? Serpent handling. Matthew will say he's going to be a serpent-handling preacher. "I just want to," he says, "because it's in the Bible. Mark 16. I feel very good about God." And Michael, he says, "I want to be a preacher because it's the right thing. And I want to be a serpent handler because it's the Word. I want to do the Word, no matter what. I want to do this because I want to go to heaven." We love our children very much, but we love them enough that we want them to make it to heaven.

Back in the old Holiness days, when they started up, children did handle young. We discourage our children from handling until they're at least eighteen. But we say, "Obey God." Now, my daughter Robin was fourteen years old. I have to tell this. She was anointed, and there was three rattlers in the box. And she walked over, and she flipped the lid back, and I took hold of her, and I said, "No, baby." She said, "Uh *huh*, honey." She went right on in. She got her a rattler, and her dad got one, and I got one. Each one of us got one. I knew she was all right, but that motherly fear always conflicts with the spirit. But when she said that, and I seen her face, I knew she was all right.

I've been out in the world. I was in Chicago for a year before I ever married. I went up there when I was nineteen. My sister Pearl lived in Ohio, and when I got out of school, I moved up there and lived with her and baby-sat for

Lucille Church handles copperheads at Jolo, 1999
Photo by Fred Brown

her. But I had enough common sense to take care of myself. I worked at General Motors in Defiance, Ohio. I worked in the cafeteria, and then I transferred out into the plant because it was more money. Then when Charles and I first married, we moved up there and lived in Ohio for thirteen years, and then we came back here and got back into the church. During that time in Ohio, I didn't go [to church]. Up north, you're not going to find this kind of religion. In Indiana, yes, and Columbus, Ohio—there's two there. Muncie, Indiana, and Fort Wayne and Indianapolis. There's more serpent-handling churches around than people know. There's some in Michigan, in Pontiac. I know, because I've been out there.

This is our point: You could be harmed by driving too fast or drinking too much. But people say we bring it on ourselves. We go out, we catch the serpents, [and] we handle the serpents. Others think we say, "Well, bite me and kill me," but that's not the intent. It's the verse, "Thou shall take up serpents." That's the intent.

Cynthia Church at a Jolo service, 1999
Photo by Fred Brown

COMING
HOME TO GOD

CYNTHIA CHURCH
B. 1962

*"[Explaining the anointing is] like trying
to explain color to a blind person. It's the
way the first astronaut must have felt
when he stepped on to the moon."*

ONE NIGHT DURING THE TIME when Cynthia Church
had backslid, she was sitting in a nightclub listening to a rock-'n'-roll band. The
air was thick with cigarette smoke, there was loud music playing, and everything seemed stale and worthless. "I was tired of the world," says Cynthia, "and
I was sitting there thinking, 'There must be something better than this,' and
suddenly I realized, 'There *is* something better than this,' and that was the
church."

It was another year and a half before she made the transition back to her
religious roots. But she says that "during that time when I was out of the church,
I had never walked very far from God, and there were times when I really missed
the Lord. Part of that time, I was married, and part of that time, I was single
with two children to support. I was working two jobs and going to school, and
sometimes I didn't know where my next meal would come from. I was smoking,
cussing, drinking. I never did take drugs. But I came to realize that there is no
high, no drink that is like the anointing you get from God. But I wasn't quite
ready yet, and I think He'd rather you'd be a sinner than a hypocrite."

For two years now, she has been back in the church, which means she is
also back in the bosom of her close-knit family at the Church of the Lord Jesus.

Cynthia is a beautiful woman with startling emerald-green eyes and naturally curly reddish brown hair. For a serpent-handling believer, she is something of an enigma, in that she is an independent and outspoken feminist who nevertheless bows to the authority of the Signs Following Church, which says that men should be the heads of households and that women should be excluded from conducting the business of the church.

"I have to obey it because it's the Word," says Cynthia, herself the mother of two sons, Kevin Charles Robert Brown, a college student, and Casey James Brown, born in 1986. "It's a man's world. The fact is, in every profession, men make more money than women who perform the same jobs. But in the beginning, when that passage was written in the Bible, there was a completely different social structure. Women didn't work. They were supposed to be the chaste keepers of the home—teachers and keepers of the children. That's why the Bible says men were a step above. Men were supposed to take care of the women and the business of the church. But society's structure has changed. For example, Phoebe was one of the first nurses in the Bible. She was a single woman who devoted her life to the Lord, but she didn't have a family, so she had the opportunity to do that."

One of the four children of Signs Followers Lucille and Charles Church, Cynthia decided early on to get an education. When she lived in Logan, West Virginia, with her first husband, who is the father of her children, she started taking classes at Southern West Virginia Community College. Even when her marriage ended and she had to support her sons by working two jobs, she kept studying. She took executive secretarial courses and worked in a doctor's office, where she was given responsibility for handling accounts and insurance billing. But these were solitary jobs, and she wanted more interaction with people.

Even when she was working full time, even when she didn't get home sometimes until eight o'clock at night and still faced hours of studying, Cynthia always tried to set aside time to read at least one chapter of the Bible. "I'm more of a reader of the Bible than a student of the Bible," she says. "I don't have time to run a reference down. Maybe later, when I'm older and have more time."

Cynthia earned her EMT's license in shock trauma, studied phlebotomy, and worked aboard an ambulance on the side. "But I couldn't do that very well in a skirt," she says. Her religion prohibits her from wearing slacks. "One day, we were called to the scene of an automobile accident, and the car was upside down. We had to crawl inside the wrecked car to get to the victims to administer oxygen, and that's hard when you're wearing a skirt."

But Cynthia didn't want to give up her ambition to help people, so she started taking LPN classes and prerequisite courses for an RN degree at Southwest Virginia Community College in Richlands, Virginia.

Now, instead of feeling that everything is worthless, she believes that every opportunity is worthy. "I was backslid for twelve years," says Cynthia. "But I've taught my kids that if they go to church, they know the way. Holiness is not a religion, it's a way of life.

"And don't call me a snake handler. I'm a child of God. Serpent handling is a Sign of the Lord's Gospel, not a person. It is a small part of my religious beliefs, not who I am."

IN HER OWN WORDS
CYNTHIA CHURCH

This religion is not David Copperfield. It's not smoke and mirrors and magic. Who would be stupid enough to lay their lives down on the line for a *show*? It makes me angry when people think serpent handlers are ignorant rednecks from Appalachia. The way people talk here is cultural. Just because some of them are uneducated doesn't mean they are ignorant, but that is the way they are portrayed by most of the press.

This is a funny story. I remember when I came back here from Ohio, people made fun of me because of my *Northern* accent. And I didn't understand some of the Southern expressions. I recall going to a friend's house, and I had all my records in a brown paper bag. My friend's dad said, "Hand me that poke." I had no idea what he meant. After about the second or third time he asked me, he finally said, "*That brown paper bag*. Hand it to me." Not too long after that, I was visiting my future mother-in-law. She asked me, "Would you like some fried poke [a green vegetable similar to mustard greens]?" I said no thanks. I couldn't imagine eating a poke [paper bag].

There are serpent-handling churches all over this country, and that's only part of the religion. Picking up serpents is only one of the Signs, but the press wants to put a certain slant on things to make it more exciting. There was even an article in *Hustler* magazine once about serpent handlers, and they used the F word, which we *never* do. That's why I don't usually give interviews. I was going to church at sixteen, and at that time, I gave an interview about serpent handling, and when it came out, it didn't sound the way I meant it to sound. It had that slant on it. No matter how well written an article is, the journalist can slant the facts to make it sound like we are ignorant, crazy people.

I have some friends who are not in this religion who know I handle serpents, and they accept the way I believe. They don't understand, but they are still my friends. But the way our women go without makeup and jewelry, and the way we wear our hair long, and the dresses—some people make fun of us. Even if you think you've made a friend, sometimes when they find out you handle serpents, they don't want to be seen with you.

I was born in West Virginia and brought up in Ohio, but we came back to Jolo in the summers and went to church here all our lives. When I was thirteen, one night in church, I felt the power of God so strong [that] I had to get up and go outside. I can't explain it. It's like trying to explain color to a blind person. It's the way the first astronaut must have felt when he stepped onto the moon. It's like an energy you get.

The summer of 1978 was when I picked up my first serpent. I was sixteen, and I had gone to a Pentecostal church in Ohio and had given my life over to the Lord. It was a Saturday night service at Jolo, and I'm not positive about this, but I think I was wearing a blue dress. During the service, the assistant pastor just looked at me with a questioning expression, like, "Do you want to take this?" And he was holding a black rattler about two and a half feet long. I just reached out and took it.

I've handled a lot but never been bitten, thank God. But the Lord will tell you when to put the serpent up. I think sometimes when the Lord tells you to pick up a serpent and you know you will be bitten, it's a test, like when God told Abraham to take his son Isaac out and offer him up as a burnt sacrifice. God meant to see how much faith Abraham had.

I learned a lot from my grandmother Barbara Elkins. She was a legacy. My grandmother was not just my grandmother, she was my *hero*. And my popaw, Bob Elkins, he's the best man in the whole wide world. Mamaw had a gift of fire and a gift of wisdom. She was the mother of all the church, and she has taught people at a lot of other churches, even if they didn't have their roots at Jolo. She loved people, and she loved her family, whether you were a sinner or a Christian. Either one, we had to set an example. We were not cut any slack in the church.

People were drawn to Mamaw like a moth to a light bulb. When she died and was laid out in the church, you could feel the power of God. There was a kind of mist in the church. You could actually see the evidence of the power of God, just like when the children of Israel saw the pillar of cloud during the day.

These miracles that happen in the church, it's not mind over matter, it's God over matter. Mamaw had the gift of fire. She would pour kerosene on a little white handkerchief—you know, the kind ladies used to carry—and she would set it on fire and burn it in her hand. The hankie would burn with fire and smoke, and Mamaw held that fire in her hand for about fifteen minutes while she danced. Finally, she closed her other hand down over it and put the fire out, and her hand was not even burned, and the handkerchief was not even burned or scorched.

I talk to my children about the church. They are not presently in the church, but my son Kevin and I were talking about it the other night. He told his girl-friend, "Even though I don't go to church, I am a religious person." My sons have seen it since they were born. They've seen the miracles.

I think there's a misunderstanding about my grandmother as to the reason she never saw a doctor. What happened was this: When she was a young woman, she had tuberculosis and cancer, and she promised God that if He would heal her, she would never go to a doctor again. He did heal her, and she kept her promise.

Some believers never seek medical attention, and others do. As a medical person, I think I would probably administer CPR if I saw someone dying of snakebite. Someone usually does, if there is anyone there that can do CPR. Also, everyone who is serpent-bit is *always* offered medical attention. They can accept or decline. The decision is theirs, but they are offered medical attention.

But if I myself got a bite, I don't know what I would do, but I really don't think I would seek medical attention. That's where the spiritual side comes in. As a nurse, it's hard to stand by and watch. You have to separate that flesh and what the Bible calls carnal from the spiritual. A snakebite is different from an automobile accident. The first one's spiritual; the second one's flesh. Luke was a physician, and Jesus said that those that are whole don't need a physician, but only those that are sick. If you have that faith, I say let the doctor take care of the little things and let God take care of the big things.

The Bible tells us we could hardly even imagine how wonderful heaven is. In I Corinthians, it says, "Eye hath not seen, nor ear heard, neither have entered into the heart of man, the things which God hath prepared for them that love him." Yes, it says we will walk on a street of gold. We will have walls of jasper and gates of pearl. But I think the idea of heaven is much greater than the natural mind can comprehend, so this idea of material jewels and riches is the closest [way] that Saint John can approximate the idea, because it's so overwhelming. But I guess my idea of heaven would be like floating on a cloud and seeing nothing but light and goodness and love and being up there in the spirit all the time.

Photo by Fred Brown

THE CHURCH OF THE LORD JESUS

JOLO, WEST VIRGINIA

"Are you ready to fly away?"

THE MEMORIAL SERVICE

LABOR DAY 1999. It is a hot September afternoon in Jolo, West Virginia, a small coal town on Route 83 in the shadow of Bradshaw Mountain. The temperature is pushing up toward ninety-five degrees. Jolo is suffering from the long drought that has withered the entire Southeast this summer. Dust coats the roadside trees and puffs up from the gravel back roads. Creeks usually fed by Tug Fork are almost dry. Even wildflowers are wilting in the heat.

It's the second day of the three-day revival that the Jolo church traditionally hosts on Labor Day weekend. This year marks its thirtieth annual homecoming celebration.

In a hillside house off a coal road for Buckeye Coal Company No. 1, Brother Bob Elkins and his granddaughter Barbie Coleman are preparing food for Sunday's dinner on the grounds, the culmination of the annual get-together for serpent-handling churches from all over the Southeast. Fragrant smells saturate the kitchen, where Brother Bob is cooking two large pork roasts and Barbie is rolling out dough for chicken and dumplings. On the stove are pots of green beans. Dishes and cooking supplies crowd the counter space. Barbie, dressed in a white T-shirt, an ankle-length flowered jumper, and a long white chef's apron, is dusted in white. Occasionally, she reaches up and pushes her dark hair back with a wrist, because her fingers are covered in flour. Bob's granddaughter Melissa Evans has just carried out a box of food to be stored in the church kitchen, and Bob's stepson Herbert "Bobie" Elkins sits in the darkened living room, kibitzing.

Barbie works at the table, rolling and cutting out triangles of dough that will be stacked in the freezer until the next day. She lifts another batch and puts it on top of the growing mountain of wax-paper layers already stored in the refrigerator. Brother Bob looks tired, but he beams his usual sweet and welcoming smile. It is the first homecoming in three decades without his wife, Barbara, with whom Bob raised six children and faced the threat of state legislation prohibiting serpent handling. The couple stood together through tragedy and victory. It's a bittersweet day for Bob, because he's also anticipating the memorial service that will be held at Barbara's grave site on the hill across the street from the church. She's been gone seven months now, but the mention of her name can still reduce any of the family members to tears. They know the memorial service will be emotional, but they'll all be there this evening at six o'clock, as will a few close friends.

More than a hundred people are expected for Saturday-night and Sunday services. "If I live," says Brother Bob with a laugh, "it will be my thirtieth homecoming." Barbie smiles and continues rolling out triangles of dough.

Brother Bob, now seventy-three, realizes that he is the holy glue that holds together this small mountain church of serpent handlers, many of them family members. The weight of his enormous loss and the increasing responsibilities of the church bear down on his stooping shoulders. Even before his wife's death, his health had been failing. As the primary caregiver for Barbara in the last year of her illness, he became physically and emotionally exhausted. Now, family members try to help him out even more than before.

At six o'clock, the family and a few friends meet in the church. It's cooler in there, thanks to the air conditioner. Dewey Chafin, Barbara's son, has not yet arrived for the memorial service, but he has been up on the hill most of the day, tending the grave, mowing the grass, and weeding. Now, he's gone home to shower and dress for church.

At about fifteen minutes past six, Charles Church, Bob's son-in-law, drives him up the hill to the little cemetery. The rest of the family climbs the rocky slope on foot. It's hot. People are perspiring and breathing hard from the climb. Charles helps Bob from the car and supports his arm as he walks the last few yards to the burial site. There, Bob sits in the chair brought for him and stares down at Barb's grave for a long time, lost in reverie. At last, he looks up at those gathered, as if suddenly remembering their presence. He is dressed in a handsome charcoal suit and a plum-colored shirt and tie. His shoes look brand-new, shiny and black.

Here at the top of the hill is a small grove marked with two young evergreens. Not far from Barbara's burial site is the grave of her granddaughter Deana Kay Evans, who died in an automobile accident. The first to be buried in this family plot, Deana was the child of Barbara's oldest daughter, Pearl, who died of Alzheimer's disease in 1988. Flowers sent by family and friends surround Barbara's grave, but the heat has already wilted many of the blooms. Although Dewey has raked the burial site, grass has not yet taken hold here because of the drought. The crumbling soil gives the unsettling impression that the grave is newly dug and not yet weathered. A dog barks somewhere in the hollow. The sound of traffic rushing by below interrupts the hushed atmosphere of the gathering.

When Bob talks about this being Decoration Day, one of his stepdaughters reminds him that he is mistaken, that this is Labor Day. "This will be our Decoration Day from here out," says Bob. "This is Labor Day, and we've always had our services on Labor Day." His lips tremble. "But we will hold it as our Decoration Day to respect Barb. She was always at our [homecoming] service. This one makes thirty services. She made twenty-nine of them." He breaks down momentarily, then continues. "I thought it would be good to have prayer and sing a song or two in respect of her. Let's everybody bow our heads for prayer." He wipes his mouth and nose with a handkerchief. The dog barks again in the hollow, and the sound seems to hang in the stifling air.

With Brother Bob in the lead, everyone begins to pray, each murmuring or calling out his or her own individual prayer. When they have finished, Bob goes on. "She always talked about the work of the Lord and having these meetings.

Really deep down in, she looked forward to having them and meeting the people. She enjoyed feeding people. [There was] nothing she liked to do any better than to feed people and meet the people and rejoice in the Lord."

He looks around. Roy Lee "Bootie" Christian, who plays the guitar in church, has arrived with his daughter and his guitar. "If you got a song you'd like to sing, we'd like for you to go ahead and sing," Bob tells him.

Charles helps Bob strap on his own guitar, and the family chooses a song that was one of Barbara's favorites. "Someday I will go to meet her,/In that bright eternal home./Oh dear love,/She knows no more on earth to roam./Mother's life was faithful/And her heart was filled with love."

Lydia Elkins Hollins, dressed in a white suit with a navy-blue blouse, leans back, takes a deep breath, and begins to sing without accompaniment. "What a time," she sings in her deep, throaty voice. "What a real good time./There'll be no sickness./There'll be no sorrow up in heaven./What a time." She begins to clap in rhythm with the beat. Slowly, others join in. Some wipe tears from their eyes.

A large truck roars by on the road below as Lydia's voice floats out across the grave site. "I am going to see all of those children up in heaven./What a time, oh, what a time./Oh, what a real good time./Well I'm going to sit down beside the Lord Jesus up in heaven./Oh, what a time, oh, what a time./Oh, what a real good time."

As Lydia's song fades away, Bob begins to preach. He looks at the grave. "One thing about it, she's not *there*. She's not there. I preached a few Sundays ago [that] she might be one that comes back to help execute Judgment. God said He'd bring 144,000 back with Him to execute Judgment upon the earth. Like I preached, it is going to be sad when mommies and daddies are going to have to judge you and look at you and tell you the things you done that you could have prevented, that you wouldn't be with her no more. Or with *him* no more, ever which way it might go. But the saints is going to help judge the world. Them that remain will be called up to meet Him in the air. And them that are dead in sin is casted into outer darkness, where there is weeping and wailing and gnashing of teeth.

"A lot of people thinks [that] when they die, that's the end of it. If you are living right, you just made a change from death into life. But if you've not lived right, that soul is cast into outer darkness. You just don't lay there and wait till Judgment Day. The minute the breath goes out of that body, you are either in paradise or you are in punishment. There's a lake of fire that's prepared for the devil and his angels. We are all going to be judged in the day of Judgment. We are no longer there when we are put in the ground, or when the breath leaves this body. That soul goes on to be with God, or that soul goes into outer darkness. People need to study where that soul is going when this life is over. This life don't mean nothing. It was made from the dust of the earth, and it goes back to the dust of the earth, but the spirit that dwells within us is what lives on somewhere. In this life, we make a choice of where we are going to spend our eternal life. We can spend it with the Lord, or we can spend it with the rich man. That's right.

"The Bible says, 'He lifted up his eyes, being tormented in the flames where the worm never dies and the fire is never quenched.' You want to know how long hell is? That's how long it is. *There is no end to it.* You want to know how long heaven is? *There is no end to it.* You choose this day, wherever you go in this life, whatever you do in this life. You've made your beds. Whatever you do here is how you are going to live. It ain't what we profess, it's what we *possess. It is what's on the inside.*

"Many a person will ask, 'Lord, didn't we do this in Your name, and didn't we do that in Your name?' And He's going to say, 'Depart from me, you worker of iniquity.' In the back of their mind, they had a plan, but their mind wasn't on God. He said, 'They would profess me with their mouth, but their hearts was their tongue.'

"People puts on a fair show [in] the name of being a Christian. But boys, in the day of Judgment, we are going to know who's been holy. You are going to know who's lived holy after a while. You are going to know who God is after a while. And don't put it off too late, because you got a choice. He said to choose *this* day. He give you a choice. It is up to you. If you are tormented, it is because you chose [the wrong] route to travel. I just praise Him, because He chose me one day to preach His Word and to live good. He spoke to all of us the same. Y'all pray for me."

Lydia begins another song, "How Happy I'll Be on the Other Shore." The others join in. Then they sing a serpent-handling favorite that goes, "It can't be the wrong number./The operator is on the line./I am giving Jesus a call./I am expecting a call most anytime."

Brother Bob speaks once more before the group moves to the church to begin the thirtieth homecoming. "We know what we are at the present time, but we don't know what the next hour holds for us. We don't know what the next day holds for us. The Bible says to be ready at all times, for we know not when the Son of Man comes. The pale horse and his rider could come by for you just anytime. The main thing is to be ready. Be ready."

THE CHURCH SERVICE

The gravel parking lot outside the refurbished Church of the Lord Jesus on Three Forks Road begins to fill up for the evening service. The building sits only a car's width off the narrow, two-lane highway. On the other side of the road is a deep ravine. The hand-painted sign that formerly hung above the back door is gone now. New white siding covers the outside of the low, one-story building. From the number of cars in the lot and alongside the road, you can tell that tonight's crowd is going to be a large one. Gathering in the sanctuary along with the members are college students, several young visitors from Wales, a group of boys from Finland, a photographer from New York, an anthropologist, a psychologist from Harvard, and a University of Tennessee professor who teaches the psychology of the Bible. An odd assortment of people gathers at the side door, which opens into the area in front of the pulpit. Several women dressed in short skirts and glowing with makeup stand in the door snapping photos. They are not church members, but curious onlookers.

Dewey Chafin arrives a little after seven, freshly showered and wearing a clean shirt and pants. The Elkins family usually dresses up for services, though many of the other church members wear everyday clothes. Long sleeves are mandatory for both male and female members, but guests are not subject to that rule. Charles Church and Bob Elkins always wear suits and ties. The women in the family wear dressy clothes and sometimes high heels. And stockings. They always wear stockings, no matter how warm the weather.

Inside, the building looks like a different place from the old Church of the Lord Jesus. There is a new chair for Brother Bob to sit in, a gift from a friend of the church. And there are almost five thousand dollars' worth of other improvements. Most of the funds were donated. "God told me to do it," says Brother Bob. "And then he give me the money, all but about twelve hundred dollars." The refurbishments include nineteen refinished pews donated by another church and reupholstered by Bob and Dewey, new carpeting, also donated, and two remodeled bathrooms with brand-new fixtures. At the end of the building, a kitchen has been added. Tonight, it is filled with cases of soft drinks for Sunday's dinner on the grounds.

Bob smiles and waves his hand toward the new altar board, a highly polished piece of wood erected in front of the pulpit. "A sister who is a friend of the church asked me if I wanted that altar piece. I said, 'Yeah, but I can't afford it.' She said, 'I didn't ask could you *afford* it. I asked you did you *want* it.' " The altar board became another gift to the church, with a bright red electric guitar thrown in.

The hardwood floor at the front of the church is freshly polished, and the new gray carpet that covers the floor under the pews looks to have been recently vacuumed. The paneled walls gleam. Everything is in place for the homecoming.

The new guitar is an addition to the already state-of-the-art musical equipment in the church. Brother Bob's stepdaughter Lucille plays the electronic keyboard; Lydia plays the organ; and Lydia's daughter Melissa Evans occasionally plays keyboard or organ. Dewey Chafin and Brother Bob both play electric guitars. Bootie adds a rock/jazz/gospel beat to the ensemble when he heats up his electric guitar. Aleen McAllister plays the electric piano.

Aleen and her husband, Ray, who have been with the church for over twenty years, are always the first to arrive. Aleen props her book on the ledge above the keyboard and turns the plastic sleeves in which the songs are preserved. Some are old mountain hymns, some are camp songs, some are new songs, and some are pieces that members of the congregation have written. Some have been improvised so often that nobody can remember their origins. Aleen went to high school with some of the other members of the church. She's seen them marry and have children and then grandchildren. She's seen some die.

Ray, who has been bitten eighty-six times, sits beside her and turns the pages of the music for her. His left hand is severely maimed from a bad bite by a Western diamondback rattler. The snake's toxin ate away part of his hand, twisted his fingers, and fused his thumb to his palm. "I can still use it, though," he says cheerfully, looking at his hand. Ray is always one of the first to head to the serpent boxes. He has handled everything from black mambas to cobras. Right now, his desire is to find that sea snake he's always wanted to handle.

Powerful amplifiers and an acoustical board are also part of the equipment owned by the church. Brother Bob paid nine thousand dollars for the organ and its amplifier a few years ago, after all the musical equipment that could be carried out of the church was stolen. That was the second robbery of the church's instruments. Each time it happens, the members have to start over. "Everybody gives what they can," says Brother Bob. "When that equipment was stolen, I gave my car payment, and so did another brother."

Settled in his new chair behind the pulpit in the spot where Barb once sat, Bob looks out over the gathering crowd. When he spots a stranger or an old friend, he hurries down from the rostrum to shake hands or embrace that person. Women welcome each other with hugs. Men greet each other with a holy kiss on the cheek or a handshake.

The rules of the church hang above the pulpit, their supporting Bible verses listed in parentheses. They read, "Women are not allowed to wear short sleeves, jewelry and makeup (I C 3:, I Tim: 2:9); No gossiping (James 1:26); No talebearing (Prov 18:8); No lying (Col 3:9, Rev 21:8); No backbiting (Rom 1:30); No bad language (Col 3:8); No tobacco users (II Cor 7:1, I Cor 3:17). Men not allowed to have long hair, mustach[e] or beard (I Cor 11:14); Men not allowed to wear short sleeves; Women not allowed to cut hair (I Cor 11:15); and wear dresses above the knees (Tim 2:9)." At the bottom of the sign, in parentheses, it says "Members only," meaning that visitors are excluded from adhering to these mandates.

The service begins with a burst of energy. Lucille is on the electric keyboard. Lydia warms up the organ. Since her husband, Kirby, has been working in Alabama, her playing has become infused with the gospel sounds of the black Holiness church she attends there. Dewey tunes up his guitar, his large hands swallowing the instrument's neck. Brother Bob begins to tune the new red guitar.

The music sends a tremor through the thinly carpeted floor and sets hands to clapping and feet to stamping. When the first song begins, the air is thick with excitement and anticipation. Some of the women remove their shoes so they can step more freely to the music. Tambourines are passed around. Some of the men perform a sliding step using toes and heels, a variation on the old mountain buck step. Melissa's husband, Richard, dances an energetic set of steps that resembles clogging, an old mountain dance in which the arms are held motionless at the sides and the footwork beats out the rhythm. The music is joyous, rapturous, and loud, and it quickly builds to a crescendo.

The Brother Bob who now stands up is more energized than the weak and somber man who earlier sat at the grave site on the hill. He's feeling the anointing, and his spirit and body are renewed. His face glows. He looks at the congregation and flashes his broad, contagious smile. "Are you ready to fly away?" he cries. "You're children of the light. You got the light!"

The church erupts into chaotic sound. Women and men come forward to dance in front of the altar. A visiting preacher's wife swoons and falls. Her head comes to rest beneath the keyboard where Melissa continues to play. Others step around her on the crowded floor, allowing her, as they say, to finish her spiritual experience. At the organ, Lydia is lost in a wild tumble of sound. Occasionally, her voice rises over the music: "Praise God! Hallelujah!" Bootie adds a few Chet Atkins licks while the drummer beats a steady, mesmerizing rhythm. Even Brother Bob dances wildly. He stumbles, falls, and is helped to his feet. He goes on as if nothing has happened.

Somebody sings "Satisfied," a song about meeting Jesus face to face: "Just as soon as I see Jesus,/I'll be satisfied./He bought my soul a place,/And you know I want the space./Satisfied, satisfied, satisfied." Lydia's high vibrato can be heard over the explosion of sound.

Suddenly, the serpent boxes are flipped open. Lydia is one of the first to handle. Then Lucille Church begins to feel the anointing. She staggers back and forth among the worshipers at the front of the church. Finally, as if in a trance, she goes to the box and picks up a knotted cluster of ten copperheads.

Visiting preacher Jeff Hagerman gets so worked up that he has to leave the church momentarily to get a dry shirt from his car. Upon returning, he shouts, "I am a child of God! I am a child of the light!" and abruptly pulls several large rattlesnakes from the box. He moves with lightning speed around the pulpit, shouting all the while. Then he hands off some of the serpents, puts one on the floor, pulls off his shoes, and dances on it.

Dewey lays down his guitar and picks up a handful of rattlers, the largest of them a six-foot canebrake. Ray McAllister hauls out a black timber rattler. The music dies out for a moment, then picks up just where it left off.

Dewey now has six or seven rattlers in his hands, and Lydia is shouting hallelujahs. Dewey suddenly tosses a big, black rattler high in the air and catches it as casually as if it were a piece of rope. He smiles, points one finger toward heaven, and reaches for more snakes. The entire floor is full of handlers with reptiles. Some hold the serpents high over their heads, while others stare at them nose to nose. There are now eight rattlers in Dewey's hands.

The music fades again. Brother Bob yells into the microphone, "Honey, we are going to the Lord tonight! We will be set free! God will bless you! All you got to do is *let* Him. *Offer* yourself. You don't have to wait on Him." He skips across the floor, grabs a rattler, and dances with it.

Lydia stops singing and begins to twirl in a circle. Lucille is back on the keyboard. Barbie claps her hands and twirls. Her sister Cynthia sits on the saints' bench against the wall, her chin resting on her hand. She watches as Barbie turns again and again and again.

Cameras flash madly, lending even more light to the inside of the small church, which seems to be afire with the spirit. And then, inexplicably, a large, pale green moth flutters through the open side door, flaps in front of the pulpit, where the handlers are circling with their reptiles, flies to the back of the church, works its way around a wall, then flies out the door by which it entered. None of the serpent handlers seems to notice.

A few minutes later, the same moth flies through the door again. Only this time, it seems to be shrouded in a barely perceptible mist, much like the mist that hung over Barbara Elkins's coffin when she lay in this church for the last time. The moth flies in front of the pulpit, then slowly flutters out of the church again.

A man in the front row looks at his wife. "Maybe," he says, smiling, "Barb made it to the thirtieth homecoming after all."

ACKNOWLEDGMENTS

WRITING THIS BOOK HAS BEEN A REMARKABLE JOURNEY toward understanding the hearts and souls of those who have generously contributed their stories. We are grateful to all of the people who agreed to be interviewed for the project, but a few need particular mention.

John, Peggy, Mark, and Shell Brown, a truly devout family that shows grace under the most grievous circumstances, spent hours helping us reconstruct the story of Punkin Brown's life, his evangelistic work, his complicated relationship with his wife, Melinda, his struggle to keep custody of his children, and, finally, his tragic death. The Browns put aside their own sorrow and openly and objectively discussed every aspect of Punkin's life to help us build an honest and comprehensive account. In addition, Punkin's friend Richard Cameron Short provided a new slant on Punkin's personality and an intuitive view of his basic character and his strong religious convictions.

Jamie Coots, preacher at the Full Gospel Tabernacle in Jesus Name in Middlesboro, Kentucky, and his wife, Linda, were helpful not only in providing extensive information for this volume but also in obtaining permission for us to interview Jamie's paternal grandmother, Louvernia Coots, for the first time in her life. Her invaluable stories, which included reminiscences about her well-known evangelist husband, Tommy Coots, have added immeasurably to the serpent-handling church lore. The humor and practicality with which the Cootses approached their interviews reflected their warm personalities and helped lighten an otherwise serious subject.

Brother Bob Elkins, minister of the Church of the Lord Jesus in Jolo, West Virginia, is a Southern treasure. He is an expert on the human condition, an awe-inspiring preacher, and, quite possibly, a living saint. His generosity and humor and his deep spirituality mark him as an extraordinary human being. His contribution added a new dimension to our manuscript.

Barbara Coleman, named for her beloved grandmother Barbara Elkins, was extremely helpful in providing information and insight not only about the Church of the Lord Jesus, but about the serpent-handling community as well. Her willingness to discuss her relationship with Punkin Brown illustrated the selflessness that pervades the serpent-handling community.

Charles and Lucille Church loaned us precious family photographs and supplied important genealogical information.

Our thanks also go to Dewey Chafin, a longtime friend whose humility and generosity of spirit reflect the serpent handlers' graciousness.

To all the serpent handlers, including those whose names do not appear in this book, we offer thanks for letting us visit their churches. Even those wary of outsiders showed a tremendous magnanimity in allowing our presence in their midst.

We are grateful as well to Ralph Hood, professor of psychology at the University of Tennessee, Chattanooga, who wrote the foreword to this work, and to Tom Burton, retired professor of English at East Tennessee State University, whose book, Serpent-Handling Believers, provided invaluable insights into the history and religious practices of the believers.

For information and statistics, we thank Victor Lawrence of the United States Equal Employment Opportunity Commission; Heather Rowe; the Kentucky State Data Center; the West Virginia State Data Center; and Betty Vickers and Vickie Cunningham of the Tennessee State Data Center at the University of Tennessee Center for Business and Economic Research.

We are also grateful to our friend Sandra Meredith for her explanations about the music and philosophy of Holiness churches and for her Biblical interpretations.

INDEX